FOREWO~~

*L*ive and Work in Spain and Portugal ~~ ~~ st
published in 1991. The aim of th ~~ ~~ guide to
buying property, work, starting a busin~ ~~ ~~ ~~ious countries
from Australia to France. However, sin~ ~~ ~~ *Live and Work in Spain*
and Portugal has proved one of the most p~ ~~ ~~e series, and this new edition
has been revised and updated for all thos~ ~~ontemplating moving to the Iberian
peninsular.

It is estimated that more than 40% of foreigners living in Spain are British (a
total of about 300,000), while another 30,000 have bought homes in Portugal.
In both Spain and Portugal, the majority of retired expatriates are living on the
Mediterranean coasts of these countries. In Portugal, which has long established
links with British commerce, most of the expatriate workers are in the commercial
hub of Oporto and around Lisbon.

Expatriates, workers, retirees and those who want a property in the sun to visit
and rent out, will find the information in this book invaluable. It covers useful
information from how to open a bank account in Portugal or Spain to how their
tax and social security systems work; from how to approach finding a job to what
to expect in social and business dealings with the Spaniards and Portuguese while
living alongside them in their countries.

Now that both Spain and Portugal are amongst the majority of EU countries
which have adopted the euro, this will also open up new opportunities for trade
and business and make prices easy to compare.

Whatever your purpose behind the wish to spend more time in Spain and
Portugal or to move there on a permanent basis, we hope you will find this book
an essential part of your preparations.

Victoria Pybus & Joshua White
April 2002

THE EURO

On January 1st 2002 the Euro became the legal currency in Spain and Portugal replacing the peseta and escudo respectively. The value of the Euro against the UK £ and the US $ varies from day to day: at the time of going to press one Euro is worth UK £0.62 or US $0.87.

TELEPHONE NUMBERS

Please note that the telephone numbers in this book are written as needed to call that number from inside the same country. To call these numbers from outside the country you will need to know the relevant international access code; these are currently 00 from the UK and Spain and Portugal and 011 from the USA.
To call Spain: dial the international access code +34 and the number given in this book minus the first 0.
To call Portugal: dial the international access code +351 and then the number in this book minus the first 0.
To call the UK from Spain: dial 00 then 44 then the number minus the first 0.
To call the UK from Portugal: dial +44 then the number minus the first 0.

LIVE & WORK IN

SPAIN AND PORTUGAL

SERIES EDITORS VICTORIA PYBUS & DAVID WOODWORTH

Published by Vacation Work, 9 Park End Street, Oxford
www.vacationwork.co.uk

LIVE AND WORK IN SPAIN & PORTUGAL
First Edition 1991 Rachael Robinson & Victoria Pybus
Second Edition 1998 Jonathan Packer
Third Edition 2002

ISBN 1 85458 285 2

Publicity: Roger Musker

Cover Design by
Miller Craig & Cocking Design Partnership

Text design and typesetting by Brendan Cole

Printed and bound in Italy by Legoprint SpA, Trento

Contents

SPAIN
SECTION I – LIVING IN SPAIN

– SECTION II –
WORKING IN SPAIN

PORTUGAL

– SECTION I –
LIVING IN PORTUGAL

GENERAL INTRODUCTION

RESIDENCE AND ENTRY REGULATIONS

SETTING UP HOME

DAILY LIFE

RETIREMENT

– SECTION II –
WORKING IN PORTUGAL

ACKNOWLEDGMENTS

This is the third edition of *Live and Work in Spain and Portugal*. The first was written by Victoria Pybus and Rachel Robinson, the second fully revised and updated by Jon Packer and the third has been updated by the Vacation Work team with Victoria Pybus and Joshua White. The book owes its origins to all of these people who over the years have contributed to the content.

Thank you to all those who provided information and the fruits of their own experience of living, working and travelling in Spain and Portugal.

The author and publishers have every reason to believe in the accuracy of the information given in this book and the authenticity and correct practices of all organisations, companies, agencies etc. mentioned: however, situations may change and telephone numbers, regulations, exchange rates etc. can alter, and readers are strongly advised to check facts and credentials for themselves. Readers are invited to write to Vacation Work, 9 Park End Street, Oxford OX1 1HJ, with any comments, corrections and first hand experiences. Those whose contributions are used will be sent a free copy of the Vacation Work title of their choice.

Spain

SECTION 1

LIVING IN SPAIN

GENERAL INTRODUCTION

RESIDENCE AND ENTRY REGULATIONS

SETTING UP HOME

DAILY LIFE

RETIREMENT

GENERAL INTRODUCTION

CHAPTER SUMMARY

- **History.** Spain was an Islamic country for 500 years following the Moorish invasion of AD718.
- Historically, Spain has been assembled from a number of states and kingdoms.
- The first charter flights landed on the Spanish costas in 1959.
  - Spain has 40 million tourists annually; the same number as its own population.
- Less than 40 years ago, Spain was classed as a developing nation.
- Between the years of 1961-73, one million seven hundred thousand Spaniards left their country to work abroad, mainly in South America.
- **Languages.** Besides Spanish (Castilian) there are three other distinct languages spoken: Basque, Gallego (Galician) and Catalan.
  - Economics: Spain is the world's ninth industrial power but its wealth is unevenly distributed.
  - Five of Spain's seventeen provinces produce half of its industrial output.
- **Politics**: Spain was a dictatorship under General Franco until 1974.
  - Fidel Castro, Cuba's dictator was born in the northern Spanish province of Galicia, as was General Franco of Spain.
  - Spain can best be described as a federalist monarchy having democratically elected parliaments in the autonomous regions, and a monarch, King Juan Carlos as the nation's representative.
- **Madrid.** The central site for the capital was chosen for strategic reasons in the seventeenth century.
  - All distances in Spain are measured from the centre of the capital.

DESTINATION SPAIN

Spain has been popular as a holiday destination since the first charter flights of 1959 which opened the floodgates to the Mediterranean Costas (from north to south: the Costa Brava; the Costa Dorada; the Costa del Azahar; the Costa Blanca; and the Costa del Sol). Every year, the Spanish tourist trade plays host to a staggering forty million visitors, the numerical equivalent of Spain's indigenous population. In 2000 it earned 20 billion from tourism, which employs 11% of the population and contributes over 10% to the country's national income.

The onset of mass tourism inevitably led on to the expatriate property buying boom which began in the 1960s and has been continuing ever since. Places like Jávea and Altea, whose climate was declared amongst the healthiest in the world by no less a body than the World Health Organisation, represent the extreme of expatriate saturation; at least a quarter of their residents are estimated to be British. Other areas are catching up fast; and the Costa del Sol, roughly from Málaga to Gibraltar, has firmly established its reputation as a centre of expatriate life; while Marbella is considered by many to be the most upmarket resort; and is still popular, with the European jet set, a Spanish equivalent of the Côte d'Azur.

Over 300,000 Britons have made their homes in Spain; many have set up businesses catering for their fellow countrymen and women; or have found employment in the tourist industry or with British, American and Spanish firms. Tourists who visit may choose eventually to make their home or to retire there. Then there is the 'halfway house' of timeshare accommodation or the current vogue for elderly British tourists-cum-expatriates to spend the winter months in a Spanish resort and avoid the heating bills and cold weather back home. About 400,000 Britons spend the winter in Spain each year, during the so-called 'swallow season'. Over 200,000 of them own property there.

There are social as well as economic consequences of this wave of emigration-cum-tourism, with some expatriates complaining of isolation and poorer quality hospital treatment and social services than they are used to back home. But the British Consulate General in Madrid reported that there are relatively few problems considering the size of the community. They live in harmony with the Spanish, who have a live-and-let-live attitude and no deep-seated antagonism towards Britons. UK residents say they prefer the warm weather (which remains the principal attraction for many Britons in Spain). Many come who are nostalgic for holidays spent there; or for a change of lifestyle; or simply for the sun.

Spain (along with Portugal and the South of France) is now the European equivalent of the American sun belt, especially for Britons and the Dutch. With its long history of welcoming British visitors, it is also considered a good starting-point for those whose international career may subsequently take them further afield and who wish to gain a first experience of living and working abroad. Communications with the rest of the world are relatively straightforward; and Spanish is one of the 'world' languages: a passport to employment and a useful asset in Latin America (which has an extensive trade with Spain) and many other countries around the world.

Younger residents, working in English teaching or tourism – and other related areas where their language and other skills are in demand – cite the way of life and more relaxed social *mores* as their reason for choosing to live there. Festivals and an enjoyment of life are part of the Spanish way of doing things, which expats also enjoy. Cafés and restaurants are plentiful and cheap; food and drink are enjoyed and understood in this country with strong rural and agricultural roots. Outside the cities, local traditions still play an important part in daily life. Everywhere, in towns and villages, the evening starts with a leisurely stroll through the main streets, where the latest fashions are on display (as in Italy); many Spaniards take a siesta; and lunches, even at work, are long and languid. In the towns and cities, and along the coast, nightlife continues into the early hours: one attraction for younger visitors.

More generally, Spain has been undergoing a series of radical reforms both political and economic – bringing it from a died-in-the-wool 36-year-old dictatorship which lagged far behind the rest of western Europe (with the exception of neighbour Portugal) to an increasingly liberal and open society where democracy is firmly established and young people look forward to the future with optimism. It was classed as a developing nation by the United Nations as recently as 1964; and is today the world's ninth industrial power. Nowadays, Spain takes its modernity for granted. Government used to be highly centralised; but power has been devolved to the regions, most notably the Basque Country, Catalonia and the Canary Islands.

Spanish people are welcoming. Most have rejected the isolationist attitudes of the past and most young people have no sense of being 'second-best'. They speak more languages and drink more beer and less wine. This cosmopolitan outlook also comes from Spain's history as one of the world's great powers (see below) and its present position within the EU (which it joined in 1986). Events like the 1992 Olympic Games held in Barcelona and Expo'92 in Seville brought Spain to international attention, as have its contemporary writers, artists, and filmmakers; these are some of the cultural reasons which may also prompt Britons and others to consider moving there.

Other recent economic developments like European Monetary Union, followed by the adoption of the euro currency in 2002 and the ongoing programme of privatisation) have brought a new wave of workers in areas like finance, consultancy, electronics, information technology and industrial design which have little to do with the service sector and tourism. These are some of the reasons for its booming economy, low inflation and low public sector deficit.

As Spain changes, so the kinds of workers and expatriates who move there are changing. In winter and summer, expatriates and shorter-term residents continue to be a familiar feature of life along the stretch of the Mediterranean coast from the Costa del Sol to the Costa Brava and the Balearic Islands (Mallorca, Menorca and Ibiza). Elsewhere, Madrid boasts a large expatriate population; so do Barcelona and, to a lesser extent, Valencia and Seville. There is a continuing interest in living and working in a country which has much to offer its older and younger residents alike. In the following pages you will find some pointers to employment in Spain, geography, regions, and history.

Pros and Cons of Moving to Spain

One distinct advantage of moving to Spain is that over the last few decades the procedures involved in buying and selling property have become well documented, with many agencies in the UK which specialise in removals and conveyancing. Nowadays it is probably best to avoid some the pitfalls simply by consulting one of the reputable relocations agencies or specialists. One established expert who has himself lived in Spain since 1971 is lawyer John Reay-

Smith. He became a bestselling author on the subject with his publications *Living in Spain* (Robert Hale) and the more recent *Spanish Real Property and Inheritance Laws – a Handbook* (also published by Robert Hale). However as even he points out, books are 'not a substitute for professional advice'. Still, despite the simplification of the procedures, the most common problems are associated with 'the language barrier and property purchases' according to the honorary British Consul in Benidorm John Seth-Smith. Another useful and practical book is *Long Stays in Spain* published by David & Charles of Newton Abbot and London; and in the United States by Hippocrene Books Inc., 171 Madison Avenue, New York, NY 10016. An expert in the field who we consulted during the editing of this book is *Cornish and Co.* solicitors (☎020-847 83300; fax 020-8552 3418/3422; email: interlex@cornishco.com).

On the employment front (where some similar legal considerations apply) the completion of the transitional period of EU membership and the removal of barriers to employment across the EU (including self-employment) mean that visitors from Britain do not need a work permit, although a residence card (*Targeta de Residencia*) will still be required. North Americans considering moving there will have to satisfy a wide range of criteria which means in practice that getting a job will be much more difficult for them. There are still many rules and regulations which British workers should be aware of, covering everything from equivalence of qualifications and setting up a business to tax and other requirements which are different to those in the UK. One advantage of the EU for those who may at present be unemployed is that there are now provisions for transferring your Job Seeker's Allowance (unemployment benefit) to a specific destination in Spain for up to three months if you are going to look for work there. Lowprice winter packages mean that this is a reasonable option (if you have paid your national insurance contributions: this is for 'contribution-based' Jobseeker's Allowance only). A winter spent job seeking on the Costa del Sol may seem a more attractive option than the same thing in Britain. Some advice: take enough money with you, to tide you over if there are problems; and visit your local employment office to make your preparations well in advance. This is a period of job seeking, not a holiday.

All of these requirements are described in detail in the chapter which follows on *Residence and Entry Regulations*; with more information about removals, renting, housebuying, mortgages, insurance, and tax and allied subjects in Chapter Three on *Setting up Home*.

In spite of the increased opportunities for work brought about by this transition to a modern and more diverse economy, unemployment (which is higher than in other EU countries, and currently estimated at anywhere between 15% and 23% depending on which figures you use) remains a problem; and employees are favoured who have a specific skill which is not locally available. Non-EU job applicants have to be 'very qualified' according to one agency; and so, despite the increasing presence of American, international and UK-based companies and the burgeoning demand for English language teachers, academic staff and so on, the prospects are not quite so encouraging in skills-orientated fields which will bring you into direct competition with Spanish workers. The strict criteria on inflation and the deficit following the introduction of the single currency could if anything make this worse. It remains to be seen what the effect of the euro will be economically, but many pundits predict falling interest rates across the Union. Economic growth for 2002 is predicted to be 2.2%.

High unemployment means that most general vacancies are likely to be taken by Spaniards. However even this major disadvantage can be mitigated by the possession of certain skills and qualifications likely to impress potential employers or which enable one to be selfemployed. A working knowledge of the Spanish language is also essential. One advantage of Spanish is that it is considered one of the easier languages for Englishspeakers to learn. Some knowledge of other Romance languages, French and Italian for example, or Latin, will also help you to recognise many Spanish words.

Those looking only for casual employment in tourism or in related fields can probably get by without Spanish, as the clientele is likely to be largely British or English-speaking. The English language is more widely spoken in Spain than neighbouring Mediterranean countries nowadays, especially in the resorts and among the young (older people are more likely to speak French); but there is still a 'language deficit' which is also one of the principle assets of English-speaking staff seeking employment there.

There are are normally plenty of more 'casual' employment possibilities, from bar work to crewing yachts to selling timeshares, where speaking English may be one of the advantages. Even without a residence or work permit some non-EU jobseekers already living there can find this kind of work. At present, the relatively high pound, and the strength of the UK economy, is favouring the tourist trade with Britain.

One of the disadvantages of working in Spain is likely to be the relatively long hours, probably far longer than would be considered tolerable in Britain, or the USA. This is particularly true of seasonal work, for those running bars or restaurants, or working as employees in them. Those working for Spanish companies may be pleasantly surprised by the long lunchbreak, although times are changing. 'Spain's entry into the European Community in 1986 in effect killed off the siesta,' one correspondent to *Live and Work in Spain and Portugal* has reported, 'at least among the urban professional classes.' But in many companies a longer and slower afternoon break lingers on. Remember that Spanish night life begins late; and usually ends in the small hours in the cities and resorts; days off for seasonal and tourism workers may prove impossible in high season.

There are no particular income tax advantages in moving to Spain, as the tax rates are roughly comparable; the personal income tax threshold is around the UK level (about £4,500); and the 56% top tax rate is significantly higher than that in Britain or the USA. Those contemplating living and working on the coast will find it reliably sunny (and Madrid residents will discover that winters can be much colder in this continental climate than Britain). However, being geographically near to Africa has a disadvantage in the south: red dust sucked up from the Sahara by the seasonal winds is often deposited on southern Spain and its coastline; this can be a recurring phenomenon for several weeks or months during the winter.

Those expatriates with gardens may grow nostalgic for the verdant lawns and flowerbeds they have left behind; and the daily battle against a harsher climate is often lost.

Culturally, every country has its advantages and disadvantages as a place to live and work. The presence of so many British expatriates in Spain may be a good or bad thing according to your point of view. It may seem superficially easier to adapt, with English-speaking friends and neighbours; but more difficult when you come into contact – as you must – with the wider Spanish community. Many Britons choose to continue with a more or less familiar way of life. But the true enjoyment of living in another country comes from discovering the local people and the way they live and in truly adapting to your new environment. This can only be done outside a narrow circle of English-speaking friends.

The following is a summary of the main pros and cons of living in Spain:

TABLE 1	PROS & CONS

Pros

O Residence and work procedures are relatively straightforward for EU citizens.

O There are wellestablished procedures for buying and selling property.

O Property prices are generally lower than in the UK or USA except in the most popular areas, e.g. the Costa del Sol.

O Spain is an interesting country with a fascinating history and a vibrant culture.

O The large expatriate population offers employment opportunities for British qualified staff, e.g. medical or in hospitality etc., to set up facilities to cater for them.

O Good employment prospects exist for those with the right qualifications in other specialised fields.

O There are plenty of casual jobs in tourism and a need for English-language teachers.

O The major cities and the most popular resorts aside, you can still live relatively cheaply in Spain (as many retired Britons and 'part-time' residents have found).

O Communications are good and air travel is inexpensive.

O The culture is vibrant; and welcoming to foreign visitors and residents.

O The economy is booming and prospects for the future are good.

Cons

O Spanish and Spanish-speaking applicants will be favoured for most jobs.

O Unemployment is still high.

O Some property may not be up to UK or US standards.

O Property prices are high in the major cities.

O Older residents in particular may find it difficult to adapt.

O Social services may not be up to British or American standards.

O There is strong competiton for jobs at the unskilled level.

O It may be difficult to find more long-term work outside tourism.

O Crime rates are quite high on the costas and in some major cities like Barcelona, Seville and Madrid.

O Language can be a barrier in dealing with officialdom and finding work.

O Tax rates at the top level are high.

POLITICAL AND ECONOMIC STRUCTURE

History

The key to Spain's recent political development lies in its rich and varied history. For those who are interested a *Concise History of Spain* (Cassell) by Melveena McKendrick outlines the main events from early times until just before Franco's demise. (And if you are going abroad some research into the history and culture is invaluable. We recommend a trip to your local bookshop or library; or a call to the *Spanish Tourist Office* brochure line – ☎09063 640 630 – for some excellent brochures on your destination or region and its history).

Important events that have shaped Spain's past (and present) include the fascist dicatorship of General Franco; its imperial expansion during the sixteenth and seventeenth centuries; as well as the earlier domination by Islamic invaders for over five hundred years from AD 718, which left it with a legacy unique in Western Europe of Moslem art and architecture in such cities as Granada, Córdoba and Seville and which has influenced musical traditions, and Spanish literature.

It took the Christians thirty-six years to complete a military reconquest of Spain in the thirteenth century (although the Arabs retained their final stronghold of Granada until the fifteenth century); there was a period of colonial expansion and the colonising of vast territories in Latin America and Asia; more recently, a bitterly fought Civil War and the right-wing military dictatorship of General Franco have coloured the Spanish experience in the twentieth century. Franco's death in 1975 ended a period of stagnation and oppression, although for some Franco embodied a 'restored' (as they saw it in the 1930's) and united Spain. Only as recently as 1996, with the election of the government of José María Aznar, can Spain be said to have entered a period of true democracy, with an elected government and a main opposition party both with experience of democratic government.

Economy

The country was exhausted by the Civil War (1936-39) during which an internal matter of a military rebellion against the elected government turned into an international affair. Volunteers from many countries (including writers from Britain like George Orwell and Laurie Lee, and of course the ubiquitous Ernest Hemingway) came to help fight against the fascists. Half a million lives and a brutal war later, the army was in power; and the consequence for Spain's economy was a state of ruin worse than that of her neighbours in the aftermath of the Second World War.

The postwar era was a lean one for all the European nations who struggled to rebuild their devastated economies; but the main protagonists of the war at least benefited from financial aid under the Marshall Plan. Spain had remained neutral and even provided active aid to the Axis Powers in return for their support for the dictatorship.

For these reasons, Spain was penalised by a UN economic blockade which lasted until 1950. The extreme hardships of the postwar years came to be known as the *años de hambre* (years of hunger), when cats and dogs disappeared from the streets, and it was said only the handouts from Perón's Argentina kept the country from total starvation. Economic isolation, combined with disastrous economic management, had a continuing negative effect on living standards throughout the fifties; a Stabilisation Plan then brought some benefits and Spain finally began to creep out of the nineteenth century in the nineteensixties.

In the latter years of Franco's dictatorship there were some signs of economic progress, particularly between 1961 and 1973, the socalled *años de desarrollo* – or 'years of development' – when the economy was growing at the rate of 7% annually, second only to that of Japan. International companies including Chrysler, John Deere and Ciba-Geigy set up in Spain; and tourism became a huge earner. An estimated one million seven hundred thousand Spaniards left their country to work abroad and their earnings, sent back to swell their bank accounts at home, contributed to their country's economic expansion (a situation which is paralleled in some of the transition economies of Eastern Europe today).

There was also an effect on the movement of the population within Spain. Traditionally, it had always had a population of migrant workers from the poorer regions like Andalusia, who moved around the harvests merely to earn enough to subsist on. However, with the new economic expansion, the disparity in living standards between the cities and the rural areas caused more craftsmen to seek their fortunes in the cities. The resulting depopulation of the countryside, in particular the *meseta* (central Spain), caused an extreme imbalance between the wealth and population of the cities and the emptiness and poverty of such regions.

By 1975, five of the nineteen provinces, Madrid, Barcelona, Valencia, Biscay, and Oviedo, were producing nearly half the country's industrial output, concentrating the wealth of the country in the north and east. Today, the position is much the same, except that Navarre (also in the north) has taken over from Oviedo as a centre for industrial development. Owing to this more recent liberalisation of the Spanish economy (compared with other western European nations) there is still a relatively uncompetitive industrial sector; and the workings of business continue to be hampered by labour laws left over from Franco's era; old-fashioned industries like the northern coal mines seem not only unviable but also permanently inviolable, even under a right-wing administration which has privatised many other companies. The tradition of political patronage is also a factor that has hampered growth and development.

Today, UK companies like BP, Cadbury Schweppes, Commercial Union, Ferodo, ICI. Lloyds Bank, Plessey and Unilever all have operations in Spain; and there is a British presence across a wide area of industries and business activities. Few Spanish companies are well-known outside Spain; perhaps Seat (the Spanish branch of Fiat) was the nearest thing to an internationally-owned company; but this was bought by Volkswagen (although the Seat marque has been retained). Spain's economic growth continued at 5% annually up to 1990 but then varied during the next decade between 2% and 5% and is currently about 2%. It is likely to grow again at the time of writing and has potential to be one of the fastest growing economies in Europe.

Government

During the years of his dictatorship, Franco held the disparate elements of Spanish politics together in a coalition; and enforced rigid centralised government. Franco himself was also a monarchist; and having made himself head of state with the power to appoint his successor he began to groom Prince Juan Carlos to take over the reins of power; in spite of these efforts it remained a generally held belief that the young Juan Carlos was not up to much; and that the political future of Spain was uncertain. During the last months of the dictatorship it became obvious that all the distinct peoples of Spain, some with their own language and culture like the Basques, Catalans and Galicians (who had experienced a measure of autonomy under the Republic) were working themselves up to bid for their old autonomy back; no doubt some of this activity resulted from the fear that the kind of monarchy envisaged by Franco was not likely to be any more liberal than his dictatorship.

Even regions which had formerly not been bothered about self-rule jumped on the bandwagon; the prospect of a loose federation of states (derived in part from the pattern of the old mediaeval kingdoms) caused a mounting *fiebre autonómican* (autonomy fever) throughout Spain.

After Franco's death in 1974, King Juan Carlos transferred power to a democratically elected parliament; and Spain has ended up as what can best be described as a federal-monarchy which the Spaniards call an *estado de las autonomías*. Their king pays taxes in keeping with his constitutional role; and has powers strictly limited to the promulgation of laws and decrees; the calling of elections and referenda; and the appointment of prime ministers and ministers. However, it is said that he wields considerable personal influence on politics; and he is Commander-in-Chief of the armed forces.

In 1978, the Spanish constitution was drawn up, largely at the behest of Juan Carlos. The most important task of the constitution was to make possible the devolution of power to the regions which were (and still are) entitled to have their own governments, parliaments, regional assemblies and supreme legal authorities. This radical transition to a democratic and devolved system of government was carried out to form the seventeen Autonomous Communities of Spain, each with their own flag, capital city and president.

However, these procedures for devolution have been carried out more slowly in some regions than others. Spain is really a mosaic of parliaments and regional identities. Catalonia, the Basque Country, Galicia and Andalusia were the first of the regions to become Autonomous Communities; nowadays there are still variations in the level of independence amongst the regions. The central parliament, or Cortes, retains overall control of such matters as foreign policy and defence, though it is true to say that in Spain local politics normally arouse more interest than national ones.

The first Prime Minister of Spain, Carlos Arias Navarro, a political appointee chosen by Franco, lasted barely six months in office; and was replaced by Adolfo Suárez, chosen by King Juan Carlos as the best person for the job of transforming Spain from a dictatorship to a democracy. Suárez was responsible for political reforms including the creation of a two-tier parliament, the Cortes, comprising a lower house, the Congress, and an upper house, the Senate. Meanwhile a plethora of political parties were formed to contest the forthcoming election in 1979. Suárez resigned shortly after the elections for a variety of reasons arising mainly from the government's proposed liberalisation of various laws. He was honoured with a dukedom by Juan Carlos in recognition of his achievement in setting up the new democracy.

Between the dissolution of the Suárez government and the creation of the next, reactionary elements of the army, alarmed by what they saw as political turmoil and the end of Spanish unity, launched a theatrical attempt at a coup when Antonio Tejero Molina, a lieutenant-colonel in the Civil Guard, marched into the lower house of Parliament at the head of his men brandishing a pistol; and proceeded to hold the entire Congress hostage for twentyfour hours.

The situation was saved by King Juan Carlos, who still commanded the loyalty of monarchists. He announced that the attempted coup did not have his backing; and this probably tipped the balance against Tejero, who was isolated from more senior officers who had orchestrated the coup attempt and he was sufficiently demoralised to surrender without bloodshed to the police.

A long period of rule by the 'moderate' socialist party the PSOE (*Partido Socialista Obrero Español*) followed; and its leader Felipe González, originally a lawyer from Seville, presided over the renewal of the Spanish economy and society and a process of privatisation and economic reform which was only partially completed. It brought riches to some but at a cost of high unemployment and discontent among those who wished to see more power at the centre; and among some other nationalists in Catalonia and the Basque Country who are still seeking full independence. There were the corruption and other scandals which are often associated with a long period in office, culminating with election in 1996 of a government led by the Popular Party of José María Aznar. General elections are held every four years; and there are plans for reform of Spain's complex and decentralised constitution.

Political Parties

The history of Spanish politics has a byzantine complexity. Suffice it to say that the main elements of the fascist regime headed by Franco in the thirties included his own *Falange* (fascist) party, the church and the monarchists who were fused into an unusual coalition. The many political parties which comprised these groups were known collectively as the *Falange Española Tradicionalista y de las Juntas de Ofensiva Nacional-Sindicalista*, mercifully shortened to *FET de las JONS* but also known as the *Movimiento Nacional*.

The Falange progressively became the most dominant element and the coalition itself was the only legal political entity under the dictatorship. Illegal opposition parties without political power could only seek influence through street demonstrations which were invariably supressed by the police. Barely a year after Franco's death, political parties were legalised; the Socialists in February 1977 and the Communists in April. Along with these reforms came legalisation of trade unions and the right to strike. The Moviemiento was abolished and the new constitution was drawn up in 1978 through all-party consultation.

While all this was going on the new political parties were organising themselves for the forthcoming election which was won by Suáarez and his coalition the UCD (*Unión de Centro Democrática*) which could be described as comprising the vestiges of Francoism with elements of liberalism. In the election of 1982, the UCD not only lost but did so spectacularly, its 168 deputies and 119 senators being reduced to 13 and four respectively. The ascendant party was the PSOE (*Partido Socialista Obrero Español*) led by Felipe González, giving the socialists an overall majority in parliament for the first time. The PSOE has its origins in the Spanish Socialist Workers' Party started in 1879 and is the oldest political party in Spain; it was reborn in the twilight of the dictatorship and held the balance of power from 1982 to 1996.

The current government party is the centre-right PP (*Partido Popular*), formerly known as the *Alianza Popular*, which has a mandate for privatisation and some economic and constitutional reforms. Television viewers in Spain can get an insight into some of the many political shenanigans and problems from a programme called *Noticias de Guiñol* – the Spanish equivalent of *Spitting Image* – including a puppet of Prime Minister Aznar whose catchphrase *España va bien* ironically echoes the mood of the country. Spain has never had it so good.

GEOGRAPHICAL INFORMATION

Mainland and Offshore Spain

Spain occupies 85% or 194,885 sq miles/504,750 sq km of the great landmass that forms the southwestern extremity of Europe, the Iberian Peninsula. Including the Balearic and Canary Islands, Spain is the third-largest European nation (after Ukraine and France); and perhaps more surprisingly is second only to Switzerland in its average altitude. The Pyrenees form a natural barrier between Spain and France to the northeast while to the west is Portugal. To the north is the Bay of Biscay, and the northwestern province of Galicia has an Atlantic coast. In the south and east is the Mediterranean; and a mere 10 miles/16 km separates it from Africa across the Straight of Gibraltar (and its two tiny enclaves of Melilla and Ceuta). The Balearics, which comprise the four islands of Mallorca, Ibiza, Menorca and Formentera, lie off Spains's northeastern coast and occupy 1936 sq miles/5014 sq km. The Canaries, about seven of which are inhabited, are situated about 60 miles/97 km off the coast of Africa and occupy 2808 sq miles/7273 sq km. Here, the population is Spanish; and a variety of climates and landscapes in each island, as well as long sandy beaches have made islands like Tenerife and Gran Canaria familiar to tourists from all over Europe.

Regional divisions and main towns

The seventeen autonomous regions of Spain and their provinces are:

> ANDALUCIA (ANDALUSIA) – Almería, Cádiz, Córdoba, Granada, Huelva, Jaén, Málaga and Sevilla (Seville)
> ARAGÓN – Huesca, Zaragoza (Saragossa), Teruel
> ASTURIAS – Oviedo
> CANTABRIA – Santander
> CASTILLALA MANCHA – Albacete, Cuenca, Ciudad Real, Guadalajara, Toledo
> CASTILLA Y LÉON – Avila, Burgos, León, Palencia, Salamanca, Segovia, Soria, Valladolid, Zamora
> CATALUÑA (CATALONIA) – Barcelona, Girona, Lléida (Lerida), Tarragona
> COMUNIDAD DE MADRID – Madrid
> EXTREMADURA – Badajoz, Cáceres
> GALICIA – A Coruña, Lugo, Orense, Pontevedra
> ISLAS BALEARES (BALEARIC ISLANDS) – Palma

ISLAS CANARIAS (CANARY ISLANDS) – Las Palmas de Gran Canaria, Santa Cruz de Tenerife
LA RIOJA – Logroño
MURCIA – Murcia
NAVARRA (NAVARRE) – Pamplona
PAIS VASCO (BASQUE COUNTRY) – Bilbao, DonostiaSan Sebastian, VizcayaGasteiz
VALENCIA – Alicante, Castellon, Valencia.

Population

While the populations of several EU countries, notably Italy, France and Germany have been falling, by contrast the population of Spain had been slowly increasing up to 1998. More recently, however, the Spanish birthrate has fallen dramatically as Spanish women work longer hours, face mounting childcare costs and delay having children until after their 30th birthday. Spain's is now reported to be so low that some estimate that on present trends the population could fall by nearly ten million over the next 50 years.

From being a nation synonymous with big families and despite the Catholic Church's hostility to contraception, Spain has seen its birthrate fall to just 1.23 children per woman of child bearing age.

It was recently reported in *The Times* that the opposition Socialist Party has proposed generous cash payments for second, and subsequent children to encourage families to have more children. It has yet to be seen whether these proposals will become fact and even if they do, whether they will be sufficient to persuade women to have larger families.

The current population is around 39.2 million with an average density of 77 inhabitants per square kilometre; which is six times less than the Netherlands. However there is wide disparity in the population density region by region: the Basque country and Madrid province together comprise only 3.02% of the total surface area but house around 16% of the population. However if you put together the provinces of Extremadura, Castile/La Mancha, Castille/León, Aragon and Navarre which, together, represent over half the surface area of Spain, their total populations would still not exceed the combined population of the Basque Country and Madrid. This population imbalance and the wide variations in prosperity between regions are the result of decades of internal and external migrations, the former from the rural to the industrialised areas, where the cities continue to expand their populations at the expense of the countryside. The largest conurbations are Madrid, Barcelona, Bilbao and Valencia.

Climatic Zones

Spain is a country of climatic extremes. However hackneyed the phrase, there is no other way to describe a country where in the northwest (Galicia) the climate is as wet and the landscape as correspondingly verdant as parts of Wales (though the mountains are higher); while in the south much of the province of Almería is so arid that westerns have been filmed there. The nearly subtropical climate of Almería means it can be a pleasant holiday destination even in December. Another sunny area not yet spoiled by tourism is the Costa de la Luz (Coast of Light) which runs from Huelva near the Portugese border in the south to Cape Trafalgar overlooking the Straight of Gibraltar. The town of Seville in Andalusia has the highest temperatures in Spain reaching 94°F/34°C between July and September and the sun normally beats down ceaslessly from dawn to dusk. By contrast, in the north of Spain, Santander in Cantabria has a climate and temperatures similar to Britain. The vast area of central Spain is known as the *meseta* (tableland); and though not a precise geographical area it embraces the Castilles (La Mancha and León) and Extremadura as well as the edges of Navarre and Aragon. Here the inhabitants are baked by the sun in summer and endure freezing temperatures in winter. The capital, Madrid, which is in the centre of Spain, also has the lowest winter temperatures and expatriates there may not be prepared for the colder conditions.

Along the Mediterranean coast there are rarely such extremes of climate as in the meseta; but the costas in the north and east may be subject to the cold winds which bring the snow to the Pyrenees and the meseta in winter. It is said that the mountainous ranges of the hinterland protect the costas in some measure from extremes of climate and funnel warm air to the costas through the summer.

The offshore provinces of Spain, the Balearics and the Canaries, have their own weather patterns. The Balearics usually have warm comfortable summers, tempestuous autumns and chilly winters, while the Canaries, situated off the coast of Africa, are nearer to the equator than the Bahamas; and their winter climate is correspondingly warm and welcoming to visitors in search of winter sun. In spite of the relatively long flying time from the UK of five hours, the popularity of the Canaries as a destination and a place to live or retire is growing, mainly the islands of Gran Canaria., Lanzarote and Tenerife.

TABLE 2	AVERAGE MAXIMUM TEMPERATURES			
Area	Jan	Apr	Aug	Nov
Cadiz	15°C	21°C	30°C	20°C
Malaga	17°C	21°C	30°C	20°C
Sevilla	15°C	23°C	36°C	20°C
Murcia	12°C	19°C	29°C	20°C
Alicante	16°C	22°C	32°C	21°C
Valencia	15°C	20°C	29°C	19°C
Barcelona	13°C	18°C	28°C	16°C
Santander	12°C	15°C	22°C	15°C
Pontevendra	14°C	18°C	26°C	16°C
Madrid	9°C	18°C	30°C	13°C
Mallorca	14°C	19°C	29°C	18°C
Gran Canaria	21°C	23°C	31°C	24°C

REGIONAL GUIDE

Unlike France, where the distribution of foreigners living and working is more widespread, in Normandy as well as the south, in Spain the expatriates are concentrated on the Mediterranean costas, and to a lesser extent on the Balearics and Canaries. The exception would be those teaching English as a foreign language and those working outside tourism, who could find work in any of the larger cities, not just the coastal ones.

Historically, Spain has been assembled from a number of states or kingdoms, making it a mixture of peoples and cultures more complex than many of its near neighbours. Apart from Spanish (Castilian), there are at least three other distinct languages spoken by the socalled 'historical nationalities': the Basques, Gallegos and Catalans. The regions described below represent the current political setup of Spain; many of them are based on the old kingdoms, like Asturias, which was founded in the tenth century. Athough most of those living and working there are likely to find themselves in the better-known areas, there are vast areas of Spain like Extremadura which seem practically deserted. *Spain Off the Beaten Track* by Barbara Mandell and Roger Penn (Moorland Publishing) is an excellent guide to some of these more out-of-the-way destinations.

Information Facilties

A good starting point is the Spanish National Tourist Office (SNTO) (in your home country) for a supply of national maps, railway guides and brochures for all the main Spanish towns and regions. In Spain itself, you will find an SNTO; in every larger town and from these you can get specific local guidebooks and information on hotels, car hire, the principal sights, and so on. In addition, there are the tourist information bureaux (*Turismo*) which are run by the municipality. Generally speaking, the tourist offices and bureaux do not carry information for places outside their region. The *Mapa de Comunicaciones España* which can be supplied by the SNTO lists each of the local tourist information offices, with information on customs posts, driving and speed limits, motorway assistance, railway information telephone numbers, and the *paradores* which are the government-run inns and hotels.

The central reservation number for Spanish paradores is 915166666; fax 915166657. In Britain, *Keytel International* (402 Edgware Road, London W2 1ED; ☎020-7402 8182; fax 020-616 0317) will send you a booking form (with, at present, some special offers for senior citizens) and general information including insurance and car hire details, and a Directory of Paradors in Spain. To arrange accommodation in advance *Room Service* also has a brochure for Spain, featuring some charming and affordable hotels and pensions from £25 a night for a double room in, say, Barcelona; or throughout the country: Madrid, Andalucia, Santander, Santiago, Toledo and so on. Flights, car hire and tailormade itineraries can also be arranged.

THE MEDITERRANEAN REGIONS

Andalucia (Andalusia)

Main cities and provinces: Almería, Cádiz, Córdoba, Granada, Huelva, Jaén, Málaga and Sevilla (Seville).

Andalusia is the second largest region of Spain covering 17% of Spain's total area. It is the most populated region with around six and a half million inhabitants and takes its name from al Andaluz, which was the stronghold of Muslim Arabs and Berbers who crossed from North Africa in the eighth century, virtually took over the Iberian Peninsula in less than four years, and were finally driven from their last stronghold in Granada by the Christians in the mid-fifteenth century. Andalusia's past glory derives from the great monuments that survive from the Moorish period, most notably the cities of Córdoba, Seville and Granada.

The Alhambra Palace in Granada is regarded as one of the world's greatest buildings. Andalusia is also the home of the gypsy guitar and the flamenco. By contrast with its rich past Andalusia today can be said to embrace extremes of poverty and wealth. Part of its coastline is the Costa del Sol, one of the playgrounds of the rich and famous and home to an estimated 200,000 foreigners, the majority of whom are Brits, while the region itself has one of the highest unemployment rates in Europe, where peasants eke out an existence on smallholdings and by seasonal work.

The advantage of the Costa del Sol for anyone thinking of living and working in Spain is that there is a ready market for anything from bookshops to barbers – it's just a question of finding a suitable gap in the market. It is also easy to get to by way of Málaga airport; and there is plenty of scope for seasonal work during the tourist season.

Most of the development so far has taken place west of Málaga, where there is perpendicular concrete virtually all the way to Marbella, amidst which may be found the infamous resorts of Torremolinos and Fuengirola. East of Málaga concrete is still proliferating principally around the resorts of Nerja, Almuñécar and Salobreña. The main coastal road, the N340, is known locally as *Caretera del Muerte* (the highway of death) because of the high number of fatal accidents. The road is virtually a motorway which runs through urban areas; and fatalities are caused by pedestrians and those unfamiliar with the Spanish highway code (often intoxicated British package holidaymakers) trying to cross it.

To the west of the Costa del Sol between Estepona and Tarifa is a less built-up part of the coastline; and about halfway between them juts the rock of Gibraltar, still British, but inevitably due to be returned to Spain. (This is the Spanish point of view at any rate). Luxury housing developments are beginning to sprout in the vicinity, notably Sotogrande and La Duquesa; and many people are choosing to live not too far from English-speaking Gibraltar now that communications between it and Spain are easier.

Occupying a similar place to the Rock in African history are the two Spanish outposts of Melilla and Ceuta which are officially parts of Andalusia; but situated on the north African coast. These may one day be returned to Morocco. Further west is another landmark of British history: the Cape of Trafalgar; and beyond that, the Gulf of Cadiz, whose unspoilt coastline eventually meets the Portugese border. Also in the area is the famed Coto Doñana wetland wildlife park.

Regions & Provinces of Spain

The Basque Country
Biscay
Guipuzcoa
Alava

Navarre

Rioja

Soria

Huesca   Lérida   Gerona

Aragon   **Catalonia**

Zaragoza   Barcelona

Tarragona

Guadalajara   Teruel

Cuenca   Castellón

Balearic Islands   Menorca

Mallorca

Mancha

Valencia

Ibiza

Albacete   Formentera

Alicante

Mediterranean Sea

Murcia

Almeria   La Palma

Lanzarote

Gomera   Tenerife

Hierro   Fuerte-Ventura

Gran Canaria

The Canary Islands

Andalusia also contains one of Spain's largest mountain ranges, the Sierra Morena; and the highest range, the Sierra Nevada, dominates Granada. There are ski resorts in both ranges. The province of Jaén behind Granada is famed for its olive growing, while Almería is partly desert. There is a small collection of foreign-owned villas in and around the hill town of Mojácar near Almeria: most are inhabited during the mild winter months as summers tend to be too hot and dry. For those interested in exploring the region from the UK *Ramblers Holidays* offers a range of walking tours through the countryside as well as the larger towns. Contact them on 01707331133.

Murcia and Valencia

Provinces and main cities: Murcia, Alicante, Castellón and Valencia.

Murcia and Valencia between them make up nearly 7% of the area of Spain and just over 12% of the population. Murcia is separate from, though adjacent to, the region of Valencia. There could hardly be a greater contrast between Murcia, the driest place in Spain, and Alicante, Valencia and Castellón which make up Valencia (País Valenciano), one of the most fertile. Valencia has strong historical associations with the Catalonian/Aragonese partnership which conquered it in the twelfth century; and shares a linguistic heritage with Catalonia, although arguments still rage as to whether Valencian is a language in its own right or a dialect of Catalan. Murcia consists of a single province of that name; and neither historically nor nowadays does it have as strong a regional identity as its Valencian neighbour. In the thirteenth century the area was a part of the united territory ruled over by the dynasties of Castille and Aragon. The Aragonese kindom at that time also encompassed Catalonia.

It was the historical linkage of Catalonia and Murcia which led many inhabitants of the region to pour into Catalonia after the Civil War, to search for jobs. It was at this time, too, that Murcians seem to have acquired an unfortunate and unmerited reputation for being uncouth and violent which has become part of national lore, to the extent that to many Spaniards '*Murcian*' is a term of abuse. The main port in Murcia is Cartegena, named after the Carthaginians who founded it. Cartagena is a large naval base whose nightlife is described by one guide book as 'lively, if somewhat dangerous.'

To the east of Murcia is the province of Alicante, more familiar to British visitors; and on whose Costa Blanca (white coast) are the beaches and resorts beloved of package tourists and residents alike: Denia, Jávea, Calpe, Altea, Benidorm and Villajoyosa to name but a few. Access to these places is easy from Alicante airport. It is not until you reach the city of Alicante, away from the hotels and villas, that you feel you are back in a truly foreign country. Inland from Alicante the landscape is more exotic, with palm groves originally planted by the Arabs centred around Elx or Elche. The fame of this town rests almost exclusively on the discovery of an ancient bust discovered at the turn of the century and known as *La dama de Elche*, although you will have to go to the Archaeological Museum in Madrid to see it.

North of Alicante is Spain's third largest city: Valencia. Somewhat confusingly, this is also the name of the province, and of the region comprising the three provinces of Valencia, Alicante and Castellón. The modernday city of Valencia has sprawling suburbs of highrise blocks and its fair share of beggars and gypsies.

By contrast, its history is linked with the romantic figure of El Cid who was once its charismatic ruler.

El Cid, otherwise known as Ruy Diaz de Bivar, was a soldier of fortune in the dark days of the Arab occupation; and he became through his chivalric exploits the hero of one of Spain's earliest epic poems the *Cantar de mío Cid* as well as the subject of folk legends and ballads. The reality was probably more mundane; he fell out with his monarch, fought on the Moorish side, and then became reconciled with his ruler by changing sides once again, and was rewarded with the governorship of Valencia. A pointer to future Spanish politics in many ways.

The coastline north of Valencia, the Costa del Azaha (coast of orange blossom), is lined with small summer resorts. Perhaps the best known to visitors is the ancient fortified town of Peñiscola. Properties along this lesser-known coastline are bought mainly by Spaniards but may well appeal to foreigners as the prices are still reasonably low and access is relatively easy from Valencia airport.

ISLAS BALEARES (BALEARIC ISLANDS)

Main town: Palma (Mallorca).

The Balearic Islands (Las Islas Baleares) off the Valencian and Catalonian coast, have been associated with Spain since the Romans incorporated them into their province of Hispania, which comprised the whole Iberian Peninsula. Together, the four main islands, Mallorca, Menorca, Ibiza and Formentera comprise less than 1% of the area of Spain with a total population of around 750,000. The biggest island is Mallorca which attracts an estimated three million tourists a year and also has an estimated 15,000 British residents and workers. Fortunately, the tourist development is concentrated in small areas of the coast, notably around Palma and in the northeast around Pollensa. The other islands are mainly summer resorts and extremely quiet (and sometimes chilly) out of season. The liveliest and most upmarket is certainly Ibiza (main town Eivissa) which gained its reputation for tolerance towards foreign visitors in the sixties when it was popular with hippies; and several pop stars bought properties there. More recently, aficionados of house music have made it a popular destination among the young. Menorca (which boasts the summer home of the entrepreneur Richard Branson) is more sedate and family-orientated; and the smallest Formentera is the quietest and least developed.

From the expatriate point of view, Mallorca is the obvious choice because of its size and facilities; but there are British communities on each of the three major islands. Access from the UK is easy as there are numerous charter flights all year round. There are ferry connections to Ibiza from Denia and from Valencia to Ibiza and Palma, as well as to Menorca from the mainland. In winter there are fewer flights to Ibiza and Menorca.

CATALUÑYA (CATALONIA)

Main cities and provinces: Barcelona, Girona, Lléida (Lerida), Tarragona.

Catalonia is one of the regions of Spain which has its own distinct historical – and some would say national – identity, with its own culture and language, Catalan. Although covering less than 7% of the total area of Spain, Catalonia is home to over six million inhabitants, or 17% of the total population. This has long been one of the most exciting and cosmopolitan parts of Spain; and

Barcelona a hotbed of politics, fashion, commerce and culture. Its first ruler was the unfortunately named Guifré the Hairy. In the twelfth century, Catalonia was an autonomous part of the kingdom of Aragon, an alliance that enhanced its political influence, and brought far ranging cultural influences to Aragon from Provence and Roussillon by way of Catalonia. The Catalan language is closely related to the Langue d'Oc, still spoken across in some parts of southern France where this once formed part of one kingdom with Catalonia. There is even a Catalan-speaking outpost in Sardinia: in the Middle Ages Catalonia was one of the Mediterranean powers.

The decline of Catalonian wealth and power in the fourteenth century weakened Aragon to the extent that Castile became the dominant regional power. For the next five centuries the Catalonians attempted to consolidate their autonomy in an on-and-off fashion as successive Spanish dynasties tried to stake a claim to it. Towards the end of the nineteenth century, the broadbased nationalist movement of Catalanism began to gather momentum; and attracted the attention of Madrid which offered a limited autonomy to the region, which was subsequently repressed by the dictator Primo de Rivera. Any further thoughts of autonomy were interrupted by the Civil War during which Barcelona became the final refuge of republicanism and anarchism; and held out against Franco's armies until the bitter end in 1939.

His retribution against the Catalan language and culture took the form of bookburning and the changing of street and place names. However, in the decades following the end of the Civil War, Catalan nationalism mellowed; and Catalanism became characterised by bravura rather than violence and extremism. Perhaps one of the reasons for this change is that, during most of this century, the Catalonian region has been settled by many migrant workers from poorer parts of Spain, attracted by the industry and wealth of the area. The result is that about half of the people of Catalonia are descended from immigrants, which has led to a bi-lingualism not unlike that of Wales, with Spanish universally spoken but Catalan favoured in schools and universities. This immigration also contributed to diluting some of the strong nationalist feelings in the region.

The town of Tarragona is a large industrial port with chemical and oil refineries and can be divided into two parts: an old walled city and an ugly modern one. Historically, Tarragona has had trading links across the Mediterranean. The Romans built a splendid city here; and many fine examples of their architecture remain in the old part of the town and its environs, notably the forum, Scipio's Tower (*Torre de Scipio*) and a triumphal arch (*Arco de Bara*).

Barcelona (the province) includes part of the Pyrenees. It is also home to one of the national symbols of Catalonia, the monastery of Montserrat built around the legend of the Black Virgin, an icon reputedly hidden on the site by St Peter and rediscovered in the ninth century amidst the sort of miraculous happenings usually associated with such shrines. During the Franco era the monastery clandestinely published the Montserrat Bible in Catalan and became a centre of nationalist gatherings. It can be visited by bus from Barcelona.

Barcelona city, much to the chagrin of the capital Madrid, is held by many to be the most lively and interesting in Spain. Not only is it a huge industrial centre and port (population three million), and the spiritual home of individuals of such startling originality as the architect Gaudí and Pablo Picasso, it is also the most liberated (or decadent depending on your viewpoint) city in Spain. The notorious red light district, the *barrio chino*, is now used as the term for similar districts elsewhere in the country. The sheer energy and sophistication of the place are a great attraction, especially for European night-clubbers; and it is near enough to the Costa Brava where many foreign residents are based to make it regular port of call for those who want a change of pace.

Rumour has it that the famous Gaudí cathedral, La Sagrada Familia started in 1882 and left unfinished after the architect was killed by a tram in 1926, will finally be completed in the not too distant future. For years it remained open to the skies – although work proceeds apace – and many Barcelonans would have preferred to see it left that way as a monument to its creator. The facilities left behind by the Olympic Games in 1992 are another attraction. Another is the Picasso Museum on the Carrer de Montcada.

Barcelona airport, Prat, is 14 kms from the city centre; and there are ferries from Barcelona to the Balearics. Of interest to jobseekers are the many English language schools in Barcelona – as in many other Spanish cities – and the recent growth of high-technology industries to match those across the Mediterranean in southern France, where the region also has many commercial as well as historical links (see the *Employment* chapter for details of English language teaching in Spain).

The whole coastline of Girona up to the French border is known as the Costa Brava (the rugged coast), home to many northern Europeans; but more for retirement and second homes than either work or business reasons.

The well-known holiday resort of Lloret de Mar is situated just south of Girona city. Girona airport serves all the Costa Brava holiday resorts; and the mediaeval walled city of Girona, largely neglected by tourists, is well worth a visit. Northwards still is Figueres, the birthplace and now museum of another Catalonian original, Salvador Dali.

The final province of Catalonia, Lerida is situated inland and is a mixture of fertile plain and a part of the Pyrenees. Lerida town has a magnificent former cathedral which has been used as a military barracks since the eighteenth century.

THE PYRENEAN REGIONS

Aragón

Provinces and main cities: Huesca, Teruel and Zaragoza (Saragossa).

The northern part of Aragón incorporates a section of the Pyrenees while the south slopes toward the Ebro valley and rises again in Teruel. The Aragonese provinces comprise 9.5% of Spain but like Extremadura are heavily underpopulated with a total of only around 1.2 million inhabitants. The historical kingdom of Aragón was created by Sancho the Great of Navarre who reigned from 1000 to 1035. Later, in the fifteenth century, Aragón and Castile became one kingdom under the joint rule of Ferdinand and Isabella. Places of interest include the magnificent castle of Loarre about 25 miles/40km from Huesca which was built by Sancho the Great as part of his forward defences against the Arabs. Pyrenean Aragón is fast becoming popular with hikers, particularly in the Ordesa National Park. There are also several ski resorts of which the most chic is Benasque. The town of Jaca, the capital in former times, was also on the pilgrim route to Santiago de Compostela.

Saragossa is a lively city with some interesting Moorish architecture notably the

Ajaferiá Palace.

Geographically the province of Teruel reaches out to the south rather than the Pyrenees and is one of the most unexplored areas with few inhabitants and poor roads.

Navarra (Navarre)

Main town: Pamplona.

Navarre is one of the smaller regions comprising 2.06% of Spain's area and home to 1.35% of the population. A stretch of the Pyrenees fills the northeastern part of the province and includes the historic pass of Roncesvalles on the route taken by mediaeval pilgrims to Santiago. The south of Navarre is on the northeastern edge of the meseta and is a region of vineyards and other agriculture. The main city of the region is Pamplona, whose bull-running festival, Fiesta of San Fermín, takes place in July and attracts capacity crowds from all over Spain and beyond.

The origins of the kingdom of Navarre can be found in a ninth century battle between the Basques and the Franks. The latter, in the process of retreating after an unsuccessful campaign against the Moors, were ambushed by some early Basque separatists who, having routed the Franks in the valley of Roncesvalles, declared the area around Pamplona independent. The event is immortalised in the *Chanson de Roland* which, however erroneously, claims the attackers were really Moors not Basques. During the eleventh century, the kingdom of Navarre included Basque territory on both sides of the Pyrenees, which links its history with that of France as well as Spain. Navarre remained an independent kingdom, playing its own part in European power politics, until 1512, when the aforementioned King Ferdinand of Aragón and Castile annexed it in order to give his armies a safe corridor to attack the French on the other side of the Pyrenees.

Once this had been accomplished he allowed the Navarrese their autonomy; which they have retained almost uninterruptedly ever since. It is probably largely due to this continued independence that Navarre never became incorporated into the Basque country, in spite of its foundation by Basques and close links with this region.

THE BAY OF BISCAY AND ATLANTIC COAST (THE GREEN COAST)

Pais Vasco (The Basque Country)

Provinces: Alava, Guipuzcoa, Vizcaya (Biscay).
Main cities: Bilbao (Vizcaya); San Sebastían/Donostia (Guipuzcoa); Vitória/Gasteiz (Alava).

The Basque Country (*Euskadi*) is one of the more heavily populated regions of Spain representing about 1.5% of the surface area and 6% of the population. Most Basques see themselves as an ethnic or national minority within Spain and in common with Catalalans seek greater autonomy, or independence. It also has the most determined separatist movement; and a terrorist organisation, Euskadi ta Azkatasuna (ETA) which came into being as a direct result of the repression of the Basques, their culture and language (*euskera*), and their national aspirations, by the Franco regime. Its campaign continues today; and ETA is in some respects the Spanish equivalent of the IRA.

It is now widely said that the Basques are descended from the original aboriginal inhabitants of Europe, who lived in the region before the farmers and settlers arrived from the Middle East 10,000 years ago. There may be some connection with the now-extinct Picts in Scotland. Early skeletal remains featuring a distinctive elongated head which is characteristic of Basque people have been unearthed in the region, although many subsequent invasions have left their mark on the Basque Country; and other Europeans have been shown to be descended from a range of migrating peoples as well.

The claim that the Basques managed to resist domination by the Romans has been disproved by historians who have ascertained that these invaders did in fact subdue the province to the extent of building roads and settlements there. After the Romans left the so-called barbarians (the Franks and the Visigoths) who settled in much of the rest of Spain never managed more than a partial conquest of the area, who clearly outfought the barbarians during their dogged resistance. This was also one of the last corners of Europe to adopt Christianity and to build towns; the Basques habitually ambushed pilgrims on the route to Santiago. Nominally ruled by the dynasties of Castile and Navarre they managed to keep a large measure of autonomy through the grass roots governorship of their own nobles and chieftains.

Through their long association with the Castilian crown, they also prospered, providing administrators for the Hapsburgs; and producing such notable historical figures as Ignatius Loyola, St Francis Xavier and the explorer Lope de Aguirre.

The strident nationalism associated with the region was unknown until the nineteenth century; and arose in response to the spread of centralist government, and ultimately as a reaction to the French Revolution. During the socalled Carlist Wars, the Basque provinces were split into the urbanised supporters of Madrid and the rural peasantry, who sided with Don Carlos (who made an unsuccessful attempt to usurp his brother's throne). As punishment, Basque areas had their autonomy rescinded; which upset the loyalists who had sided with Madrid; and caused a festering discontent. In the early twentieth century, Basque industry, based around rich natural resources such as iron ore and timber, made the area around Biscay a hub of wealth, industry and banking. The Basque Nationalist Party, the PNV, was founded in 1910 with support broadly based in the liberal middle stratum of society. The Civil War of 1936 reopened the old gulf between the peasantry and the middleclasses: the coastal provinces of Guipúzcoa and Vizcaya sided with the republicans who rewarded them with autonomy, while the inland province Alava sided with the government.

In 1936, the Basque Country was the scene of the most appalling brutality when the small but historic town of Guernica was bombed; and over a thousand of its inhabitants massacred as they fled. It took four hours to reduce the town centre to rubble; the bombardment was carried out by the German airforce, a premonition perhaps of the greater conflict which was to follow. Miraculously perhaps, the ancient *Guernikako Arbola* (Tree of Guernica) under which the Basque Parliament used to meet survived the attack.

Franco's attempt to bludgeon the Basques into submission has become immortalised in the Picasso painting depicting nightmarish scenes juxtaposed with modern technology representing the horror of war and the artist's reaction to it. The huge canvas was only brought to Spain after the dictator's death – as Picasso had requested – and now hangs in the Prado museum.

In recent years, the industrialised north of Spain has suffered economic setbacks, with iron and steel works around Bilbao being put out of business by the recession. With high unemployment, and its reputation for terrorism, the Basque country may not seem an attractive prospect for living and working. However, there are some possiblities: away from the main industrial areas around Bilbao there are rural areas characterised by a greenness reminiscent of the Emerald Isle, while Basque farmhouses resembling Swiss chalets may appeal to some.

The greatest drawback to living in this part of Spain would probably lie in mastering the Basque language, which bears no resemblance to other European languages, and would prove more difficult than learning Spanish. The port of San Sebastián is a well-known and attractive but not particularly sophisticated resort.

CANTABRIA & ASTURIAS

Main towns: Santander, Oviedo.

The spectacularly mountainous regions of Cantabria and neighbouring Asturias were considered too remote and inhospitable by the eighth century Moslem invaders, who left the area unconquered. The result was that Christians and the remnants of the Visigoths fleeing the Moors found it a useful place of refuge. Protected from the south by the natural barrier of the Cantabrian Cordillera, one of Spain's highest mountain ranges, the Christian northerners were slowly able, by a combination of violent sorties and general creeping encroachment, to push back the frontier of Moslem Spain.

In 718, there was a notable Asturian victory at Covadonga under Pelayo, who founded a small Asturian kingdom. From these modest beginnings the kingdom of Asturias spread out westwards and southwards until it reached León on the meseta. Eventually expansion reached the point where it allowed the Christian north to make a determined push against the Arabs and complete the reconquest of most of Spain in the eleventh century.

In the nineteenth century, Asturias became a centre for mining and steel production; today the main industrial town of Avilés has become the worst source of airborne pollutants in Spain.

Asturias was fiercely republican during the civil war; and produced one of its greatest heros, the communist *La Pasionaria* (the Passionflower), an Asturian miner's wife, Dolores Ibarruri, who incited the housewives of Asturia to defend their homes with boiling oil. A legendary orator in her lifetime, she returned to Spain from exile on Franco's death. On the falangist side, Franco sent Spanish legionnaires and north African troops with a reputation for barbarity to subdue the region; an irony which was not lost on the Asturians who prided themselves on their historical resistance to the Moors.

Another range of mountains, the Picos de Europa, form a natural barrier between Asturias and Cantabria to the east. The small region of Cantabria, of similar area and population size to La Rioja, is centred on the port of Santander. Once patronised by royalty, Santander is an elegant resort, popular with Spaniards from the capital. There are many smaller resorts east of Santander including Laredo which is to the French what Benidorm is to the British.

Galicia

Provinces and main towns: A Coruña, Lugo, Orense, Pontevedra.

It is hardly surprising that Galicia rates with Andalusia as one of the least developed and poorer regions of Spain. Its inland provinces of Lugo and Orense have a reputation as among the most backward in the country. Galicia sits in the northwest corner of the peninsula, isolated geographically and with poor communications with the other regions. Its sizeable, mainly rural population of nearly three million has steadily diminished through emigration, while those who remain survive at subsistence level on agriculture and fishing. Galicia has a twilit Celtic past of which traces survive, including the bagpipes (*gaita*), and the Galician language, *galégo* (which also gave rise to Portuguese); this it is a separate language from Spanish spoken by about 80% of the inhabitants, in a variety of dialects. This region is often compared to Ireland because of a shared Celtic heritage, similar climate and a west coast shaped by the Atlantic into deep inlets. Other similarities include a past in which famines led to emigration in Spain and abroad. Cornered by the Atlantic to the north and west and Portugal to the south, the emigrants were forced southwards into Léon, Castile and Portugal, or to Latin America, to seek their fortunes.

In contrast to the countryside, the coastal cities of Coruña, Pontevedra, Vigo and Santiago are relatively prosperous; and tend to be Castilian speaking.

Before history made Galicia such an an isolated backwater, it had been the focal point of Christian nationalism in Spain by virtue of a miracle which took place on its soil: a shepherd was supposedly led by a guiding star to discover the remains of St James the Apostle, who, legend has it, preached there. From that moment, the Christians gained a holy patron *Santiago matamoros* (St James the moorkiller) in whose name they waged battles against the infidel. Near the site of the miracle a city, Santiago de Compostela (St James of the Field of the Star) grew up; the saintly relics were housed first in a church and then in a great cathedral. The latter became a famous place of pilgrimage throughout Europe in mediaeval times (even Chaucer's Wife of Bath had been there); and this cathedral remains – along with the city surrounding it – one of Spain's premier tourist attractions.

Is there something in the soil of Galicia that produces dictators? Certainly, two of Galicia's most famous sons are such: Fidel Castro in Cuba was the product of Galician emigrants; and General Francisco Franco was a nativeborn Galician.

Although in 1936 Galicia voted for home rule in a regional referendum, the Civil War interrupted its implementation. There is virtually no heavy industry in the area and, without the radicalism that organised labour and industrialisation can produce, the politics of the region have remained largely conservative.

INLAND SPAIN

Castilla y León (Old Castile)

Provinces and main cities: Avila, Burgos, León, Palencia, Salamanca, Segovia, Soria, Valladolid, Zamora.

The nine provinces of the region of Castille/León make it the largest region of Spain, covering almost a fifth of the surface area; but it has less than half the population of the next largest region, Andalusia. Modern Spain grew out from the old kingdom of Castile which was an independent country ruled by its founder Count Fernán Gonzalez in the tenth century, and a kingdom ruled by King Ferdinand in the eleventh century. The new kingdom quickly swallowed up León, becoming the combined kingdom of Castile and León on and off until the thirteenth century. In the fourteenth century, by the marriage of King Ferdinand of Aragon and Isabella of Castile, the three kingdoms of Portugal and Aragon-Castile were united. Castille/Léon is frequently referred to as Old Castile while the region of Castile/La Mancha to the south is New Castile. AragonCastile became known as Spain in the wider world.

The great river Douro flows right across the meseta of Castille/León and on through Portugal to Oporto at its mouth. The meseta is characterized by its huge prairies, given over largely to cereals, and by its lack of inhabitants.

Some of the most beautiful cities in Spain are to be found here: Salamanca, León, and the walled city of Avila. The most scenic province is probably Soria which is full of the fine castles (*castillos*) which give rise to the region's name. Burgos, the city as opposed to the province, was the former capital of Old Castile, though its significance nowadays derives from its position as a main garrison of the military.

La Rioja

Main city: Logroño

Rioja to most Britons means wine. La Rioja is the smallest of the Spanish regions occupying just 1% of its surface area; and home to a mere 0.67% of the population, or just over 50,000 souls. Historically part of the mediaeval Castilian kingdom, La Rioja has nevertheless so far chosen to remain independent. This single-province region takes its name from the Rió Oja, a minor tributary of the great Ebro river which provides the water for the famous vineyards of the region. The main city of Logroño is on the pilgrim way to Santiago; and is the next main stop on the route after Pamplona in Navarre.

MADRID

It is not by chance that the capital looks like a bull's eye on the map of Spain: located on a high plateau with impossible extremes of climate, the town had little else going for it other than its strategically central and easily defended position, until, that is, the capital was moved here in the seventeenth century. Madrid is 2200 feet/670 metres above sea level. All distances in Spain are measured from Puerta del Sol in the city centre. It is the seat of the Spanish parliament and famed for the Prado museum and its dizzy nightlife, which lasts from dusk till dawn.

Madrid and the surrounding area together form the autonomous community of Madrid, which is the most densely populated region of Spain, with about 600 inhabitants to the square kilometre. Madrid city, as opposed to the region, has a population of around five million inhabitants – referred to as *Madrileños*. Unfortunately, in common with other giant metropolises, Madrid has its fair share of eyesore highrise suburbs. And, to its chagrin, it is considered by some as runner-up to trendy Barcelona as a place to live and work.

But living in the capital has many advantages for those not wedded to the sun, sea and sand lifestyle offered by the Mediterranean coast: limited heavy industry and strict pollution controls, and a programme of tree-planting which has transformed the cityscape, have quite literally given Madrid a better atmosphere; there are scores of English language schools, and various UK and American companies operating here, as well as all the job opportunities provided by any capital city, with a wide range of commercial and business activities.

Last but not least, some of Spain's most stunning sights are within easy visiting distance of the capital, notably the cities of Segovia, Avila and Toledo.

Extremadura & CastillaLa Mancha (New Castile)

Main towns and provinces: Badajoz, Cáceres, Albacete, Cuenca, Ciudad Real, Guadalajara, Toledo.

Extremadura and Castile/la Mancha are two of the regions of the meseta (the central tableland) which together comprise about a quarter of Spain's surface area; but contain just over a sixth of its population. Extremadura is dominated by ranges of mountains and reservoirs. There are plans to enhance the agricultural prospects of this little known and bleak region, which is passed through by travellers between Madrid and Portugal, but otherwise virtually ignored by outsiders. Cáceres, the main town, was originally built with spoils from the activities of the local nobles in the New World. There is a famous six-arched Roman bridge at Alcántara near the Portugese border; and further extensive Roman remains at Mérida.

The plain of La Mancha is probably best known for its windmills, and Cervantes' mournful Don Quixote who tilted at them and brought the word 'quixotic' into the English language. Nowadays, the plain is highly cultivated; and agriculture an important part of the local economy as in much of Spain.

Castile/La Mancha contains what is probably one of the most beautiful towns in Spain, Cuenca, perched precariously on the side of a cliff. It also has one of the most famous, the medieval capital of Spain, Toledo, which sits on a craggy rock in a loop of the Tajo River. Toledo was once synonymous with crafted steel, especially swordblades; but its fame rests also on other achievements including scholarship, architecture, building, and the paintings of El Greco. This city also has connections with El Cid, who captured it in the eleventh century. Although redolent with history, Toledo's importance declined in the sixteenth century when the capital was moved to nearby Madrid.

ISLAS CANARIAS (THE CANARY ISLANDS)

Principal islands and resorts: Gran Canaria Las Palmas; Lanzarote Arrecife; La Palma Santa Cruz; Tenerife Santa Cruz.

The Canary Islands (*Las Islas Canarias*) became Spanish territory as long ago as the fifteenth century. The central island, Gran Canaria, is described as a 'miniature continent', with a range of climates from sandy and desert-like around the periphery to lush and subtropical, to a more temperature climate as you climb the central mountains. These are volcanic, like the islands themselves, which emerged from the Atlantic some 40 million years ago. There are legends which have been woven around them, or become enmeshed in their history, like Homer's Garden of the Hesperides, or Atlantis (which we can report did not sink into the sea around here). The ancient Greeks and Phoenicians both knew these islands. There were aboriginal inhabitants, whose fate when the Spanish arrived is not recorded in the guidebooks. They were probably related to the Berbers of nearby North Africa. Gran Canaria also has a *Columbus Museum* in its bustling main town (and port) Las Palmas which records the visit of the explorer who discovered America, and thought it was India. It is in the atmospheric Governor's Residence in the Old Town, where some brightly coloured parrots also commemorate the link with the New World. Colonists from the Canary Islands also went on to settle in North and South America; and the atmosphere today is surprisingly cosmopolitan, with an important fishing industry and import-export companies (taking advantage of the islands' favourable tax regime); and tourists from continental Europe as well as Britain thronging its beaches, notably in the modern tourist developments around the Playa del Inglés and Maspalomas in the south.

More suitable for expatriates are the capital, with all the facilities of any large Spanish city – and its own beach which is a centre for sunbathing and socialising – or the coastline further to the southwest (where Puerto de Mogan retains its old-fashioned charm and is a favoured stopping-off point for the yachts which ply these waters); or to the north, less developed and with strong local traditions. Getting away from it all would mean living inland, near the town of Teror with its famous annual fiesta. Gran Canaria is not a backwater. Ikea is here; and Benetton; and Il Corte Inglés, the ubiquitous Spanish chainstore. The facilities make this an excellent place to live and work, especially away from some of the overcrowded resorts. The *Patronato de Turismo Gran Canaria* can be contacted at: León y Castillo 17, E35003 Las Palmas de Gran Canaria; ☎362222/2422/2622; fax 362822.

The best-known Canary Islands are also the largest: Gran Canaria, Lanzarote and Tenerife. There are seven altogether, located around 70 miles off the Western Sahara coast. The smaller ones are Fuerteventura, Hierro, Gomera and La Palma. Confusingly there is also a Las Palmas on Mallorca in the Balearics which is why you have to write Las Palmas followed by one or other island name. With the exception of Lanzarote, which is comparatively flat, all these islands are characterised by high central mountains, and the consequent change of climate and spectacular scenery which are a legacy of their volcanic origins. The climate is surprisingly mild considering their location, with the North East Trade Winds bringing moistureladen air, the 'horizontal rain' which supports much of the vegetation. Ferries run by *Tranmediterranea* link each of the islands, and latterly jetfoils; and communications with the UK (with all the charter flights) are good.

The Canaries have greater autonomy from central government than other regions of Spain and the two provinces they form are regulated from Las Palmas-Gran Canaria and Santa Cruz-Tenerife. The three main islands have long been popular with tourists from all over the world. In recent years, they have also become increasingly popular with timeshare and perhaps more surprisingly villa owners, many of whom holidayed in the islands before settling there. The all-year round warm climate is a great attraction that outweighs the inconvenience of a comparatively long flight from the UK.

Apart from the scenery and the wildlife there is much of interest culturally and historically; and if you are interested is sailing and ships this is a good place to be. Other points of interest are the mysterious aboriginal inhabitants, and the (almost) unique whistled language which used to be 'spoken' by shepherds in

Gomera. In past times, the Canaries were a useful last-stop for ships bound across the Atlantic. Today, the Japanese tuna fishing fleet and many cargo vessels still stop off here.

The most popular places for foreign residents are also the tourist centres: Tenerife especially the Orotava Valley, and the south of Gran Canaria where there are several tourist developments (as mentioned above) including the aptly named Playa del Inglés and San Agustin. Apart from the three main islands there are also smaller British communitites in Fuerteventura, Lanzarote and La Palma.

Hierro and Gomera are less visited; and further from the facilities and services which make expatriate life possible; a long winter break may be a more attractive option, here and on the other islands.

RESIDENCE AND ENTRY REGULATIONS

CHAPTER SUMMARY

○ Spain joined the European Union after a six-year trial period.

○ **Residence Card.** EU citizens need to have a residence card if they are staying longer than 90 days and they have to apply for it 30 days after arriving if they know they are staying longer than 90 days.

   ○ You apply for a residence card at the local police station.

   ○ It is a good idea to take a Spanish-speaking friend along when you apply for the residence card as documents and procedures vary from place to place.

○ Alternatively, you can employ an intermediary to do all the time consuming legwork and there are companies called *gestorías* that specialise in this.

○ **Non-EU Citizens.** Non EU or EEA nationals should apply for a visa and work permit through the Spanish Consulate in their own country.

   ○ Americans can stay in Spain for 90 days without a residence or work permit.

○ If you are entering Spain for retirement or with nonworking status you will be means tested.

The Current Position

Spain is a current member of the European Union. Immigration for Britons follows the pattern of the other EU countries. EU citizens can enter Spain as a tourist; go to the local police station and apply for a residence card. For workers and residents, this process is fairly straight-forward, although you cannot expect English or other foreign languages to be spoken there: taking along a Spanish-speaking friend is probably a good idea. Those purchasing a business or setting up their own will have to meet some more complex regulations, which also are no more difficult than those facing a Spanish citizen.

No work permit is required, as in the other EU and EEA – European Economic Area – countries; but you do need a residence card (*tarjeta de residencia*) to stay for more than three months (90 days); and should apply for this within thirty days of arrival if you intend to stay for three or more months; or you can go, when you have found a job, to the nearest police station with a *Departamento de Extranjeros* (foreigners' department) and get your residence card and tax/fiscal number sorted out there. Those entering Spain to set up their own business, or who are already in some form of self-employment, do not require a work permit, or any special visa either; but do have to register with the local police after their arrival. All British citizens in Spain, and indeed anywhere in the world, would also be well advised to register with the nearest British Consulate office.

However, non-EU citizens will require a visa to live in Spain (but not always to visit the country) and both a residence and a work permit. Work permits can cost up to 300 euros and will be issued for 15 years

Visas for EU and Non-EU Citizens

Anyone – including EU citizens – who intends to take up permanent residence in Spain may apply for the residence card or 'visa' as it is sometimes known (*visado de residencia*) which is mentioned above. Before entering the country this can be obtained at the relevant Embassy or Consular Office; or, if they are already legally there, at the Bureau for Foreign Persons (run by the Ministry of the Interior in each province – usually at the local police headquarters *(Comisaría de Policia);* or at a Foreigners' Registration Office *(Oficina de Extranjería)* which in Madrid is at C/ Madrazo 9; this office now gives out appointment times for presenting applications; ring 900 610 620. There is also a 'Provincial Directorate for Labour, Social Security and Social Affairs' which may process your application; or the Directorate General for Migration in Madrid where larger employers with more than 100 workers would have to file the application for you (see below).

In recent years, the Spanish authorities have tightened up on entry and work regulations for non-EU or European Economic Area citizens; which in practice means that many temporary or short-term workers do not bother to apply; and more and more mainly young people who work in tourism or seasonal jobs and come from outside the EU are being expelled. Illegal residents run the risk of being thrown out of the country straightaway; and forbidden to return for three years. It is wise to make sure that all the procedures described below are followed, without taking any 'shortcuts' or trying to drift insidiously from tourist to resident status.

For non-EU citizens, the process covers both the residence and work visas required. For applicants from the EU – or those with leave to remain in these countries for an indefinite period stamped on their passports – it is simply a matter of obtaining your residence card, as outlined above. All are supposed to complete the process which legalises their work and residence status in Spain before starting work.

Americans and others from outside the EU will also have to know which work permit to apply for: Class A, which covers seasonal or cyclical work; Class B, for 'a given occupation and activity in a given territorial area;' Class C, for those who have already been resident in Spain for some time and covering all categories of employment; Class D, for self-employment in a specific location for up to one year; and Class E, for all categories of self-employment. Class F only concerns you if you live close to the Spanish frontier and commute to Spain. Excellent detailed information on the legal processes can be seen on the website of *The Broadsheet*, an English-language monthly magazine in Madrid (www.thebroadsheet.com). The American organisation, InterExchange (161 Sixth Avenue, New York, NY 10013; 2129240446 ext. 109; www.interexchange.org) arranges language assistant programmes in Spain for a placement fee of $400$600.

British and other EU citizens will be relieved not to have to know about all of this!

The Spanish Embassy or Consulate can advise on preferences in granting these permits (and the strict rules which stop you doing work which could be done by Spanish people, or undercutting the wages and conditions which apply locally). They will advise on the documents you need; and forms to be filled in. These include some which your employer will have to give you; as well as your own qualifications or diplomas; photocopies of your passport and visa application; a certificate relating to your criminal record (or preferably the absence of one); a medical certificate; as well as evidence which can show, for example, that your work is needed to 'organise and start up a foreign enterprise moving entirely or partly to Spain'; or other preferences which can favour your application (which include being a close relative of the employer).

Non-EU nationals are not meant to go to Spain to work without prior permission. But it is worth noting that Canadian and American visitors with a valid passport do not require a visa to visit there for a period of up to 90 days; a time which may allow for the organisation of these other visas and permits if you do happen to find work, and therefore cannot make these arrangements in advance.

Residence and Retirement

Those who are going to Spain to retire – and 'those of independent means' – will need to present proof of a substantial pension or sufficient means of support (possibly a standing order from a bank stating that the said amount is being transferred to Spain each month). This declaration can be given when they apply to the relevant Consulate in the home country for their residence card. Information as to the amount required currently (and for each additional member of the family) can be obtained from the Spanish Consulate. Currently this is around £500 ($700) a month for a single person. Pensioners would also be well-advised to note that the standard British pension may not always be enough to cover all future needs; The Department of Work and Pensions offices and charities like Help the Aged can be sources of advice on this aspect of moving there.

For the British and Irish and other EU nationals, EU rules have made this process much simpler. Documents needed to apply for your residence permit (whether you are at home or in Spain) are: a full valid passport; proof of residence; completed application forms; marriage documents; four passport-sized photographs; a standard medical certificate from your doctor (these are needed by all those applying for a residence card); bank certificates showing your regular income where these are needed (get your UK bank to call the documents they send you 'bank certificates': this may help); and details of health insurance (you will need a certificate from the health insurance company stating that full hospitalisation and treatment are covered, or evidence of registration with the Spanish equivalent of the Departments of Health/Social Security, the INSS). There is more about *Health Insurance and Hospitals* in the chapter on *Daily Life* later in this section.

Other documents which will be needed by non-EU retirees include: a full passport with a minimum validity of six months, and with at least one full blank page to affix the visa; and three completed application forms, with three photographs attached. Visa and residence applications for all retired people may be made in person or by post in the USA and Canada; and the Consulate will advise on the forms and fees needed. Consulates in the UK, Ireland and North America are generally open from 9.30am to 12 noon Monday to Friday. In Spain, the local police office may be contacted for one of these residence permits and/or visas.

Using a Gestor

Although this process is theoretically speedy and uncomplicated, in practice it may involve a lot of queuing and legwork. In this and other transactions when you are in Spain, you may wish to employ the services of an intermediary known as a *gestor* (please see below) who can help to facilitate many other arrangements as well. He or she is available to deal with the mountain of paperwork, red tape and bureaucracy which needs be worked through, to purchase a business, for example. And a gestor can help you avoid endless queuing; assembling piles of unnecessary documents; and having to deal with the Spanish authorities in Spanish (a unique and not always rewarding experience).

Gestors' offices (*gestorías*) are listed in the local telephone directory (*Las Paginas Amarillas*); the prices they charge vary, so it's worth shopping around.

It is important to stress that although there are some small advantages (e.g. concerning bringing your car into Spain) which are available to those who keep their tourist status, it is much better for those intending to live permanently here to operate within the letter of the law. This applies especially to those outside the EU or EEA areas. Some of the latter may try to deceive the authorities by applying for a *permanencia* – a 90 day extension to their original visa – and then darting out of the country in another 90 days' time and then slipping back in again, and so on, in order to legalise another 90 days 'visit'.

Apart from the likelihood that you will one day be exposed by some unusually alert border guard while on one of these clandestine jaunts, there are also definite advantages to having, or to intending to apply for, a residence permit. This allows you to import furniture, household goods and personal possessions free of all customs duties; or to get a loan from a Spanish bank to buy a house, flat or car. Since in practice there are no restrictions on this anyway for EU-citizens – only proof of identity and a list of the items to be imported – there is no incentive for them now to find a way around these regulations.

Additionally, EU pensioners in possession of a residence permit can join the Spanish state health service free of charge. And if you are living or working in Spain, and then want to bring in your car, you will just have to import it (as the locals would). The procedures are complex; but basically there is no prohibition on importing cars for personal use in Spain. It may be cheaper to buy one there though.

Extending Work Permits and Other Procedures'

Once in Spain, you are able to apply for permanent residence immediately and must apply before the expiry of 90 days. As with many administrative matters, this may be more conveniently tackled by a *gestor* (also see above). For those who prefer to obtain the residence permit themselves, they should assemble all the documents mentioned above, and evidence of income and photographs etc; and go to the *Oficina* or *Departamento de Extranjeros* at the *Comisaría Provincial de Policía*; the same applies to renewing residence or work permits.

Unfortunately, the list of required documents can vary in its details from office to office; and will also depend (for non-EU citizens) on whether a work permit is being renewed at the same time. The simplification of procedures for Britons and Irish and other EU citizens does not mean you will be able to do without the services of a gestor; even for something as relatively simple as renewing a residence permit. If you are less certain, or are newly arrived in the country, the only way for you to find out precisely what is required in many administrative matters is to queue at the counter along with your Spanish neighbours – this is why the gestor is such a busy person!

Renewal of temporary residence permits should simply be a formality (and most Britons and Irish citizens can receive a five-year or permanent one). If you move out of Spain, or back to your country of origin, then once the residence permit has been handed in at the police station, your right to residency in Spain automatically ceases.

Work Permits for Non-EU Applicants

For non-EU/EEA applicants, the procedure for obtaining a visa for those who also need a work permit is different, and the process of obtaining the residence/work visa takes considerably longer, usually several weeks. Applicants should specify what kind of work permit they are applying for (the five different types are listed in the *Visas* section above). There are exemptions, for categories of workers from the USA or Canada and elsewhere for foreign academic staff and media correspondents, for example, or representatives of religious organisations. A full list of these can be obtained from the nearest Spanish Embassy or Consulate. There are also categories for group work permits, trainees and au pairs.

Applications are not accepted by post in any circumstances; and instead should always be made in person or by a representative who has written consent from the applicant to act on his or her behalf. The following documents are required for each application: a certified copy of your passport details; a report on the employer's business and a job profile; four recent photos; a duplicate copy of your visa application; any relevant degrees and qualifications; evidence if applicable that you fall into one of the preferential categories (see above); evidence that the employer is registered with the Social Security Administration; the completed application forms; a medical certificate; a certificate of your criminal record; written proof of the offer of employment (in the form of a pre-contract of employment stamped and signed by both parties or a letter written on headed paper of the employing company in Spain) and a stamped addressed envelope.

If all the documents are in order, a copy of the application form, medical certificate and the photocopies of the passport, certified by the Consulate, will be returned to the applicant as proof that he or she has applied for the visa. All three documents must then be sent to the prospective employer in Spain; who in turn should apply immediately for the work permit at the district department of the Ministry of Labour (*Minesterio de Trabajo*) or the relevant department. The granting of the visa is subject to the approval of the work permit by the Spanish authorities and this usually takes several weeks, or longer.

Successful applicants should collect their visas in person as soon as the Consulate advises them to do so and must take with them their passports with at least one blank page to affix the visa, the consular fee, and the communication from the Consulate stating that the visa is ready for collection. Once in Spain, a work permit can be picked up from the local police station or from the provincial departments of the Ministry of Labour and Bureaux for Foreign Persons; there will be no problem in obtaining this if the residence/work visa is presented.

The type and duration of the work permit will vary according to certain factors, e.g. the type of work undertaken, and the area in which it is done, but in no case will it exceed five years. Work permits will always be issued for the same duration as the residence permit.

The granting and renewal of work permits will depend on the following considerations: the level of unemployment in the specific activity for which the permit is applied for; and vacancies available in the profession in which the proposed activity is to be carried out.

It is worth making the point that UK and Irish and other EU citizens are exempt from these work permit procedures and only require a residence permit.

Entering to Start a Business

The form required for EU citizens planning to set up their own business in Spain is called the *tarjeta comunitaria*. This is an EU document; and there is no need for a work permit as such. However, in order to acquire the tarjeta, anyone planning on opening a small business (e.g. a shop, bar, or restaurant) must first obtain a business licence, the *licencia fiscal*, from the tax authorities, as a Spanish citizen would. This authorises the setting up of new businesses.

The criteria for the granting of the licence vary from profession to profession, and include the existing provision of the services one intends to offer in the region and the applicant's own professional experience. It is worth noting that the authorities tend to regard with favour applications to start businesses which employ local labour or which 'promote job creation among Spanish workers'. Anyone planning to continue working within his or her own profession (e.g. a doctor or lawyer) must apply for membership to the relevant professional association in Spain; such associations can often be less than helpful when asked to admit foreign competition within their own ranks. Note that although self-employed EU nationals do not need a work permit as such, they must register with the district police station and also with the local tax office (*hacienda*).

That means, although the bureaucratic process for the self-employed is less complex than for those of different status, it can be just as fraught with difficulties and delays. The whole process may take months to complete as the tax authority grinds its way laboriously to granting all the necessary forms and documents.

Equivalence of Qualifications

These are coordinated in Spain by the National Institute for Employment; and there are a wide variety of leaflets on comparability of qualifications available in the UK in Jobcentres and business libraries. For more about this, see under *Skills and Qualifications* in the *Employment* chapter.

Transfer of Jobseeker's Allowance

Those who have been registered as unemployed in Britain for four weeks can go to other EU countries (including Spain) to look for work and still receive the UK benefit. See leaflet UBL222 available from Job Centres; and there is an application form to transfer benefit abroad: E303. First of all, you should select the town where you intend to look for work in Spain; and then notify your local unemployment benefit office which will tell you if you are eligible (and have paid enough National Insurance contributions). You should certainly make these arrangements as far as possible in advance; receipt of the form E303 means that the Spanish social security department the INSS can pay your benefit, through the local *Oficina de Empleo*; which is where you should take your E303 form on arrival if it has not been sent directly there (and make sure the British authorities have notified their Spanish opposite numbers).

For more about this scheme you can ask at your local Jobcentre. At the time of writing, the system for paying 'JSA' and unemployment benefits in Britain is under review; but EU regulations which the British government has already signed up to mean that the general outline of this scheme will remain the same.

This approach to becoming a resident of Spain and looking for work there can seem attractive to people who are currently unemployed; and provides a financial cushion which will allow you some time to find work (it also allows the UK government to 'export' your unemployment benefit /JSA and, cynics would say, to reduce the unemployment totals). Your time will be limited; so some preparation is advisable. For further information see *Claiming UK Jobseekers Allowance in Spain* in the *Daily Life* chapter.

Spanish Residency – Registering with your Embassy

Once resident in Spain, as anywhere in the world, it is also advisable to register with your local National Embassy or Consulate: a list of these is provided below. This registration enables the authorities to keep emigrants up to date with any information they need as citizens resident overseas; and also to trace individuals in the event of an emergency. They can also help with information regarding an emigrant's status overseas; and advise with any diplomatic or passport problems; and they may also help in the case of an emergency, e.g. the death of a relative overseas. However, consulates do not really function as a source of general help and advice; they can certainly not act as employment bureaux.

As a rule, British embassies and consulates interpret their role helping British citizens overseas more strictly than those of many other countries, as many who have needed their help in an emergency have found they tend to keep within the letter if not the spirit of their duties. Appeals for assistance in matters which fall outside these duties – explained in a leaflet available from embassies/consulates or the *Foreign and Commonwealth Office*, Consular Department (Room CL 605), Clive House, Petty France, London SW1H 9HD, ☎020-7270 4137 or 020-7270 4142 – often fall on deaf ears.

Residency and Citizenship Rights

Residence in Spain is not the same as citizenship of that country. Those who wish to become a citizen of their new host country will need to have lived there for ten years first. Residents of Spain with overseas nationality have most of the rights and obligations of a Spanish national in employment, health and other fields; but no right to vote in elections and no liability to military service.

Non-EU or EEA Nationals

Non-EU or EEA nationals applying to take up residence in Spain have much more red tape to cope with (as this chapter may already have made clear). However, the volume and variety of the bureaucracy will vary according to nationality (and if there are reciprocal health and tax agreements for example). All non-EU nationals should first of all apply for a visa and work permit through the Spanish Consulate in their own country if they are intending to live and work there.

Spanish Embassies and Consulates in the UK

Spanish Embassy: 30 Chesham Place, London SW1X 8SB; ☎020-7235 5555; fax 020-7259 5392.

Spanish Consulate General: 20 Draycott Place, London SW3 2RZ; ☎020-7589 8989; fax 020-7581 7888.

Spanish Consulate General: 1A Brooke House, 70 Spring Gardens, Manchester M2 2BQ; ☎0161-236 1233; fax 0161-228 7467.

Spanish Consulate General: 63 North Castle Street, Edinburgh EH2 3LJ; ☎0131-220 1843; fax 0131-226 4568.

Consular Section: Spanish Embassy, 17A Merlyn Park, Ballsbridge, Dublin 4, Ireland; ☎ +353 1269 1640.

British Embassies and Consulates

British Embassy: Calle de Fernando el Santo 16, E28010 Madrid; ☎913190 208/190 200; www.ukinspain.com

British Consulate: Plaza Calvo Sotelo 1/2, 03001 Alicante; ☎965 216 022/216/190; fax 96514 05 28.

British ConsulateGeneral: Edificio Torre de Barcelona, Avenida Diagonal 47713, E08036 Barcelona; ☎93419 9044; fax 93405 2411.

British ViceConsulate Benidorm: to be contacted through Alicante.

British ConsulateGeneral: Alameda de Urquijo 28, E48008 Bilbao; ☎94415 7600; fax 94416 7632.

British ViceConsulate: Avenida de Isidoro Macabich 451°, E07800 Ibiza; ☎97130 18 18/30 38 16; fax 97130 19 72.

British Consulate: Edificio Duquesa, Calle Duquesa de Parcent 81, E29001 Málaga; ☎95221 7571; fax 9522 11 30.

British Consulate: Plaza Mayor 3D, E07002 Palma de Mallorca; ☎97171 24 45; fax 97171 75 20.

British ViceConsulate: Sa Casa Nova, Cami de Biniatap 30, Es Castell, E07720 Menorca; ☎97136 33 73.

British Consulate: Edificio Catalunya, Luis Morote 63, E35007 Las Palmas; ☎928262 5080; fax 92826 77 74.

British ViceConsulate: Plaza Weler 81, E38003 Santa Cruz de Tenerife; ☎92228 68 63; fax 92228 99 03.

British Consulate: Paseo de Pereda 27, E39004 Santander; ☎94222 00 00; fax 94222 29 41.

British Consulate: Plaza Nueva 8 (Dpdo), E41001 Seville; ☎95422 8875; fax 95421 0323.

British Consulate: Plaza Compostela 236, E36201 Vigo; tel/fax 98643 71 33.

Spanish Labour Office: 20 Peel Street, London W8 7PD; ☎020-7221 0098; fax 020-7229 7270; email spanlabo@globalnet.co.uk. For advice on work and social security in Spain; and publishes *Regulations for British Nationals Wishing to Work or Reside in Spain.*

Job Centre Plus: Overseas Placing Unit,, Rockingham House, 123 West Street, Sheffield S1 4ER; ☎0114-2596192; www.employmentservice. gov.uk; www.jobcentreplus.gov.uk. Publishes information sheet on *Working in Spain.*

Other Embassies and Consulates

Spanish Embassy: 2375 Pennsylvania Avenue, NW, Washington DC 20037; ☎2024520100; fax 2028335670.

There are Consulates in Boston, Chicago, Houston, Los Angeles, Miami, New Orleans, New York (☎2123554090), Puerto Rico and San Franciso.

Spanish Embassy: Suite 802, 350 Sparks Street, Ottawa, Ontario K1R 7S8; ☎61323721934; fax 6132369246. Consulates in Burnaby, Calgary, Halifax, Montréal, Québec, St John's, Toronto and Winnipeg.

United States Embassy: Serrano 75, E28006 Madrid; ☎915774000; fax 915641652.

Canadian Embassy: Edificio Goya, Calle Nunez de Balboa 35, E28001 Madrid; ☎914314300; fax 914312367.

In all your dealings regarding residence and entry, whether to start a business, work, or retire, you should find the process nowadays is relatively straightforward, if at times somewhat time-consuming. Where difficulties do arise while you are in Spain you are recommended to contact solicitors *Cornish & Co.* at their Marbella office (Edificio Alfil, Avda Ricardo Soriano 19, 29600 Malaga).

SETTING UP HOME

CHAPTER SUMMARY

O Most of the foreigners in Spain live on the Spanish costas.

   O The popular Mediterranean coasts of Spain are the most expensive places to buy property and are beginning to price themselves out of the market.

   O The best property bargains are away from the Costas.

   O The Balearic island of Majorca is a favourite spot for the super rich.

O **Outstanding debts on property.** When buying property in Spain it is essential to make sure that there are no outstanding debts on it.

   O Under Spanish law the purchaser is liable for any debts on property he or she has purchased.

   O Many expatriates persist in trying to maintain a well-manicured lawn, when the climate and frequent water shortages are against them.

   O The Spanish property contract or conveyance deed is prepared by a notary (*notario*) who is a public official.

O **Buying Land.** Buying a plot for building in Spain is hedged with a multitude of regulations.

O Once private building work has been completed, another barrage of paperwork is involved in order to be connected to the utilities and to bestow legal ownership.

O **Importing a car.** It is generally easier and cheaper to buy a car in Spain than to import yours.

Overview

For many years Spain has been the property buyer's paradise. Traditionally, cheap property, the availability of timeshares, as well as offshore banking and a welcoming atmosphere for expatriates, have all contributed to its attraction for secondhome buyers and potential residents. Many have bought property there which they would never have been able to afford at home. Currently, however, although many bargains are still available, the Spanish property market, especially in the tourist-saturated areas along the coast, is in the process of upgrading itself; and Spain is not the buyer's market it once was (except in some of the less well-known regions where expatriates are still thin on the ground). There is the possible risk of the mass-market costas pricing themselves out of reach of many who would wish to live or retire there.

On the other hand, the fall in the value of the euro has had a countervailing effect for those nationalities with stronger currencies, including the UK. Exchange rate fluctuations in the future and the various effects of your own country adopting the euro (if applicable), are just a couple of the factors you should take into consideration before you decide to buy. Those outside the Eurozone will also have to consider the effect of differential interest rate fluctuations on the amounts they must pay on their mortgages: Spanish interest rates are currently similar to those in the UK.

The costas are becoming less fashionable than they once were and with the bad publicity which mass tourism has attracted, many of the major housing developments are now inland, or on sites adjacent to golf clubs or similar facilities to attract the more 'upmarket' purchaser. There are purpose-built complexes nowadays for retired people as well; and estate agents have become almost like travel agents, offering everything from inspection visits, car hire, resale and even paying all the bills. Many property developers are now copying the tourist trade and offering an all-inclusive service with the same leisure facilities and amenities that a holidaymaker might expect.

Prospective buyers can keep up with trends by reading the property and travel sections of some of the broadsheet and Sunday newspapers. Obviously, property costs vary greatly according to location. Some of the cheaper areas include the depressed market of the Costa Blanca, while the periphery of the Spanish hinterland (e.g. Castilla La Mancha) is at last beginning to open up to the international property buyer (and more tourists) through the extensive refurbishment of road communications and the revival of interest in these little-discovered and scenically unspoilt areas.

Future development is another potential pitfall to be taken into account. British residents from Fuengirola to Estepona on the Costa del Sol are presently up in arms about a proposed new motorway that 'might put paid to the area's reputation as one of the Mediterranean's most sought-after locations for leisure and retirement homes', according to one commentator; some are even being made homeless to make way for the road. The E15 Euroroute could yet rouse some elderly and retired expats to become road protesters; and some others are complaining about promised road connections and motorways which have not materialised.

Fashion also dictates property prices. Marbella, once the dream destination of the more affluent expatriate, is now out of favour with the same; so some real

CORNISH & Co.
SOLICITORS

The Spanish Specialists

- **Buying property in Spain**

- **Selling property in Spain**

- **Spanish Wills**

- **Offshore Companies/Trusts**

- **Foreign Mortgages**

LONDON
Tel: +44 (0) 208 478 3300
Fax: +44 (0) 208 553 3418/3422
e-mail: interlex@cornishco.com

SPAIN
Tel: + (34) 952 866830
Fax: +(34) 952 865320
e-mail: cornish@mercuryin.es

GIBRALTAR
Tel: +(350) 41800
Fax: +(350) 41931
e-mail cornish@gibnet.gi

www.cornishco.com

property bargains are currently available. For instance, at the time of going to print, a one-bedroomed maisonnette with a large patio, next to the Conception Lake in the Marbella mountains would cost about £55,000 ($80,000). The price range in Marbella is from £30,000 for a one-bedroom flat to £50,000-£55,000 for a larger twobedroom flat with patio or garden to £100,000 ($145,000) for a three-bedroom town house. In nearby Sotogrande, a luxurious three-bedroom house with private pool costs considerably less than its British equivalent, with one advertised for £150,000 ($215,000). In contrast, Majorca, which was once relatively unspoilt (especially the north of the island) is enjoying a period of renewed popularity, reflected in its often younger visitors and the escalating property costs. All the Balearics seem to have become home to the very rich; who manage to live in secluded isolation from their less affluent British neighbours and can easily pay one and a half million pounds for a holiday home.

Here and elsewhere, living costs have risen; and in Majorca your everyday expenses will be noticeably more (around 20%) than they are even in London; although prices for food, electricity, water charges, and so on are more or less the same as those in Britain away from the islands, and outside the more expensive Madrid and Barcelona areas.

Property buying procedures in Spain are bound to be unfamiliar to the majority of aspiring expats; and although this chapter explains the main procedures, and some of the pitfalls, **it is essential that professional and local advice is taken before any financial commitment is made.** This is the first rule of house or villa-buying in Spain; and good advice is easily obtainable from property agents in the UK as well as on-the-spot; from solicitors as well as from others who have already set up home there.

What are the problems? One house buyer who failed to take professional advice ended up paying out an extra £10,000 ($14,500) in rates which the previous owner had failed to pay. Another case involved a woman handing over money to a Spanish estate agent for a property without any consultation with a solicitor, only to find that the agent and seller had disappeared along with the money a few weeks later. More generally, you should ensure that a title to resell the property is a part of the contract; and be aware of any outstanding debts on your new house or villa, which in Spanish law are likely to become your responsibility when ownership is transferred. You should also take professional advice on property and home insurance.

This chapter contains listings in the relevant sections for various UK-based companies who specialise in various specific services such as removals or offering legal advice. But one company, *Spanish One Stop Shop*, that defies any such simple classification. Its activities relevant to this chapter include marketing and selling freehold property; arranging UK, offshore and Spanish mortgages, offering legal advice by a UK-based solicitor from an office in mainland Spain, arranging buildings contents insurance and shipping property to Spain three times a week. Its address is Mansion House, Acadia Hall, High Street, Dartford, Kent DA1 1DJ; ☎ 01322-391 040; fax 01322-228 178.

How do the Spanish Live?

Increasingly, the trend in Spain is towards home ownership as opposed to rented property which was still the norm some years ago. It is estimated that over half

Looking to buy a home overseas?

exhibitions

Visit one of the Homes Overseas exhibitions throughout England, Ireland, Scotland, Norway, Sweden, Denmark, Belgium and Germany.

Blendon Communications are Europe's largest independent organisers of multi-exhibitor property exhibitions.

Visit our website at www.homesoverseas.co.uk for the full calendar of events.

For the most comprehensive property search on the web visit www.newskys.co.uk

1000s OF PROPERTIES FOR SALE IN MANY OF THE WORLD'S PRIME LOCATIONS INCLUDING

- THE CARIBBEAN • CYPRUS • FLORIDA
- FRANCE • GREECE • ITALY • MALTA
- SOUTH AFRICA • SPAIN AND ITS ISLANDS • PORTUGAL

PROPERTY FOR RETIREMENT, HOLIDAYS AND INVESTMENT, LEGAL, FINANCIAL AND REMOVAL ADVISORS

24 hour information line: +44 (0) 20 7939 9852

HOMES OVERSEAS MAGAZINE

The complete monthly guide to buying property overseas including destination and lifestyle reports from some of the world's most popular destinations. Regular features include legal, financial, removals, golf and money matters plus news on industry trends. Available at most newsagents, Homes Overseas exhibitions or via subscription: +44 (0) 20 8709 6690

For trade enquiries call the Homes Overseas sales team on + 44 (0)20 7939 9888

 207 Providence Square, Mill Street, London, SE1 2EW
Tel: +44 (0) 20 7939 9888 Fax: +44 (0) 020 7939 9889 www.blendoncommunications.co.uk ae

01452-770199. Costa Blanca specialists.

Casa Del Sol Properties: 51 High Street, Emsworth, Hampshire PO10 7AN; ☎01243-397797; fax 01243-379737.

Costa Blanca Choice: Hersal House, 77 Springfield Road, Chelmsford, Essex, CM2 6JG; ☎01245-496644; fax 01245-495454

Courciers: 4 & 6 Station Road, South Norwood, London SE25 5AJ; ☎020-8653 6333. Country homes as well as coastal properties on the Costa Blanca.

Diamond Sun Resorts: Diamond House, Main Street, Markfield LE67 9UT; ☎08009-757198; fax 01530-2241242; www.diamondsunresorts.com. Offer a onetoone specialist service.

Gran Sol Properties: Summerville House, Heatley Street, Preston, Lancashire; ☎01772-825587; fax 01772-251902; email:gran.sol.europe@zetnet.co.uk. Spanish office: Edificio Apolo 1, Calle Corbeta, Calpe, E03710 Alicante; tel/fax 965835468.

Iberian International: Atlas House, Station Road, Dorking, Surrey RH4 1EB; ☎ 01306-870961; fax 01306-870994. Specialise in all kinds of property in Torrevieja, including apartments, villas, bungalows, townhouses etc.

MASA International: Airport House, Purley Way, Croydon CR0 0XZ; ☎020-8781 1995; fax 020-8781 1922; wwwmasainter.com. Specialise in the southern Costa Blanca.

Garrison Resorts: Marlborough Court, Pickford Street, Macclesfield SK11 6JD; ☎01625-613681/0800975 7198; fax 01625-613737.

McCallum SL UK: ☎Spain 971866615; www.ihh.com. Specialists in Mallorca.

Nyrae Propeties (Overseas): Old Bank House, 1 High Street, Arundel, West Sussex BN18 9AD; ☎01903-884663; fax 01903-732554. Deals with agencies throughout the world.

Philip Lockwood: 71 Coventry Street, Kidderminster DY10 2BS; tel 01562-745082; fax 01562-740202. Philip Lockwood specialise in villa construction and sales of all types of property to the east of Malaca near Lake Vinuela.

Propertunities: 13/17 Newbury Street, Wantage OX12 8BU; ☎01235-772345; fax 01235-770018; email villas@propertunities.co.uk. Specialists in villas on the Costa Blanca and Costa Calida.

Solymar Estates S.L: Urb. El Saladillo, Oficina Solymar Estates S.L., Estepona 29680, Malaga; ☎95290 4020; solymarestates@hotmail.com

Spanish Connexion: The Old Vicarage, Leigh, Sherborne, Dorset DT9 6HL; ☎01935-872222; fax 01935-873094; email fscx@tovic.com. International removal.

Names of other agents dealing in Spanish property can be obtained from the *National Association of Estate Agents*, Arbon House, 21 Jury Street, Warwick CV34 4EH; ☎01926-496800; wwwnaea.co.uk (select the international section. They can send a list (ask for their 'Homelink' department) of members specialising in Spain. Or contact the *Royal Institute of Chartered Surveyors*, 12 Great George Street, Parliament Square, London SW1 3AD; ☎020-7222 7000.

Timeshare Advice. Advice on timeshare properties is issued by the *TimeShare Council*: 23 Buckingham Gate, London SW1E 6LB; ☎020-7821 8845; fax 020-7828 0739. *The Organisation For Time-Share in Europe* (☎020-7291 0901; www.oteinfo.com; info@oteinfo.com) are helpful. A leaflet *Your Place in the Sun* is published by the Department of Trade and Industry in London which recommends that timeshare purchasers should only sign contracts which include a coolingoff period during which they can change their mind without incurring a penalty. **When buying a property, as with your mortgage and other transactions, you are strongly advised to take professional advice and to check the credentials of the organisations concerned.**

Translations: Often documents relating to property purchase, residence, import/export etc. may be in Spanish. If you have a problem with these contact *Verbatim Language Services*, Clifton House, 6 Clifton Terrace, Southsea, Hants P05 3NL; ☎02392-833121.

FINANCE

Exchange Risks

Now that Spain is in the 'eurozone' and Britain is not, British expatriates are at some risk of euro fluctuations against sterling. There is a greater risk involved in purchasing property in another EU country such as Spain – and a danger of your investment losing its value – although it is hoped that the single currency will remain stable against other currencies. You should bear in mind that

if the euro increases in value against sterling then a UK purchaser may have to make higher mortgage repayments on a monthly, or, preferably, quarterly basis: however the value of the property in sterling will also have increased. Similarly, if the value drops, then payments are reduced, as is the value of the property and the loan.

Although a mortgage (*hipoteca*) in euros on a Spanish property provides better security against fluctuations in currency values, the fluctuation in interest rates may serve to counteract this advantage. One of the main and uncomfortable aspects of Spanish-based mortgages in the recent past is interest rates which have been maintained at a higher rate than other comparable European countries (along with Spain's higher unemployment). Sometimes a fixed UK mortgage will be a better bet, and will usually be quite easy to organise. Among those who can arrange a mortgage you may contact UK building societies like the *Halifax* (head office: Trinity Road, Halifax, West Yorkshire HX1 2RG) at their high street branches. International and Spanish specialists include *Conti Financial Services*, 204 Church Road, Hove, Sussex BN3 2DJ; ☎01273-772811; fax 01273-321269;www.overseasandukfinance.com and *Philip Lockwood* (71 Coventry Street, Kidderminster DY1 2BS; ☎01562-745082; fax 01562-740202) both of whom are able to arrange both euro and sterling-based mortgages and explain the relative benefits and risks of each type.

Spanish Mortgages

Many Spanish banks offer euro mortgages either within Spain or through branch offices in the UK. The conditions relating to Spanish mortgages differ from those in the UK in that a deposit of at least 30% is usually required; a maximum of 70% of the property value being provided as a loan, unlike the 95% or even 100% available from UK banks. Non-residents usually have a lower limit of borrowing of 50% imposed and the mortgage repayment period also tends to be shorter, the norm being fifteen years. The method used to assess your mortgage is also a little different from that in the UK. Basically, you will have to put all your UK and Spanish earnings and income forward; and get references from your UK bank. Any other borrowing you have will also be assessed. Although repayment mortgages still predominate, there are endowment and pensionlinked options as well. The arrangement fee is usually around 1%. Interest rates (and any changes in them) could be a disadvantage, even though you have escaped most of the risks associated with exchange rate fluctuations (at least if your move is permanent). And you will find that the cheaper interest rates and special deals on offer usually only apply to more highlyvalued properties of between £100,000 and £200,000; and not to the more modest end of the property market.

UK Mortgages

A number of people planning to buy second homes in Spain arrange loans in the UK, remortgaging or taking out a second mortgage out on their UK property and then buying with cash in Spain. Alternatively, it is now also possible to approach London-based banks for a sterling loan secured on the Spanish house. If you are considering borrowing in the UK, then the method of calculating the amount that may be borrowed is worked out at between two and a half or three and a half times your primary income plus any secondary income, less any capital amount already borrowed on the mortgage. Sometimes two and a half or three times joint income, less outstanding capital, is possible.

Naturally the mortgage would be subject to a valuation on any UK property and you could expect to borrow, subject to equity, up to a maximum of 100% of the purchase price of the overseas property. A second charge, or a new first charge would be taken by the lender. Some lending institutions charge a higher rate for a loan to cover a second property. A final word of warning is that you should ensure that if a loan is arranged in the UK then all of the details of this are included in the Spanish property contract (*escritúra*).

TABLE 3	MORTGAGE COMPARISON TABLE	
	UK Mortgage	**Spanish Mortgage**
Types available: pension mortgages etc.	Repayment, endowment or	Mostly repayment
Maximum % of value:	100% (can remortgage, i.e. clear existing loan and the new advance becomes a 1st charge or second mortgage.)	70% of valuation
Maximum compared to income:	2.5 x joint or 3.5 x 1.	30% of diposable income.
Period of mortgage:	5 to 25 years	5 to max 20 years
Interest rate:	fixed, discounted, variable or capped.	4%-5% above UK base.
Repayments made:	Monthly	Monthly or quarterly

Legal and Other Advice

A useful contact for further advice and information on any queries concerning the Spanish property market is *Mackenzie Wemyss Associates*, Overseas Property Consultants (Stable Grange, Cliftons Lane, Reigate, Surrey RH2 9RA). This is a firm of Spanish property and mortgage consultants which offers practical advice to anyone intending to buy property in Spain. A *Guide to Buying Property in Spain* is a useful publication while *Bennett and Co* solicitors, 144 Knutsford Road, Wilmslow, Cheshire SK9 6JP, ☎01625-586937, fax 01625-585362, www.bennett-and-co.com; handle all property purchasing and finance legalities. Bennett & Co. have associate offices in Lisbon, Almancil, Madrid, Alicante, Marbella, Torrevieja, Javea, Tenerife, Girona, Barcelona, Majorca, Ibiza and Lanzarote. A firm of solicitors specialising in Spain is *John Howell & Co*, 17 Maiden Lane, Covent Garden, London WC2E 7NL; ☎020-7420 0400; fax 020-7836 3626; email info@europelaw.com. They are the only firm of English solicitors to do nothing but work involving Spain, France, Portugal and Italy. They will answer your enquiries on all aspects of buying property in Spain and send you a free information pack. Another specialist is *Fernando Scornik* of 32 St. James's Street, London SW1A 1HD; ☎020-7930 3593; fax 020-7930 3385.

Also specialising in Spain is *Florez Valcarcel*, Notary Public and Licentiate in Spanish Law (130 King Street, Hammersmith, London W6 OQU; ☎ 020-8741 4867; fax 020-8741 4867), with professional contacts in the most important places in Spain and more than 35 years' experience in the field.

Cornish & Co., a firm of solicitors with offices in London, Marbella and Gibraltar, can also offer comprehensive legal advice on everything from setting up home to retirement matters or the creation of business structures (Lex House, 1/7 Hainault Street, Ilford, London IG1 4EL; tel 020-8478 3300; fax 020-8552 3418/3422; e-mail interlex@cornishco.com; www.cornishco.com; tel (+34) 952 866830; e-mail cornish@mercuryin.es in Spain; and (+350) 41800; e-mail cornish@gibnet.gi in Gibraltar). See also the section below. They have a range of legal services for overseas residents, from advice on forming trusts and companies to tax planning, wills and probate advice as well as dealing with all property-related matters. An information pack is available on request or visit their website www.cornishco.com where you can obtain an estimate of legal fees for your property purchase online. The *Allied Dunbar* publication *Buying and Selling Your Home in Spain* by Per Svensson (Longman) also contains some useful tips, although some of the information may be a little out of date.

Offshore Mortgages

The principle of offshore companies involves turning a property into a company, the shares of which are held by an offshore bank based in a tax haven such as Gibraltar or the Channel Islands, as collateral against a mortgage of up to 75% for a repayment term of up to 20 years. The property owner's name is confidential; and the property company is administered on his or her behalf by the offshore trustees. Previously, the advantage of offshore property purchase was that it reduced tax liability in the country of purchase, as, if and when the property was resold, it merely became a question of transferring the shares confidentially to a new owner, thus avoiding transfer taxes and VAT (sales tax in the country in question).

However there are risks. For example, due to legislation passed in 1991, thousands of Britons who bought property in Spain through offshore companies ended up facing potentially huge tax bills in the event of either their selling the property, or of their death. Although, in the majority of cases, offshore property purchase has resulted in the legitimate avoidance of wealth tax, succession duty, transfer tax and capital gains tax, a minority of cases has clearly crossed the fine line between tax avoidance and tax evasion at the cost of the state coffers. **You should certainly not try to enter into such an arrangement without the advice of an accountant, solicitor, or other professional adviser.**

The Spanish government has always been relatively powerless to trace tax evasion carried out in this way, as the confidentiality of the ownership of offshore companies is protected by law. Now, however, even if they are unable to meet this problem directly, the authorities have opted to at least make the avoidance of tax and death duties a costly business for those involved. Offshore companies which own property in Spain are now subject to an annual 5% tax on the property's rateable value (approximately 70% of its market value) unless the owners are prepared to submit the name of the ultimate beneficial owner and proof as to the source of the money used to buy the property. Once this information has been established and the tax levied – or so it is intended – the owners will then not find it so worthwhile to avoid capital gains and inheritance taxes; and the transfer of ownership of property through sale or death will become obvious.

One of the main reasons for Spain clamping down on its own residents is that many have been using money from unpaid taxes to buy property through offshore companies. There is also evidence that offshore companies have been used to launder the proceeds of crime and drugs, and as a convenient way of buying property anonymously. Although the restrictions on offshore companies have seriously inflated some residents' tax bills, tax consultants who advise foreign property owners in Spain have generally welcomed the legislation. They say that it does nothing to alter some of the legitimate advantages of using an offshore company in order to avoid or reduce some taxes, and is deterring those who wish to operate illegitimately.

So, potential property buyers in Spain should be wary of any organisations which advertise schemes claiming to be able to circumvent the current legislation or claiming huge tax advantages. In the light of the Spanish authorities' determination to improve tax collection, and considering that all Spanish property is within the territory of the Spanish Revenue, which has the right ultimately to seize homes in order to collect the tax which it is owed, it is just as well to take some unbiased professional advice before entering into such an arrangement. In all circumstances, paying for this advice before you make a purchase will almost certainly save you money in the long run; and is the best approach.

Owners or potential purchasers should use a Spanish financial adviser; or one with experience of dealing with Spain. And any non-resident Portuguese property owners – an offshore company qualifies as such – should be sure to have an appointed fiscal representative in Portugal, as this is required by the law there; and readers should refer to the section on *Offshore Mortgages* in that section for details of offshore companies there. The same applies in Spain.

Offshore property mortgages are now available through many British building societies which have moved into offshore mortgaging; one such is *Abbey National* which has offices in Gibraltar (237 Main Street, PO Box 824, Gibraltar; ☎76090; fax 72028) from where it can provide its free booklet *Buying your home in Spain or Portugal* and Jersey (PO Box 545, Abbey National House, 41 The Parade, St Helier, Jersey JE4 8XG; 01624-644500). Your local high street branch should be your first port of call. Another is the *Halifax Building Society. Halifax International (Isle of Man) Ltd.* at PO Box 30, 67 Strand Street, Douglas, Isle of Man; ☎01624-632500. The Halifax, like most high street building societies and banks, has leaflets on offshore mortgages, and other financial matters like international payments, which will be worth consulting. *Lloyds Bank Overseas Club*, which offers a range of services, is based at the Offshore Centre, PO Box 12, Peveril Buildings, Peveril Square, Douglas, Isle of Man IM99 1SS; ☎01624-638104; fax 01624-638181.

One organisation which specialises in Spain is *Conti Financial Services* (see the beginning of this section on *Finance*). A solicitor which can help you set up an offshore mortgage or overseas trust in Spain is *Cornish & Co* whose website is www.cornishco.com (Lex House, 1/7 Hainault Street, Ilford, London IG1 4EL; tel 020-8478 3300; fax 020-8553 3418/3422. They have offices in Marbella (Edificio Alfil, Avda Ricardo Soriana 19, 29600 Malaga); Gibraltar (Hadfield House, Library Street); and associate offices in Portugal and the USA. An information pack is available on request or visit their website www.cornishco.com where you can obtain an estimate of legal fees for your property purchase online.For other companies, see under *Offshore Banking* in the *Daily Life* section which follows.

THE PURCHASING AND CONVEYANCING PROCE-DURES

Professional Assistance

Notarios. The Spanish property contract or conveyance deed, known as the *escritura de compraventa* is prepared by a public official called a *notario*. Notarios are trained in specialised property conveyancing work and have no exact counterpart in the UK but are similar in function to the French *notaire*. The notario is responsible for ensuring that the contract is drawn up correctly and that the purchase price is paid to the vendor in the appropriate currency. He or she will then witness the signing of the deed, arrange for it to be registered in the local property registry in the name of the new owner, and collect any fees or taxes due. In addition to dealing with all property transactions, the notario draws up Spanish wills (see the section *Wills and Insurance* below) and authenticates copies of important documents. However, in no way does the notario remove the need for a lawyer. The former is an impartial public official acting on behalf of neither the seller nor the buyer, whereas the latter is paid to protect his or her clients' interests in the purchasing process.

His or her fees charged to legalise the *escritura* will be on a sliding scale based on the declared value of the property.

Lawyers. A Spanish lawyer (*abogado*) should be consulted before any agreement or deposit (usually 10% of the purchase price) is made on a property. Although the vendor frequently doesn't require the services of a lawyer, the purchaser will always need one; this is the only way to be entirely sure that you are not buying a property which owes back rates or buying from a vendor who is behind with his or her own mortgage payments; a necessity in Spain as the new purchaser becomes responsible for these. In these cases, the bank which is providing the vendor's mortgage even has the right to take possession of the property and to sell it to repay the debt. Although a lawyer is at least partly employed to check the notario's work and in some ways the purchaser is paying twice for the same service, at least he can then be sure that all the necessary safeguards and precautions have been observed. Obviously, it is preferable to employ a separate lawyer to that of the vendor, as it is quite likely that, at some point, interests will clash. A list of English-speaking lawyers may be provided by the *Law Society* (113 Chancery Lane, London WC2A 1PL; ☎ 020-7242 1222; www.lawsociety.org.uk) – ask for the 'Records' department. Alternatively, a list of Spanish law firms is given in the section on *Working in Spain*, in the business and industry report, under *Law Firms*. Also see *Cornish & Co.*, *Fernando Scornik*, *Florez Valcarcel* and *John Howell & Co.* above. *Bennett & Co.* solicitors provide a wide range of legal services for UK residents and expatriates in Spain or those thinking of moving there (144 Knutsford Road, Wilmslow SK9 6JP; ☎ 01625-586937; fax 01625-585362; www.bennett-and-co.com; also see above). Lawyer's fees in Spain would normally be expected to be 3% or 4% of the purchase price for cheaper properties.

Land Registry

The notario will first of all investigate the seller's title to the property. All property sales and purchases in Spain must be registered at the local property registry; and before signing a final contract on any property a title check must be made to confirm the legal ownership of the property (it is surprising how often the *escritura* is not actually registered in the name of the seller) and to reveal any unpaid property taxes or mortgages. Please note that, the notario does not have to tell you whether there are plans to develop a factory or to construct a busy main road close to what is to be your home; this is something which a lawyer will be able to check for you; and is a standard part of the service a Spanish lawyer should be able to provide.

The Contrato

If the land registry check passes smoothly, then the lawyer will proceed to draw up a preliminary agreement for sale: the *contrato*. Although Spanish law does not require a preliminary written agreement for property purchase, it is advisable to have one, as it may well save trouble later on in the purchasing procedure. For instance, if a deposit is demanded, the contrato can provide that the deposit be returnable in the event of the vendor defaulting and the transaction falling through. The contrato also gives a date for the new owners to move into the property and specifies whether the balance of the purchase price is payable in full and immediately or by instalments.

The Escritura de Compraventa

The *escritura de compraventa* is a legally-binding property contract which is signed by both vendor and buyer in the presence of a notario. It often takes weeks before the escritura is ready to be signed and if, for instance, you agreed to buy a property when on holiday in Spain and find that it is inconvenient to return for the signing, you can appoint an agent to act on your behalf. The agent can be any trusted friend, need not be a Spanish national, but must officially be granted a special power of attorney, known in Spanish as an *escritura de poder de compraventa*. The cheapest and easiest way to obtain the power of attorney is to have the deed prepared by the notario as soon as you have agreed to buy. Remember that if the property is being bought in the joint names of a husband and wife it is important that the agent is expressly authorised to sign on behalf of both.

Once the escritura has been signed it remains only for a notarised copy of this document to be submitted to the land registry office in order for the new owner's name to be inserted on the registry deed, and for the property to be registered with the local tax office (*hacienda*), for eventual payment of annual rates. Depending on the complexity of the property purchase in question, the whole procedure will take anything from between two and four months to complete.

Selling Spanish Property and Repatriating Funds

The home owner is entitled to repatriate the proceeds of any future sale of the property subject only to tax clearance. The same provision holds true for any non-speculative capital gains accruing on the disposal of the investment after the relevant taxes have been paid. Income from rent may also be transferred back to the UK, providing that the purchase price has been paid in full and that the owner is up to date in his or her Spanish tax payments.

Expenses

A variety of fees will arise separate to the actual purchase price of the property. The most substantial of these include the notario's fee and the registration fee; both costs are calculated relative to the registered value of the property which is normally less than the purchase price. New property owners will also be liable to pay a purchase tax of 6.5% of the registered property value in VAT (IVA) if buying the property from a company; or transfer tax of 6% – known as the ITP (*impuesto de transmisiones patrimoniales*) – if buying from a private seller. These rates may change in future years. The percentage is on the value declared in the *escritura* (transfer deed) mentioned above; and under-declaration of this value may result in penalties, and potentially in increases in capital gains tax on subsequent resale.

It used to be expected that the purchaser would pay the capital gains tax (*plus valía*) involved in the transaction. This is a provincial not a national tax, levied on the notional increase in the value of the land since the last change of ownership. However, this is no longer a charge against the property and nowadays is usually payable by the seller. Or this can be a matter for negotiation when the contract is being drawn up.

As a general guide, expect to pay out approximately 10% of the purchase price for expenses like taxes and fees over and above the property cost. This figure includes the notario's fees, transfer tax, VAT and the property registry cost, but will not take into account all the legal fees which will be anything up to a further 2% of the purchase price for a straightforward sale.

Having bought the property, you will become liable to various local rates; and should certainly establish what these are in advance, as they can differ from region to region (as well as to Spanish income and wealth taxes, the exact details of which will depend on if you become a Spanish resident – see under *Taxes* and *Property-Related Taxes* below).

REGULATIONS GOVERNING OWNERSHIP AND DEVELOPMENT OF PROPERTY AND LAND

Buying a Plot of Land

When considering buying a piece of land to build on, you will need to bear in mind that all Spanish land is subject to a law ruling what purposes it can and cannot be used for. The various plans and rules pertaining to local land usage are kept at the town hall and are available to the general public. Once you have ensured that the piece of land which you are interested in is not designated purely for agricultural use (*finca rustica*), and that it has been approved for building purposes (*finca urbana*), you can proceed to apply for a building permit.

Planning Permission

It is essential that anyone planning to buy a plot of land on which to build his or her own home first applies for planning permission from the local town hall. Although twelve years ago it was very easy to obtain planning permission in Spain for virtually any property, the myriad of badly-designed developments which have sprung up all over the country since has resulted in local councils drawing a far tighter rein on property development as a whole. However, your application should not be turned down so long as the building specifications are safe and follow any good planning rules which apply to the area, and which will often be less strictly drawn up than in Britain. The cost of the licence will vary regionally and according to the size of the property but an average charge is about 90 euros.

Paperwork

Although a special permit is no longer needed to buy development land in Spain, anyone intending to purchase a plot of land is required to complete a form (TE7) available at any notario's office. On completion of the building work the land owner will have to work through a minefield of paperwork for which it is essential that professional advice is taken. The first document is the certificate of completion of building works, which is a certificate issued by the architect supervising the building work. This is then used to obtain the Habitation Certificate (*Cédula de Habitabilidad*) from the Town Hall which is in turn necessary to obtain the *Boletin de Instalaciones Electricas* and the *Certificado de Fin de Obra* – the Certificate of Electrical Installation and the Certificate of Completion of Work respectively. The latter two forms are necessary to ensure the supply of electricity, gas bottles and the installation of a water meter to the new property, while the

Habitation Certificate is similar in purpose to an escritura in that it bestows legal ownership of the property onto the holder.

RENTING PROPERTY

There are thousands of apartments and villas for rent in Spain, both through commercial agents and private owners. So for those who are intending to live there permanently, it may be a good idea to rent a property initially, before buying, just in case you find that the reality of Spanish life doesn't quite meet your expectations. One classic problem arises when expatriates who have only ever holidayed in Spain move to live there permanently, forgetting that holiday villas are built for the sun, and that even in southern Spain winter does exist! Marble floors can be unpleasantly chilly on the feet over the winter months. Anyone considering moving to one of these holiday villas should definitely try out a winter let first; or even holiday there for a few months over the winter: the major tour operators like *Thomson* and *First Choice* offer many longer-term stays like this, especially for older travellers. The *Spanish Tourist Office* can supply a list of many companies which offer self-catering holidays in villas, apartments and rural houses on request.

These winter sun holidays can be an enjoyable break from cold weather and heating bills at home, as well as a prelude to a more permanent stay for some. In Spain, and all around the Mediterranean, the dividing line between a holiday and more permanent residence is becoming increasingly blurred, as many choose to spend part of the year in warmer climes. Officially, it is when you spend more than 180 days in Spain in any one year that you need to become a resident.

Renting can mean a less permanent commitment; allowing you time to make up your mind. In the cities where many Britons live and work it will often be the only option and will also suit single people and those in less secure professions, or who have not yet moved on to house-buying. This is recommended for those who are not ready to make the commitment to living there permanently which buying a property involves. But the disadvantage of Spanish rentals generally is that, pricewise, they are fairly exorbitant, with prices in expensive Majorca starting at a minimum of 200 euros per week. Madrid rents are uniformly expensive; and to live in a pleasant and more upmarket area of Barcelona (of which there are not too many) you would be looking at about 4,600 euros a month, or more, for a spacious two or three-bedroom house in one of the more affluent suburbs. Prices are comparable to London. More modestly priced house and apartment rentals tend to be advertised in the *to rent* columns of the local newspapers.

Agency rentals, which include an extra month's rent in advance, and a commission for the agency service itself usually of one month's rent, will tend be more expensive but offer more security and are a way to avoid what can be the interminable, soul-destroying and foot-wearying search for the 'right' place. Many rentals which are part of a block or condominium work on the *comunidad* principle where the sharing of communal facilities is involved. Tenants will have to pay a monthly fee for the maintenance of these services; and should find out about them in advance. As in Britain, personal recommendation and the 'friend-of-a-friend' approach may be best way of avoiding unexpected problems and help you to get the best deal.

Tenancy Laws

Spanish renting and letting laws were extensively updated with the enforcement of regulations passed in 1985. These were revised in the Rent Law of January 1995. These regulations have ended some very strict forms of tenant protection, which included what was in effect the tenant's right to an indefinitely extendable rental contract and rents in some circumstances can now be raised by more than the cost of living index. But there are still some third-generation Spanish families in Madrid paying these low, protected rents for downtown apartments; and even subletting them. This situation was regarded as unfair to landlords and made many owners think twice about renting out their property in the first place.

The new legislation means that the rights of tenants are very similar to those in Britain, with some additional protection which stops your landlord raising the rent unfairly. When a rental contract specifies that the rental period ends in July, it means just that. But if the tenant fails to vacate the property when the temporary contract (*por temporada*) expires, the owner no longer has the right to evict you if a renewal has been sought; and all tenants now have a right to renew their tenancy for an initial minimum period of five years. In Spain, as elsewhere, all evictions involve the rather time-consuming and costly (for the landlord) process of getting a court order first.

So, the landlord must offer you a new contract; these can either be temporary or long-term (*vivienda*). It used to be that they could raise the rent as much as they liked in the process. However, the present situation is that most rent rises are in line with inflation and the Consumer Price Index. These arrangements are often administered by the rental agency itself and this is where payments are made. On the other hand, it is the reponsibility of the tenant to give one month's clear notice, even before the end of the contract or he or she may have to make up the difference and pay compensation to the landlord.

There is provision for the tenant to pay a deposit of one month's rent for unfurnished accommodation or two months for furnished accommodation. This would be lodged with the local Autonomous Community; additional guarantees may also be negotiated.

The Rental Contract

A rental contract is a prerequisite to renting any kind of property in Spain; both short and long-term lets are available. Short-term leases are known as *por temporada*; and long-term ones, which generally give tenants more rights than a short-term lease, are known as *viviendas*. Another difference between the two is that longer-term contracts often require tenants in blocks of flats to pay the *comunidad* fees (there is more about this below).

However, if these charges are not mentioned in the contract then they are wholly the owner's responsibility and the tenant is under no obligation to pay for them or to have these imposed subsequently.

All tenants are legally required to take out house insurance on the property they are renting, although the choice of which insurance company to take out a policy with is entirely his or her own decision and cannot be dictated by the landlord.

Contracts are drawn up through the standard, state-sponsored tenant/landlord agreements which are available from street kiosks: it is really your responsibility as the tenant to obtain one of these; and to make sure the contract type matches the rent you will pay over a year, as they vary. **It is better to have the contract checked by a solicitor or someone who really knows about rentals before signing.**

Anyone who feels that they have a complaint to make regarding their rental contract can – perhaps surprisingly – apply to the local tourist office – this is more suitable for those in short lets – while semi-permanent and permanent residents will do better at the nearest OMIC (*Oficina Municipal de Información al Consumidor*), the consumer information office run by the local government or Autonomous Community. Although the OMIC's primary function is to deal with consumer problems, they will at least be able to put you in contact with the most effective place to register a formal rental complaint.

Communal Apartment Blocks

Many of the apartments for rent in Spain are part of a block of flats or condominium which work on the *comunidad* principle which is very similar to the concept of *copropriété* in France, neither of which will be too familiar to those who have not lived in another European country. Both concepts involve the sharing of certain communal facilities (e.g. swimming pool, car park, garden areas) towards the upkeep of which tenants pay a monthly fee. This fee includes such costs as stair cleaning, rubbish disposal, garden maintenance, etc; and the level of the fee varies according to the size of the flat: the smarter and larger the flat, the more you pay. This fee can be as high as £150 ($215) a month for the more upmarket areas and apartment blocks.

When purchasing a property with a 'community of owners' as it is known, it is important to see the deed establishing this communal ownership (called the Deed of Horizontal Division) and the rules of the Community, which should be explained to you and which you have approved.

For owners and tenants, a meeting of all the residents of these communal apartment blocks is usually held once or twice a year to plan next year's budget, elect representatives, and to discuss maintenance, refurbishment, and the like. It is your legal duty to attend these meetings, which may be regarded as a useful way to meet the neighbours or as an interminable waste of time according to your point of view.

Letting Out Property

Letting property is often a good way of paying off the cost of a second home while you are on holiday yourself or back in the UK. It's a boom area at the moment, with many UK purchasers buying properties simply to rent. When you do this you have to 'lock away the emotion and look at the maximum return available,' according to one estate agent; who also advises buying a property for rent first; and if you are considering moving into it later to sell up and buy a new property which is suitable for you. The requirements of the rental and residence markets are very different, he says and it is well worth remembering that in northern Spain the holiday rental period is really only July and August, although the hotter weather in the south means the season can extend into spring and autumn – and even through the winter – so the potential income you can earn is – much higher.

There is a local rental market as well with prices rocketing as more and more foreign nationals are buying in the holiday areas; so this may be another option.

There is a lot of competition, too, with literally hundreds of companies renting out villas and offering a similar service; so some business acumen and the right choice of property will be important if you want to make money from your property purchase in Spain. Word-of-mouth is one way of going about it, as good as any other; or advertising in Spain or in the UK; or asking friends to advertise your holiday home in shop windows (probably the cheapest and often a successful method). Many villas are now advertised for rent on the internet.

Newspapers like *The Sunday Times* are another option; but again the competition seems fierce. A pleasant, out-of-the-way location will certainly be an advantage. Other, identical villas along the costas may in practice be unrentable; so you should find out about the neighbouring properties if you can, and their letting potential. For holiday rentals, a good position within sight and sound of the sea will be an advantage. Grouped houses or apartments in lowrise complexes tend to do better than individual villas; with very high occupancy rates in places like Alicante during the summer there is a rising demand for long-term leases and quality residences to rent as well. Again, there is no substitute for actually going there and doing a little research on the spot.

It is standard practice to charge your prospective tenants rent in advance for their stay and to ask for a deposit against possible damage when letting out any property. Telephones and electricity bills can often cause friction between tenant and landlord and it may be as well to remove or lock the phone with one of the convenient devices that are available for this; and to include an estimated electricity or bills charge in the advance payment, whether this be for two weeks, two months, or longer, to avoid mis-uderstandings later.

To avoid any future disputes, it is also a good idea to have a fairly exhaustive inventory of the contents of the property drawn up, and a description of their condition. In case of disaster, a landlord or lady is entitled to evict a tenant for the following reasons: failure to pay rent (although courts have a frustrating – for landlords – habit of ruling that the arrears must exceed six months before any action can be taken); damage to the property; use of the property for immoral purposes; subletting the property where no such provision has been made in the contract and for causing a social nuisance to neighbours. As the arrears can be as much as six months before a court will rule in your favour, an efficient approach to managing your property will be probably your best protection; and the legal approach only a last (and often unsatisfactory) resort.

Apart from advertising in the local newspaper for tenants for your Spanish property it is also worth contacting the local letting agencies, if indeed they exist, and doing something to check their credentials. Be sure that you are dealing with people who are competent and who you can trust; all too often you can find that extra fees and charges from the agency soon add up; or that the maintenance of the property is not attended to properly in your absence. Additionally, some UK estate agents which deal in Spanish property will arrange lets for Spanish property in the areas in which they specialise (some advertise in UK and expatriate newspapers, or see the section *Estate Agents* above). Remember that VAT (at 16%) for short-term lets, and income tax, will have to be paid.

Taxes

It is perfectly legal for owners of private houses, villas or flats to rent out their property without paying any advance taxes or making any business declarations.

However, owners are liable for Spanish income tax if the income from the rent exceeds a certain sum (about £5,000) per year, as this is then regarded as taxable income arising in Spain). For more information about this and other tax matters you can contact one of the Consulate offices in the UK; or your local tax office (*hacienda*) when in Spain. From the UK, you can also write to the *Ministerio de Economia y Hacienda* about tax matters (c/ Alcalá 11, E28071 Madrid; ☎915221000); or from Spain to the *Direccion Genmeral de Tributos* (c/ Alcalá 5, 28014 Madrid; ☎91522 1000).

Although the non-taxable limit or threshold for earned income is similar to that in Britain's, this limit is much less when the income originates from investments or real estate; and will depend, too, on whether you are resident in Spain. Non-residents renting out property are liable for income tax at the rate of 25% from the very first euro of rental income. Even if you are paid by your tenant outside Spain in a non-euro currency, legally this income arises in Spain because the property itself is situated there. Although many owners undoubtedly do let their property out on the quiet – and although the chances of being caught are slim – taking this risk is really not recommended; and it is advisable to keep records of all your income through renting.

Anyone intending to make a business of letting their property, who provides sheets and other hotel-type services like B&B – or dealing with a lot of tourist visitors on a short-term basis – is moving into a new area legally. You have created a business; and must therefore declare all income received, setting aside 25% of the rent as a witholding tax to the Spanish government; and adding an extra 16% VAT (IVA) to the rent which must be paid to the Spanish Finance Ministry. This tax is declared on Form 210, available from your local hacienda. The more positive side of your new business status is that you can now deduct maintenance expenses from your rental income before tax is calculated.

INSURANCE AND WILLS

Insurance

Either the owner or tenant should always arrange appropriate insurance for a property. Apart from being a sensible precaution, third party insurance for property is also a legal requirement. Most insurers prefer a multi-risk policy which covers theft, damage by fire, etc. If the insurer has bought into a development it may well turn out that the building as a whole is already covered. It is advisable to check this before taking out an individual policy. In any event, it is unlikely that the existing cover will include the private property of individual inhabitants.

Anyone who has purchased property from a previous owner may find the seller's insurance may be carried on to the next owner. However, the new owner will have to check whether the policy is transferable, or indeed, whether they wish to cancel it in order to take out a new policy. If you are planning to let the property then you must inform your insurers, otherwise the policy may be void; an extra premium may be payable. Note that you won't be covered for theft by your tenant unless you take out a policy which covers larceny. Additionally, the policy will only pay out on theft it there are signs of forcible entry.

It is possible to arrange insurance for your Spanish home through many UK insurance companies and travel agencies (e.g. *Towergate Holiday Homes Underwriting Agency,* Towergate House, St. Edwards Court, London Road, Romford, Essex RM7 90D; ☎01708777720; fax 01708777721), or contact *Derek Ketteridge & Associates,* 1st Floor, 130A Western Road, Brighton BN1 2LA; ☎01273720222; fax 01273722799. They offer a wide range of travel-related policies and schemes. The head office addresses of several major British insurance companies which operate in Spain are given below; and these may be worth contacting on arrival.

Useful Addresses

Axa Arora: Paseo de La Castellana 79, 28046, Madrid; ☎915551700. Mortgages and insurance.

Commercial Union Assurance Co: Via Augusta 281285, 08017 Barcelona; ☎932534700. Mortgages and insurance.

Direct Seguros: Ronda Poniente 14, 28760, Tres Cantos; ☎918069500. Insurance.

Eagle Star Insurance Company: Oficina de Santiago, Erraez, Calle de Vasquez, Madrid; ☎915062860.

Guardian Assurance: Numero 158, Piso 1A, 28002, Madrid; ☎934053344.

Plus Ultra, Anonima de Seguras y Resuguras: Plaza de Cortes 8, 28014, Madrid;

☎915899292.

Royal Insurance España: Paseo de la Castellana 60, E28046 Madrid.

Union Española de Entidades Aseuradoras, Reascuradoras y de Capitalizacion[ac]n: (Association of Spanish insurance companies) Calle Nunez de Balboa 101, E28006 Madrid.

In the UK, contact *Towergate Sharp Brokers Ltd.* Towergate House, St. Edwards Court, London Road, Romford, Essex RM7 90D; ☎01708745196; fax 01708742524. For general insurance, private cars, commercial insurance and homes insurance.

Wills

After buying any property in Spain, the purchaser should be sure to draw up a Spanish will with a Spanish lawyer. This is essential as under Spanish law if the foreign resident dies intestate or without having made a Spanish will – as it is a difficult and lengthy process for a British will to be recognised in Spain – the estate may end up being claimed by the Spanish state. When making a Spanish will it is unwise to include any property held in the UK or outside Spain, as this could lead to further complications. In other words, British and Spanish property should be kept entirely separate.

One company which does work with property and wills etc. in both Portugal and Spain is *Bennett & Co. Solicitors,* (144 Knutsford Road, Wilmslow, Cheshire SK9 6JP; ☎01625-586937; fax 01625-585362; www.bennettandco.com). Also see *Cornish & Co., Fernando Scornik , Florez Valcarcel* and *John Howell & Co.* above.

UTILITIES

It is essential to understand that although all public services are widely available in Spain and that the service in question will always be provided in the end, when it will arrive is far less certain. Moreover, unlike in the UK where several polite reminders for unpaid bills are issued before supplies are cut off, in Spain no such civility is offered. Electricity, telephone and water bills must all be paid promptly or one morning you could simply wake up to find that your telephone line, water supply or electricity supply has been cut off.

Electricity

The domestic electricity supply in Spain is mostly 220v or 225v AC, 50Hz, and less commonly, in the more remote country areas, 110v or 125v AC. Once all the plugs have been changed on UK electrical appliances to fit Spanish sockets (these are often two-pin in older properties and three-pin in more modern ones) the UK appliances should perform quite adequately, if a little more slowly than in the past. Make sure to choose the right socket: flat pins for 220v or 110v. Light bulbs are usually 110v and are the continental screwin type.

Electricity is supplied by the Compañia de Electricidad through the overhead lines of an extensive grid system linking the hydroelectric and atomic power stations with cities, towns and villages throughout the country. It is essential to organise meter installation or reconnection through your regional branch of Compañia de Electricidad well in advance, as the waiting lists for both services can be very long.

Electricity is priced on the international system of a small standing charge and a further charge per kilowatt-hour consumed, the rate for which diminishes as consumption increases. Bills are issued bi-monthly and VAT at the standard rate is added.

Generally, you will find that electricity is similarly priced to the UK or USA, bearing in mind that if you decide to live in a summer-built holiday villa through the winter months, your heating bill is going to be substantial. Surprisingly, the economical form of solar heating is something which is relatively uncommon, although becoming less so, in most areas of Spain.

Gas

The use of gas is not as common in Spain as in the North of Europe and, except in the larger cities, there tends to be no main household supply. However, readily available bottled gas (supplied in cylinders known as *bombonas*) is cheap and commonly used for cooking and heating in most homes. The bombonas can be easily refilled through the butane delivery service which operates in most areas. As with electricity, gas bills (for piped gas) are rendered bi-monthly and VAT is added.

Water

Spanish water is perfectly safe to drink in almost all urban areas as government regulations require public water supplies to be treated with anti-pollutants. However, for this same reason the water does have an unpleasant taste of chlorine and most foreign nationals follow the example of the Spanish and drink bottled mineral water instead. This is cheap, of good quality and sold at practically every corner shop in Spain; *con* means carbonated and *sin*, non-carbonated.

Although Spain has an adequate natural water supply, water shortages do occur over the summer months as the water system is still not administered well enough to guarantee a constant unrestricted water supply. The problem mainly arises because the municipalities control the supply, and plans to lay national pipelines are continually frustrated by local issues. Consequently, although there is surplus rainfall in the north, there is a scarcity along the Mediterranean coast and in the Balearic Islands in the dryer months which involves a corresponding shortage of water supply in these areas.

The mains service to private premises is metered, with charges calculated per cubic metre used or at a flat rate. To have a water meter installed, apply to the local water company office with your passport, habitation certificate and the number of your Spanish bank account. A deposit is payable, as is the cost of installing the water meter. Again, bills are issued bi-monthly. Owing to the extreme hardness of the water it is essential to have filters installed, preferably within the system (as opposed to just on the outlets), to prevent the furring up of pipes, radiators etc.

Telephones

Spain has an increasing number of private telephones; but cajoling the national (although now privatised) company *Telefónica* to actually install a phone can still take time. Outside the major cities you should be prepared to wait for a month or two. Bills are sent out every two months; but while Telefónica is not slow to cut you off if the bill is not paid within twenty days; they are distinctly slow to reconnect – at an additional charge; so these bills may be best arranged by standing order. Or you can go to their high street shops to pay.

In addition, Spain has all the telecommunications services which are now a feature of life all over Europe: with many retail outlets offering mobile phones, as well as public telephones which may be used (payment afterwards) in shops and exchange bureaux as well as throughout the country. There are also telephone cards, which will prove useful, available in post offices and elsewhere. Competition, with the privatisation of *Telefónica* and deregulation of the market, is having some of the efficiency-inducing effects it had in Britain. The equivalent now of Mercury or Comtel which is emerging as a rival to the former monopoly held by Telefónica is Retevisión, which is currently offering mainly business-orientated services in the major cities.

PROPERTY RELATED TAXES

The Contribución Urbana

Just as property prices have increased greatly over the past thirty years, so have property taxes; and the main property-related tax is the *contribución urbana* or *el impuesto municipal sobre bienes immeubles*, otherwise known as the *IBI*, which is a significant cost if you are thinking either of buying a property to live in, or to rent out. On a typical two-bedroom apartment in the Costa del Sol region, you can expect to pay this Spanish equivalent to the rates in the region of £300/$420 at present per year, we are advised. There is also an inconvenient 20% late payment surcharge; so direct debit is a good way to pay. If you are buying a house it is your responsibility to check to see if the property is registered for this tax; ask to see a recent receipt to avoid being liable for all kinds of back taxes and penalties.

The Valor Catastral

This is the term for the rateable value of your property; on this will depend the other main property tax, local capital gains tax or *Plus Valia*. This is calculated on computed land values given for the vicinity in which the particular property is located, the land value in that particular area in other words. This is greater than the contribicíon urbana, and assessed at around £1,000 ($1450) on the typical two-bedroomed property mentioned above. In Spain, another tax which will have unfortunate echoes of the past for British residents still exists: the Wealth Tax. The Wealth and Income tax payable in Spain is also based on a valuation of the property, which is perhaps a disincentive to local housebuyers as the value of your property also has an effect on other taxes. The question of property valuation is therefore highly controversial in Spain. At present, 2% of the rateable value is computed as notional income when this is taxed; so owning property means you pay more in income tax. Upon that 2% of the ratable value of the property income tax is levied at 25%. Wealth tax is charged at a rate of 0.2% of the total ratable value of the property.

For example, if a property has a rateable value of £50,000 then income tax of £250 would be payable, while the wealth tax you pay would be about £100 per year. It is essential to know what this charge will be before you purchase a house or apartment in Spain; and to make clear in any rental agreements you are involved in as to whether this is or is not included. The advice of an expert solicitor in the field (like *Bennet & Co.*, *Fernanco Scornik*, *Florez Valcarcel* or *Cornish & Co.* – see above) should certainly be sought if you are in doubt about any of these tax matters relating to property.

Inheritance Tax

Legislation passed by the socialist government considerably softened the impact of what was hitherto the exceedingly high rates of Spanish inheritance tax. Previously inheritance tax started at 12% for a ludicrously low limit of around £50; the tax spiralled to nearly 80% for inheritors related by neither blood nor marriage to the deceased. However, the *Ley de Sucesiones* readjusted the nontaxable inheritance limit to the more realistic sum of about £10,000 increasing about £2,500 for each year for those under the age of 21 to a maximum of about £35,000. This legislation is likely to come under review of centre-right administations.

In effect, the revised legislation ensured that the majority of inheritors did not have to pay any inheritance tax at all. Moreover, the exemption applied to each individual who benefited from the bequest, not to the estate as a whole. It is worth noting that the taxfree exemption (which your solicitor or accountant should advise you of) is reduced for relations other than immediate family (i.e. uncles and aunts, cousins, nephews and nieces). Spanish inheritance tax is hard to calculate, which is why you will need the services of an expert; and it is worth noting that there is no exemption between spouses as in the UK.

Only those who are already very rich will suffer from these revised inheritance tax laws as the tax rates are based on a sliding scale according to the amount of net worth which the inheritor possesses, separate from the bequest in question. Although the usual top inheritance tax rate is 34%, this can rise to a maximum of 85% at the top rate, and where the total estate is left to a non-relative who already has a net worth of more than £2,500,000.

Various schemes have been used in the past to avoid inheritance tax; in the light of the new legislation these should not now be necessary for most British residents there. These schemes included transferring legal ownership of a property to a relative, as a gift, during the owner's lifetime (although the owner would remain in the property until his or her death); this is known as reserving a *usofructo*.

Although this approach may save the inheritor some tax, the inheritance tax is actually named *impuesto sobre sucesiones y donaciones* (a tax on inheritances and gifts); and under Spanish law this transaction qualifies as a taxable gift if it is made within three years of the death of the bequeather. Similarly, selling property to relations or friends will save some tax if the house owner lives long enough, but again if the sale is made within five years of his or her death, the new owner will be taxed at the full value of the property.

Offshore property purchase has, in the past, been the most popular and sometimes notorious way to avoid paying inheritance tax. Property bought through offshore companies is officially owned by the company which, in legal terms, can never die and is thus not liable to inheritance tax. However, the legislation passed in regard to offshore banking in Spain has done much to reduce the attraction of this option (see above).

REMOVALS

If you choose not to transport any of your belongings to Spain this will certainly make things easier both as regards expense and customs formalities. Having said this, nearly everyone possesses something to which they feel inextricably attached and it is always comforting to have something to remind one of home. Additionally, this is an opportunity to make considerable savings on certain goods which are cheap in the UK but very expensive in Spain. Start with a list of essential items and then try and cut this down again. Electrical items are slightly more expensive in Spain and it may be worth taking your UK ones as long as they are compatible, as discussed earlier. However, there may be difficulties with electrical repairs as some home appliances in Spain are of particular Spanish design and manufacture.

Anything of substantial weight will be very expensive to move and some furnishings may not be suitable if moving to a warmer part of Spain. Basically, any item is liable to breakage, no matter how careful the removers, and anything one decides to take must be carefully considered to ensure that it really is practical. A good removal company can avoid or deal with most of the disasters which inevitably coincide with uprooting you and all your possessions to a foreign country – see the section *Removal Companies* below. Additionally, the British Association of Removers (3 Churchill Court, 58 Station Road, North Harrow, London HA2 7SA; ☎020-8861 3331; www.bar.co.uk) provides a free and useful leaflet offering practical advice for anyone preparing to move abroad. They can also provide the names and telephone numbers of reputable overseas removal companies throughout the country which are members of BAR. The addresses and phone numbers of companies which deal with Spain, whether directly or by subcontracting to other agencies, are given in the *Removal Companies* section below.

General Conditions of Import

Any EU citizen intending to take up permanent residence in Spain may import their household effects and personal possessions free of customs duty. All reputable international removals firms should be fully aware of the regulations concerning the transport of personal and household items. But anyone thinking of bringing them out in a privately hired or owned truck should first consult the Spanish Embassy or Consulates for current advice.

For permanent residence, you will need to have proof of intended permanent residence in Spain, in the form of a residence permit; if you haven't received this before leaving home the initial *visado de residencia* will suffice but a deposit may have to be paid. This deposit exempts the holder from customs duties and will be returned once the permit has been produced.

You need an application form (*Cambio de Residencia*) requesting the Head of Customs to allow the goods free entry into Spain (obtainable from the Consulate) as well as an itemised list of the contents in duplicate, written in Spanish, which shows the estimated value in euros. These should accompany the goods or shipment and should have been legalised at the Spanish Consulate. If you are sending the goods with a removals company, they will also need a photocopy of your passport which has been similarly legalised. To import wedding gifts, you will also need a copy of your marriage certificate; and there are similar special requirements for diplomats' removals; inheritance; and, for example, new furniture whose value is greater than 3,000 euros.

Other conditions for the exemption from duty for non-EU citizens include not having been resident in Spain during the two years prior to the importation of the goods; that the goods enter Spain within three months of your own arrival and that the goods are for your use, being at least six months old; and will not be sold when in Spain for at least two years.

Under the provisions outlined above, you are able to import anything it is possible to even think about taking abroad: furniture, books, works of art, personal effects, musical instruments and a bewildering variety of household and electrical items ranging from washing machines and electric or gas cookers to floor polishers and radios. However, if you decide to leave Spain within two years of your arrival, you will have to export your goods again (a relatively simple process within the EU) or pay the duty on them.

Another form of concession on import duties is available for those who wish to import furniture for a second residence or holiday home; this is known as the *vivienda secundaria*. Entitlement to this exemption does not include taking Spanish residency and involves making a deposit which will be returned on the expiry of a two year period.

Useful Address

Verbatim Language Services: Clifton House, Clifton Terrace, Southsea, Hants, PO5 3NL; ☎02392-833121. Specialise in translating documents relating to removals abroad, property purchase, residence, import/export etc.

The Import Procedure

This basically consists of compiling a signed inventory, written in Spanish, of all the goods to be transported to Spain. This list should then be presented to the Spanish Consulate with a completed customs clearance form and the former will be stamped for a small fee. The removals company should handle a good deal of the paperwork required. However, the basic procedure is outlined below:

> O Make two copies of a complete inventory of all the items to be taken, valuing all of the items at their present value, not cost new, and opting for the low side of the estimate. Even if there are some things you want to take now and others which will not follow for several months include the latter on the inventory as once the list is compiled, it can't be added to later. Remember to include the makes, models and serial numbers of all electrical items on the inventory and two copies of a declaration of ownership of the goods in Spanish.
> O The customs clearance form, *la Dirección General de Aduanas* must be completed; this is available from your nearest consulate.
> O You may also need to present either a copy of the escritura to the new Spanish property or, if you have had your own property built, a copy of the habitation certificate from the local authority in Spain which granted the planning permission for building.
> O A full passport; and photocopies of the first five pages which have been stamped at the Consulate.

Although it is obviously more economical to transport all of your possessions in one fell swoop, newly-fledged Spanish residents are allowed to import all household goods in as many trips as are required. It is worth remembering that it may be difficult to import goods after the expiry of the one year period; it can take up to a year to obtain a separate import licence and the duty on the import for non-EU citizens can be astronomical. For those who have bought a second home or holiday residence, the procedure for importing personal effects and furnishings is similar to that for long-term and permanent residents except that the home owner is required to draw up a notarised declaration that he or she will not sell, hire out or otherwise transfer ownership of the property or personal goods within the twelve months following importation.

Finally, it is a commonly-held misunderstanding that if you buy an item in Britain (or other EU country) and pay the VAT (sales tax) and then subsquently export it to another country in the EU such as Spain, there is an entitlement for a refund of the VAT paid on purchase – this is simply not true. However, the misunderstanding arises from the fact that if you are buying anything to take with you, such as a fridge or stereo, it can be supplied VAT free if the goods are delivered direct to the remover as an export shipment from the dealer.

Removal Companies

The British Association of Removers can provide advice on choosing a removal company; and members offer a financial guarantee if they go out of business through the Association. Write to *BAR Overseas* at the address above. *FT Expat* magazine has articles of interest to all expatriates, with details of planning and preparation, personal finance and investment services; and other practical

CHECKLIST BEFORE MOVING

Confirm dates with mover
Sign and return contract together with payment
Book insurance at declared value
Arrange a contact number
Arrange transport for pets
Dispose of anything you don't want
Start running down freezer contents
Contact carpet fitters if needed
Book mains service for disconnection
Cancel all rental agreements
Notify dentist, doctor, optician, vet
Tell your bank and savings/share accounts
Inform telephone company
Ask the post office to reroute mail
Tell TV licence, car registration, passport offices
Notify HP and credit firms
Make local map for friends/removal company
Clear the loft
Organise your own transport to new home
Plan where new things go
Cancel the milk/newspapers
Clean out the freezer/fridge
Find and label keys
Address cards to friends and relatives
Separate trinkets, jewellery and small items
Sort out linen and clothes
Put garage/garden tools together
Take down curtains/blinds
Collect children's toys
Put together basic catering for family at new house

information. Subscriptions for one year from the UK and Europe are £59; for two years £79.50. The magazine is published by the Financial Times Business Department, subscription address: FT Expat, Subscription Dept., Units 12 & 13, Cranleigh Gardens Industrial Estate, Southall, UB1 2DB; ☎020-8606 7545.

Removal companies can take away much of the hassle out of moving if you choose the right one; as one successfully-moved expatriate put it:

> *The secret is to use a really good removal company. Ours was superb and handled everything for us – all the paperwork, form filling, everything we could possibly worry about was handled by the firm.*

You should remember also to do all the planning which is necessary and check on the import / customs procedures mentioned above. The *British Association of Removers* publishes a useful leaflet *Now that you're ready to move...* which covers most of the issues; and ends with the advice that no-one moving home will find easy to follow: 'Relax...'

Although Spanish Consulates will supply information concerning the export of household goods and personal effects on receipt of an s.a.e, you may find that their own information is out of date as more than in any other European country (with the exception only of Portugal) Spain constantly amends and alters its regulations regarding the importation of personal and household effects. The most up-to-date information will come from a removal company specialising in exports to the Iberian Peninsula (see *Useful Addresses* below). These can provide quotes; but should also be able to give information on Spanish import procedures on request.

It is particularly important to shop around for a wide variety of quotes as general removal companies sometimes subcontract jobs to other companies which are going to the country in question, thus incurring all of the extra expense of fees picked up along the way. The approximate charge from the UK to Spain is £120 to £150 per cubic metre plus a fixed fee for administration and paperwork.

The amount will vary greatly on either side of this estimate, however, depending on where in Spain the shipment is going, and where it is coming from in the UK. And the price per cubic metre should decrease with the volume of goods you are transporting.

Remember to make the photocopy of the first five pages of your passport, with the Spanish visa if you are a non-EU national, and give this to the removal agents, as they will need to present it at the customs office at the Spanish border when they enter with your shipment of goods. It is worth taking out comprehensive insurance against damage to your possessions incurred while in transit. Your removals company can advise you about cover and make arrangements on your behalf – the cost is usually quite modest. Another fact to bear in mind is that the customs clearance charges involved in exporting and importing goods can sometimes be more expensive than the shipping charges themselves (also something which a good removal company should advise you of and deal with on behalf of the client).

Useful Addresses – Removal Companies

Allied Pickfords: 345 Southbury Road, Enfield, Middlesex BN1 1UP; ☎020-8219 8000. A worldwide network with many branches in Britain. Rep-resentative in Spain: *Arthur Pierre*, Calle Urogallo 12, Pol. Ind. Matagal-legos, E28940 Fuenlabrada (Madrid); ☎91642 2080; fax 91642 2538.

Andrich Removals: ☎01283-761990. Based in Derbyshire with branches throughout the UK. Regular service to Spain and Portugal with full and part loads.

ARTS International: Unit 37, Belbrook Industrial Estate, Uckfield TN22 1QL; ☎01444247551. Spain and Portugal.

Avalon Overseas: Drury Way, Brent Park, London NW10 0JN; ☎020-8451 6336.

Britannia Lanes of Devon: Hennock Road, Marsh Barton, Exeter EX2 8NP; ☎01392-494966. Fortnightly service to Spain and Portugal.

Britannia Removals: Britannia House, Alington Road, Little Barford, St. Neots, Cambridgeshire PE19 6YH; ☎01234-272272; fax 01480-218430.

Clark & Rose Ltd: Barclayhill Place, Portlethen, Aberdeen AB12 4LH; ☎01224-782800; fax 01224-782822.

Crown Worldwide Movers: Freephone 0800 393363, with offices in; Birmingham (01827 264100; Glasgow (0123644 9666); Heathrow (020-8897 1288); Leeds (0113-277 1000); London (020-8591 3388); Montrose (01674-672155).

David Dale Removals: ☎01423-867788; fax 01423-324450. Takes part and full loads, has a regular weekly service, and storage available in Spain in Malaga and Alicante.

Four Winds International Group: The Georgian House, Wycombe End, Beaconsfield, Bucks HP9 7LX; ☎01149-4675588.

Harrow Green Removals Group: Merganser House, Cooks Road, London. E15 2PW; ☎020-8522 0101; fax 020-8522 0252. Full removals service, but they can also make arrangements for pets.

Interpack Worldwide Plc: Hannah Close, Great Central Way, London, NW10 0UX; fax 020-8324 2096. Services include pet shipping, full/part house contents, motor vehicles, air freight and storage.

Luker Bros (Removals & Storage) Ltd: Shelley Close, Headington, Oxford OX3 8HB; ☎0186-5762206.

Meadows International: Suite 501, 223 Regent's Street, London W1 R8QD; ☎020-7474 1000 or 7000. A worldwide service including Spain and Portugal with doortodoor or doortodepot rates on request and storage facilities.

Movers International (of Preston) Ltd: ☎01772-651570; fax 01772-654570. A weekly trade service to Spain and Portugal.

Northover's Removals and Storage: ☎01428-751554; fax 01428-751564. Has a regular service to Spain and some storage available in Almeria.

Pink & Jones Ltd: Britannia House, Riley Road, Telford Way, Kettering, Northants. NN16 8NN; ☎01536-512019.

Robinsons International Moving and Storage: Nuffield Way, Abingdon, Oxon OX14 1TN; ☎01235-552255.

Branches in London: ☎020-8208 8484; Basingstoke: ☎01256-465533; fax 01256-24959; Birmingham: ☎01527-830860; fax 01527-526812; Bristol: ☎0117980 5800; fax 0117980 5828; Manchester: ☎0161-766 8414; fax 0161-767 9057; and Southampton: ☎023-802-20069; fax 023-800-31274; Darlington ☎01325-348700; fax 01325-485186; Glasgow: ☎0141-779 9477; fax 0141-779 9486.

Spanish Connexion: The Old Vicarage, Leigh, Sherborne, Dorset DT9 6HL; ☎01935-872222; fax 01935-873094; email fscx@tovic.com. Regular deliveries to and from Spain and throughout the UK.

Union Jack Logistics Ltd: Unit 4, Hill Barton Business Park, Sidmouth Road, Clyst St Mary, EX5 1DR; ☎01395-233486; fax 01395-233686. Costa Blanca ☎(96) 686 62 10/fax (52) 564 385. Costa del Sol ☎(96) 52 446 639/fax (52) 564 385. Specialists in removals to and from Spain with offices on the Costa Blanca/Costa del Sol.

Importing a Car

Anyone thinking of importing a foreign-registered car into Spain should first of all consider carefully the drawbacks: the inconvenience of having a righthand drive car in a country which drives on the right and the inevitable tortuous red tape that the import procedure gives rise to.

A UK or Irish citizen who feels that they cannot possibly part with their UK car and decides to import this permanently into Spain does not need to apply for authorisation to use the vehicle for a period of up to six months.

Outside this six-month period, they must apply for an import licence from the Ministry of Economy and Finance (Ministerio de Economia y Hacienda, Castellana 162, Madrid) or seek further advice from the Consulate. One big advantage of bringing your own car from the UK is that the car can be imported duty free, providing that the vehicle has been used and registered in your name for at least six months prior to moving. Exemption from VAT (currently 28% levied on cars imported into Spain) can also be obtained on the same basis, after providing proof of having paid VAT on the vehicle in the UK. Should the amount of VAT you paid be less than that levied in Spain, the difference will have to be paid once you have arrived there. Note that the exemptions are given on condition that the vehicle will not be sold or transferred within a period of one year after the registration date in Spain.

Exemptions should be applied for from the *Dirrección General de Aduanas*, Guzman el Bueno 137, E2804 Madrid; ☎915826229.

Importing Pets into Spain

If you decide to take your pets with you to Spain, the move should be as smooth for the four-legged expats as for the two-legged ones, providing that the procedures outlined below are followed and the relevant documentation obtained. In 2001 'Passports' for pets were introduced for bringing pets back into the UK from other countries. This means that many more people will consider taking their animals to Spain because they can bring them back and forth to the UK without enduring the compulsory six-month quarantine that was formerly in force.

The latest details of import conditions for taking your pets to Spain can be obtained by contacting the Pet Travel Scheme (Dept. for Environment, Food and Rural Affairs, Area 201, 1 Page Street, London SW1P 4PQ; ☎0870 241 1710; fax 020-7904 6834; email pets.helpline@defra.marff.gsi.gove.uk) and requesting the contact details of your nearest Animal Health office, who will then supply you with the information you need to take your animals with you.

Although the PETS scheme makes travelling with pet animals more straightforward, it is a lengthy process. At the time of press DEFRA (the new name for MAFF) was understood to be working to a six month deadline, so you need to plan ahead.

TAKING PETS OUT OF THE UK

The procedures involved are:
- Vet inserts a tiny microchip just under the animal's skin (cost £20-£30).
- Vet administers a rabies shot, (or two, given two weeks apart). (£50 x two; possibly second shot cheaper).
- Vet takes a blood sample and sends it to a DEFRAapproved laboratory. (£70-£80 including Vet's handling charge).
- Vet issues a PETS 1 Certificate, which you have to show to the transport company (e.g. airline, ferry, Shuttle etc).
- When taking pets out of the UK to Spain you will need a PETS 5 certificate (this replaces the separate Export Health Certificate) which is issued at the same time as PETS 1 (see above).
- Total cost about £200.

Dogs in some Spanish cities will require a licence or tax to be paid for them.

Importing Pets Back into the UK

The Pet Travel Scheme (PETS), has been running since 2000 and 12,000 or more animals have travelled under its procedures. PETS allows dogs and cats to visit certain countries in mainland Europe and rabies free areas like Australia and New Zealand, provided that they are vaccinated against rabies. Additionally, they are required to have been treated against tapeworm (*echinococcus multilocularis*) which can pass to humans and the tick known as *Rhipicephalus sanguineus* which also carries disease transferable to humans.

To get your pet back into the UK you will need a PETS Certificate to show the transport company when checking in your pet. A PETS Certificate is valid six months after the date of the blood test and is valid up to the date the animal's booster rabies shot is due. In France you should obtain the PETS Certificate from a government-authorised vet. You can obtain a list of these while still in Britain from DEFRA's website (www.defra.gov.uk/animalh/quarantine/pets/contacts.shtml).

Immediately (24-48 hours) before you travel from Spain the animal must be treated against ticks and tapeworm by a vet. This has to be done *every* time your pet enters the UK. The vet should issue an official certificate (i.e. government authority printed) with the microchip number, date and *time* of treatment, the product used and the vet's stamp.

Pets Originating Outside Britain

If your pet originated out of Britain where different systems for identifying dogs and cats are in force it will still have to be microchipped for entry to the UK. Pets which have another form of registration (e.g. ear tattoo) can be vaccinated, blood-tested and then finally micro-chipped. To enter the UK the animal must have PETS Certificate that shows the veterinary has seen the registration document.

For other information about Pets, see the relevant section in *Daily Life*.

Useful Contacts

Airpets Oceanic: Shipping Agents, Willowslea Farm Kennels, Heathrow TW19 6BW; ☎01753-685571; fax 01735-681655; www.airpets.com. Pet exports, pet travel schemes, boarding, air kennels, transportation by road/air to and from all UK destinations.

AirSupply shipping agents (0800 137 321) produces a free leaflet about moving abroad with pets.

D.J. Williams: Animal Transport, Littleacre Quarantine Centre, 50 Dunscombes Road, Turves, Nr Whittlesey Cambs PE7 2DS; ☎01733-840291; fax 01733-840348. Pet collection and overland delivery service. Will collect from your home, arrange all the necessary documentation. Also return home service from Europe provided.

Independent Pet and Animal Transport Association: fax 903 769 2867; email: Ipata@aol.com. Citizens of the USA can contact this address for a list of agents dealing in the transport of pets from the USA to Spain.

MRL: Lumbry Park, Selborne Road, Alton, Hants GV34 3HF; ☎0800 917 1091.

ParAir Services: Warren Lane, Stanway, Colchester, Essex C03 0LN; ☎01206-330332; 01206-331277; www.parair.com parair@btinternet.com. Handles international transportation and quarantine arrangements. Can arrange door to door delivery of pets by specially equipped vans.

Pet Travel Scheme, Department for Environment, Food and Rural Affairs, Area 201, 1 Page Street, London SW1P 4PQ; ☎0870 241 1710; fax 020-7904 6834; email pets.helpline @defra.maff.gsi.gov.uk.

Pets Will Travel: www.petswilltravel.co.uk.

Travelpets: (020-7499 4979; www.travelpets.net

Note that as the PETS scheme is fairly new at the time of press, regulations may change. Some ferry companies and airlines will take accompanied pets and the list of them is growing so check with your carrier. For the latest information contact the PETS Helpline (see above).

Pet Travel Insurance

With the PETS scheme, a niche market in Pet Travel Insurance has opened up. No doubt there will soon be a host of pet travel insurers. Pet Plan (020-8580 8080; www.petplan), a well-known UK animal health insurance company offers cover for pets taking trips abroad. The minimum 30 days' costs about £16 for dogs and £10 for cats; 60 days and 90 days' cover also available. Petwise Insurance (0870738333 930), Rapid Insure (www.rapidinsure.co.uk), Pinnacle Pet Healthcare (www.pinnacle.co.uk), MRL Insurance Direct (www.mrigroup.co.uk) also offer travelling pet insurance.

DAILY LIFE

CHAPTER SUMMARY

○ **Languages.** The language spoken throughout Spain is Castilian but there are several other languages and dialects spoken in their respective regions.

○ **Education.** women outnumber men in secondary education and in the first years of university.

○ **Media.** Under Franco the Spanish press was subject to 30 years of censorship which was not lifted until 1978.

   ○ Only one in ten Spaniards buys a daily newspaper – one of the lowest readership rates in Europe.

   ○ The Spanish are tele-addicts and come just after the British in the number of hours of television watched.

○ **Tax.** The Spanish tax system is based on a vital minimum allowance plus a series of other allowances depending on your age and other circumstances before you start paying any income tax.

○ **Spanish health service.** Everyone who pays social security contributions, pensioners, the unemployed and those under 18 get free treatment under the health service.

   ○ Free treatment is only available in some hospitals and waiting lists are long.

   ○ Most Spanish nationals and expatriates have private health insurance.

○ **The Spaniards.** the Spaniards embrace several traditions and a range of cultural differences from Celts and Basques in the north to Mediterranean in the south.

When going to live in a foreign country, one will immediately find that there is a multitude of daily rituals, previously taken for granted, which now pose a seemingly insurmountable challenge. The intention of this chapter is to provide all of the practical information required to successfully cope with various aspects of Spanish life. The information provided can help you decide if Spain is for you. Note, however, that in most of the aspects covered there are bound to be regional and local variations – so do not then take this or any other advice you read or are given necessarily as law. In Spain there are particularly striking differences between town and country which may affect the procedure required in doing even the most mundane things. The key to unravelling daily life in Spain lies essentially in the ability to speak the language reasonably well. Thus, the first section of this chapter covers this area, with subsequent sections dealing with all of those aspects of daily life, which, if handled successfully, can make living in another country an exciting rather than a daunting experience.

This chapter contains listings in the relevant sections for various UK-based companies who specialise in various specific services such as private health insurance or offering legal advice. But one company, *Spanish One Stop Shop*, that defies any such simple classification. Its activities relevant to this chapter include offering qualified investment advice, offering legal advice by a UK-based solicitor from an office in mainland Spain, providing a Spanish translation service and access to Spanish lessons, offering advice on private health insurance from both UK and Spanish insurance providers, and providing access to a car purchase service. Its address is Mansion House, Acadia Hall, High Street, Dartford, Kent DA1 1DJ; ☎0132-2391 040; fax 01322-228 178.

THE LANGUAGES OF SPAIN

The language that we call Spanish is actually Castilian spoken throughout the country including in the Autonomous Communities which also have their own languages, i.e. Catalonia, Galicia and the Basque Country. In the province of Catalonia, the principality of Andorra, parts of the French Pyrenees and the Balearic Islands, Catalan (*català*), and the various dialects of this language, are widely spoken. The province of Valencia also has its own language which developed out of Catalan when in the 16th century huge numbers of Catalan-speaking labourers were moved from the north and never returned.

Catalan. Catalan dates back to the ninth century and is currently spoken by six and a half million people (and is therefore more widely spoken than either Danish, Finnish or Norwegian). It is worth noting that there is no surer way to offend a Catalonian than to refer to his or her language as a dialect. Although Catalan bears a close resemblance to Provençal and therefore to French and Spanish, it is as distinct from each of these as, say, Italian; and has as long a history. School children in Catalonia are now taught both Castilian and Catalan; and in this region you will find that many road signs and documents (as well as tourist office maps) appear in both Catalan and Castilian.

Basque. The Basque provinces also have their own language, known as *euskera* or *euskara*, now spoken by about 700,000 people in total. Although some words have been absorbed from French and Spanish, the basic vocabulary and structure are completely unrelated to any known tongue and therfore predate the Roman conquest of Spain. Very few English words derive from Basque; one exception is 'bizarre' from the Basque word for beard.

Galician. About four-fifths of the 3,000,000 inhabitants of Spains northwest province speak Galician (*Galego*) as at least their second language; it includes elements of both Spanish and Portuguese (with Celtic roots). Again this is a separate language not just a dialect; within Galicia three dialects of Galego are spoken.

Knowledge of literary Spanish (Castilian) is much more useful than a knowledge of Catalan, Basque or Galego, since all Spaniards understand Castilian but very few outside their communities can communicate in the regional languages. If you choose to live in the great Catalan city of Barcelona or in rejuvenated Valencia, Castilian Spanish will usually be understood. In the more chauvinistic parts of Catalonia and the Basque Country, Castilian is reviled; however foreigners are forgiven more easily than Spaniards for speaking Castilian. If you have children who are going to go to local schools, be aware that it will be compulsory for them to learn the language of the region, possibly to the exclusion of Castilian.

It is strongly advised that anyone planning to move to Spain try to make some headway learning this useful language before leaving home. Castilian Spanish is one of the easiest languages to learn at a basic level, especially if the student has a prior knowledge of any of the Romance languages (e.g. French, Italian) and some understanding of the basics of phonology. Beginners will find that tentative attempts are met with a helpful, if sometimes bemused, response once in Spain.

Spanish is also an international language. After Chinese and English, it is the most prevalent language on earth, spoken by about 250,000,000 people, and as the primary tongue in 20 countries, mainly in Latin America. 'We Spanish and Hispano-Americans are the owners and users of one of the four great languages of the future, the others being English, Arabic and Chinese,' the 1989 Nobel laureate from Spain, Camilo José Celar, has said. The Latin American variants of Spanish may differ in pronunciation but Castilian Spanish is both widely understood and appreciated there. The difference is not unlike that between British and American English.

Many types of course are offered by language schools and organisations both in the UK and in Spain; and some of the most popular forms of language-learning and the organisations which offer these courses or language-learning materials are listed below.

Self-Study Courses

The advantage of self-study is that it allows students to work and absorb material at their own pace and in their own time. The BBC produces excellent workbooks and audio cassettes at various levels. Further information is available from BBC Customer Services (☎08700-100222) or via the websites www.bbcshop.com or BBC Education (www.bbc.co.uk/education/languages/spanish). The BBC now offers an online beginners' course called 'Spanish Steps' as well as the self-study course *España Viva* (among others), an introduction to everyday Spanish based on recordings of what Spaniards actually say.

Linguaphone (0800-282417; www.linguaphone.co.uk) distributes more elaborate (and more expensive) self-study courses in the form of books, cassettes and compact discs which tend to be geared towards holidaymakers rather than prospective residents. Consequently, the lessons focus on such subjects as sightseeing, how to order meals and drinks, shopping, making reservations, explaining symptoms to a doctor, etc.

Other books with cassettes currently on the market are *Teach Yourself Spanish* (Hodder & Stoughton), *Colloquial Spanish* (Routledge) and *Teach Yourself Spanish* (Hugo). These and other book-with-cassette courses are generally priced between £20 and £40 and are available from larger bookshops or in selected libraries.

The *Open University (OU)*, Central Enquiry Service, PO Box 724, Walton Hall, Milton Keynes MK7 6ZS, ☎08709-000305; www.open.ac.uk (which also runs many courses for expatriates in Spain and around the world) offers courses leading to an undergraduate degree in Spanish. For example 'A Fresh Start in Spanish' is a level 1 course aimed at people who already have a grounding in the language; it runs from February to October and costs £325.

Language Courses in the UK

Evening language classes offered by local authorities and colleges of further education usually follow the academic year and are aimed at hobby learners or those wishing to obtain a GCSE or A level. Intensive Spanish courses offered privately are much more expensive. Consider using a self-study programme with books and tapes (which usually cost £25-£35), though dedication is required to make progress. Even if you make slower headway with the course at home than you had hoped, take it with you since you will have more incentive to learn once you are immersed in the language.

A more enjoyable way of learning a language (and normally a more successful one) is by speaking it with the natives. The cheapest way to do this at home is to link up with a native speaker of Spanish living in your local area, possibly by putting an ad in a local paper or making contact through a local English language school. Remember to check that the tutor can speak enough English to communicate with you in your own language if your grasp of Spanish has a tendency to collapse sporadically.

Spanish Societies. It is a good idea to find out if any Anglo-Spanish clubs or societies exist in your area, as these will organise various social events and discussion groups and hopefully function to soften the culture shock on arrival in Spain. Check with your local further education institute, university, or local library. It is also worth obtaining details from the Hispanic and Luso Brazilian Council mentioned above of its cultural and educational programme. It also has a library of 50,000 books on Spain, Portugal and Latin America, covering geography, history, current affairs, economics, sociology, natural history, literature, art, music and religion. The *Canning House Library* is open to the public from 2pm to 6.30pm on Mondays and 9.30am to 1pm, then 2pm to 5.30pm Tuesdays to Fridays. Borrowing facilities and a postal service are available to members only. The Council also distributes a free list of Spanish language conversation classes in and around London including addresses of organisations and private tutors offering day or evening language and conversation classes.

Additionally, the Spanish equivalent of the Alliance Francaise or the Goethe Institute of Germany is the non-profit *Instituto Cervantes,* now the largest worldwide Spanish teaching organisation, with headquarters in Madrid (C/ Libreros 23, 28801 Alcalá de Henares, Madrid; ☎918856100; www.cervantes.es).

The Cervantes Institute in London, sometimes referred to as the Spanish Institute (102 Eaton Square, London SW1W 9AN; 020-72350353), has an information and audiovisual department to which members have full access. Manchester also has an Instituto Cervantes at 322330 Deansgate, Manchester M3 4FN; ☎0161-6614200). The membership fee includes admission to events on their cultural programme such as flamenco performances, classical guitar concerts and exhibitions of paintings.

Total immersion courses in Spanish are offered by international language organisations like *Berlitz UK* (913 Grosvenor Street, London W1A 3BZ (☎020-79150909; www.berlitz.com) and inlingua (Rodney Lodge, Rodney Road, Cheltenham, Glos. GL50 1HX). Both offer incompany tuition and executive crash courses in Spanish which can be started in Britain and completed in Spain on request. The Berlitz School in Madrid is at Gran Via 80/4, while inlingua Madrid is at Calle Arenal 24 (☎915413246/7).

Language Courses Abroad

Almost all large Spanish towns, language schools and universities offer residential courses for foreigners to learn Spanish. Courses at all levels of ability normally last two or four weeks. The classes tend to comprise a maximum of ten pupils and accommodation can be arranged in halls of residence, in local pensions or with Spanish families.

An annotated list of schools and universities that offer Spanish language courses in Spain is available from the *Hispanic and Luso Brazilian Council* (Canning House, 2 Belgrave Square, London SW1X 8PJ; ☎020-72352303; www.canninghouse.com) for £4. The current list, which was last updated in 2000, includes the current prices and details of the courses, including accommodation if available. Various regional associations of language schools can put you in touch with their member schools, for example the Associacion de Escuelas de Español para Extranjeros de Andalucía has links to 16 schools in the main towns of Andalucia such as Cadiz, Cordoba and Granada from its website www.aeea.es.

Serious language schools on the continent usually offer the possibility of preparing for one of the internationally recognised exams. In Spain the qualification for aspiring language learners is the D.E.L.E. *(Diploma de Español como Lengua Extranjera)* which is recognised by employers, universities, officialdom, etc. The D.E.L.E is split into three levels: *Certificado Inicial de Español, Diploma Básico de Español* and the *Diploma Superior de Español*. Most schools say that even the Basic Diploma requires at least eight or nine months of study in Spain. A prior knowledge of the language, of course, allows the student to enrol at a higher level and attain the award more quickly.

Typically a four-week residential course will cost between £600 and £800 with accommodation in host family, shared apartment or hall of residence. Most schools put on a programme of social, cultural and sporting activities to supplement academic study while others offer classes on Hispanic history, culture and art in conjunction with the language course. You may even be tempted by a specialist combination course and in addition to learning Spanish pursue another interest like Flamenco dance or riding, literature or golf.

Latin America has in the last few years become another possible destination for those considering Spanish language courses, with lower living costs somewhat offsetting the higher costs of travel to get there; and these courses can be of equal quality. It makes little difference in Spain – if you speak Spanish as a second language – if you have a Latin American accent, although for native speakers there may be some greater problems. In the end, you are learning an international language, rather as those learning English as a second language usually do so to communicate internationally and not just in one country. Most British language agencies have contacts in Latin America as well as Europe.

UK Language Travel Agents. UK-based language organisations and advisory services that may be of assistance for arranging language courses in Spain include:

Cactus Language: 9 Foundry St, Brighton BN1 4AT; ☎01273-687697; www.cactuslanguage.com.

Caledonia Languages Abroad: The Clock-house, Bonnington Mill, 72 Newhaven Road, Edinburgh EH6 5QG; ☎0131-6217721/2; www.caledonialanguages.co.uk.

CESA Languages Abroad: Western House, Malpas, Truro, Cornwall TR1 1SQ; ☎01872-225300; www.cesalanguages.com.

Challenge Educational Services: 101 Lorna Road, Hove, East Sussex BN3 3EL; ☎01273-220261; www.challengeuk.com. Total immersion language courses in Madrid, Barcelona, Marbella and Salamanca suitable for all ages and abilities.

Don Quijote: 24 Stoneleigh Park Road, Epsom, Surrey KT19 0QT; ☎020-87868081; info@donquijote.co.uk; www.donquijote.co.uk. Intensive (20 lessons a week) and Super Intensive (30 lessons a week) courses for all levels throughout Spain: Barcelona, Granada, Madrid, Malaga, Puerto de La Cruz (Tenerife), Salamanca, Seville and Cuzco (Peru).

EF International Language Schools: 1 Farman Street, Hove, E Sussex BN3 1AL; ☎01273-201410; www.ef.com.

EuroAcademy Ltd: 24 Clarendon Rise, Lewisham, London SE13 5EY;

☎020-82970505; fax 020-82970984; www.euroacademy.co.uk. Vacation courses and allyear courses for young people and adults in Málaga, Seville, Valencia, etc.

Euroyouth Abroad Ltd: 301 Westborough Road, WestcliffonSea, Southendon-Sea, Essex SS0 9PT; ☎01702-341434; fax 01702-330104. Intensive summer courses in Madrid, Salamanca and El Puerto aimed at anyone over 17.

Gala Spanish in Spain: Woodcote House, 8 Leigh Lane, Farnham, Surrey GU9 8HP; tel/fax 01252-715319. Information, advisory and placement service for students of any level from age 16 in a number of Spanish cities. Sample prices of family stay with halfboard would be £570-£770 or with self-catering residence £500-£630 for 4 weeks.

Living Spanish: The Barley Mow Centre, 10 Barley Mow Passage, London W4 4PH; ☎020-8747 2018; info@livingspanish.com; www.livingspanish.com. Spanish courses in Spain and Latin America. Sample onemonth intensive course including accommodation with a local family costs £660.

SIBS Ltd: Beech House, Commercial Road, Uffculme, Devon EX15 3EB; ☎01884-841330; www.sibs.co.uk.

Homestays. Another possibility is to forgo structured lessons and simply live with a family. Several agencies arrange paying guest stays which are designed for people wishing to learn or improve language skills in the context of family life. Try *En Famille Overseas* (The Old Stables, 60b Maltravers St, Arundel, West Sussex BN18 9BG), *EIL*, a non-profit cultural and educational organisation, offers short-term homestay programmes in more than 30 countries (287 Worcester Road, Malvern, Worcestershire WR14 1AB; ☎01684-562577; www.eiluk.org), *Home Language International* (www.hli.co.uk) and *International Links* (145 Manygate Lane, Shepperton, Middlesex TW17 9EP; ☎01932-229300) all of which arrange homestays in Spain with or without a language course.

The youth exchange organisation *Relaciones Culturales Internacionales* at Calle Ferraz 82, 28008 Madrid (915417103/fax 915591181), places native English speakers with families who want to practise their English in exchange for providing room and board; they also arrange voluntary work for English assistants on summer language/sports camps. Two other agencies involved in making this sort of live-in placements are *GIC,* Pintor Sorolla 29, Apdo. 1080, 46901 Monte Vedat (Valencia) and *Castrum,* Ctra. Ruedas 33, 47008 Valladolid (983222213). The latter makes placements in Castille and Leon whereby participants undertake to spend at least four hours a day teaching English to members of the family and to enrol in a Spanish course (minimum five hours a week).

Language Schools in Spain. Out of the thousands of language schools offering Spanish courses for foreigners, a small selection is listed here. If you decide to pursue the language after you are established in Spain, look for relevant adverts in the press, for example in *Lookout* magazine, a useful source of information on living and working in Spain published in Malaga.

Aula Magna Castellana: Santo Tomas 1 3D, 40002 Segovia; ☎921412155; www.aulamagnacastellana.com). Specialised and Intensive courses, Academic Vacation and Individual courses in Segovia. From €1,200. Also tries to assist graduates find paid work or traineeships in local companies.

Centro de Estudios de Castellano: Avda, Juan Sebastian Alcano, 120, 29017 Málaga.

CLIC International House: Albardea 19, 41001 Seville; ☎954502131; clic@clic.es; www.clic.org. Recreational Spanish courses.

Colegio Maravillas: Salvador Vicente 9, 29630 Benalmádena, Málaga; ☎952577550; www.maravillas.es. Vacation courses for teenagers include sports and other activities.

Eat, Sleep & Study Español: C. Doctor Fleming 4, Bjos 2a, 08960 Sant Just, Barcelona; ☎933718725. Specialises in onetoone tuition, living, learning and socialising with the tutor. Full-board accommodation and excursions included.

ENFOREX   Spanish   Language

School: Alberto Aguilera 26, 2°, 28015 Madrid; ☎91594 3776; www.enforex.es. Courses at 10 locations yearround.

Malaca Instituto: Calle Cortada 6, 29018 Málaga; ☎952293242; www.malacainstch.es.   Variety of Spanish language and culture courses including practical Spanish for the older student, Spanish and Dance lessons (Sevillanas or Salsa), Commercial Spanish and intensive or onetoone tuition.

Proyecto Español: C/ Garcia Morato 41, 03004 Alicante; ☎966697847/ 639926210; proyespa@aol.com.

Sociedad Hispano Mundial: Palacio de Congresos, Paseo del Violón S/N, 18006 Granada; ☎958246892/ 010172; www.shm.edu. Spanish language courses, plus Spanish civilisation and Hispanic studies courses.

Trinity Language School, PO Box 720, Calle Ave del Paraiso 6, 11500 El Puerto de Santa Maria, Cadiz; ☎956871926; info@trinitylanguage school.com. A Mediterranean resort favoured by Spanish holidaymakers.

Spanish Societies

It is a good idea to find out if any AngloSpanish clubs or societies exist in your area as these will organise various social events and discussion groups and hopefully function to soften the culture shock on arrival in Spain. Check with your local further education institute, university, or local library. It is also worth contacting the Hispanic and Luso Brazilian Council which has a library, open only to members, of 50,000 books on Spain, Portugal and Latin America, covering geography, history, current affairs, economics, sociology, natural history, literature, art, music and religion. The *Canning House Library* is open to the public from 2pm to 6.30pm on Mondays and 9.30am to 1pm, then 2pm to 5.30pm Tuesdays to Fridays. Borrowing facilities and a postal service are available to members.

The Council also runs an information service on courses and opportunities in the UK and abroad and organises a cultural and educational programme from September to June. There are special rates for schools and student membership. Membership includes full use of the library facilities, access to the Council's publications on the Latin American countries and free admission to the cultural events (exhibitions, concerts, lectures) which the Council organises. Further details are available from the Education Department at the above address. Additionally, the *Instituto Cervantez* (102 Eaton Square, London SW1 9AN; ☎020-7235 0353) has an information and audio-visual department to which members have full access. There are also Cervantez Institutes at: The University, 169 Woodhouse Lane, Leeds LS2 3AR and at Brook House, 326 Deansgate, Manchester M3 4FN; ☎0161-661 4200. The membership fee also includes admission to all the events on their cultural programme.

The kinds of events they sponsor cater for all tastes and include subjects as diverse as exhibitions of flamenco dancing, classical guitar concerts and exhibitions of paintings, or trips to Spain for old age pensioners. Applications for membership and further information should be made to the above address.

SCHOOLS AND EDUCATION

The decision of how and where to educate your children is something which has posed a quandary for parents wherever or however they live. Moving abroad with children of a young age is in some ways easier than moving with teenagers as younger children are remarkably adept at picking up languages and fitting into new situations. Furthermore, as their education has not yet begun in earnest, the problem of juggling two curricula does not exist. Although the Spanish education system is perfectly adequate, it will obviously not follow the same as the UK or American one; and this will create difficulties if a child in the middle of a GCSE course is suddenly uprooted to Spain and expected to do well in Spanish examinations. For this reason, many parents choose to send their children to international schools while abroad (see below), while families who can afford it sometimes choose to keep their children at UK boarding schools so as not to disrupt their education. However, the opportunity to mix with Spanish children and to attend a Spanish school is both rare and exciting and one well worth considering.

The Spanish education system has undergone a radical transformation in recent years. Previously elitist and badly-organised, the system is now built on a structure which has opened up education to all classes, and to people of all abilities. Responsibility for education in Spain is shared between the state and the seventeen autonomous communities or regions. Some of these autonomous regions have assumed full control over education, and it is likely that decentralisation will go further in future.

It is ironic that a country which for so many years has fallen behind its European neighbours in education should at the same time possess a deep and inherent respect for study and education not found in many other countries, including the UK. The structure of the Spanish education system is still based primarily on Article 27 of the 1978 Constitution and also on the *Ley General de Educación y Financiación de la Enseñanza Obligatoria* (LGE) 1970. Two more recent laws, the *Ley de Reforma Universitaria* (LRV) of 1983 and the *Ley Orgánica del Derecho a la Educación* (LODE0) 1985 have served to adapt this structure; and there was another reform in 1992 following a complete review of the existing system (*la Ley de 70*). The law which changed it is known as the *Ley Organica de ordinación General del Sistema Educativo* otherwise known as the *LOGSE*. In general terms, the Spanish education system has moved away from a centralised and highly traditional system to a decentralised and more modern one.

School attendance in Spain is compulsory by law between the ages of six and sixteen (and it is no longer possible, as it was, to opt out of education at 14). Both state and private education exist; families in state education are expected to pay only for school books (which are only free in special cases), school supplies, a certain proportion of transportation services and for some voluntary extra-curricular activities. The academic year usually runs from September to June, with vacations at Christmas and Easter; religious instruction is voluntary.

The spectacular growth of the Spanish educational system over the past few years has resulted in many changes; but there are still the four basic levels of education in Spain: pre-school, primary (*Educación General Básica*) known as *EGB*, secondary, and university level.

At the end of compulsory secondary education (*Educación Secundaria Obligatoria*) or *ESO* students are faced with a choice between a more academic or a more vocational route. The former usually means going on directly to do the *Bachillerato* – otherwise known as the *Bachillerato Unificado Polivalente* or *BUP* – which is a two-year course covering four areas of study: arts; natural and health sciences; humanities and social sciences; and technology.

An alternative route is to leave school and go in for the *Profesional de Primero y Segundo Grado*, the two levels of vocational training, with Intermediate and Higher Grades each comprising two years of study. Those leaving school without qualifications would have to go in for an initial year of training called the Social Guarantee Programme (*Garantia Social*) which would act as a foundation course for the Intermediate Grade Training Cycles (*Ciclos formativos – Grand Medio*) and subsequently the Higher Grade Training Cycles (*Ciclos Formativos – Grado Superior*). In contrast to the present non-elitist structure of education, what pre-school education existed in the 1970's was very limited and secondary education, beginning at the age of ten, was mostly restricted to private sectors.

It was true at that time that a significant number of Spaniards were illiterate. But the new system has brought levels of illiteracy more into line with other European countries. Nowadays, university is no longer seen as nothing more than a place of study for the privileged minority; and both of these routes – the vocational and academic – allow the student to apply for the university of their choice, dependant of course on their results, and their passing the entrance exam.

The reformation and improvement of the system when Spain became a democracy has resulted in nearly all children from four to five years old attending pre-school education; compulsory education up to sixteen years of age is universal; and more than 70% of young people stay on until the age of eighteen while 40% receive professional training. University has become a form of education which anyone may enter, with a student body of over one million people. Interestingly, this growth is principally a result of the number of female students at university, who exceed the number of males in secondary education and in the first years of university. The presence of females is less only on the professional training courses where they constitute 45% of the student body.

State and Private Education

Both state and private education are available in Spain, although the former accounts for by far the larger percentage of students. However, the fees charged by the private schools are usually not monstrously large, as these schools also receive a subsidy from the state. State education is free and is available by law to all children resident in Spain. More details of the Spanish education system (state and private) can be obtained from the *Spanish Embassy Education Office* in London (20 Peel Street, London W8 7PD) or the *Ministerio de Educación* in Madrid (see address above). At present, a large minority of of all non-university education is private and Catholic education represents approximately 20% of the whole educational system, but is more widely prevalent in school than university education.

The Structure of the Education System

Pre-school. This is divided into playschool (23 years of age) and kindergartens (45 years); both groups are voluntary and free in public centres. Private schools charge a fee which tends to be most expensive in the unsubsidised international schools. Despite the rapid growth in recent years in the number of state pre-school facilities, anyone considering this form of education for their children will have to research the area of Spain in question to find out what facilities are available as these tend to vary greatly from region to region. Although it is not always the case, children who have been to pre-school classes do tend to be at an advantage over those who have not, once they enter primary school.

The objective of pre-school education is to develop basic personal aptitudes and cooperative social attitudes through games and other nondidactic methods; instruction in reading and writing tends to be left to the primary schools. In most areas, plans to transform pre-school education into what are known as infant schools (*escuela infantiles*), have been carried out; these are conceived of as for children from birth through to six years of age, and divided into two groups, ages 0-3 and 3-6, each with its own specialised teachers.

Primary. Catering for children from the age of six, primary education is both compulsory and free in Spain in the state sector. Those who have completed the last year of primary school receive the *Título de Graduado Escolar*; this is a prerequisite for secondary education and then university. Those who do not receive the Título are given the *Certificado de Escolaridad* which can be used for entrance to technical training courses. Thus, at a very young age Spanish schoolchildren are forced into an irreversable decision which will to a great degree determine the course of their future careers. The technical training is largely practical while the two or three years of secondary education leading to the baccalaureat is purely academic. Having to make this kind of decision so young is one of the strongest criticisms levied at the Spanish education system.

Secondary. The *Bachillerato Unificado y Polivalente* (BUP) provides its students with a three-year, academic training as a preparation for university. The first and second years are divided equally between the natural sciences, mathematics, languages and the humanities, while a specialisation is made in the third year. The *Título de Bachiller* is awarded at the end of the course if no more than two subjects have been failed in the final examinations and this certificate may be used to enter the second stage of the technical training course or to attend a one year, pre-university course, the *Curso de Orientación Universitaria* (COU). Students who enter for this level must pass all subjects as COU is an essential preliminary to university. Some students go on to technical training centres rather than entering the COU course.

Technical Training. The *Formación Profesional* comprises two levels, known simply as FP1 and FP2, and is free for most students, whether they attend a public centre or a private institution financed by the state. The technical training courses have a strong practical emphasis and take students from the age of 14. FP1 consists of a two year course and is compulsory for those who fail to gain the *Título de Graduado Escolar.* The course provides a general introduction to a specific vocation such as clerical work, electronics, etc. FP2 is the second level or cycle of technical training and offers specialised vocational training. In the past about twice as many children chose to take BUP over the FP course, but as vocational training becomes more and more precious the balance is changing and the ratio is now closer to three to two.

Additionally, the high percentage of failures and dropouts combined with the reluctant acceptance of the certificate in the job market and the class consciousness in the make-up of the student body have made FP1 the most problematic and criticised area in the Spanish education system. However, those who continue to FP2 and successfully complete the course receive the further *Técnico Especialista* certificate; and this enjoys a much better reputation in the job market. Usually, students on this course have divided their time between school studies and working in some kind of business concern.

Study and Exchange. The *ASSE* programme gives school students in Britain the opportunity to spend a year in Spain (and other countries), living with a local family and attending school there. This is for sixth-form students aged between 16 and 18. They can provide details of possible placements and have representatives on the ground to assist students once they are there. Contact: *ASSE UK*, PO Box 20, Harwich, Essex CO12 4DQ; ☎ 01255-506347.

In addition, teachers interested in exchange programmes should contact the *Schools and Teachers Team, Education and Training Group,* The British Council, 10 Spring Gardens, London SW1A 2BN; ☎ 020-7389 4916. Internationally, the *European School Exchange Database* also has a list of schools seeking partners throughout Europe: contact the *Centre for International Education* (CEVNO), Nassaauplein 8, 1815 GM Alkmaar, The Netherlands.

University. The Spanish university system, like many of its European counterparts, dates back to the Middle Ages. The oldest Spanish university is Salamanca, founded in 1218. In the last twenty years, the university system has experienced its greatest growth in history while at the same time advancing towards a self-governing and decentralised system. There are presently 30 or so state universities in Spain and four private ones. All four of the private universities are tied to the Catholic Church, one of which, the Opus Dei University in Navarre, carries far more influence than its size would warrant, the majority of its intake comprising the sons and daughters of the powerful, wealthy and aristocratic. The Complutense in Madrid and the Central in Barcelona are by far the largest Spanish universities; the former comprising nearly 100,000 undergraduates while the latter has a total intake of nearly 80,000. Despite their size, these two universities are generally regarded as being the best in Spain.

To enter a Spanish university, a student must have passed either the educational or vocational levels of secondary education (see above); a university entrance exam must also be taken (this is held in the university itself). The subject of study is determined by academic criteria and depends on the average grades received and on the grade received in the university entrance exam.

There is a clear division between academic and practical courses; some universities (*Facultades* and *Colegios*) offer five or six year academic courses while the *Escuelas Universitarias* provide shorter, three-year, vocational courses (for teachers, nurses, etc). The latter courses are regarded less favourably than the purely academic ones although this is a trend which is changing as the demand for students trained in a specific vocation rises each year. Currently, many more students undertake purely academic courses than those who enter for vocational ones, and those who have high enough academic grades will usually choose to enter the former. A high percentage (80%) of all Spanish students who complete secondary education go on to university.

Foreigners who choose to work within the courses offered by the Spanish education system at university level must sit the *selectividad* examination either at the university where they wish to study or, if they live abroad, at the Spanish Embassy in that country. Before taking this entrance exam, foreign students must have their qualifications (GCSE's, A levels, etc.) officially validated through the *Ministerio de Educación y Ciencia* in Spain (see address above) or through the Spanish Embassy in the applicant's native country. Alternatively, almost all Spanish universities offer special courses for foreign students. It is not necessary to validate foreign qualifications for these courses but the certificates gained through following this type of course are not recognised within the state education system. Courses take place both during summer vacations and throughout the year and universities may be able to offer accommodation in student halls of residence or at least provide some assistance in this respect. Information on both standard Spanish courses and those specially designed for foreigners and details of how to apply for them, may be obtained directly from the universities in question. Note that a prior knowledge of Spanish will be required by most universities.

Study and Exchange Schemes. There are a number of such schemes for those already studying or intending to study at a British university and wishing to spend up to a year at college in Spain as well. The *British Council* in London should be contacted (see address above) or your UK university. The *Erasmus* scheme is part of the EU's Socrates programme, intended to encourage cooperation between universities as well as student exchanges. Students and UK institutions should contact the *UK Erasmus Students Grants Council*, The University, Canterbury, Kent CT2 7PD; ☎01227-762712. There are also British Council offices at 3 Bruntsfield Crescent, Edinburgh EH10 4HD; ☎0131-447 8024; and 2nd Floor, Norwich Union House, 7 Fountain Street, Belfast BT1 5EG; ☎02890-233440.

International Schools

International schools tend to be regarded as the best alternative by expatriates who are considering the long-term education of their children. This is primarily because they offer the qualifications better known to selection bodies for UK or American universities. Spanish law requires all foreign schools to be supported by their embassies. For this purpose, The *National Association of British Schools in Spain*, Arga 9 (El Viso), E28002 Madrid, works with the British Council to arrange that all its member schools are visited regularly by British inspectors who then report to the Spanish Ministry of Education. On receipt of a satisfactory report, the school is authorised to continue as a foreign centre of education.

The following is a list of international schools in Spain which either teach the UK or American curriculm or a combination of the Spanish and international systems; the age range of the pupils is also listed. The list is updated constantly at the website of the *European Council of Schools (ECIS)*, 21 Lavant Street, Petersfield, Hants GU32 3EL; ☎01730-268244 or 263131; fax 01730-267914; email ecis@ecis.org; internet: http://www.ecis.org. (The most recent updated ECIS list can be found at this internet address). The *ECIS Iberian Office* can be contacted at: *ECIS*, PO Box 6066, E28080, Madrid; ☎915626722; fax 917451310; email ecismadrid@ecis.org. Alternatively, you may buy their *Directory of International Schools* from www.johncatt.co.uk.

International schools also teach French and German curricula; and ECIS also lists such schools. There are around ten American schools in Spain which are a possible choice for all expatriates. However, the multitude of British schools in Spain, along with what is the overall high quality of education which they offer, will probably make this unnecessary in the majority of cases, as it easier to switch back into the British education system from a UK, rather than a US, school abroad. Other schools offer a dual system of Spanish and English language teaching and curricula which provide the opportunity for children to be equally well qualified to live and work in Spain or in the UK in future life; these schools are required to allocate at least 20% of the total number of places available to Spanish students. Different again, are those schools which teach the UK curriculum but also include some Spanish studies, taught in English in the same curriculum.

Please note that in the list below the area code for each school is provided, this should be prefixed by 00 and then 34 – the international dialling code for Spain. The address and phone number are generally followed by the age range of the pupils. If the school offers teaching in both Spanish and English, and the curriculum offered covers both UK and Spanish subjects, then this is indicated by the words, 'mixed curriculum' at the end of the entry. Most of the American schools are also included. The great majority of schools are day--schools only but the few which do take boarders have been marked as doing so.

Caxton College: Ctra Barcelona S/N, E46530 Puzol, Valencia (☎961464500; fax 961420930), 3-14.

Sierra Bernia School: San Rafael S/N, Alfaz del Pi, Alicante E03580 (☎966875149; fax 966875149).

Xabia International College: Apartado 3-11, E03730 Javea, Alicante (☎965790253; fax 965790252), 2-18+, UK-based curriculum.

ESCAANEscola Catalano Anglesa: Passeig de les Acacies S/N, E08870 Barcelona (☎938942040; fax 938942072).

Oak House School: San Pedro Claver 1218, Barcelona E00817 (☎932038624; fax 932057021), ages 3-18 ;mixed curriculum.

AngloAmerican School: Apartado 172, E08860 Castelldefeis, Barcelona (☎936651584; fax 936651584); ages 3-18. US and UK curriculum.

Izarra International College: Finca Arguitza, Izarra, Alava E01440 (☎94537100; fax 94537214), 3-16. Boarding facilities.

British School of Gran Canaria: PO Box 11, Tafira Alta, E35017 Las Palmas de Gran Canaria (☎928351167; fax 928351065); ages 4-18.

Oakley College: Ctra a Los Hoyos 130, Tafira Alta, E35017 Las Palmas de Gran Canaria (☎928354247; fax 928354267; email dmorgan@idec.es), ages 2-11.

International British Yeoward School of Tenerife: Apartado 332, Puerto de la Cruz, Tenerife (☎922384685; fax 922373565) 3-18.

British Council School of Madrid: c/ Solano 3, 5y7 Prado de Somosaguas, Pozuelo de Alarcon, E28223 Madrid (☎913373612 or 3608; fax 913373634); ages 3-18.

English Montessori School: Avda La Salle S/N, Aravaca, E28023 Madrid (☎913572667/8; fax 913071543); ages 3-18. Mixed curriculum.

Hastings School: Paseo de la Habana 204, E28036 Madrid (☎913599913; fax 913593521); ages 3-18.

International College Spain: Apartado 271, E28100 Alcobendas, Madrid (☎916502398/99; fax 916501035; ages 3-18).

International School of Madrid (formerly the International Primary School): Rosa Jardon 3, E28016 Madrid (☎913592121/0722; fax 915195623), ages 3-14. Mixed curriculum.

King's College Madrid: Paseo de los Andes, Soto de Vinuelas, E28790 Madrid (☎918034800; fax 918036557); ages 2-19. Takes boarders.

Runnymede College: Camino Ancho, 87 La Moraleja, E28109 Madrid (☎916508302; fax 916508236; 2-18).

The Academy International School: Apartado 1300, E07080 Palma de Mallorca, Mallorca (☎971605008; fax 971605008; email acad@ocea.es); ages 2-14.

Baleares International School: Calle Cabo Mateu Coch 17, San Agustin, E07015 Mallorca (☎971401812; fax 971700319; email bispmi@ibm.net), 3½-18. US and UK curriculum.

Bellver International College: 5 Jose Costa Ferrer, Palma E07015 (☎971401679/404263), 3-18.

Queen's College, The English School: Juan de Saridakis 64, Palma de Mallorca (☎971401011; fax 971400153) 3-18.

Aloha College: El Angel, Nueva Andalucia, Malaga, E29600 Marbella (☎952814133; fax 952812792), 3-18+.

New English International College: Urb Ricmar, C.N. 340 Km 189.5, E29600 Marbella (Malaga), ☎952831058; fax 952838992; ages 3-18.

Swans International Primary School: Capricho 2, E29600 Marbella (Malaga) ☎952773248; fax 952776431), 2½-12.

International School at Sotogrande: Apartado 15, Sotogrande Province de Cadiz (☎956795902; fax 56794816), 3-18. Takes boarders.

Sunny View School: Apartado 175,

Cerro de Toril, E29820 Torremolinos, Malaga (☎952383164; fax 952372695), 4-18.

El Centro Ingles: Apartado Correos 85, Carretera Fuentebravia Km1.2, Puerto de Santa Maria, E11500 Cadiz (☎956850560; fax 956873804), 2-18. Takes boarders.

El Plantio International School of Valencia: Urbanizacion El Plantio, C/233 No.36, La Cañada, Paterna, Valencia (☎961321410; fax 961321841), 3-16.

English School 'Los Olivos': Avda Pino Panera 25, E46110 Godella, Valencia, 3-15.

American Schools.
American School of Barcelona: Calle Balmes No 7, E08950 Esplugues de Llobregat, Barcelona (☎933714016; fax 934734787), 3-18.

Benjamin Franklin International School: Martorell i Peña 9, E08017 Barcelona (☎934186545/6609; fax 934173633; email bfis@goliat.upc.es), 3-19.

American School of Bilbao: Soparda Bidea 10, E48640 Berango, Bizkaia (☎946680860/1; fax 946680452; email amschbil@sarenet.es), 3-16.

American School of Las Palmas: Apartado 15, Tafira Alta E35017, Gran Canaria (☎928430023; fax 928430017); ages 3-18.

International School of Cartagena: Bellavista, La Manga Club, Los Bellones, CP E30385 (☎968564511 ext 2238; fax 968564511); ages 4-13.

Evangelical Christian Academy: Calle Talia 26, E28022 Madrid (☎917412900; fax 913208606); 5-18.

American School of Madrid: Apartado 80, E28080 Madrid (☎913572154; fax 913572678; email spa0130@appleli nk.apple.com); ages 3-18.

American International School of Mallorca: Calle Oratorio 4, Portals Nous, Mallorca (☎71675850/1; fax 71676820), 3-18+. Takes boarders.

Colegio HispanoNorteAmericano: PO Box 9, Puzol, Valencia (☎961421412; fax 961464639).

MEDIA AND COMMUNICATIONS

Newspapers

Freedom of the press was not established in Spain until 1978, in the aftermath of thirty years of censorship under the Francoist dictatorship. However, the removal of the censorship laws have not changed what can only be described as the apathy of the Spanish towards newspaper reading, at least compared to their more voracious British and American cousins. The circulation of the daily press is far lower than in most other European countries; the only countries in Europe with a lower newspaper readership than Spain are Greece, Portugal and allegedly Albania. The most popular daily newspaper in Spain is *El País* (Miguel Yuste 40, E28017 Madrid), which has a reputation for liberalism and for being supportive of more 'leftwing' causes; it is one of very few Spanish national newspapers to offer any serious political analysis and competent foreign news coverage.

El País has an average daily circulation of about 450,000 – which compares not too unfavourably with the most widely read quality newspaper in Britain *The Daily Telegraph*, which has a daily circulation figure of over a million. Apathy towards politics is another reason for the mixed popularity which newspapers as a media form receive throughout the country. Only eight papers in Spain sell more than 100,000 copies a day. The statistic that only one Spaniard in every ten buys a daily newspaper is also fairly staggering. However, as newspapers in Spain tend to be handed around and read second, third and fourth hand, this statistic is based only on sales figures and is thus not wholly accurate as to readership.

ABC is the other leading daily newspaper of national circulation; similarly to *El País*, this is published in Madrid (Serrano 61), with some regional editions in some of the Autonomous Communities. This, however, is where the similarity ends as *ABC* is aligned very definitely right of centre in its politics as well as in its stringent moral dictums. Other leading national papers include, *La Vanguardia Española* (Pelayo 28, Barcelona), *El Mundo* (Pradillo 42, E28002 Madrid), *El Periódico* (published in Barcelona and read mostly in Catalonia and to a much lesser extent in other parts of Spain) and *AS* and *Marca* – both of which are dedicated to sports coverage. In Spain, the newspapers circulated in the week are also published on Sunday; Sunday sales are generally 50%100% higher than those for the rest of the week.

Shocking though it may seem to those whose literary staple diet is *The Sun* or *The Daily Mail*, Spain has no real equivalent of our tabloid newspapers. Instead, national curiousity tends to be aroused, not by the latest on the royals, but by current affairs of a rather less frivolous nature, and by sport. The Spanish popular newspapers do cover the lives of the rich and famous, but these articles are left to the back pages rather than taking the role of lead stories as often happens in the UK.

Franco's death brought with it, amongst many other changes, the recreation of a vernacular language daily press. The Catalan newspaper, *Avui* is one such newspaper which has gradually gained a solid and established following. The Basque papers, *Eja* and *Egin* are mostly printed in euskara, the latter paper being a supporter of independence. However, Franco's death left followers as well, and *El Alcázar* is a popular, blatantly ultra-right wing, national newspaper whose circulation soared during the 1980s.

Magazines

As none of the Spanish newspapers has an equivalent of the social diaries or gossip columns that are found in such abundance in British and American papers, the Spanish magazine market has sucessfully exploited this gap in the market. There are now countless glossy and profitable womens' magazines devoted to the lives and loves of the famous; a few of the most well-known include, *Hola!* (which spawned *Hello!* magazine in the UK); *Pronto*; *Diez Minutos*; *Lecturas*; *Semana*; and *Garbo*. These magazines are known as the *Prensa de Corazón* (Press of the Heart) and account for six of the ten most popular magazines in Spain.

Specialist Newspapers

So far as employment is concerned, those who speak Spanish can turn to *Mercado de Trabajo* (which itself has a number of newspaper guides for employment elsewhere in Europe: Germany, Belgium, Denmark, France, Holland, Italy and Norway). They also publish *Guia de las Empresas que Ofrecen Empleo* which you can order direct from *Mercado de Trabajo*, Plaza de las Acacias, 3, 1°, E28005 Madrid.

English Language Newspapers

Spain is well served for English-language publications, which also have their Situations Vacant and Situations Wanted columns. *SUR in English* is one of the bestknown English-language newspapers in the country. It has a large employment section in the classified ads which is used by many foreign residents in the south of Spain and also a large section of the Spanish population. It is a free weekly paper distributed on Fridays through outlets such as supermarkets, bars, travel agencies, banks etc. and is published by *Prensa Malagueña*, Avda. de Marañon 48, E29009, Málaga; ☎952 649 600; www.surinenglish.com.

As mentioned in Chapter Three, property is also advertised in *SUR in English*, although this is often for those looking for a holiday home in Spain. *Spanish Homes Magazine* is a magazine and newsletter covering residential and business property, legal and financial services, removals, and information and advice for expatriates in Spain (Paragon Place, Blackheath, London SE3 0SP; ☎020-8297 9194; fax 020-8297 1094); www.spanishhomesmagazine.com. Also see *Lookout* magazine below, Another local English-language magazine is *Absolute Marbella*, (Office 602, Edif. King Edward Ramón Gómez de la Serna 22, 29660 Malaga; ☎952 820 065; www.absolute.marbella.com).

English-language publications in Spain include the weekly *Costa Blanca News* (Apartado 95, Benidorm, 03500, Alicante, E03500; ☎966 812 841); The *Majorca Daily Bulletin* (San Felio 25, Apdo. 304, E07012 Palma de Mallorca; ☎971716 110; fax 971719706); *The Island Gazette*, C/Iriarte 43 2°, Puerto de la Santa Cruz, Tenerife, Canary Islands; *The English Press* (Andrés Mellado, 46, 2°D; ☎915490429; fax 915499350) and *Spain Now* (Abedul 16; ☎9913506617; fax 9913504503) both in Madrid; and *The Island Sun*, based in Las Palmas de Gran Canaria, Realidad 3; ☎928561650); as well as *Lookout* magazine, a source of a wide range of information on living and working in Spain: Urb. Molino de Viento, C/Rio DarroPortal 1, E29650 MijasCosta, Málaga; ☎952 473 090; email lookout@jet.es;. A useful glossy magazine for Barcelona residents is *Barcelona Resident* (distributed free in the city). Articles are on all aspects of Barcelona life; and various useful services for expats are advertised.

Lookout is another very useful magazine for anyone thinking of living in Spain, with general interest articles, property trends, and useful legal advice; and various property and other community services are featured. The same group also publishes *SunGolf* for golf enthusiasts; *SunProperty*; and the annual *Property Guide for Southern Spain* (in English and German). Similar newspapers and magazines are to found in all those areas where there is a UK expatriate population.

Finally, for those to whom a British newspaper is an indispensable commodity, even when abroad, British newspapers and the *International Herald Tribune* are available in most of the larger Spanish cities. *The Guardian Weekly* current subscription rates for Europe are currently £39 from Spain for six months (£71 for a year) available from *The Guardian Weekly*, 164 Deansgate, Manchester M60 2RR; 0161-832 7200. *The Weekly Telegraph* is a similar digest of news culled from *The Daily Telegraph* (01454-620070; subscription is £61 for six months and £104 for a year).

Books

Libraries in Spain usually work on a closed-shelf system where readers need to know exactly what they want and then ask for this at the counter. Often, Spanish libraries do not allow readers to take books away, even if they are members of the library. English-language bookshops are scattered along the costas (try Julian's Library, Calle España 11, Fuengirola) and are also to be found in Madrid (try Booksellers, José Abascal 48 or the Turner English Bookshop, Calle de Genova 3) and Barcelona (try ComeIn, Proventa 203).

The Spanish National Tourist Office in London also publishes an information sheet on *Books about Spain* including general and regional guides, city guides, books on specialist subjects and the Spanish language. Some expatriates may also wish to subscribe to UK book clubs with an overseas department. One extremely useful organisation in this respect is *The Good Book Guide Ltd.* which produces a bi-monthly magazine. This publication contains independent reviews on a wide selection of books, videos, audios, CDROMs and also gifts which can be mailed anywhere in the world. For a complimentary copy of *The Good Book Guide Magazine* and information on subscriptions you can contact them on 020-7490 0900 or at 61 Frith Street, London W1D 3GB. A year's subscription costs £19.

Televison

The Spanish are a nation of tele-addicts; after the British they watch more television than any other country in Europe. Nearly every Spanish household contains at least one television set, sometimes where the household lacks several more essential facilities, and approximately 90% of Spaniards over the age of 14 watch television every day. The influence which the television has as a media form is intensified by the fact that the Spanish do not read newspapers with the same avidity as the British.

So far as the history of Spanish TV is concerned, Television Española (TVE), the main Spanish television station, set up as a state monopoly in 1956, was subject to heavy censorship under Franco's regime. This censorship continued well into the 1980s and had the effect of lowering the general quality of the programmes aired. TVE's two channels are called TVE1 and TVE2. The first is directed to a more general public. TVE2 has a flexible programming which lends special attention to sports broadcasts and live broadcasts of important cultural events. Its television coverage and audience have grown considerably over the last few years, reaching a daily audience of almost 12 million viewers in 1994. However, TVE1 has the larger audience with more than 20 million spectators (80% of total viewers). Various regional television channels also exist in Catalonia, the Basque Country, Galicia, Andalusia, Madrid and Valencia.

Light entertainment does not enjoy the same popularity among the Spaniards as it does with most other viewing publics and the audience figures reflect the same interest in current affairs and serious discussion programmes as mentioned earlier. Documentaries are particularly popular, as are TVE's two main current affairs programmes, *Informe Semanal* on TVE1 and *La Clave* on TVE2. An aspect of Spanish television which seems odd to foreigners is that programmes are often shown half an hour after or half an hour before the scheduled time – and sometimes, although rarely, not at all.

Today, the introduction of commercial television and the formation of three new private channels is raising the standards of both professionalism and of the programmes themselves. As in the UK, the arrival of satellite and digital TV has sparked some political controversy. The Grupo Prisa (which also owns *El*

País) has launched a cable channel called *Canal Satélite Digital* (soon to be available by satellite) with pay-for-view football, something which the government is currently attempting to limit. A rival digital service has also been launched called *Via Digital* which plans eventually to offer 35 more channels to an already sated Spanish public.

Radio

Spanish radio has a reputation for high-quality and entertaining programming and its audience is greater than that in any other European country. The first state network, Radio Nacional de España (RNE), created by Franco in 1937, paralysed the development of the radio as news broadcasts were produced only by this government-controlled station and prohibited on any others. Only groups close to the Franco regime were given licences and in 1960 all radio stations were legally obliged to broadcast simultaneously the news programmes produced by RNE. However, once the censorship laws had been removed, the growth of new networks was so prolific that at one point Spain hosted some 450 radio stations. Currently, however, Spain has a far smaller number nationally, around ten. The largest public network so far as budget, number of stations and personnel are concerned is still RNE which merged with *Radio Cadena Española* in 1988, although the audience level is still lower than that of some of the private networks.

The most popular radio networks include SER which has three different stations, Los 40 principales, directed mainly at young people, Radio Minuto which alternates music and news, and Radio Corazón which is aimed primarily at housewives. COPE (Cadena de Ondas Populares Españolas) is the second-largest system of private stations and is owned by the Church. Antenna 3 is a more recently-established national network and groups together a number of FM stations, which appeared after the concession of new licences in the 1980's. Most of the stations and networks are now on FM rather than medium wave (Spain has no longwave stations); and many, like the newspapers and TV channels, also have their own political stance and alignments as well.

Post

As in the UK, urgent or registered letters and packages must be taken to a post office in Spain. Post is delivered to your door if it weighs less than 500g and by paying a surcharge if the package weighs in excess of this limit. If the excess payment is not made then the package must be picked up from the local post office. For those who have no fixed address the poste restante (*lista de correos*) service is useful; just write the addressee's name, then lista de correos and the place name on the envelope; the addressee can then pick up his or her mail from the post office after providing a passport as identification. A PO Box service (*apartado de correos*) also exists whereby, for a fee, correspondence can be picked up directly at the post office most convenient for the addressee.

Airmail letters (*aerogramas*) are available at the post office. Letters may also be sent by registered mail (*carta certificada*); this will guarantee their arrival. It is possible to send money through the post by money order (*giro postal*). Post office business hours are generally from 9am to 2pm, although large cities or towns usually have a main post office with longer opening hours.

Postboxes often have two parts; one marked *ciudad* for local mail and another marked *provincias y extranjero* for the rest of the country and abroad. Stamps are sold at post offices and at tobacconists, easily spotted by the Spanish flag painted outside.

A telegraph service (*servicio telégrafo*) which dispatches telegrams and urgent money orders around the world is also available. A telegram can be sent from the post and telegraph offices, or by telephone for a slightly higher amount. Enquiries should be made at the post office..

The Spanish have a similar postcode system to that of the French; the town name is prefixed by either one or two digits which have been attributed to that area and these digits comprise the first two or three digits of the postcode. The same digits are also printed on car licence plates to indicate which area of Spain the car is from.

Telephones

Most of the Spanish telephone service, both national and international, is automatic and the majority of European countries are connected to it. Codes for national and international dialling are given in the telephone booths and can also be obtained by dialling 1003 – Directory Enquiries for national and provincial calls (there is a charge for this service); dial 025 for Directory Enquiries for international calls. The national number for the police is currently 091 and 092 for local police. Reverse charge and person-to-person calls are made through the operator. Telephone directories are available free of charge and there is an English-language telephone directory for the Costa del Sol. It is called ESTD (English Speaker's Telephone Directory) and this is available, free of charge, at distribution points along the coast. Special sections are devoted to financial services and restaurant guides. The deadline for advertising each year is October.

When telephoning inside Spain, dial the complete nine-digit number for the area you are calling. You also need to use the complete number if you are dialling from abroad. To telephone the UK from Spain dial 00 44 and the UK number, omitting the first number of the UK area code. For example, to ring Vacation Work Publications from Spain you would dial: 00 441865241978. To telephone Spain from the UK dial 0034 and the nine-digit Spanish number.

TABLE 4		AREA TELEPHONE CODES	
Alicante	96	Madrid	1
Avila	920	Málaga	95
Barcelona	93	Murcia	968
Bilbao	94	Marbella	952
Burgos	947	Oviedo	985
Cádiz	956	Salamanca	923
Castellón	964	Santander	42
Cordoba	957	Seville	954
Granada	958	Toledo	925
Huelva	959	Valencia	96
Jaen	953	Tenerife	922
León	987	Zaragoza	976

CARS AND MOTORING

Roads

The Spanish road system is radial, stretching out in all directions from the centre point, Madrid. The country's system of motorways presently has several branches, stretching out along the Mediterranean coast and up to Barcelona in the east; to the west of Madrid as far as the Portuguese frontier; and linking up with the Basque country, Valladolid and Burgos in the north. Some statistics illustrate the extensive road revision, stimulated by the need to transport cash crops quickly, and spurred on by Spain's rapid modernisation: in 1984, the country had only 1,800 kms of motorways; by the end of the twentieth century it had 11,000 kms. The road revision programme also includes widening roads, to introduce special lanes for heavy traffic, improving traffic signs and road markings, and to build town bypasses in the most builtup areas.

Tolls are required on all motorways except urban ones; a useful map of all the Spanish toll points is available, free of charge, from ASETA, Calle Estébanez Claderón 3, Madrid 20; or may be supplied by local tourist offices. The rate for tolls is currently around Ptas 15 per kilometre.

The essential driving signs to recognise in order to avoid chaos and potential disaster on the Spanish roads include: *Peligro* (danger) and *Cuidado Estacionamiento Prohibido* (no parking). Car parks are indicated by the letter P in towns. In blue zones the maximum waiting period is 1½ hours; parking permits for 30,60 or 90 minutes are available from tobacconists. A more arcane regulation concerns parking in one-way streets. On dates which are an odd number, you should park on the side of the road with odd house numbers; on even-number dates you should park on the opposite side of the street where the even-number houses are, leaving it an open question where you should park if you are staying more than a day.

Driving Regulations

The minimum driving age in Spain is 18. Drivers and front-seat passengers are required by law to wear seat belts in built-up areas and it is recommended that children under 14 do not travel in the front seat of the car. New plans have been drawn up to enforce the wearing of seat belts in the back seats of cars also. Three-point turns and reversing into side streets are forbidden in towns; and at night sidelights alone must be used in built-up areas (unlike in the rest of Europe where dipped headlights are required). In daylight dipped headlights must be used on motorways and on fast dual carriageways. A spare set of headlight bulbs must also be carried. One tip is always to carry enough cash with you to pay on-the-spot fines. And lorry drivers in front of you will indicate right when it is safe for you to pass. If they then switch the indicator off or are indicating left – but heading straight on – then this means there is oncoming traffic.

Speed limits are 50kph in towns; 90kph out of town; and 100kph on dual carriageways. In Spain, the alcohol limit for drivers is 80mg per 100ml of blood. The Guardia Civil, or Civil Guard, has set up a roadside rescue service which operates on major roads throughout the country. The roadside SOS telephones are connected to the nearest police station which sends out a breakdown van with first aid equipment. The van driver can also radio for an ambulance if needed. There is a small charge for labour and any spare parts required. Alternatively, in cases of accident, contact the nearest Guardia Civil station.

New Traffic Laws. A recent sharp rise in accident figures (January 2002, 363 killed plus 700 injured) has led to some fairly draconian new fines for offending motorists. New penalties now in force include a 600 euro (£370/$530) fine for using a mobile phone while driving, failing or refusing to take a breath test, exceeding city speed limits by more than 18mph. Excessive speed in poor weather conditions will also bring stiff penalties.

Driving Licences

Non-UK and non-EU nationals may drive with their own driving licence for up to six months in Spain. Alternatively, if intending to live permanently in Spain, they can extend this period by applying for an international driving permit or an official translation of their original licence, both of which are valid in Spain for one year. An official translation of the licence can be obtained from the Spanish Consulate in the home country. However, after one year they will need a Spanish driver's licence.

Unsurprisingly, a mountain of paperwork is involved (as for those seeking work there from outside the EU). Just for starters, Americans and others will need to present a medical certificate, a letter specifying which kind of licence they are applying for, the residence permit, current driving licence, and the inevitable three or four passportsized photos. During the few months it takes for the new licence to be processed you will be given an official receipt for your old one and a photocopy of it.

For Britons and EU citizens the procedure is much easier. All licences issued in the EU are now valid in any other EU country. This means if you got your licence in France, Britain, Ireland etc. you no longer have to exchange if for a Spanish one if you decide to take up residence in Spain. Official regulations governing motoring matters are available at the local traffic department in Spain, the *Jefatura Provincial de Tráfico*.

Note that licences in Spain are not sacrosanct until the driver reaches the age of 70 as in Britain. Instead they have to be renewed according to your age and the type of licence held. A car licence is usually granted for ten years if the driver is under 45, and for five years if he or she is between 45 and 70. Drivers over 70 years old must renew their licence each year.

Buying a Car in Spain

Many new residents manage to avoid paying the hefty VAT charged on cars bought in Spain by buying a car in Spain with tourist plates; this is quite legal as anyone who moves to Spain is classified as a tourist for the first six months of residence anyway. Many residents manage to renew the tourist registration plates for more than four years, even though they have now become fully-fledged Spanish residents. The disadvantages of this are that although a greater VAT cost is avoided, the buyer must pay for the total cost of the car in foreign currency and immediately; the car cannot be bought through a hire purchase agreement.

Although, strictly speaking, the tourist registration is only valid for six months of each year, it is fairly straightforward to obtain an extension called a *prórroga* which will allow the owner to use his or her car for the remaining six months of the year. To be eligible for such an extension, the car owner must usually have brought approximately 6,000 euros into Spain in the previous year and not be working in Spain. After obtaining the maximum number of five extensions permitted it shouldn't be a problem selling the car on, as the extension limit applies to the owner of the car, not to the car itself. The next owner can continue renewing the tourist plates just as the previous one did. A word of warning however – it is well worth checking that the province to which you are moving does not ban Britons who have a resident's permit from obtaining the *prórrogas*, as is the case in some areas.

In many ways, selling a UK car and simply buying another one in Spain, with Spanish registration plates, saves a lot of paperwork and bother. Many makes and models of cars are available, although these tend to cost rather more than similar cars in some other European countries. In theory, anyone buying a car in Spain should have a residence permit; in practice, Spanish car dealers often don't mind at all if you don't have one. However, you will need a Spanish driving licence to drive a Spanish car. For this it is necessary to have a residence permit.

Prices are often advantageous if you buy in Spain. At present, the comparatively strong pound has meant a difference of up to 20% between Spanish and UK prices.

Insurance

The basic legal requirement for Spanish car insurance is third party only; thus drivers are insured for claims made against them, but not for any accident which may befall driver or car. This type of insurance can cost as little as 120 euros a year and covers third party claims for bodily harm and about for collateral damage. Anyone who feels that they don't have enough security with only third party insurance can take out more comprehensive insurance which either raises the limit on the amount the insurance company will pay out on third party insurance, or insures the car owner, his or her family and the car. Coverage can also be bought against fire, theft and damage.

A comprehensive car insurance policy will cost more. If the policy holder agrees to pay an excess (i.e. they are liable for the first hundred pounds or so) of the costs in any accident not only will they receive substantial protection in return but this protection will cost less than it would without this agreement. As in the UK, policy holders are entitled to a no-claims bonus – a discount on their insurance premiums if there have been no claims against the policy.

In the case of an accident, either party must bring any charge against the other within two months. This simply involves going to the local police station, making a statement (you must know at least the registration of the other car involved) and then letting the insurance companies on either side battle it out. However, if it comes to a court case then you may have to wait, literally, for years as the Spanish judicial system heaves its way towards justice.

For those on a temporary visit to Spain, the country's membership of the EU has made the international insurance certificate (green card) no longer necessary. However, you may find that your individual policy gives only minimum coverage without it, so check to be sure. Green cards are available on request from all insurance companies. For those travelling by car to Spain, *Derek Ketteridge & Associates* (1st Floor, 130A Western Road, Brighton BN1 2LA; ☎01273-720222; fax 01273-722799) can arrange European breakdown assistance insurance with Green Flag at net rates from £12.90.

TRANSPORT

Railways

The Spanish national rail network, RENFE (Red Nacional de los Ferrocarriles Españoles) has a length of around 13,000kms; it stretches out from the centre point of Madrid where its three principal lines begin, two of which extend to the French frontier crossing the Basque country and Catalonia and the third to Andalusia and Levante. The junctions within the rest of the network are Medina del Campe Venta de Baños and Zaragoza in the northern half and Alcázar de San Juan in the South.

All train fares and times can be viewed on the website www.renfe.es or telephone 902 240 202 (domestic) or 934 901 122 (international) for information and reservations. A monthly publication, *Guía Horarios*, contains details of all rail, bus, air and sea services in Spain and is available from station bookstalls.

Trains are graded and priced according to their speed. Talgo 200, TER, AVE, InterCity, and Estrella require the largest supplements. A smaller supplement is payable for the deceptivelytermed *rapido* grade, and the *correo* is the slowest of all and to be avoided at all costs for long journeys. Look out for the blue, white and red days. The former is when there are the greatest reductions. Normal fares are applied on white days; and on red days the fares increase by 10%; this is applied also to supplements and reductions.

An ongoing project (which began with the 1992 Seville EXPO 92 exhibition) is the *Alta Velocidad Española* (AVE) which is the Spanish equivalent of the TGV in France, a high-speed train linking initially Madrid and Seville but destined to cover most of the intercity routes in Spain. Then there are the single track lines (FEVE) which still crisscross much of the north and east, picturesque for tourists but for the locals more often frustrating as they are highly susceptible to delays.

Almost all trains have first and second class compartments: first class costing approximately 50% more than second. Supplements can almost double this. Then there are a wide range of saver tickets, reminiscent of British Rail in its heyday, including young saver, child saver, large family and family pass tickets etc. In addition, there are many more local and long-distance tourist train routes which will be of interest to enthusiasts, like the Al Andalus Express and, in the north, El Transcantabrico. A list of all these RENFE services, and how to make reservations for them, is available from the Spanish Tourist Office in London.

Trains are clean, comfortable and generally reliable. Booking in advance is best. But if you should board a train without a ticket you may be able to pay the conductor on the train itself; but are liable to be charged double for this. It is always advisable to reserve your seats; reservations should not be relied on to be made at stations, since ticket offices have erratic opening hours. Instead, go to the RENFE office in town or to any travel agent.

Children under four travel free on Spanish trains; and children aged between four and twelve travel for half fare. Discounts of up to 20% are available on return journeys of over 200km and on the offpeak blue days (*dias azules*) mentioned above. Residents may choose to take advantage of the RENFE Card. Holders who travel frequently will receive vouchers entitling them to a 10% reduction; and it offers 'a more convenient form of payment' – a little like a credit card. The tourist card (*tarjeta turistica*) is available to anyone residing outside Spain (perhaps useful for a speculative visit before deciding to move permanently) and allows unlimited

1st or 2nd class rail travel for 8, 15 or 22 consecutive days' travel on scheduled RENFE trains and on international trains throughout Spain (with the exception of the Paris-Madrid Talgo). Reservation fees are payable additionally, as with other European rail passes, as are any other fast train and sleeper supplements etc. but holders of 1st class tourist cards are exempt from paying 2nd class couchette supplements on RENFE domestic trains. The price for the same tickets locally may be cheaper, though. Ten-day passes are also available at a special price.

Booking in advance is probably more convenient if you are planning your itinerary through Spain; and a train route through France – or by ferry to Santander – is one way to get there without a car (the alternative being a Eurolines or similar coach – see below); information about the tourist card and other rail passes is available from RENFE stations in Spain and most major travel agents in the UK.

A map of the Spanish railines is available from Thomas Cook. Enquiries should be made to Thomas Cook Publications, PO Box 36, Peterborough PE3 6SB; or one of the large specialist shops like Stanfords Ltd., 1214 Long Acre, Covent Garden, London WC2E 9LP. This should be available in most travel bookshops as well. Another invaluable publication is their International Train Timetable. Alternatively, see the *The Rough Guide to Spain* (£13.99) or the *Cadogan Guide to Spain* for 'getting there' information by train or boat or plane.

Air

Almost a third of the millions of international passengers who visit Spain each year travel by air; and of these more than 70% arrive by charter flights. To some destinations like the Canary and Balearic Islands a charter flight will be the only suitable option. The UK and Spain are the only two countries in the world to record such a high percentage of international charter flights; and the relatively cheap tickets are one reason why many Britons choose to live there. There are also lowcost scheduled services to major cities like Madrid and Barcelona, a trend which looks like continuing with the proliferation of budget airlines following the deregulation of air travel within the EU.

A huge investment plan for Spanish airports has resulted in many improvements and in particular those at Seville and Barcelona airports (a spinoff from the World Exposition and the Olympic Games which were held in those cities). Madrid's Barajos Airport is the centre of domestic traffic (airport information tel: 913058343/4/5/6) and Barcelona is becoming increasingly important (airport tel: 934785032). A regular hourly shuttle service – from 7am to 11pm in Madrid, from 6.45am in Barcelona – operates between these two cities which transports over two million passengers each year. There are also frequent connections between all the main cities in Spain, including flights between Barcelona, Madrid and the Balearic and Canary Islands which, after the shuttle service, are the most frequently used.

At the time of writing, the national Spanish airline, Iberia, is also offering reduced price return tickets to Spain – its response to increased competiton; and flight-only charters to the tourist destinations are available for as little as £69. These kinds of tickets may be useful if you are planning a preliminary trip to Spain before moving out there, as well as for keeping in touch with friends and relatives at home; and it is worth contacting Iberia to find out if they are offering any reductions on flights currently. There are routes out of Dublin, London and many UK regional airports; and a range of international connections and onward domestic flights from Madrid, Bilbao, Valencia, Málaga and Barcelona.

The booking number for Iberia is a call centre 08456012854 (head office in the UK: Iberia House, No 10, Hammersmith Broadway, London SW6 7AL; www.iberia.com.

It is also worth contacting Flight Club (Guildborne Centre, Chapel Road, Worthing BN11 1LZ; ☎ 01903-231857; fax 01903-201225; www.flightclub.co.uk.

Scanning the travel pages of newspapers like *The Guardian* and *The Independent* as well as the free London magazine *TNT* or your local press is another way of keeping in touch with the best flight deals including the many new budget airlines offering amazingly cheap flights to Spain.

The Metro

Barcelona, Madrid and Valencia each have their own underground railway network, known as the metro. These are open from around 6am until midnight or 1am the following day. There is a 'carnet' ticket you can buy which is valid for ten trips. Most metro stations have ticket-vending machines but you can also buy tickets at the counter. You may occasionally see the odd dubious-looking character selling cut-price tickets at station entrances; these are usually tickets which have been bought at a reduced rate (e.g. for children) and are being sold as full fare tickets. Definitely worth avoiding. Information numbers are: 915225909 (for Madrid); and 933187074 (for Barcelona).

Coach and Bus Services

RENFE and numerous private operators run long-distance bus services with similar fares to trains. Many cities have two or more bus stations. Buses also have fixed fares; or you can buy a *bonbo bus* ticket which is valid for 10 journeys and can also work on the metro: the price is the same. The entrance door in buses is marked *Entrada*; and if this is at the front, pay the driver; if it's at the back, pay the conductor who usually sits by the door; or alternatively use the ticket machine. Buses usually run until 11 or 11.30pm. For details of bus services from Barajas Airport in Madrid call 14019900. They leave from the Plaza de Colón. Generally, bus and coach tickets within Spain cannot be booked from the UK; and seat reservations for the long-distance routes can be made only a day or two in advance from the bus/coach station or departure point. The relevant local tourist office can supply details of bus services in the area.

From the UK, regular coach services can be booked with: Eurolines, 4 Cardiff Road, Luton, Beds. LU1 1PP; ☎ 01582-404511; www.gobycoach.com. Also try STS, 138 Eversholt Street, London NW1 1BL; ☎ 020-7387 5337. Or contact your local travel agent. At the time of writing *Siesta Travel Europe* is offering reduced-price family breaks to Spain by coach, again suitable for speculative trips out there perhaps, with apartment accommodation in Salou or Estartit. Please contact them for information and a brochure on 01642-227711.

Ferry Services

Getting there by boat used to be the preferred option for the intrepid mediaeval travellers who took the pilgrim's way to the shrine of Santiago de Compostela (avoiding the marauding Basques). These were some of the first visitors from Britain to Spain, who relied on hearsay, not guidebooks. For travellers today, a much more comfortable ferry can take you by much the same route to the Bay of Biscay in the north. Brittany Ferries have a service from Plymouth to Santander twice a week on Mondays and Wednesdays (☎0870-5360360); and P&O European Ferries go to Bilbao from Portsmouth (☎0870-5980980).

Out to the islands, *Tranmediterranea* operates passenger and car services as well as interisland ferries. In the UK, telephone Southern Ferries on 020-7491 4968; or contact Tranmediterranea directly in Spain. They also operate car and passenger services to Melilla and Ceuta (the Spanish enclaves on the North African coast) and to Tangier.

Taxis

Taxis are cheap, reliable and – most important – metered. These prices can vary from area to area, though; and drivers should have an approved list of charges for intercity or airport journeys. There is usually a surcharge for luggage; or travelling at night, weekends, and during public holidays.

BANKS AND FINANCE

On paper, opening an account in Spain can seem complicated. But in fact those opening resident bank accounts in Spain should encounter nothing strikingly dissimilar to procedures elsewhere and it is a surprisingly simple operation compared to some other European countries. You will only require a letter of introduction from your UK bank and your passport. The largest Spanish banks (the equivalents of Barclays, NatWest and Midland in the UK) include Banco Central, Banco de Bilbao, Banco de Vizcaya, Banco de Santander, Banco Exterior and Banco HispanoAmericano. All of these banks can be found in most towns and cities and offer all the usual banking facilities, including mortgages. Standard bank opening times are from 9am to 2pm on weekdays and from 9am to 1pm on Saturdays, although these may vary from bank to bank.

It is advisable to open your Spanish account immediately on arriving – or even before leaving Britain. This can easily be arranged through the major UK banks – which all have branches in Spain – or through a UK branch of the larger Spanish banks just mentioned (see below). This will enable you to make payments for any professional advice taken and for day-to-day bills. It also saves some time as you will be leaving for Spain with a bank book and cash card in hand. UK banks will also offer Visa and similar cards which can work in Spain; and will have a variety of leaflets of interest to travellers and residents there. So your local bank in the UK should be your first port of call; and you should compare the different charges carefully as well as the exchange rates they quote for using a credit card in Spain.

Exchange Control

Britain abolished all its laws on exchange control in 1979; there is no limit on the amount of currency which can be taken into and out of the UK. Spain followed this example in 1993; presently there is no limit on the amount of foreign currency or euros which can be brought into Spain and no limit on the amount of currency and euros which anyone is allowed to take out of the country. There is more information on income arising from property transactions or salaries under *Non-resident Accounts* below.

Savings Accounts

The Cajas de Ahorros saving banks have branches throughout Spain and they issue a bank card which enables the holder to withdraw money at any time from the automatic cash dispensers which they operate.

For a short-term savings account you can open a deposit account (*libreta de ahorro*) from which withdrawals can be made at any time; interest is added twice yearly to the average credit balance but this will be negligible unless the balance is £1,000 or more. For larger amounts, a savings account (*cuenta de plazo*) will earn more interest as the money has to be left in the account for a previously agreed period of time; perhaps six months, perhaps six years. Obviously, the longer the set period, the greater the rate of interest earned by the account.

The *libreta de ahorro* account is useful for casual workers who are only in Spain for a few weeks or months and do not want to open a long-term bank account but who want to store their money in a bank and also need to have easy access to it.

The address for the Spanish Confederation of Cajas de Ahorros is: 16 Waterloo Place, London SW1 4AR; ☎020-7925 2560. They can send you details of their members in Spain. For other UK contacts for Spanish banks see below.

Banking Procedures

Bank statements are usually sent out to all customers every three months and are available on request at any time. Unlike in the UK, charges are levied on day-to-day banking procedures in Spain, with charges being made on all credit card and cheque transactions. Overdrafts and loans are available on request. All the usual services, such as standing orders and direct debit transferrals, are also available from Spanish banks; but again you should be careful to check the charges, as you would in the UK.

Most Spanish banks will provide cash on presentation of an international credit card (e.g. Access, Visa, American Express). Card holders are able to withdraw the credit balance of their personal limit, which is checked through a central international computer in Madrid. This method only takes a few minutes but is an expensive way of buying euros; and it is cheaper, although not as quick, to pay in a Sterling cheque to the Spanish bank where the commission charged will usually be less.

Opening a Spanish Bank Account from the UK

There are about 150 banking establishments in Spain, of which a third are foreign. Although this comprises a relatively insignificant international presence, the facilities do exist to open up a Spanish account with a UK bank. However, although some people may be more confident opening an account with a Spanish branch of a UK bank, they will find that the Spanish branches function in just the same way as the Spanish national banks. National Westminster (now part of The Royal Bank of Scotland) and Barclays Bank are the most widely represented British banks with approximately 200 branches apiece throughout Spain. Those who wish to open an account in Spain should contact their local branch which will provide the relevant forms to complete. Alternatively, the London offices of the largest Spanish banks are also able to provide the forms necessary to open an account with their Spanish branches. The banks which will provide such a service include Banco De Santander (48 Haymarket, London SW1 Y4SE; ☎020-7332 6900); Banco De Bilbao Vizcaya (100 Cannon Street, London EC4; ☎020-7623 3060)

Offshore Banking

Offshore banks offer tax-free interest on deposit accounts and investment portfolios through banking centres in tax havens such as Gibraltar and the Channel Islands. More and more high street banks and building societies along with the merchant banks are setting up offshore banking facilities and the list given below offers only a handful of the most widely-known which offer such services.

The minimum deposit required by each bank will vary; ranging from £500 to £10,000, with the norm being between £1,000 and £5,000. Usually, a minimum of £10,000 is needed for the yearlong deposit accounts while the lower end of the minimum deposit range applies to 90-day deposits; instant access accounts are also available. The deposit account interest rates work on the basis that the more inaccessible one's money the higher the rate of interest paid. Full details about offshore property mortgages are given in Chapter Three on *Setting Up Home*.

Useful Addresses

Abbey National Offshore: Carrick House, PO Box 150, Douglas, Isle of Man; ☎01624-662244.

Abbey National (Gibraltar) Ltd: 237 Main Street, PO Box 824, Gibraltar; ☎76090; fax 72028.

BDO Stoy Hayward: 8 Baker Street, London W1V 3LL; ☎020-7486 5888. Sixth biggest accountancy firm in the world providing tax advice from offices throughout Europe and overseas.

Bradford and Bingley International Ltd: 30 Ridgeway Street, Douglas, Isle of Man IMI ITA; ☎01624-695000; fax 01624-661962.

Brewin Dolphin Bell Lawrie Ltd: Stockbrokers: 5 Giltspur Street, London EC1A 9BD; ☎020-7248 4400.

ExPat Tax Consultants Ltd: Suite 2, 2nd Floor, Shakespeare House, 18 Shakespeare Street, Newcastle-upon-Tyne NE1 6AQ; ☎01912-30 3141.

Halifax International (Jersey) Ltd: PO Box 664, Halifax House, 31/33 New Street, St Helier, Jersey, Channel Islands JE4 8YW; ☎01534-613500; fax 01534-759280.

Halifax International (Isle of Man) Ltd: PO Box 30, 67 Strand Street, Douglas, Isle of Man IM99 1TA; ☎01624-612323; fax 01624-670086.

HSBC Group: International Business Centre, 5th Floor, 62/76 Pack Street, Southward, London SE19 9DZ.

Lloyds Bank Plc: Isle of Man Offshore Centre. PO Box 12, Peveril Square, Douglas, Isle of Man IM99 1SS; ☎01624-638104; fax 01624-615408. One of their services is the *Lloyds Bank Overseas Club.*

Wilfred T. Fry Limited: Crescent House, Crescent Road, Worthing, Sussex BN11 1RN; ☎01903-200868; fax 01903-200868. A comprehensive tax and compliance service. They may send a copy of their useful free guide *The British Expatriate.*

Useful Publications

The British Expatriate: see above.

Lookout magazine: Urb. Molino de Viento, C/Rio DarroPortal 1, E29649 MijasCosta, Málaga; ☎952473090; fax 952473757; email lookout @jet.es.

Nexus Expatriate Magazine: Rose House, 109A Southend, CR0 1BG; 020-8760 2028; fax 020-760 0469.

Spanish Property News: 2 Paragon Place, Blackheath, London SE3 0SP; ☎020-81297 9194; fax 020-81297 1094. Includes articles on finance, tax, business, and the law as well as Spanish property.

TAXATION

Despite all you may have heard to the contrary, Spain is no longer a tax haven for those with a lot of money and few nationalistic or altruistic tendencies. Over recent years the Spanish taxation authorities have tightened up on foreigners coming to Spain in order to dodge income tax in their own country by not declaring certain assets and income. Currently, foreigners resident in Spain will find that they pay approximately the same amount of tax as they would have done in the UK; and more at the top rate of tax. There is no special tax relief for foreigners residing in Spain; capital gains and disposable assets are included as part of income and are taxed accordingly; and residents are liable for Spanish tax on their worldwide income. This means that all income is taxable, whether it be a pension, private investments, dividends, or interest.

Any person who spends more than 183 days a year in Spain is considered a resident and will be liable to pay Spanish tax. Contrary to popular belief this unpleasant reality holds true whether or not one is in possession of a formal residence permit; faking tourist status will not, therefore, exclude unwilling contributors from paying their share of taxes (see above). Another refinement of the 183 day rule is that anyone who is not resident in Spain, i.e. who spends less than 183 days in the country each year, is still liable for Spanish tax on income arising in Spain, e.g. from renting out property. In this case, the recipient of the income will be taxed in Spain and will have to apply for relief when they pay income tax in their own country.

The Tax System

The Spanish system of personal taxation is based on three kinds of levies: *impuestos* (true taxes); *tasas* (dues and fees); and *contribuciones especiales* (special levies). The last two are much lower; and residents will mainly be concerned with the *impuestos*. Income tax is called the *Impuesto sobre la Renta de las Personas Físicas* (IRPF) or simply 'la renta'. Central, regional and local governments may all levy taxes; and the key factor is residence in Spain. Non-residents may also be taxed if they are regarded as having a permanenet establishment in Spain or are carrying on some kind of business there.

Income Tax

Income tax has been going down in Spain in the last decade and rates now compare favourably with most European countries. The system has also been reorganised and a vital minimum (*mínimo vital*) introduced. Before you become liable for tax you deduct the vital minimum from your gross income and also deduct various other allowances depending on your circumstances. If your income is less than a certain amount per year amounts vary according to the category (over 65, under 65 etc) you do not have to pay income tax or complete a tax declaration.

TABLE 5   DEDUCTIONS ALLOWABLE FROM GROSS INCOME

Vital Minimum   approx. 305 euros (under 65s)
Vital Minimum   approx. 390 euros (over 65s)
Vital Minimum   approx. 550 euros (unmarried or legally separated with dependant children)
Disability Allowance approx 510 euros (one to two thirds disabled)
Disability Allowance approx 700 euros (over two thirds disabled)

There are also allowances for professional and trade union fees, Spanish company pension schemes, child support that you may be paying etc. Up to date information about the minimum earnings before tax is liable can be obtained on the Spanish tax office website www.aeat.es. Local provincial tax offices (*oficina de información al contribuyente*) in areas where there are many expatriates may be able to deal with your questions in English.

Double taxation agreements. Fortunately, Britain has a reciprocal agreement with Spain which avoids double taxation and thus the possibility of someone being taxed twice, once by the Spanish and once by the British tax authorities on their income, pension, etc. The exception to this is during the initial period of Spanish residency when, as the UK and Spanish tax years run from April to April and from January to January respectively, UK nationals in Spain may be taxed by both the Spanish and UK authorities in the overlapping months of their first year in the new country. In this case, you are able to claim a refund of UK tax by applying to the Inland Revenue through your local tax office. They will supply you with the elusively-titled SPA/Individual form, which offers relief at source for tax refunds concerning interest, royalties and pensions, or with the yet more obscurely-titled SPA/Individual/Credit form which provides repayment on dividend income for anyone who has suffered double taxation on moving to Spain. Once the form has been filled out, take it to the local *hacienda* (tax office); they will stamp it and then you can return it to the British tax authorities as proof that you have paid Spanish tax and are therefore no longer liable for British tax. It is a procedure which obviously should be carried out while you are in Spain and not after your return to the UK; and it is important to keep good records of your income etc. while in Spain, to meet any problems should these arise.

The main point is to keep these records of salary and other income; and there are specialist accountants who can advise you on your tax situation in Spain, mainly for those starting or running a business (see the chapter on this for some useful addresses).

For more information on the Spanish tax system, contact the Spanish Embassy or Consulate; or the *Ministerio de Economía y Hacienda*, C/Alcalá 11, E28071 Madrid;

☎915221000. More detailed advice may be forthcoming from the *Direccion General de Tributos*, C/Alcalá 5, E28014 Madrid; ☎91522 1000 (as above) or your local tax office (see above).

Tax Returns

Those whose financial situation is relatively uncomplicated can draw up their own tax return; advice on how to do this is available from the local hacienda. Tax returns should be made between May 1 and June 20 (or June 30 for those who are expecting a tax refund). To do this, you will need to have your most recent receipt for the payment of your *contribucíon urbana* – if you are a property owner – as a percentage of the official value of your property is calculated as if it were income and then added to your income tax total. You will also need your end-of-year bank statement which will show any interest you have been paid and your average balance. The interest is counted as part of your income and the average balance is counted as an asset for the wealth tax (see below). You must also take documents pertaining to any other property you own, or any other shares or bonds which you have, as well as the ubiquitous passport and residence permit.

Various deductions are available from income tax totals for those who are married and/or whose children, parents or grandparents live with them; invalids also receive a deduction. Additionally, if you have bought a house in the current tax year or if you are making payments on one, you can deduct 15% of that amount from your income tax total. Further information about tax or any changes in rates can be found in a leaflet entitled *Taxation Regulations for Foreigners*, available from any hacienda.

In Spain the *aesor fiscal* deals with all tax business, unlike in Britain where accountants, solicitors and bank officials all have some knowledge of tax matters. For those with complex tax returns or those for whom the word 'tax' succeeds only in producing blind panic and a feeling of slight nausea, the aesor fiscal offers invaluable assistance. For fees beginning at around £50 for relatively straightforward tax returns, this godsent official will complete the form on your behalf and frequently save you a lot of money by virtue of his or her wisdom and general expertise. Tax advice is also available from the relevant organisations listed under *Useful Addresses* above.

Wealth Tax

Unlike in France, where wealth tax is something which affects only the lucky or unlucky few, the Spanish wealth or 'net worth' tax (*impuesto extraordinario sobre el patrimonio*) is a small tax (0.2% rising to 2.5% for the super-rich) levied on every individual's worldwide assets and property. The tax was originally introduced as a means through which to force many Spanish citizens to declare previously hidden assets, especially property; anyone who does not declare all his or her assets is subject to fines.

As all residents have an exemption on a certain amount of their capital assets and many deductions concerning children and property value are available, most residents actually end up paying very little, if anything at all, under this tax. However, the raising of assessed property values for many (the *valor castral*) has led to fears that this will push many people over the limit, therefore making them liable to pay the wealth tax where before they were exempt. Full details of the valor castral and of all other domestic taxes in Spain are given in the chapter on *Setting Up Home*, under the heading *Property-Related Taxes*.

VAT

VAT, known confusingly as IVA (*Impuesto sobre el Valor Añadido*) was introduced in 1986, as a prerequisite to Spain joining the then EC. Transactions subject to VAT are sales and importation of merchandise and services rendered; exports are exempt from the tax. There are currently two main rates of IVA, ranging from a reduced rate of 7% for basic necesities e.g. water, medicines and food (items which are often zero-rated in the UK); through to a standard rate of 16% for most goods and services. There is a super-reduced rate applying to some of the necessities of life: bread, milk, pharmaceutical products, books and magazines (although why this should not apply to water is not clear). Health, education, insurance and financial services are all exempt from VAT as is the transfer of any business providing the buyer continues the existing business concern, rental of private property etc. It is worth mentioning that VAT is not levied in the Canary Islands, Ceuta and Melilla. The Canary Islands have an equivalent Canary Islands Indirect General Tax ËCIIGT.

Capital Gains Tax

There is no special Capital Gains Tax as such in Spain, but it is worth giving a mention to legislation which requires that Non-residents who make a profit from the sale of a second home in Spain, or a business, are liable to be taxed on this profit. For example, a non-resident who purchased Spanish property through imported foreign currency would be subject to this tax on the profits of any future sale of the property. Moreover, Spanish tax laws have attempted to eliminate tax evasion by chasing the tax due on property transactions made between foreigners, in foreign currency, and even outside Spain.

There is a tax on gains from shares and real estate, ranging from 5.26% to 11.11%, a percentage of which is however taxfree; and gains on these types of assets will be completely taxfree if held for a period of between ten and 20 years. Capital gains on sales of assets are also generally taxfree if proceeds do not exceed about 3,000 euros.

HEALTH INSURANCE AND HOSPITALS

The National Health Service

The Spanish health service combines both public and private health care and everyone who makes social security payments or who receives a state pension, is unemployed, or under the age of 18 is entitled to free medical treatment. The government's public healthcare policy has been oriented towards the universalisation of health care, through the recent extension of coverage to a million low-income group residents who have not been protected until recently (98% of the population is now covered by the state health system, in contrast to 86% back in the 1980's). Recent laws have also included illegal immigrants and their dependents in the category of persons given free health care. However, free treatment is still only available in certain hospitals, whose waiting lists tend to be long (particularly for those who need hospital treatment for terminal diseases); and coverage for psychiatric illnesses in particular severely limited.

The shortcomings of the system are well exposed by the fact that such preventable diseases as TB, tetanus and diptheria are still around in Spain. There are not enough hospitals available (especially in the poorer areas) and the emphasis still lies with curative rather than preventative medicine. The root of the problem lies in the inefficient way in which the social security resources are administered and distributed; it is primarily because of this that various attempts at reform of the system have failed in recent years. Not surprisingly then, many Spanish residents, both nationals and expatriates, take out private health insurance, details of which are given below.

Anyone living and working in Spain who is below retirement age must make a monthly contribution to the Spanish national health service. This contribution is included in social security payments (see below) which are deducted from an employee's gross salary by the employer; social security payments account for approximately 6% of a worker's gross income.

The benefits which anyone subscribing to the Spanish national health service is entitled to include free hospital accommodation and medical treatment much as in Britain. As some hospitals (approximately 40%) only treat private patients, it is as well to know which hospitals in your area provide national health treatment. A list of national health centres and hospitals in your area is to be found in the local office of the *Insituto Nacional de la Seguridad Social* (INSS) in Spain, or indeed in the local Yellow Pages. Or write to your Consulate there.

Using the NHS

It is essential that all UK nationals who are intending to move to Spain – whether to work or retire – register their change of address with the Overseas Branch of the Department of Health before leaving the country. These are the main people to contact. They will then be sent the paperwork to be completed in order to receive the Spanish national health card (*cartilla*) from the Spanish social services. This card (or a photocopy of it) must be produced whenever you need medical treatment; and will cover the holder for 100% of medical treatment and 90% of prescription charges. The cartilla will also entitle you to full benefits when on holiday in Britain or in any other EU country. The two systems of national insurance in the UK and social security in Spain are transferable insofar as – if you return to Britain at any future time – payments towards one count towards the other; and vice versa. What happens in detail is explained in various leaflets available from the Pensions and Benefits Overseas Directorate in Newcastle (☎0191-218 7777), or the Euroadviser in your local Jobcentre may be able to advise. In Spain, further information about social security can be obtained from the *Instituto Nacional de la Seguridad Social (INSS)*, Servicios Centrales, Padre Damián, 4, 28036 Madrid; ☎915 688 300.

The E111

Reciprocal medical arrangements which exist between the UK and Spain under EU regulations make it possible to obtain mainly free medical treatment for shorter-term visitors to Spain for no more than three months at one time. This arrangement may well be helpful for those going on a home-searching trip to Spain or those who already have holiday homes there. However, this agreement only covers temporary residence, not the first three months of permanent residence in the new country and applies only to emergency medical treatment. To qualify for such treament you need form E111, (known as the Eone-eleven). The form T6 *Health Advice for Travellers* contains the application form for the E111 and is available from post offices, or the Inland Revenue, National Insurance Contributions Office (International Services, Longbenton, Newcastle-upon-Tyne NE98 1ZZ; ☎0191-225 4811; international services helpline: 0845-9154811; fax 0845-915 7800; www.inlandrevenue.gov.uk/nic/intserv/ose.htm).

Happily, the Spanish authorities have simplified the procedures necessary for foreigners to obtain medical treatment and now you have only to present your E111, and a photocopy of this, to the ambulance, doctor or practice when treatment is required. The original E111 will be returned after it has been checked but the photocopy will be retained. Be sure to carry spare copies of this all-important form, as they will be needed if further treatment is required. If you do not have the E111, you will be expected to pay for medical treatment and you will still, anyway, have to pay for non-emergency treatment, e.g. prescribed medicines and dental treatment. Moreover, the E111 is not a substitute for travel insurance which should still be taken out for short trips abroad, as this will provide financial protection against costs which are not regarded as emergencies.

An E111 normally expires after a three-month period and is not valid once you have left the UK permanently or are employed in Spain. It can sometimes be renewed and it is also possible to get an 'open-ended' E111 if you make frequent trips abroad for a longer period than three months. However once a residence permit has been applied for (i.e. after three months) permanent arrangements should have been made. Explanatory leaflet SA29 gives details of social security, healthcare and pension rights within the EU and is obtainable from main post offices and also from the Department of Work and Pensions, Overseas Directorate, Tyneview Park, Whitely Road, Benton, Newcastle-upon-Tyne NE98 1BA. It may be of use to those intending to move to and work in Spain.

Residents should also take out private health cover (see *Private Medical Insurance* below).

Also, if you are transferring your Jobseeker's Allowance to Spain (see below) you have the advantage of being automatically entitled to free health care. Make sure you apply for the appropriate form, the E119, before you leave the UK (and take this along with the Jobseeker's Allowance form you need, the E303).

The E101 and E128

The Inland Revenue, National Insurance Contributions Office, International Services in Newcastle, issues an E101 to UK nationals working in another EU country to exempt them from paying social security contributions in that country because they are still paying them in their home country.

The E128 entitles you to medical treatment in another EU country where you are working, or if you are a student. You have to obtain an E101 *before* you can obtain an E128.

Sickness and Invalidity Benefit

Anyone who is moving out to Spain permanently and who claims sickness or invalidity benefit in the UK is entitled to continue claiming this benefit once in Spain. Strictly speaking, to claim either benefit, you must be physically incapable of all work, however, the interpretation of the words 'physically incapable' is frequently stretched just a little beyond literal truth. If the claimant has been paying National Insurance contributions in the UK for two tax years (this may be less depending on his or her level of income) then he or she is eligible to claim sickness benefit. After receiving sickness benefit for 28 weeks, you are entitled to invalidity benefit which is paid at a higher rate. Although it may seem something of a Catch 22 when you can only claim sickness benefit if you are incapable of working and yet you are only entitled to the benefit through the last two years of National Insurance payments deducted from your income, the benefit is primarily used by people who have had to stop work due to severe illness.

Anyone currently receiving either form of benefit should inform the Department of Work and Pensions (formerly the DSS) that they are moving to Spain. They will then send your forms to the DWP International Services department (Newcastle-upon-Tyne NE98 1YC) who will then make sure that a monthly sterling cheque is sent either to your new address or direct to your bank account. The only conditions involved are that all claimants submit themselves to a medical examination, either in Spain or Britain, on request.

Child benefit may also be claimed if the child goes abroad for more than eight weeks. Ask for leaflet CH 6.

Private Medical Insurance

Although the level of convenience, comfort and attention offered through private insurance schemes is superior to that received by national health patients, the treatment itself will not necessarily be of a higher quality. However, a growing number of foreign residents in Spain are opting to remove themselves from the long waiting lists and sometimes chaotic conditions of the Spanish national health service and to take out private health insurance. It is easy to do this through a UK organisation.

Those who are going to Spain seeking work, or who spend a few weeks or months a year there, will require private medical insurance to cover the balance of the cost not covered by the E111 (see above). If you already hold private health insurance you will find that most companies will switch this for European cover once you are in France. With the increase of British and foreign insurance companies offering this kind of cover, it is worth shopping around as cover and costs vary.

Useful Addresses

British United Provident Association (BUPA): (Russell House, Russell Mews, Brighton BN1 2NR; ☎01273-208181; www.bupa-intl.com). BUPA International offers a range of worldwide schemes for individuals and companies of three or more employees based outside the UK for six or more months.

For a copy of the **International Health Plan** brochure for individuals or groups (minimum of 5 employees) please email **info@expacare.net** or visit **www.expacareworld.net**

ExpaCare is a trading name of JLT Healthcare Limited. Regulated by the General Insurance Standards Council.

ExpaCare – high-quality health insurance cover, for individuals or families living abroard. To find out more...

Expacare: e-mail: info@expacare.net or visit www.expacare.net. Specialists in expatriate healthcare offering high quality health insurance cover for individuals and their families, including group cover for five or more employees. Cover is available for expatriates of all nationalities worldwide.

Goodhealth Primary International Ltd.: Springfield House, Springfield Road, Horsham, West Sussex RH12 2RG, offers private healthcare plans to expatriates worldwide.

Private Medical Insurance – Spanish Providers. Those interested can set up the policy from the UK before moving to Spain or on arrival in Spain through a broking agency. One of the advantages of UK health insurance schemes is that their policies cover the claimants for treatment incurred anywhere in Europe, not just in Spain itself.

Spanish insurance policies are widely available and have a distinct advantage over UK ones in that payment for medical treatment is made in the form of vouchers provided by the insurance company rather than having to pay initially and then claim back the treatment cost from the insurance company afterwards. However, although the premiums on Spanish insurance policies may appear much cheaper and more attractive than those offered by the British companies you may well find that the policy is limited to specific local hospitals – not very helpful if you are in urgent need of treatment and are driven to a hospital not on their list and refused treatment. Additionally, the small print needs to be read very carefully; perhaps treatment is only refunded if surgery is performed, or outpatient treatment is not included in the policy (i.e. visits to the local GP and the dentist). Other policies may offer limited cover on surgery, medicines and accommodation.

SOCIAL SECURITY AND JOB SEEKER'S ALLOWANCE

Social Security

The Spanish system of social security (*Seguridad Social*), which was set up in 1966, is not the only welfare system in Spain but it is the largest. There are separate social security systems for members of the civil service and the armed forces and a variety of other bodies like the Fondo Nacional de Asistencia Social (FONAS) which provides old age pensions for those who do not qualify under any of the other schemes. The national social security system covers over 80% of the population and offers a complete range of welfare provision. Cash benefits (for unemployment, sickness, housing, etc) are distributed through the Instituto Nacional de Seguridad Social (INSS); medical care is administered through the Instituto Nacional de Salud (INSALUD) and the Insituto de Servicios Sociales (INSERSO) is responsible for social services.

The standard rate of social security deducted from an employee's gross salary is low, set at approximately 6%, with the employer's contribution of over 30.2% forming by far the greatest chunk of the total. However, the total government contribution is relatively small with a contribution percentage of approximately 25%; as compared to 30% by the German government and 40% by the British. In Spain, just under two thirds of the total revenue from social security each year is spent in providing cash benefits; of these the greatest share is accounted for by pensions – old age, disabled, orphans and widows, all of which are very generously provided for. Standing in rather stark contrast to this, less than a third of total revenue is spent on health and social services. The remainder, a paltry 34% accounts, in theory, for adminstrative costs and, combined with what is the insufficient total revenue claimed for the tax from all sources, must account to a large extent for the administrative chaos which swamps the entire system.

It is possible to keep up national insurance contributions (the equivalent of Spanish social security) in the UK on a voluntary basis on moving to Spain. This can be quite a canny move for anyone who isn't working but who hasn't yet reached retirement age. If you do keep your payments up then you will be eligible to claim a UK pension from the age of 65 (for men and women) throughout your time in Spain. However, this will be unnecessary for those who intend to work in Spain as EU regulations ensure that social security contributions made in one member state are counted as a contribution period to the contributor's own country's social security system for the purpose of determining their future benefits from that system. The two systems are supposed now to be more or less interchangeable.

Unemployment Benefit

Currently, Spain has one of the highest unemployment rates in Europe (see the *General Introduction*). Nearly half of the total number of unemployed, are young people who have never had a job and who, because of this do not qualify for benefit. The thinking behind this is that young people can remain with and be supported by their family until they do find a job. Many in fact choose to go abroad, where prospects may be brighter. Although the amount of benefit provided to those entitled to it is generous by any standards, paid at 70% of the claimant's previous salary, it is only available to approximately 50% of those who need it. Furthermore, entitlement to benefit lapses in nearly all cases after a period of between one and two years; the only exception to this is that those who have a family to support may claim a severely reduced allowance. Since Spain has no equivalent of the UK's more comprehensive Job Seeker's Allowance, the unfortunate rest are forced into taking any odd jobs that come their way, living off friends and relatives and accepting charity from wherever and whomever they can get it.

As Spain is a full member of the EU, it is possible, however, for someone claiming unemployment benefit in the UK to transfer this claim to Spain. As discussed earlier, sickness and invalidity benefit as well as child benefit can be maintained and transferred to Spain at the present time.

Jobseeker's Allowance

If you are currently unemployed and receiving UK Jobseeker's Allowance (JSA) it is possible to have this paid to you in Spain. Payment of JSA is not automatic to anyone unemployed in the UK. You have earn your entitlement by paying a certain number of contributions into the country's unemployment insurance organisation. In Britain these contributions are represented by Class 1 National Insurance contributions. Class I are paid only by people who are either employees earning at least £62 per week. Other groups of people may pay either Class 2 and contributions (for the selfemployed) or Class 3 (a voluntary payment for those who would otherwise not be covered by national insurance) which entitle them to some social security benefits, but not JSA.

Income Support. In the UK people who are not eligible for the JSA may claim income support, if they have no other means of support. All countries in the EU except Greece and Portugal have equivalents. However, the right to have your claim transferred to another EU country, unlike the JSA, is not possible.

To be eligible for the Spanish equivalent of income support is at the discretion of the municipal authorities who normally expect the claimant to have been resident in their district for several years.

Claiming UK Jobseeker's Allowance in Spain

Any EU national who has been registered unemployed for a at least 4 weeks and is entitled to received JSA can arrange to receive it for up to three months, paid at the UK rate, while looking for work in Spain. It is helpful if you have a precise date of departure and definite destination, preferably with an address. Note that if you go on holiday to Spain and decide to stay on to work, the benefit cannot be transferred. Your local job centre should have a leaflet (ref. JSA 22)for people going abroad or coming from abroad, plus an application form for transferring benefit. When you have told your local job centre your plans, they will supply a letter in English and Spanish explaining you are eligible to claim benefit. This letter is called a DLJA 402/403. Within seven days of arriving in Spain you must register with the Instituto Nacional de Empleo (INEM).

Your local job centre will inform the Department of Work and Pensions in Newcastle, who will then decide if you are eligible for an E303 which authorises INEM to pay JSA for up to three months. The E303 is sent directly by the DWP to Spain. Further details can be obtained from the Department of Work and Pensions, Jobseekers & Benefit Enhancement, Overseas Benefit Directorate, Tyneview Road, Benton, Newcastle-upon-Tyne NE98 1BA; ☎0191-218 7147 and they can send you a fact sheet if your local job centre has not supplied you with one.

You are also entitled to free health care, and need to apply for the appropriate form for this, the E119, before you go.

LOCAL GOVERNMENT

'Autonomy' is a difficult word in a political context. The heady, near neurotic drive for local home rule which gripped Spain as the years of Franco's repressive dictatorship drew to a close was to cause years of political controversy, unrest and negotiation. The result of these troubled years (which climaxed in the failed military coup of 1981, the military's response to the seemingly all-embracing move to a federal Spain) was the carving up of the country into seventeen Autonomous Communities. The devolution of power to the regions was the outstanding innovation of the 1978 Constitution although this was not effectively achieved until 1983.

The definition of 'autonomy' is also tricky, as some of the Communities enjoy greater powers of self-rule than others. Although the 1978 Constitution ruled that each Autonomous Community was to have a President, a Governing Council, a Legislative Assembly and a Supreme Court, the central government was still to be exclusively responsible for foreign affairs, external trade, defence, justice, criminal, commercial and labour law, merchant shipping and civil aviation. However, many grey areas, such as education were not allocated specifically to either central or federal government; and this is one issue which is handled differently in different regions.

The Basques and Catalans were the first to achieve home rule; they were both given control of education in their area and won the right to plan their own economies and set up their own police forces. A difference between the two is that in the Basque country the regional government collects taxes and hands them over to the central government, retaining what it needs for its own purposes, whereas in the Catalan provinces, as in the rest of the country, the central government collects the money and then gives the regional government its share.

Although all of Spain is now divided into Autonomous Communities, and each of these enjoys a varying degree of autonomy, the concept of self-rule has come to have very little direct effect on the man in the street. Locals and expatriates often find that power is really devolved further in Spain, down to the city administration; and to get things done will find a visit to the *ayuntamiento* (town hall) more useful. This functions as part of the regional administration; and will answer queries on local taxes, and dispense advice on both central and federal government matters.

CRIME AND THE POLICE

Crime

Sadly, democracy in Spain has appeared to come hand-in-hand with a crime rate, which has been rising steadily over the last thirty years (at a rate of up to 10% each year). However, despite this unpalatable statistic, the Spanish figures for car crime and burglary are still significantly lower than Europe's most crime-ridden country in this respect: Britain. These are lower than in much of the rest of Europe as well.

One factor which has contributed to the increase of crime in Spain is a more sympathetic police force; which now deals with reports of offences 'more professionally,' it is said. Another is the growing drug problem. Drugs are relatively easy to come by and cannabis (apparently known as *chocolate*) is widely used among the young, and largely tolerated by the Spanish police. Again, this problem is one which was born in the transition to democracy, and the relaxation of social *mores* which followed. It was the Socialists who, in 1983, effectively decriminalised the use of cannabis for a time; a measure which was largely responsible for the 'easy-going' attitude taken towards the use of soft drugs in the 1980s. This law was then revoked; and now all non-prescribed drug use is illegal; but the effect has been irreversibly stamped on drugusers and police alike. The core of the drugs epidemic, however, lies in the spread of hard drugs such as cocaine and heroin; Madrid's Barajas airport is a particularly popular entrance point for drugs from Latin America destined for the whole of Europe; and other soft drugs tend to be smuggled in from Morocco.

One focus for crime is, unsurprisingly, tourism, with much petty theft located along the costas and directed at the thousands of tourists who visit them each year. The varieties of crime indulged in range from purse snatching and car breakins to theft of property left on the beach to armed burglary (a favourite with Spain's teenage generation apparently). There is little you can do after the event; and it is best to prevent such unhoped-for traumas by taking sensible precautions. And you should ensure that you have a good insurance policy. It is better to 'travel light', preferably without a large, inviting-looking hand or carrier bag. However, in pleasant contrast to this rather bleak picture, those who choose to live away from the popular and tourist-saturated coastal areas will most probably enjoy a blissfully crime-free existence.

Police

Spain has three different types of police. The Policía Municipal (the approximate equivalent of Britain's local police forces – with a gun) is the least intimidating and most sympathetic force; and can be found in every small town. These are definitely the people to approach in cases of minor disaster; if you are hopelessly lost; or need to ask the time. In contrast, the Guardia Civil, a 60,000man force which patrols the rural areas of Spain – who also act as customs officers and frontier guards – are definitely to be avoided unless you have had a road accident, in which case you must report this to them and just grin and bear it.

Established in 1844 to combat banditry in the countryside, the Guardia Civil is a predominantly military force which has failed to lose its reputation as an reactionary and somewhat hostile militia, called out to combat riots or strikes as well as more peaceful demonstrations. (It was a Guardia Civil colonel, Tejero, who held the Cortes hostage in the unsuccessful coup of 1981).

The third police force, the Policía Nacional, was much hated for the violence and repression for which it was responsible in the Franco years. However, in what was a largely successful effort to clean up their image, the government renamed and redressed the Policía Nacional in 1978 (they were previously known as the Policía Armada). The Policía Nacional, and their machineguns, can be found mounting zealous vigil over embassies, stations, post offices and barracks in most cities. Serious crime, such as theft, rape or mugging should be reported to the nearest Policía Nacional station.

Lastly, the Basques and Catalans both have their own police forces; a result of the Spanish experiment with devolution in which both these Communities were granted home rule. Spanish police are permitted to hold anyone suspected of a serious crime for up to ten days before charging or releasing them; and they have 72 hours before they are required to bring the suspect before a court. In practice, however, three days can easily become three weeks, months or even years in some, more notorious cases.

Although everyone is entitled to some legal advice in prison, whether it is provided privately or by the state, those who cannot afford their own solicitor often forgo even the smallest hope of gaining legal representation. What may seem the chaotic nature of the Spanish prison system is largely (as in Britain) due to overcrowding; this is being tackled by the present government. Obviously, however, it is not a very good idea to run the risks involved in drug smuggling or of committing any other dire crime and ending up in a dilapidated Spanish prison awaiting trial for the next indefinite number of years. Lorry drivers returning from Morocco should pay particular attention to what they are carrying; bags should not be carried for others at airports; and so on.

RELIGION

The Catholic Church in Spain has a long and rich, if sometimes intolerant history; which reaches far back to the Church's spearheading of the Counter Reformation. The years of the Inquisition resulted in the virtual elimination for a time of Protestantism in Spain (and forced Jews and Muslims to convert). The right to worship freely and of freedom of conscience was not granted to other religious denominations until as recently as 1978; and even then the centuries of power and influence which the Catholic Church had enjoyed through its close association with the state (particularly in the early Franco years) persisted, meaning that by this time there were few strongholds of any other religious denomination left.

The lay religious order, Opus Dei, was primarily responsible for the influence over the secular authorities which some would say the Catholic Church still wields in the twentyfirst century. Founded in 1928 by José María Escrivá Balaguer, this semi-secret organisation succeded in infiltrating Spanish society at many professional levels, in schools, government and business, and became tremendously powerful in the 1960's. A tax scandal exposed in 1969 by a government official succeeded in reducing but not extinguishing the rather sinister power of this group. One of their greatest strongholds is in the education sector; and their four universities and colleges provide an initiatory education for the sons and daughters of the many aristocratic and influential Opus Dei members.

Unsurprisingly, newly fledged Spanish residents will find themselves immersed in Roman Catholicism in almost every town in the country. Notices of services are posted not only outside the churches, but at strategic viewing points throughout the town to attract as many churchgoers as possible. There are many festivals and holy days whch are popular with visitors and locals, as in Seville. In fact, the effect of Catholicism in Spain is not only to be felt in the church (with the number of churchgoers now in sharp decline); its culture and values are an integral part of many social attitudes within the country. Even those Spaniards who claim agnosticism have the Catholic culture as part of their heritage.

Christianity in Spain is all but synonymous with Catholicism. There are a mere 250,000 Protestants in the country; while 95% of the population is Catholic. However, there are resident Anglican clergy in a number of tourist and retirement areas; and many Anglican services take place throughout Spain which are attended by expatriates and visitors; these are usually listed in the local paper. Such services often take place in buildings borrowed from other denominations or in schools or church halls, even in hotels. There are also synagogues in the main towns and cities.

SOCIAL LIFE

Despite the tens of millions of foreign tourists visiting Spanish resorts each year making Spain one of the most popular tourist destinations in the world, surprisingly few of these visitors have ever explored beyond the confines of the most 'touristy' areas. The limitations of visiting Spain on a package tour can be overcome by consciously making an effort to travel even a little way from the coast, where social distractions are geared to British and other national tastes as much as local demands. The radically improved road network has succeeded in making the interior accessible to everyone; and as the costas experience a slight decline in popularity, so the National Tourist Office in Spain is successfully promoting a rather different image of the country and its many unspoilt and undiscovered regions inland, as a destination for cultural and special interest holidays, as well as a summer vacation by the beach.

Anyone thinking of living and working in Spain certainly needs to experience some of the real Spanish flavour which is amongst the liveliest and most colourful in Europe. If you are now living on the coast, you can plan excursions inland; getting away from it all will now, for many, mean getting away from all those tourists! And the Spanish Tourist Office *Turespaña* can provide some helpful leaflets. To do this successfully, it is also helpful to have a knowledge of Castilian (or perhaps one of Spain's other languages, see the earlier section on *The Spanish*

Languages). To understand the Spanish character and attitudes, a knowledge of the history, ancient as well as recent, is also a must. Spain has changed so rapidly in the last twenty odd years that it is hard even for the Spanish themselves to come to terms with all these changes; and the liberties they now possess after decades of repression.

This is so among older people at any rate. The greatest changes have been in the lifestyle of the young. The 'economic miracle' of Spain has been achieved in part through these changes in society; and some degree of dislocation as well, in particular the movement of inhabitants from one region to another to fulfil the labour demands of the big cities. Spain, like Britain, is now mainly an industrial country (with an agriculural sector in decline). This has left vast tracts of countryside virtually abandoned; and the customs and traditions pertaining to them may soon require scholarly research to preserve their memory, as Spaniards become increasingly homogeneous and separated from their roots.

Meanwhile there are still plenty of traditional customs to be found in the villages and smaller towns, where the social life often revolves around cafés and bars, and also outdoor fiestas, in which the whole community takes part. In the bars and clubs of the big cities, life is more like that in any city, anywhere in the world. One difference is that nightlife begins late (perhaps because of the daytime heat), and goes on into the early hours.

The two main categories of foreign resident in Spain are the retired expatriate who may or may not run a small business, and the person who goes there to take up employment, temporary or long term. The expatriate community for either has its own social network. For those who arrive without any contacts there are ways of forming them: through the local English churches and through activity clubs (bridge, golf, painting, etc.) and pubs and bars in the area. The newspapers and magazines which serve the English-speaking community in Spain (see under *Newspapers* in the *Daily Life* chapter) provide an invaluable source of information, listing various social activities and events taking place in the area.

The Spaniards

It is very difficult to generalise about Spanish people as they embrace at least three different traditions and a range of cultural differences: from the Celtic and Basque peoples of the north to the more typically Mediterranean Spanish of the south. However it is likely that many of those living and working in Spain will do so on the Mediterranean coast and in the great cities in the southern half of the country.

Traditionally, Spaniards have a reputation for self-reliance and self-centredness; for being smouldering and quarrelsome by turns; for being macho, (petulant for women), proud and flamboyant, and on occasions capricious. Having a good time has always been a part of Spanish life. These national traits are still in evidence, but among younger Spaniards especially, an increasing prevalence of a more liberal tolerance of those with differing opinions or a different way of life is noticeable. Better educated, democratised and with a wider outlook than their forbears, Spaniards can afford to show a certain magnanimity towards the world.

Towards foreigners, Spaniards tend to be open and genuinely helpful. They are as warm and friendly, and show less formality, than the Italians or Portuguese. As in the other Mediterranean countries, even today, it is regarded as an honour to be invited to a Spaniard's home as he or she tends only to ask close friends.

Social Attitudes

Nothing else in Spain has changed as much as attitudes towards sex and sexuality. Sexual liberation came late to Spain, in the late seventies and eighties, and reached a stage of startling openness in recent years, especially when viewed against the ultra-stringent repression of the Franco era. As recently as 1959 engaged couples (*novios*) were prohibited by the leaders of the Church from physical contact of any kind; kissing between novios was finally permitted by the Church only in the sixties. Since over 70% of Spaniards are practising Catholics, even today it is not difficult to see that the Church in Spain regards itself as the keeper of the nation's morals. In the past, its sphere of influence even extended to censorship, which reached extraordinary limits in films, television and newspaper photography; even the half-naked male torso was taboo.

The more conservative attitudes of the Catholic Church at that time can be summed up by the view of one leading churchman who condemned moving pictures as the greatest evil unleashed in the world; in his own words 'worse than the atomic bomb.'

There may be those who think he was right. Now Spain has gone to the other extreme in matters sexual: government licences are granted for sex cinemas and prostitutes; brothels (credit cards accepted) advertise in the quality newspapers; and the heady days when one of the Guardia Civil's duties was to arrest girls for wearing bikinis (after first wrapping them in blankets) seem very far away.

One of the much-needed changes of social attitude to come out of this sexual revolution has been the steady demise of *machismo*. This often parodied phenomenon has in fact some deep roots in Spanish society, in a code of honour which in our own more northerly countries died out with the rise of Protestantism (which brought a greater informality in social relations to northern Europe). In the Catholic countries this has lingered on. Honourable behaviour in Britain and America (and our rather outmoded idea of behaving like a 'gentleman') is not quite the same thing as being honourable in Spain, which is a more starkly black-and-white affair.

This peculiar Spanish approach to honour is perhaps best illustrated by the film *Chronicle of a Death Foretold*. The code demands – or demanded – that a man who has been dishonoured by a woman's infidelity or her loss of virginity before marriage, retrieve his honour by challenging his rival. The woman who has prompted this action would subsequently be abandoned. If she were from the aristocratic class she would be hidden away in a nunnery but if from the poorer classes she would almost certainly end up joining the ranks of the world's oldest profession.

The other iniquitous element of machismo (which is the descendant of this ancient code) is that men were (and often are) respected by their peers for the plurality of their sexual conquests. There are strong overtones of mediaeval Muslim culture in this concept that women can be rated as little more than chattels. Perhaps such attitudes arrived in Spain by way of the Moorish occupation; or perhaps it has more ancient origins. From Spain, machismo spread with the conquistadores to the New World (where it is notable that the Spaniards and Portuguese married the local Native Americans to a much greater extent than the British colonist did in North America). Perhaps theirs is a more liberal and 'open' way of looking at things after all...

Fortunately for Spanish women, social progress has wrought encouraging changes in the way society regards them today, in their work and other relations. In fact there is probably less sexism in the workplace in Spain than anywhere else in southern Europe. Such an about-turn has been effected by a combination of circumstances, including better education and the subsequent emergence of women in the professions (as a rule rather than the exception) as well as the election of women to positions of power in the cabinet, academic institutions and the higher echelons of the police force.

One way in which Spanish women lag behind their counterparts in the rest of Europe is to do with abortion; this remains a contentious issue (although legalised in 1986) and is still available only in certain circumstances: where the pregnancy endangers the life of the mother; or the baby will be severely deformed; or the pregnancy has resulted from rape. The outcome of these restrictions is that Spanish women have had either to resort to backstreet terminations; or, if they can afford it, to go abroad.

Manners and Customs

In these days of air-conditioning and global markets, the siesta is not as prevalent as it used to be; many hard-pressed executives, shift workers and busy mothers no longer have time for this once essential afternoon nap. The long, lunch-time siesta break is now being replaced by a shorter, one-hour lunch break in the larger companies and businesses of Spain. However, in line with the shorter lunch hour the working day is finishing earlier; and instead of the traditional 9am-2pm and then 4.30pm-8.30pm day (still maintained, particularly in the summer, by smaller shops) most Spaniards now work what is a comparatively relaxed 9am-6pm or 7pm day with one or two hours for lunch. As in France, it is customary for Spanish families to take a one-month holiday, usually in August, which effectively shuts down the country for that month.

Even the lack of a siesta does not seem to affect the Spaniards' passion for nightlife, though. The climate is one cause of this custom; hence the fact that northerners burn less midnight oil than southerners perhaps. In Spanish bars, as elsewhere in Europe, it is customary to pay the bill when you leave, and not for each drink.

Not all Spanish men are as liberated as their womenfolk; the former will almost always open doors for women or stand aside to let them past. The Spaniards are also far more tactile than northern Europeans; men embrace their male friends, as well as patting them on the back. Male and female aquaintances kiss each other on the cheek; both cheeks in Madrid and northwards; one cheek in the south.

One aspect of Spanish behaviour which can lead to misunderstanding with the British is the Spanish aversion to queuing. Their style is more of an anarchic mass of humanity of which the queue-jumper is king. In Spain, it is not a question of lining up politely, but of being first.

The Spaniards are very indulgent towards their children and like to spend as much time with them as possible. On fiesta nights children accompany their parents to restaurants and bars, and stay up with them until the small hours. Children are not, however, allowed into bullfights.

Entertainment and Culture

Bullfights. By far the most notorious Spanish entertainment is highly-ritualised bull killing. Regarded as a disgusting spectacle of cruelty by many foreigners, its popularity shows no sign of abating amongst Spaniards themselves, who continue to flock to the *corridas* (bullrings). A bullfight is also an indispensable part of many village fiestas, when main squares become improvised corridas. At the other end of the spectrum from the village fights are the main corridas of Seville and Madrid where the stars of the art (it is not really considered a sport in Spain), the matadors, are treated and paid like opera stars; and have enormous followings. Fans of what Hemingway called 'Death in the Afternoon', are treated to six deaths (usually of bulls) per fight, dispatched by three matadors with assistance from picadors and apprentice bullfighters. Spectators should try to get a seat on the shady side of the ring in the *tendidos* (shaded stands) as, if the blood and evident suffering doesn't bring on faintness, heatstroke will.

Cinema. Before José Luis Garcí won an Oscar for *Volver a Empezar* in 1983, the reputation of the Spanish cinema had rested on the undisputed and surreal mastery of Luis Buñuel. Recent Spanish 'classics' enjoyed by an an international audience include the anarchic, urbane comedies of Pedro Almodóvar (*Women on the Verge of a Nervous Breakdown, Tie me up, Tie me down*) and the *Carmen* of Carlos Saura. Sexuality and repression are themes of modern Spanish cinema as they are in many ways in Spanish life. Only about 25% of films shown in Spanish cinemas are homegrown. The rest are usually dubbed into Spanish, which can be a problem for foreigners with a minimal grasp of the language. Going to see real Spanish films can be one way of improving this though. Watching how a language is spoken and how its sounds are made can be as instructive as listening to it; even if you do not always understand all the dialogue!

Foreign films shown in the original version are indicated, as in France, with the letters 'vo' (versión original).

Art. Spain is universally recognised as having produced some of the world's greatest and most startlingly original painters: Velásquez, El Greco, Murillo, Ribera, Picasso, Dali and Miro to name but a few. One of the most famous art museums in the world is the Prado in Madrid which houses works by all the great Spanish artists and Flemish and Italian masters. Near the the Prado is the Reina Sofía National Museum which was opened in 1986, basically as a museum of contemporary art. In Barcelona there is the excellent Picasso Museum and the Museum of Catalonian Art. In recent years modern art has become something of a passion with the Spanish and the annual Contemporary Art Fair (ARCO) in Madrid arouses huge national interest.

Music. Perhaps Spain's best-known music is the Flamenco, which originated amongst the gypsies of Andalusia. This flamboyant dance, with its accompanying guitar music and songs, is performed in theatres and night clubs, especially in the tourist resorts. It can be seen also at fiesta time being performed spontaneously in the streets.

Another traditional musical entertainment is the *Zarzuela*, a form of comic opera which can be seen in the Teatro de Zarzuela in Madrid.

Spain's best-known piece of classical music is probably the hauntingly beautiful,

Concierto de Aranjuez para guitarra y orquesta, by Joaquín Rodrigo (usually known as Rodrigo's Guitar Concerto), which even reached the British Top 20. This remarkable composer outlived his two great friends, the composer Manuel de Falla and Spain's most famous classical guitarist, Andrés Segovia. Latterly, the country has produced some popular dance hits as well.

At present Spain has almost completed a massive construction programme for musical auditoria, which has meant more halls for symphony and chamber orchestras around the country. For opera fans there are regular seasons in Madrid at the Gran Teatro de Liceo; also in Barcelona, Oviedo, Bilbao and other cities.

Theatre. The most important theatres in Madrid are the Teatro de Zarzuela, the Teatro Español, the Centro Dramático Nacional, the Teatro María Guerrero, the Centro de Nuevas Tendencias Escénicas and the Compañia Nacional de Teatro Clásico. Unfortunately much will be incomprehensible to foreigners, unless they are already familiar with the works being performed. However, English translations of the works of Frederico Garcia Lorca, Spain's famous precivil war playright and poet, and Lope de Vega, a sixteenth century playwright, are available.

In areas where there are expatriate communities, English and American plays are regularly performed by amateur theatre groups. Details of forthcoming productions in English may be found in the English-language publications (e.g. *Lookout*).

Shopping

It is worth remembering that although the cost of living in Spain a couple of decades ago was one of the foremost reasons why Brits chose to move out there, especially in retirement, this situation has changed. Prices have risen with inflation, while salaries have not; and now in the most expensive areas of the Balearics e.g. Majorca, the cost of living is even higher than the UK, while on the mainland it is approximately the same. However, markets and small villages still offer bargains; these are the areas the newly arrived resident should also explore to get a flavour of the country, and to live more economically. The Rastro Market in Madrid is particularly recommended; there are similar local markets everywhere; and Catalonian textiles are famous around the world. In general, all leather goods are of a high quality. Handmade wooden furniture is one of the traditional products of Valencia; and fine rugs and carpets can be found in markets and shops in the south.

Food Shoppping. For the less adventurous, Spain's thriving import market means that many of the international, brands of canned and frozen foods and drinks are also available in Spain. All large towns have modern, selfservice supermarkets which, as well as stocking usual supermarket items, also carry a wide variety of goods as diverse as tablewear, clothes, toiletries and hardwear. Supermarkets still tend to close for the afternoon siesta (from 2-5pm) but then reopen from 5-8pm every day except Sunday.

However, for those who are determined to integrate more fully into the Spanish way of life, there are the smaller shops which sell food and drink without the extras; and the municipal markets (*ventas*), controlled by the local government, which offer the best prices and often the highest quality fresh produce. These ventas can provide a whole new world of gastronomic discovery. For example, handmade (as oppose to industrially produced) sausages can still be found, offering a staggering variety of names, textures and tastes. The red *chorizo* sausage is the bestknown Spanish sausage, consisting of ground pork and fat, paprika or peppers; and pepper, garlic, oregano and nutmeg. *Longaniza* is the long, thin version of the chorizo, and the *chorizo de Pamplona* is a smoked variety. These, however, are all merely variations on a theme; the *sobrasada, salchichón, morcilla* and *butifarra* sausages are still to come.

Indoor or outdoor markets are found in every town and in many of the larger villages, and function as the centrepoint for the exchange of local news and gossip. They offer a real and rare insight into Spanish, small-town life. A helpful hint is to investigate any nearby countryside, where prices can be lower still than in the markets, which although good value, sometimes raise their prices to suit the look of the foreigner's pockets. Here, the smaller, more parochial shops have managed to retain a genuine local charm, as is shown by the politeness and willingness to help of the various salespeople. Shopping here will bring you more closely into contact with the locals.

Some of the remoter areas of Spain are also served by mobile shops (*ventas ambulantes*). These vans travel around, between them selling most things required by the average household, including really fresh fish and meat. This service, amounting to what is practically a door-to-door supermarket, is especially helpful for those of restricted mobility; whether this be due to old age, lack of transport or a young baby to look after.

The tax on alcohol is considerably less in Spain than in the UK; and most of the prices in the Spanish shops are lower than the dutyfree prices back in Britain. If the temptation is to indulge in the alcoholic delights of Spain – wines, sherry, brandy, and Spanish champagne – you have only to open your local English-language publication to find a warning: in the lists of discreet advertisements for Alcoholics Anonymous societies (which are located all along the costas).

Non-Food Shopping. Spain, once famous for the quality and low price of its leather goods, is still known for the quality, but no longer the bargain prices (especially in the larger, tourist areas). The mass-market department stores and boutique-like souvenir shops dominate the larger cities; to find real bargains which combine quality and value for money with authenticity and originality, you will need to travel out to the smaller towns and villages,and into the backstreets. Consumer durables, such as refrigerators, washing machines, electronic and electrical equipment and cameras, tend to be as expensive in Spain as in the UK; while food, electricity, gas, public transport, tobacco and alcohol, and presently cars, all tend to cost less.

Sport

Soccer rates highest on the list of spectator sports for Spaniards. The major teams, Real Madrid and FC Barcelona have large and fanatical followings; and foreigners may join the crowds without worries for their safety. Even the British expatriate community in Spain is represented by its own football club, FC Britanico, not yet known in international competition, but which has participated in one of the Madrid amateur leagues for many years.

Sports facilities in Spain are excellent around the main tourist areas, where communal swimming pools and tennis courts are nearly always attached to apartment blocks. Golf clubs abound, especially on the Costa del Sol; However, as in France, golf is somewhat exclusive if the fees are anything to go by. Consequently many British aficionados prefer to take golfing trips to neighbouring Portugal, which is cheaper.

Spain has several skiing resorts in the Pyrenees: Cerler, La Molina, Formigal and Panticosa. However, perhaps the bestknown resort is Sol y Nieve (Sun and Snow) in the Sierra Nevada, a mere 30km/19 miles from Granada. The mountains are also popular with walkers in summer. Detailed maps and guides to these areas can be obtained from the Spanish Mountain Federation (*Federación Española de Montañismo*) or the Spanish Tourist Office.

TABLE 6	PUBLIC HOLIDAYS
1 January	New Year's Day
6 January	Epiphany
March/April	Good Friday
1 May	Labour Day
15 August	Assumption
12 October	National Day
1 November	All Saints' Day
6 December	Constitution Day
8 December	Conception
25 December	Christmas Day

The total number of legal national holidays per year, including the many regional ones, is 14. In addition, the various regions and localities have their own festivals and carnivals which may not officially be public holidays but when most facilities will be closed.

CONVERSION CHART

LENGTH (NB 12inches 1 foot, 10 mm 1 cm, 100 cm 1 metre)

inches	1	2	3	4	5	6	9	12	
cm	2.5	5	7.5	10	12.5	15.2	23	30	

cm	1	2	3	5	10	20	25	50	75	100
inches	0.4	0.8	1.2	2	4	8	10	20	30	39

WEIGHT (NB 14lb = 1 stone, 2240 lb = 1 ton, 1,000 kg = 1 metric tonne)

lb	1	2	3	5	10	14	44	100	2246
kg	0.45	0.9	1.4	2.3	4.5	6.4	20	45	1016

kg	1	2	3	5	10	25	50	100	1000
lb	2.2	4.4	6.6	11	22	55	110	220	2204

DISTANCE

mile	1	5	10	20	30	40	50	75	100	150
km	1.6	8	16	32	48	64	80	120	161	241

km	1	5	10	20	30	40	50	100	150	200
mile	0.6	3.1	6.2	12	19	25	31	62	93	124

VOLUME

1 litre = 0.2 UK gallons		1 UK gallon = 4.5 litres
1 litre = 0.26 US gallons		1 US gallon = 3.8 litres

CLOTHES

UK	8	10	12	14	16	18	20
Europe	36	38	40	42	44	46	48
USA	6	8	10	12	14	18	

SHOES

UK	3	4	5	6	7	8	9	10	11
Europe	36	37	38	39	40	41/42	43	44	45
USA	2.5	3.3	4.5	5.5	6.5	7.5	8.5	9.5	10.5

RETIREMENT

CHAPTER SUMMARY

O There are more retired foreigners living along the Spanish coasts, than retired Spaniards.

O For every British person happily retired in Spain there are several others suffering financial hardship and loneliness, especially when one partner dies.

  O On the positive side, expatriates have created strong communities in many areas and organise many amusements, so there is no need to be lonely.

O Anyone intending to retire to Spain should be prepared to improve the quality of their Spanish before arriving.

O **Residence permit.** Anyone intending to retire to Spain must obtain a residence visa either before they leave their country or 30 days after arrival.

  O Anyone just spending the winter in Spain (i.e. not longer than 90 days) need not apply for a residence visa.

O Most Spanish towns and some villages have a pensioners' club with a bar, television, magazines etc. Anyone over 65 is eligible and foreigners are made welcome.

O **Pensions.** Spanish pensions are very generous. However most British pensioners will be receiving a UK pension.

  O If you move to Spain before retirement age it is essential to maintain your national insurance contributions to qualify for a British state pension.

O **Spanish Health Care.** The Spanish health system covers hospital care and surgery but does not include visits to the doctor or dentist.

There are, at present, more retired foreigners than retired local people along the Spanish coasts; and a staggering 80% of all expatriates in Spain are said to be of retirement age. However, although these statistics certainly guarantee no lack of companionship for the older expatriate, anyone considering such a move should first of all thoroughly investigate the main issues involved. There have recently been a plethora of programmes describing the dire straits in which many British expats find themselves after a few years of what was to be their ideal retirement in Spain. The difficulties of coping on a fixed income with spiralling inflation – and living costs and a dismal absence of welfare and aftercare services for the elderly – can, in the worst cases, combine to make life in Spain more like a fight for survival. Financial hardship can be even worse when you are away from home. Emotionally, loneliness and isolation can often set in, especially when one partner outlives the other, leaving the survivor alienated and often without enough funds to return to family and friends in the UK.

But the prospect for most is brighter. A recent survey of retired British residents living in purposebuilt estates in areas such as Torremolinos, Mijas and Fuengirola found most to be 'happy with their move' and even 'pleasantly surprised' in most cases. Retirees to Spain often become more 'robust, independent and sociable' than their British counterparts. There are predictions that soon the Costa del Sol could develop into Europe's equivalent of America's retirement sunbelt, for those from Britain and other European countries who prefer a life in the sun. Some would say this has happened already.

Naomi Greatbanks, who spent many years selling property to retired couples in Spain, explains that although there is no doubt that moving to Spain and living in its wonderful climate is therapeutic for many, living costs and inflation have succeeded in bringing both hardship and regrets into the lives of many retired couples. However, the experience of a British journalist, Bettina Brown, who lived and worked just outside Marbella for seventeen years paints a far more positive picture of retirement life. Strong expatriate communities have a habit of springing up in most areas of Spain and as she writes:

> There are clubs for just about everything you can think of: bridge, chess, amateur dramatics, classical music and the sporting facilities are excellent. There are so many charities which need helpers that those who are not sporty, loathe bridge and have few hobbies still have an opportunity to socialize and to make friends. There is no need to be lonely.

However, Mrs Brown has made the reservation that although the Spanish are much more immediately friendly towards foreigners than, for example, the French, it is still not easy to establish deep friendships with them unless your grasp of the language is fluent and you have a real interest in and knowledge of Spanish culture.

Still, there is no need for a retirement in Spain to be anything but a happy experience if all the necessary and sensible precautions are taken before departure; and sufficient homework is done as to where, when and how you intend to live once in Spain. Some of the very real advantages which can result from a retirement in Spain include a quality of life which is quieter and often higher than that offered in the UK. Property costs are often lower than the equivalent UK prices and while the climate is generally more temperate, the attraction of a new culture and way of life may act as a great incentive to Brits who are tired of the endless rain, traffic and distinctly uncontinental ambiance which often seem to be a part of British life. This chapter endeavours to deal with all of the procedures and decisions which apply specifically to those planning a retirement in Spain and which, if followed, should facilitate the transition between the two countries.

The Decision to Leave

First and foremost, anyone considering retiring there must be able to afford the move financially; and secondly, possess copious amounts of energy and enthusiasm to deal with the move practically and emotionally as well. And all emigrants should be prepared to improve the quality of their Spanish before arriving in the new country. As many decisions to move abroad are based on a love of the country discovered through past holidays, it is quite a good idea to consider a long stay of say six months which includes the winter period, in the area in which one is interested before moving permanently.

Many retired people have a lifestyle which takes them to Spain during the winter months (when holidays and longer stays are cheap) returning to Britain only for the more pleasant spring and summer. Alternatively, if you have sufficient funds, you could buy a second home in Spain; and then sell your UK residence and move abroad permanently after a trial period of staying there. Both of these suggestions should be considered as many parts of Spain which are bustling and cheerful in the summer are correspondingly deserted and desolate in the winter.

Residence Requirements

Anyone intending to retire to Spain must either obtain a residence visa, the *visado de residencia*, from the Spanish Consulate before leaving the UK or make these arrangements there. Senior citizens can apply for the visa by post rather than in person, provided that they are still resident within the UK at the time of application. Proof of a substantial pension or other means of support, with an additional amount for each member of the family, as well as a standing order from a bank stating that the said amount is being transferred to Spain, will also be required. Full details of all residence and entry requirements for Spain are given in Chapter Two, *Residence and Entry Regulations*. Some may find the detailed advice available from the UK Department of Work and Pensions offices helpful; and the Spanish Consulate-General in London can supply a separate leaflet of general information for pensioners who wish to retire in Spain.

Hobbies and Interests

You will find a pensioners' club (*Hogar de Pensionistas*) conveniently and centrally located in most Spanish towns and villages. Each club has its own bar, television and newspaper facilties, while some are so well organised as to arrange for a local doctor to call on the club, for the convenience of its members. While membership is primarily Spanish, the warmth with which expatriates are received within these clubs is a testament to Spanish hospitality. Anyone over 65 is eligible to join; and apart from the obvious social possiblities which such a setup offers, drinks are usually subsidised and offered at prices slightly lower than those found in most other bars or cafés.

There will be many English-speaking community organisations, wherever you are, centred around churches and places of worship, cultural organisations, newcomers clubs, theatre groups and so on. A sample of these in Madrid includes Anglican as well as Catholic and Baptist churches and the synagogue; the British Hispanic Cultural Foundation (☎913456344); the British Ladies Association (☎918034713) and the English-speaking amateur theatre group the Madrid Players (☎915620588 or 914072245).

As far as sporting activities go, these will be many and varied. Golf enthusiasts in particular need look no further: in southern Spain the climate lends itself ideally to the sport; and you will find that virtually all of the popular resort and retirement areas have golf courses within easy reach, as do many of the new housing complexes, although the membership fees are becoming more and more pricey. A list of golf clubs can be found in the local *Yellow Pages* (*Paginas Amarillos*) and the national or local tourist offices can provide information about courses.

Beach life in Spain offers yet more opportunities for the more sporty contingent; and swimming, sailing and fishing are all easily available along the coasts. Tennis is very popular; and hard courts, both public and private, can be easily found in most areas.

So, a retirement in Spain can be as sociable and gregarious as the person considering it. The life around the pubs and bars offers another way to meet people and form a circle of friends and acquaintances; but this carries its own dangers. Then there is travel. Being based in Spain offers a good opportunity to explore this vast and scenically diverse country. Camping and caravanning facilities are generally good and most public transport and other leisure facilities offer generous discounts for senior citizens. The Spanish railway authority (RENFE) issues Gold Cards (*Tarjetas Doradas*) and various other discounts which entitle anyone over the age of 65 to a reduction of 50% off the normal fare. On long-distance journeys these concessions tend to be limited to blue days (*dias azules*) which are usually weekdays rather than weekends or public holidays. However, the cards are normally valid year-round on local journeys. The card will only cost you a few euros, is valid for one year and is available from any RENFE office on presentation of a passport to prove that the applicant is 65 or over.

Choosing and Buying a Retirement Home

The main and very obvious point to make regarding buying a retirement property in Spain is to choose something which is both within your scope financially and which, unlike a holiday home, is suitable for year-round living. However, you will also need to take into consideration the running and upkeep costs of the property in question. Buying an apartment within a block of flats which works on the comunidad principal, for instance, can help ease some of the budgeting costs involved in house maintenance. You will find that there is an abundance of sheltered housing and retirement developments in Spain, all of which work according to this timesaving and economical principle. Proximity to health services and other facilities is also an important consideration for anyone reliant on public transport. The availability of buses, and general accessibility – even if you yourself own a car – should be part of your decision to buy or not to buy. Once you have decided on your new home you will need to follow all of the procedures regarding property purchase which are explained in full in Chapter Three, *Setting Up Home.*

Pensions

Spanish pensions are among the highest in Europe after Sweden's; the average monthly pension is about £750 ($1,050)a month.

Anyone who moves to Spain before reaching retirement age should continue to pay national insurance contributions in the UK in order to qualify for a British state pension once they do reach 65. Having established an entitlement to either a UK or a Spanish pension, depending on which country you have paid the majority of contributions in, you are eligible to draw the pension in either country.

Before moving to Spain, contact the Pensions and Overseas Benefits Directorate of the Department of Work and Pensions in Newcastle-upon-Tyne, NE98 1YX; ☎0191-218 7147 to obtain a couple of forms which must be completed in order to arrange the transfer of your UK pension to either an address in Spain or a bank account in either the UK or Spain. Note that pensions are not frozen at the level they reached on arrival in Spain; instead the pension will rise in accordance with any increases which take effect in the UK. The DWP Overseas Benefits Directorate office in Newcastle also publishes Leaflet SA29 (available on receipt of an s.a.e.) which provides details on EU pension and social security legislation.

In the case of someone being employed by a UK company but working in Spain, they should check on how long they are able to contribute to their UK company pension scheme; normally, employees would be able to remain within the UK scheme for at least three years, and with the approval of the Inland Revenue, for longer after that. But this will depend on the pension. Finally, it is worth checking whether your employer's pension contributions, if your are subject to tax in Spain, are taxable in that country. Previously as a UK taxpayer, you would not be taxed on your employer's contributions. Also take advice from an independent financial adviser as to whether it is best for you to continue with a personal pension scheme in the UK and for how long, and what other conditions and/or restrictions may apply to the scheme once you are resident in Spain.

Finance

Anyone considering retiring to Spain should take specialist financial advice regarding their own situation. Most people in a position to retire overseas have an amount of capital to invest, or will have once they sell their UK home; and it is essential to take good advice on how and where this may best be done. Moreover, those who intend to maintain connections with both the UK and Spain will need advice on how their taxation affairs can be sorted out to their own advantage. Usually, there is no reason why one should not continue with bank accounts or investments already established in the UK; and in most cases interest will be paid on deposits paid without deduction of tax where one is nonresident.

Taxation

Taxation is inextricably linked with investment considerations. Reasonably impartial advice can be obtained from the UK Inland Revenue (the Spanish equivalent tends to be less helpful), which has no wish to tax people on income to which they are clearly not entitled. Those in need of taxation advice should contact the Inland Revenue Office with which they last dealt.

Because the UK tax year runs from April to April and the Spanish one from

January to December there are certain advantages and disadvantages, from a tax point of view, in choosing a particular removal date. Whereas employees are not usually able to indulge in such freedom of choice, the retired person should consider this seriously. Generally speaking, if their affairs are properly managed, most people will not either be substantially better or worse off under a Spanish tax regime than a UK one.

UK pensions paid to British expatriates are subject to Spanish tax; unless the pensioner is exempted by a double tax agreement; or he or she is a former public service employee who worked abroad (in which case the pension is taxable in the UK, although sometimes not liable to any tax at all). The double taxation agreement only relates to pensions in Spain if you are resident there. Whether your pension is liable for UK income tax or Spanish tax, it may be better in either case to elect to take a tax-free lump sum pension option, thereby reducing the level of pension liable to tax.

Offshore Banking

From a retired person's point of view, if he or she has a sum of money which they wish to invest or put into a long-term deposit account (for a minimum of 90 days) it is well worth looking at the tax-saving options like PEPs (Personal Equity Plans) and TESSA/ISAs (Tax-Exempt Special Savings Accounts/ Individual Savings Account) which the high street banks and building societies all offer in Britain in addition to the offshore account. Banks, building societies and merchant banks all offer accounts through offshore banking centres in tax havens such as Gibraltar and the Channel Islands. The basic difference from an onshore account is that these investments pay income gross of tax which of course is ultimately taxable but they do offer legal ways of paying less tax.

These ways of paying less tax are mainly through roll-up funds, an investment vehicle in which you buy shares; and offshore life insurance, which practitioners like to stress is really an integral part of Britain's tax planning industry. So far as roll-up funds are concerned, supposing that you invest £10,000 in a fund yielding 7.5% and want to draw an income of 7.5%, with the shares going up in value accordingly, a suitable number of these are sold; and the effect, even if you pay tax on your gain at the top rate of 40%, is a tax bill currently of £20.80 on your £750 income. For what and when to sell you certainly need the advice of a financial planning expert; or a company to administer the fund for you. You can also defer paying tax to a time of your own choosing, perhaps when you anticipate you will need the money; or when you enter a lower tax bracket incomewise. Offshore life insurance policies offer similar tax savings.

For these offshore accounts, the year-long deposits tend to demand a minimum sum of £10,000. As with all deposit accounts, interest rates work on the basis that the more inaccessible one's money, the higher the rate of interest paid. Interest can be paid monthly or annually; and although the account holder will receive much the same gross amount of interest either way (although slightly less on the monthly payments because of the number of transaction charges involved) the monthly payments which bring with them a steady income flow seem invariably more popular with retired account holders. A list of banks and other organisations which offer offshore banking facilities is given under the *Offshore Banking* heading in Chapter Four, *Daily Life*. Most of the highstreet banks and building societies offer useful explanatory leaflets.

Social Security

Although the Spanish social security system is covered in detail in the relevant part of the *Daily Life* chapter, the aim of this section is to outline the range of benefits which is available specifically to those at or approaching retirement age.

Anyone who moves to Spain from the UK and is of retirement status is entitled to the health benefits of social security free of charge. This assumes, however, that the individual is entitled to, or claiming, a pension in the UK. For example, someone who had retired and moved there before official retirement age would not yet be covered. To claim free entitlement to Spanish social security one must first complete form E121 available from the DSS and then register with social security in Spain. Free benefits include health care and hospital treatment, although a financial contribution may be required in some cases (see the section, *Health Insurance and Hospitals* in the chapter on *Daily Life*).

If a UK national moves to Spain while working, and then later retires there, he or she should be entitled to a Spanish state pension rather than a UK one. However this is dependent on the claimant having paid all outstanding National Insurance contributions before leaving the UK. The main advantage of a Spanish state pension is that it should, theoretically, always match the cost of living in Spain, whereas a UK pension payable in Spain could potentially fail to do this.

As discussed elsewhere, most employees in Spain pay into private insurance schemes which will top up their social security benefits. Such schemes will not only comprise a great part of the patient's contribution to medical treatment but they will also increase the state pension payable. In many cases, the state pension added to the amount payable under a 'top-up' insurance scheme will give the retired person a pension of 100% of their past salary. However, note that such schemes must generally be started well in advance of retirement age. The few schemes available to those who have already retired and which usually provide further medical benefits only, are likely to be quite expensive.

Expacare: email: info@expacare.net or visit www.expacare.net. Specialists in expatriate healthcare offering high quality health insurance cover for individuals and their families, including group cover for five or more employees. Cover is available for expatriates of all nationalities and ages worldwide.

Or BUPA (Russell House, Russell Mews, Brighton BN1 2NR; ☎01273-208181; www.bupaint.com) also provide worldwide cover for all ages.

Health

One serious drawback of the medical treatment provided by Spanish social security from a retired person's point of view is that although it provides financial cover for operations and hospital treatment, it does not include funding for general medical treatment such as trips to the dentist or to a general practitioner. Moreover, the Spanish social security system caters particularly poorly for out patient and aftercare treatment and facilities. Social security will only cover about 75% of a patient's treatment costs; thus the patient has to meet 25% of the costs him or herself, or budget for payments for insurance to cover this instead. As discussed above, those who have worked in Spain and paid into a private top-up scheme, as most people do, have the bulk of this contribution covered; those who are already retired and move to Spain may not.

A list of English-speaking doctors will be available from the local British

Consulate: this will, however, often involve using private facilities.

Wills and Legal Considerations

It is very important that anyone who buys property in Spain should make a Spanish will in order to avoid the time-consuming and expensive legal problems which will other otherwise result from Spanish inheritance laws and taxes. Moreover, it is advisable to make two wills, one which disposes of Spanish assets and another which deals with any UK assets, rather than trying to combine the two. As long as a will is left specifying requirements, then heirs will not be subject to the Spanish law of 'compulsory heirs' in which two-thirds of the deceased's estate must be left to his or her children. However, if an expatriate dies intestate (without having made a will) then Spanish law will be applied to the deceased's Spanish assets. A Spanish will does not exempt the inheritors from Spanish inheritance tax, although this will only effect those who have inherited a sum which exceeds the non-taxable tax threshold currently; and even then inheritance tax rates are only really very high in the case of property being left to nonrelatives. For further details of inheritance tax regulations and other useful contacts, see Chapter Three, *Setting Up Home*. To validate a Spanish will you will need to obtain a certificate of law (*certificado de ley*) from your consulate which will state that the will is being made under the terms of UK national law which includes a provision for the free disposition of property. Any lawyer (*abogado*) will be able to organise this for you.

Death

In the unfortunate event that a relative or close friend should die while in Spain there are a few essential formalities which you will have to deal with. Firstly, you will need two death certificates: one issued by the local judge which must be prepared and signed by the doctor attendant at the death and another one from the British Consulate. Both certificates will be needed for any insurance claims and to carry out any instructions in the will of the deceased. You will need to contact a funeral director who will often deal with a lot of the paperwork on your behalf. For example, it is quite common for a funeral director to obtain the consulate death certificate on behalf of the deceased's relatives. He or she will frequently also ensure that the necessary official certificates are delivered to the family and contact a British pastor to perform the burial service.

A foreigner can be buried in most Spanish cemeteries, whether or not he or she was a Catholic. However, other options include a British cemetery in Málaga; an international one in Benalmadena and crematoriums in Madrid, Seville and Málaga. You will find that the British and international cemeteries have the familiar subterranean burial plots to which we are accustomed, while Spanish cemeteries consist of raised graves with the bodies placed in niches. A funeral service will cost a basic rate of around €1,000 although this can rise quickly with transport costs and other fees. Most Spanish cemeteries rent out burial plots for varying time periods and, while you will find that municipal cemetery rates are quite inexpensive, purchasing a plot can be very pricey; so it's worth enquiring at the town hall for price details. If the body is being flown back to the UK, then funeral directors will arrange transportation and embalming.

Section II

WORKING IN SPAIN

EMPLOYMENT

BUSINESS AND INDUSTRY REPORT

TEMPORARY WORK

STARTING A BUSINESS

EMPLOYMENT

CHAPTER SUMMARY

○ **The Employment Situation.** Spain has the highest rate of unemployment in the European Union.

  ○ The Spanish government keeps inflation down at the cost of high unemployment.

○ **The Economy.** Spain has a lot of potential as it is still an expanding economy.

  ○ Spain was a late starter in developing newer industries in the last quarter of the twentieth century following the end of General Franco's era of dictatorship.

○ **Staffing.** It is very expensive to dismiss staff in Spain.

  ○ Redundancy payments are some of the highest in Europe.

○ **Wages.** Salaries have not kept pace with the cost of living in Spain.

○ **Employment prospects.** Information Technology, Teachers of English and bilingual secretaries are some of the main areas for vacancies in Spain.

  ○ Spain has the largest number of private language schools in Europe.

  ○ If you speak Spanish it is preferable to look for jobs on the internet or to visit the empoloyer in person if at all possible.

  ○ Spanish companies are notoriously bad at answering letters and faxes for job applications.

○ **Casual jobs.** Grapepickers for the wine harvest may be accommodated in the local bullring.

  ○ There is a lot of local competition for casual farm work but some villages are very hospitable and will take on foreigners.

The Employment Scene

Some of the statistics concerning employment in Spain may seem unpromising when viewed in isolation. Unemployment remains the highest in the European Union at over 13%, though this marks a significant drop over the past five years. The economy has been growing 3% or 4% year on year since 2000. Inflation is currently projected at 2.2% (which meets the target for European Monetary Union, but at the cost of high unemployment). Labour costs for employers are high. It costs more to dismiss a worker in Spain than in any other European country (with the maximum compensation for unfair dismissal equivalent to 1,200 days' pay, and the average compensation also the highest of the EU countries). One of the main projects of José María Aznar's right-wing government has been labour reform and the reduction of labour costs along 'Thatcherite' lines; but Spain still has a long way to go.

In the meantime salaries look like falling behind rising living costs in unskilled areas, and rising with demand in areas of skills shortage, as in the flexible labour markets of Britain or the United States. It may be that the Spanish economy needs reform and a good dose of privatisation; and that the weakness of organised labour here provides the best opportunity for this programme of liberalisation in continental Europe. When considered against the political background of years of dictatorship and relative economic and industrial isolation, Spain has already achieved a massive step forward in attaining its current, stable form of democracy and low inflation.

Although pockets of relative poverty still exist, and despite the commonly held image of a rural and backward country – which still holds true in some more remote areas – wealth is gradually spreading; poverty itself nowadays is as much urban as rural; whole new industries have sprung up; in information technology for instance. Others (like the telephone company Telefónica and the public utilities) are being or have been privatised. All of this is subject to the vagaries of politics, and economic progress throughout the rest of Europe; but already Spain boasts the position of fifth largest industrial power in Europe.

The reason industrial expansion has been slowing recently, though, is that the government has been reducing its public deficit to the target of 3% of Gross Domestic Product required by EMU (see under *European Monetary Union* in the *Business and Industry Report* for Portugal). Spain is now competing on a level playing-field with the other EMU member countries. But what will be the costs of the single currency? Also, with the election of its right or centre-right government, the official policy is to promote de-regulatiom and to encourage all types of investment. Is this a bubble which will burst? Great progress has been made in streamlining the laws which regulate foreign investment, which is encouraging (both for foreign investors and foreign jobseekers) in the longer term. Foreign exchange regulations are also liberal in line with Spain's EU membership.

This is a generally favourable climate for employment; at least in the foreseeable future the situation looks likely to get better (some unemployed Spaniards would say that it couldn't get worse!). So whether you intend to work in Spain as an employee, employer or entrepreneur, the opportunities available in this economically young but rich country are constantly diversifying; and the time is ripe for foreigners to make the most of this favourable moment in Spain's economic development. Despite the unemployment, job prospects for expatriates in Spain look like improving in future.

Residence and Work Regulations

Full details of the visa requirements are given in Chapter Two, *Residence and Entry Requirements*. EU nationals are at liberty to enter Spain to look for and take up work. However, people without a European passport will find it extremely difficult to find an employer willing to tackle the immigration bureaucracy with no guarantee of success. Note however, that au pairs, academics employed by Spanish universities, teachers employed at American or international schools etc., – as in Portugal – are all in categories where work visas may be more easily granted.

Skills and Qualifications

Recent UK legislation has enforced the EU directive on the mutual recognition of professional qualifications between EUmember countries. A very wide range of professions and trades are included in the legislation; and within these categories or professions any British citizen with UK qualifications who wishes to live and work in Spain is eligible to join the equivalent Spanish professional or trade association; and to continue in the same line of work without having to take any new tests or exams in their aptitude or a new training programme. At present, these categories include architects, dentists, doctors, lawyers, midwives, nurses, pharmacists, veterinary surgeons and many others. Is yours covered? Appropriate professional bodies in Spain may be contacted through the UK professional association or trade union.

Here are two organisations which might help: the UK National Academic Recognition Centre or *NARIC* (0800-581591) provides information on the comparability of overseas qualifications. UK NARIC also publishes fact sheets, including one called 'Studying, Training and Doing Research In Another Country of the EU.' NARIC can be contacted at ECCTIS Ltd., Oriel House, Oriel Road, Cheltenham, Glos. GL50 1XP; ☎01242-260010; fax 01242-258611; naric@ecctis.co.uk; www.naric.org.uk. Then there is the *European Community Certificate of Experience Scheme* which assists EU citizens wishing to work in another member country in an 'independent or self-employed' capacity, if they have suitable experience and training which meets the criteria for mutual recognition etc. mentioned above. This Certificate of Experience is just that, a certificate which takes account of your actual work experience and what you have done in your trade or profession, which is accepted elsewhere in the EU as a substitute for a formal qualification. Contact the *British Chambers of Commerce* for a guidance pack and application form, at their Certification Unit, BCC, Westwood House, Westwood Business Park, Coventry CV4 8HS; ☎0247669 4484; fax 0247669 5844.

For information about language training, see the *Daily Life* chapter of this book which includes a list of schools and relevant organisations. For further details on the subject of professional and employment organisations see below.

SOURCES OF JOBS

Newspapers

UK Newspapers and Directories. Although trans-European or even global advertising for vacancies is a trend which is catching on in some specialist areas like computing and multimedia – encouraged by developments like the Internet – it is unlikely that many readers of this book will currently find vacancies in Spain this way, in the near future at any rate. The Internet can help in your job search, though. See the chapter *The Creative Job Search* in the *Directory of Jobs and Careers Abroad* (Vacation Work) for more about this.

A more likely route for most jobs will be through the newspapers. Although some jobs for Spanish-speakers are advertised in the UK press, these tend in the main to be UK-based (with perhaps some potential for relocation to Spain in future). It is quite reasonable, though, to consider working for an international company with Spanish connections. Use your own contacts; or the list at the end of this chapter. An exception to this general rule is teaching English abroad, which will certainly mean that you are based in the country. Vacancies for English language teachers are to be found in the *Times Educational Supplement*, published every Friday and the Education pages of the *Guardian* on Tuesdays.

Moreover, the specialist bi-monthly publication, *Overseas Jobs Express* (available by subscription from 20 New Road, Brighton, W Sussex BN1 1UF; 01273 699611; UK subscription £39.95 for six issues; €68 from Spain and the rest of Europe) boasts, in addition to many wideranging, well-researched travel and other articles about all aspects of living and working abroad, a substantial *Jobs* section covering a wide and diverse range of jobs in Spain and elsewhere: accountancy, banking, EFL or English as a Foreign Language teaching, management consultancy, telecommunications, nannies, au pairs, doctors, engineers, secretaries and dancing teachers are only the beginning. This is where to look for these kinds of jobs in Spain, and internationally as well. Alternatively, a wide range of casual jobs, including hotel work, campsite leaders and nannies and au pairs are advertised in the annual directory *Summer Jobs Abroad* published by Vacation Work. *Teaching English Abroad* lists schools worldwide which employ English-language teachers each year. These books are available in most bookshops or contact Vacation Work Publications, 9 Park End Street, Oxford OX1 1HJ; www.vacationwork.co.uk.

A wide range of Spanish and international newspapers is now available in most cities across the UK as well. Some can be contacted through the advertising agencies which represent them in Britain (see below). Also see the chapter *Getting the Job* in *The Directory of Jobs and Careers Abroad* for more details of newspapers and directories which carry international recruitment advertising.

International and European Newspapers. International newspapers are a fairly new development in newspaper publishing; these publications circulate editions across several national boundaries and usually carry a modest amount of job advertising. Again, the amount of ads carried and the number of these publications is likely to increase in the near future. Presently, the newspapers to consult include the *Wall Street Journal, Financial Times* and the *International Herald Tribune*. The major US newspapers carrying international recruitment advertising are the *Chicago Tribune, The Los Angeles Times* and the *New York Times* (see below). As well as employers advertising in these papers, individuals can place their own adverts for any kind of job, although bi-lingual secretaries and assistants, marketing managers and other professionally qualified people looking to relocate abroad are in the greatest demand. With the current vogue for privatisation and restructuring in the Spanish economy, UK management consultants are presently much in demand; as are more traditional areas of expertise like engineering and information technology, or tourism.

Obviously, advertising rates vary, but are usually under £10 a line for a week's coverage. This kind of advertising can become expensive, though, so readers should go through the more conventional channels first, of replying to situations vacant ads and so on; and then trying more 'creative' approaches, which include contacting individuals and companies direct, before investing heavily in situations wanted ads. Anyone interested in doing so should contact the advertising department at the addresses listed below.

Additionally, some English-language newspapers in Spain, e.g. *The Costa Blanca News* in Alicante and *The Weekly Post* for the Costa Blanca, and *Costa Del Sol News* for the Costa del Sol (all published by CB News SI at Apartado – PO Box 95, E03500 Benidorm; ☎95855287; fax 95858361), as well as *SUR in English* (Prensa Malagueña SA, Avda. Dr. Marañon 48, 29009 Málaga; www.surinenglish.com), are all useful sources for those seeking temporary jobs. For the Canaries, check out the *Island Sun* (www.islandsunnewspaper.com). Unfortunately, hard copies of these publications can be difficult to get hold of within the UK, even at places like the Spanish Embassy and Hispanic and Luso Brazilian Council library. It will be best to write directly to the publishers to obtain copies.

Even if you do not speak Spanish well, it may also be worth looking at the *Mercado de Trabajo*, a newspaper which covers the field of employment and recruitment in Spain; and has a wide range of jobs both temporary and permanent on offer, as well as an extensive *demandas de trabajo* or situations wanted column covering everything from lawyers to translators. It can be bought from kiosks for €1.80 or consulted on the internet (www.mercadodetrabajo.com) which has links to employment agencies.

Useful Addresses

Chicago Tribune: 435 North Michigan Avenue, Chicago, Il 60611, USA.

International Herald Tribune: 181 Avenue Charles de Gaulle, 92521 Neuilly-sur-Seine, France.

Financial Times: 1 Southwalk Bridge, London SE1 9HL; ☎020-7873 3000; fax 020-7407 5700.

The Los Angeles Times: Times Mirror Square, Los Angeles, California, CA 90053, USA.

The New York Times: 229 West 43rd Street, new York, NY 10036, USA.

Overseas Jobs Express – OJE: 20 New Road, Brighton, W Sussex BN1 1UF; ☎01273-699611.

Wall Street Journal: 1st Floor, 90 Long Acre, London WC2E 9PR; fax 020-7842 9650 (the number for their sales and marketing department. The International Press Centre itself does not help with enquiries about foreign newspapers).

Advertising in Newspapers. Job offers resulting from advertisements placed in either the Spanish press of English-language newspapers published in Spain are not very common. If you try, a job wanted ad in many Spanish newspapers can be placed through the London-based publishers representative, *Powers Turner Group,* 100 Rochester Row, London SW1P 1JP; ☎020-7630 9966; email: jblacksell@pub licitas.com who deal with many Spanish newspapers ranging from the nationally-read *El País* and *La Vanguardia* published in Barcelona to the more obscure regional publications. But they do not deal with any English-language newspapers in Spain; and these will have to be purchased while on a reconnaissance trip or directly from the publishers (or again you can request an inspection copy). The addresses of some of these newspapers are given under the heading *International and European Newspapers* above and in the chapter on *Daily Life* under *Media and Communications.*

Professional Journals and Magazines

If you are a member of a professional or trade body, or even if you are not, but one exists, then there may well be a professional journal or magazine which carries advertisements for jobs in Spain. Examples include *Architects' Journal* and *The Bookseller.*

Many professional journals and magazines circulate free of charge and are not tied to any specific professional body. Some such magazines may carry suitable advertisments, for example, those in the air transport industry should consult *Flight International,* while those in the catering trade could try *Caterer and Hotelkeeper*; and anyone working in agriculture, *Farmers Weekly.* Some of these magazines, although they are published in the UK, are considered world authorities in their field; and they are widely available in public libraries and newsagents.

An exhaustive list of trade magazines can be found in media directories, for example, *Benn's Media* directory Europe volume which is available from major UK reference libraries. To track down all UK-based professional and trade publications *British Rates and Data* (known as 'BRAD') will be your source; and the *European Media Directory* also covers Spain, with entries for journals and periodicals arranged by country and subject category.

Professional Associations

Many professional associations do not provide any official information on working overseas as such. However, many of them will have had contact with their counterpart associations in other EU countries, often during negotiations involving the mutual recognition of qualifications mentioned above; and should be able to provide names and addresses for their opposite numbers in Spain, or even some individual help. Trade unions are also generally members of international bodies and have useful contacts overseas. You may consider joining one, if you are not already a member and already in employment. Many have sections for unemployed and freelance workers as well. Their publications and vacancy lists sometimes include jobs abroad as well as in the UK.

Details of all professional associations are to be found in the directory, *Trade Associations and Professional Bodies of the UK* edited by Patricia Millard, available at most reference libraries. In more specialist libraries the *European Directory of Trade and Business Associations* may also be consulted; and as mentioned above, it is also worth trying to contact the Spanish equivalent of UK professional associations: the UK body may be able to provide a contact. Alternatively, consult the Spanish Yellow Pages (*Las Paginas Amarillas*)at major UK reference libraries, or approach your trade union for information about its counterpart organisation in Spain.

Specialist Publications

A few specialist publications in both the UK and Spain contain job vacancies. In the UK, *Nexus Expatriate Magazine* handles many foreign vacancies; and provides other valuable information for expatriates. This publication is available from *Expat Network Limited* at Rose House, 109a South End, Croydon CR0 1BG; ☎020-8760 5100; fax 020-8760 0469; www.expatnetwork.com; email nexus@expatnetwork.com. Membership in the Expat Network costs £66 a year in the UK, £72 in Europe.. The Hispanic and Luso Brazilian Council (Canning House, 2 Belgrave Square, London SW1 8PJ; ☎020-7235 2303; email: enquiries@canninghousee.com, www.canninghouse.com) publishes a useful and quite comprehensive leaflet entitled *Spain: A guide to employment and opportunities for young people* which, although really aimed at the young worker/traveller, is useful for anyone contemplating working in Spain. The leaflet costs £4 from the above address.

Your local Jobcentre should not be overlooked. It will have access to useful resources such as the Eurofacts and Globalfacts series of International Careers Information, and Exodus, the Careers Europe database of international careers information produced by Careers Europe (Fourth Floor, Midland House, 14 Cheapside, Bradford BD1 4JA; 01274 829600; www.careerseurope.co.uk). Another source of information on European programmes is Eurodesk (Community Learning Scotland, Rosebery House, 9 Haymarket Terrace, Edinburgh EH12 5EZ; 0131-313 2488) which has an online database (www.eurodesk.org).

Employment Organisations

A Europewide employment service called EURES (EURopean Employment Service) operates as a network of more than 400 EuroAdvisers who can access a database of jobs within Europe. These vacancies are usually for six months or longer, and for skilled, semiskilled and (increasingly) managerial jobs. Language skills are almost always a requirement. On average, 500 new posts are registered with EURES each month though if you have a specific destination in mind, they are unlikely to be able to offer much choice of vacancy. For example at the time of writing there were 133 registered vacancies in all fields throughout Spain. These can be accessed through the EURES website given below.

Rather than settle for consulting a EURES Adviser at home, you might get a more complete picture by telephoning the EURES office in your destination. Again the EURES website provides contact details for all EURES Advisers including the 41 in Spain, indicating which ones speak English. Otherwise, ask at your local Jobcentre how to contact a EURES Adviser either at home or abroad. In the UK most of the expertise is based in the headquarters of the national Employment Service. The Overseas Placing Unit, Level 4, Skills House, 37 Holy Green, Off the Moor, Sheffield S1 4AQ (0114259 6051/fax 0114259 6040) coordinates all dealings with overseas/EU vacancies. The websites http://europa.eu.int/jobs/eures and http://eu.int/europedirect have extensive information for Eurojobseekers.

UK Employment Agencies. Details of employment agencies that belong to the national organisation, the Recruitment and Employment Confederation (3638 Mortimer Street, London W1N 7RB; ☎0800320588; www.rec.uk.com) can be obtained for a fee. The agencies listed deal mainly with specific sectors, e.g. electronics, secretarial, accountancy, etc., and will recruit only qualified and experienced staff.

Nexus Expatriate Magazine (see above) also runs regular features on specific areas such as telecommunications with extensive listings of international recruitment agencies in that field.

Spanish Employment Agencies. The state-run *Instituto Nacional de Empleo (INEM)* used to be the only employment and recruitment agency which was allowed to operate officially in Spain. Private employment agencies – as in many other European countries – may only technically function as temporary employment bureaux – which obviously limits their role – although many offer more permanent positions. Those who are interested in temporary work should contact these agencies (the majority of which are based in Madrid and – for Englishspeakers – in Málaga) which are listed in the Spanish Yellow Pages *(Paginas Amarillos)*. Bear in mind, however, that there is little point in applying for most jobs unless you are bilingual or have specialist skills needed for the job.. Only some of the agencies listed below have English-speaking staff.

The Manpower temporary employment agency (www.manpower.co.uk in the UK and www.manpower.com in the US). has twenty or so branch offices in Spain but specifies the following conditions to potential applicants; their Spanish offices deal only in temporary work, they will accept enquiries from within Spain only, and all applicants must have references with them and be able to speak fluent Spanish as their service largely provides office, catering and industrial jobs where communication skills are essential. Some of Manpower's Spanish addresses are listed below. For further information on temporary work and recruitment agencies for Spain see the section, *Temporary Work* and these useful addresses.

Useful Addresses

Private Employment Organisations in Spain:

ALG (Acción Labor Group S.I.): C/ Comandante Zorita 46, Esc. Dcha. 1° C, E28020 Madrid; ☎915708605/ 5712284.

Agio T.T.: Fuencarral 33, E28013 Madrid; ☎915322129; fax 95323972. Offices and branches also in Barcelona, Guadalajara, Huelva and other cities.

Attempora E.T.T.: C/Marques[ac]s de las Valdavia 42, 3° 5, E28100 Alcobendas (Madrid); ☎914574949; fax 94571898.

Cenpla E.T.T. S.A.: Leganitos 9, E28001 Madrid; ☎915599441. Branches in Las Palmas, León, Salamanca, Valencia and other major cities.

Denci Trabajo Temporal: C/Velázquez 19, E28001 Madrid; ☎914318400;

fax 915760693. Offices throughout Spain.

Faster Iberica, E.T.T. S.A.: C/Orense 11, 2°B, E28020 Madrid; ☎915561528.

Flexiplan T.T.: C/Doctor Fleming 12, E28820 Cosiada (Madrid); Lezama 4, E28034 Madrid; ☎916310900; fax 916310890. Over 50 branches throughout Spain.

Gonzal Gestion E.T.T.: C/Doctor Esquerdo 166, 1°G, E28007 Madrid; ☎915015500; fax 915016060.

Human Group: Velázquez 146, E28002 Madrid; ☎95626010; fax 95624118. Also at: Cristo 1, E28850 Torrejonde de Ardoz; Madrid 5, E28902 Getafe; Gran Via 2, E28220 Majadahonda Getafe.

Intereuropea de Trabajo Temporal: Gran Via 624°, E28013 Madrid; ☎915426791;

fax 915471394. Another agency with branches nationwide.

Laborman: Francisoc Silvela 21, bajo, E28028 Madrid; ☎93093855; fax 94026308. National agency.

Manpower: Genova, 5 Bjos, Madrid; ☎915424875; fax 915597210. Offices throughout Spain including Alicante, Barcelona, Málaga, Seville and Zaragoza.

RHEM: C/Francisco Silvela 44, escalera B, 1°, E28028 Madrid; ☎917258120.

People: Avda. de América 331°, E28002

Madrid; ☎915199157; fax 915198589. More than 80 offices throughout Spain.

Select: Gran Via 1, E28013 Madrid; ☎9102490490; fax 915319033.

Trabatem E.T.T. S.A.: Avda. de América 8, E28028 Madrid; ☎9153610320; fax 917264698. 20 Branches throughout Spain.

Umano E.T.T. S.A.: C/Pajaritos 24, E28007 Madrid; ☎9102214161. Regional offices in Barcelona, Bilbao, La Coruña, León, Seville and Valencia.

Spanish Government Job Centres. As mentioned above, the Spanish equivalent of UK Jobcentres is the *Instituto Nacional de Empleo,* and branch offices are pretty evenly distributed throughout Spain. In addition to operating a job placement service they also give assistance to budding entrepreneurs. Although primarily a service for Spanish nationals, the job centres have an obligation, imposed by EU regulations, to be of assistance to nationals of other EU countries. It is worth seeking out the more important centres with a EURES Adviser on staff. However, once again, they are unlikely to help anyone who is unable to communicate in Spanish. As elsewhere in Europe, government employment offices can be unhelpful to foreigners; so don't expect them to bend over backwards to help, even if you do speak the language well. The INEM service is administered by the Ministry of Employment and Social Security whose list of addresses and telephone numbers is available from Spanish Consulates.

Chambers of Commerce

The Spanish Chamber of Commerce (5 Cavendish Square, London W1G ODP; ☎020-7637 9061; fax 020-7436 7188) publishes a list of addresses of its member companies, many of whom recruit in Spain. Information is provided free of charge to members; and charged to the general public to cover administration, printing and postage costs. They may send you their *Trade Directory, Directory of Chambers of Commerce in Spain* and can be helpful in providing other useful information. The *Directory of Employers* at the end of this chapter is based, among other sources, on the list published by the Spanish Chamber of Commerce.

Chambers of Commerce exist to serve the interests of businesses trading in both Spain and the UK; and most should provide a lot of potentially invaluable information about their member companies for those enmeshed in the job-hunting process. Your local UK Chamber may also have Spanish contacts. In Spain, local and regional branches can be found throughout the country, in virtually every city and town. Many of these provide enthusiastic support for local industries and companies and, on request, will provide details of these and a list of government incentives for new industry (see the section, *Government Incentives,* in Chapter Seven *Starting a Business*).

It is even possible that the local chamber of commerce might know which companies currently have vacancies in that area, although in the process they will no doubt rightly inform any hopeful jobseeker that they don't function as an employment agency. For those interested in doing business in Spain, too, these will be invaluable contacts. The addresses for the main chambers of commerce (*cámara oficial de comercio e industria*) in each region and in areas popular with British expatriates are listed below.

Useful Addresses

Cámara Oficial de Comercio e Industria: Huertas 13, E28012 Madrid; ☎915383500; fax 915383718/3677.

Cámara Oficial de Comercio e Industria: Casa Lonja del Mar, P° de Isabel 11, E08003 Barcelona; ☎933192412/16/54; fax 934169301 (Oficinas y Servicios). For enquiries write to: Av. Diagonal 452, E08006 Barcelona.

Cámara Oficial de Comercio e Industria: Alameda Recalde 50, E48008 Bilbao (Vizcaya); ☎944104664.

Cámara Oficial de Comercio e Industria: C/ Tesifonte Gallego 20, E02002 Albacete; ☎967228505; fax 967235345.

Cámara Oficial de Comercio e Industria: C/ San Fernando 4, E03002 Alicante; ☎965201133; fax 965201457.

Cámara Oficial de Comercio e Industria: C/ Antonio López 41°, E11004 Cádiz; ☎956223050/4; fax 956250710.

Cámara Oficial de Comercio e Industria: Plaza de Castellini 5/7, E30201 Cartagena (Murcia); ☎968507050; fax 968102692.

Cámara Oficial de Comercio e Industria: Avda. Hermanos Bou 79, E12003 Castellon; ☎964356500; fax 964356510.

Cámara Oficial de Comercio e Industria: C/ Pérez de Castro 1, E14003 Cordoba; ☎957296199; fax 957202106.

Cámara Oficial de Comercio e Industria: Gran Ví Jaime 1, 46, E17001 Gerona; ☎972418500; 72418501.

Cámara Oficial de Comercio e Industria: Instituto 17, E33201 Gijon (Asturias); ☎985356945/6; fax 985346275.

Cámara Oficial de Comercio e Industria: C/ Paz 18, E18002 Granada; ☎958263020/117; fax 958262214.

Cámara Oficial de Comercio e Industria: Sor

Angela de la Cruz 1, E21003 Huelva; ☎955245900; fax 955245699.

Cámara Oficial de Comercio e Industria: Tornéria 22, E11403 Jerez (Cádiz); ☎956340791/348740; fax 956344965.

Cámara Oficial de Comercio e Industria: Calle de la Alameda 30 y 321°, E15003 La Coruña; ☎981222133; 81225208.

Cámara Oficial de Comercio e Industria: C/ Fajeros 1, E24002 León; ☎987224400/4; fax 987222451.

Cámara Oficial de Comercio e Industria: Anselmo Clavé 2, E25007 Lerida; ☎973236161; 973247467.

Cámara Oficial de Comercio e Industria: C/ Cortina del Muelle 23, Palacio de Villalcazar, E29015 Málaga; ☎952211673/213785/6; fax 952229894.

Cámara Oficial de Comercio e Industria: Mallorca, Ibiza y Formentera, Estudio General 7, E07001 Palma de Mallorca; ☎971727851; fax 971726302.

Cámara Oficial de Comercio e Industria: Miguel Verí 3A, E07703 Mahon (Menorca); ☎971363194; fax 971368416.

Cámara Oficial de Comercio e Industria: Plaza de San Bartolomé, E30004 Murcia; ☎968229400; fax 968229425.

Cámara Oficial de Comercio e Industria: Yanguas y Miranda, 27 Bajo, E31003 Pamplona (Navarre); ☎948241100/4/8; fax 948242894.

Cámara Oficial de Comercio e Industria: Quintana 32, E33009 Oviedo (Asturias); ☎985223309; fax 985224566.

Cámara Oficial de Comercio e Industria: Plaza de Sexmeros 1, E37001 Sala-

manca; ☎23211797; fax 23280146.
Cámara Oficial de Comercio e Industria:
Plaza Contratación 8, E41004 Seville;
☎954211005; fax 954225619.
Cámara Oficial de Comercio e Industria: Av.
Pau Casals 17, E43003 Tarragona;
☎977219676; fax 977218977.
Cámara Oficial de Comercio e Indus-
tria: Plaza de la Candelaria 64°,
E38003 Santa Cruz de Tenerife;
☎22245384/5; 22241176.
Cámara Oficial de Comercio e Industria:
Poeta Querol 15, E46002 Valencia;

☎963511301; fax 963516017.
Cámara Oficial de Comercio e Industria: C/
Velázquez Moreno 221°, 36202 Vigo
(Pontevedra); ☎986222530/3; fax
986435659.
Cámara Oficial de Comercio e Industria:
Calle Isabel la Católica2, E50009
Zaragoza; ☎976552298; fax
976357945.
Consejo Superior de Cámaras de Comercio,
Industria y Navegación de España: C/
Claudio Coello 19, E28001 Madrid;
☎915752306/7; fax 914352392.

The Application Procedure

Speculative letters of application to Spanish companies can be made, using as a source the *Directory of Employers* list which follows. The *Directory of Jobs and Careers Abroad* (Vacation Work) also has a useful list of British companies with Spanish connections and subsidiaries. If you feel that the letter should be sent in Spanish, then a Spanish-speaking friend can help. Or the *Institute of Translation and Interpreting* (Exchange House, 494 Midsummer Booulevard, Central Milton Keynes, MK9 2EA; ☎01908 255905; www.iti.org.uk) can put people in touch with freelance translators who will provide a fluent translation, for a fee. Letters of application will be expected, much as in the UK, to be formal, clear and polite with little creative or personal content. The letter, whether speculative or direct, should always be sent with a CV.

Services which assist in the preparation and presentation of CV's can be found under the heading *CV* or *Secretarial Services* in your local *Yellow Pages* or in employment and expatriate publications like *Overseas Jobs Express* and *Nexus Expatriate Magazine*. After the CV has been compiled (and usually translated), any abbreviations etc. which may confuse a foreign reader should also be looked at; there should be a clear presentation of your qualifications and what these actually mean. Generally it is better to provide a CV that is too short rather than too long! This might prompt further enquiries from an interested employer. Don't send any original certificates or documents with an enquiry or application, of course, as these stand little chance of being returned.

And another word of warning: Spanish companies are notoriously bad at answering letters or faxes; and copious amounts of persistence and patience will have to accompany each speculative application. See the chapter *The Creative Job Search* in the *Directory of Jobs and Careers Abroad* published by Vacation Work for more about this aspect of your jobseeking.

If you are offered an interview, remember that first impressions and appearances count. Whatever the number of interviewers, the meeting is still likely to be a formal one in Spain; you will find that a casual approach to interviews is an Americanism which has yet to find a vogue with most Spanish employers. Obviously, an interview in Spain can also be a test of language ability as much as job ability. This applies in the case of more basic jobs, as well as to more high-flying executive positions, and will sometimes be the major challenge. Remember that handshaking is popular in Spain; and that it is polite to shake hands both on arrival and departure.

As with any job in any country, it is important to find out as much background information as possible about the company and the position for which you have applied, in advance of the interview. An interest in the company and its activities (based on knowledge and hard facts) is more likely to impress your potential employer than your general enthusiasm; and it wouldn't hurt to give a good shot at your best Hispanophile impression either.

A general estimate is that even today 70% of Spanish business people don't speak English; this figure is much higher throughout the general population. Adverts for English language courses abound in Spanish newspapers, as older people try to catch up. In the past, it was French which was taught as the main second language. The amount of English spoken, however, will vary enormously depending on your location. For instance, virtually no English is spoken (even in the world of business) in the Bilbao region, only some in Madrid, substantially more in Barcelona, and an awful lot in tourist-saturated Málaga or the islands. The level of English ability will also vary with the different professions: for example, much more English is spoken as the norm in chemical and engineering or computer industries, where it is part of the job, and a lot of the textbooks and information required are only available in English. This 'globalisation' of the language is a worldwide trend.

Young people generally are more proficient than their parents, as in many other countries. These demographic and professional variations are something which the less linguistically talented jobseeker may do well to consider when considering what job they are most suited to in Spain.

The *Directory of Jobs and Careers Abroad* (£12.95) available from good general bookshops is an invaluable source for anyone who feels that they need a hands-on guide on how to research the job market, or what career direction to take, with advice on CV's and the best ways to go about your job search, with sections on *Specific Careers* and *Worldwide Employment*, and including a chapter on Spain.

TEMPORARY WORK

TEACHING ENGLISH

The unprecedented economic growth experienced by Spain during the 1990s prodded businesses of all descriptions into a frenzy of English language learning. But the emphasis has shifted to adapt to changing conditions in the market. The majority of language academies are now involved with the teaching of children starting with the pre-school age group. There is a national push to introduce English early; it is compulsory in state schools from the age of nine, and the Spanish Ministry of Education in conjunction with the British Council has been recruiting experienced EFL teachers to work in nearly 50 participating primary schools. This trend has filtered through to private language providers, some of whom organise summer language camps for adolescents.

Despite a decline in the adult market, there are still thousands of foreigners teaching English in language institutes from the Basque north (where there is a surprisingly strong concentration) to the Balearic and Canary Islands. The entries for language schools occupy about 18 pages of the Madrid Yellow Pages and 585 listings in the online Yellow Pages. Almost every back street in every Spanish town has an *Academia de Ingles*. Technically *academias* are privately run and largely unregulated and *institutos* teach children aged 16 to 18.

All schools prefer their teachers to have European Union nationality (and most will not consider applicants without it) and to have a university degree, Cambridge Certificate (or equivalent) and knowledge of Spanish. Although some may be prepared to consider less, especially from candidates with some business experience or experience teaching children, the ever-increasing number of qualified applicants means that the occasions when schools need to do so are diminishing. The days are gone when any native speaker of English without a TEFL background could reasonably expect to be hired by a language academy. Many schools in the major cities echo the discouraging comments made by the director of a well-established school in Barcelona who said that he has found that there is a large supply of well-qualified native English speakers on hand so that his school cannot possibly reply to all the CVs from abroad that they receive as well.

Other schools report that the number of applications from candidates with a TEFL Certificate has soared simply because so many more centres in the UK and worldwide are offering the training courses. Opportunities for untrained graduates have all but disappeared in what can be loosely described as 'respectable' schools, though there are still plenty of more opportunistic language academy directors who might be prepared to hire someone without qualifications, particularly part-time. A great many schools fall into this category. To take a random example, the expatriate director of a well-established school in Alicante estimated that of the 20 or so schools in town, only four operate within the law (i.e. keep their books in order, pay social security contributions for their staff, etc.)

Many Britons and Irish people with or without TEFL qualifications set off for Spain to look for work on spec, preferably in early September. A high percentage of schools, especially those which have been termed 'storefront' schools, depend on word-of-mouth and local walk-ins for their staff requirements. Anyone with some experience and/or a qualification should find it fairly easy to land a job this way. With a knowledge of Spanish, you can usually fill one of the many vacancies for teachers of children (with whom the total immersion method is not always suitable). Some of the big chains like Wall Street Institutes and Opening Schools (see Useful Addresses below) are a good bet for the novice teacher on account of the stability of hours they can offer. The usual process is to put together a timetable from various sources and be reconciled to the fact that some or all of your employers in your first year will exploit you to some degree. Those who stay on for a second or further years can become more choosy.

Candidates who know that they want to teach in Spain should consider doing their TEFL training with an organisation with strong Spanish links such as *Windsor Schools* or *Oxford House College*. Better still, do a TEFL training course in Spain. An independent training organisation whose courses are patronised mainly by Americans is the International Career Center (ICC) in Barcelona; in the US ring 8882562519 or look at www.teflbarcelona.com for details of their monthly courses which come with ongoing job assistance and advice on obtaining work visas.

For a listing of English language schools in Spain, a good place to start is the Education Department of the Spanish Embassy (20 Peel St, London W8 7PD; ☎020-7243 8535/020-7727 2462; asesores@dial.pipex.com/ www.cecspain.org.uk). As well as sending an outline of Spanish immigration regulations and a one-page handout 'Teaching English as a Foreign Language', it can send a list of the 350 members of FECEI, the national federation of English language schools *(Federación Española de Centros de Enseñanza de Idiomas)*, though they may not always have the most uptodate list available. FECEI is concerned with maintaining high standards, so its members are committed to providing a high quality of teaching and fair working conditions for teachers. In order to become a member, a school has to undergo a thorough inspection. Therefore FECEI schools represent the elite end of the market and are normally looking for well qualified teachers. FECEI comprises 16 regional associations integrated in ACADE (Asociación de Centros Autónomos de Enseñanza Privada, Calle Ferraz 85, 28008 Madrid; ☎915500102; fax91 5500122; www.acade.es).

Check the TEFL advertisements in the Education section of the *Guardian* every Tuesday, especially in the spring and early summer. *EL Prospects* is the employment supplement which comes free with the monthly publication *EL Gazette* (Dilke House, 1 Malet St, Bloomsbury, London WC1E 7JN; ☎020-7255 1969). A separate subscription costs £9.95 for six issues within Europe. Searching for *Escuela Idiomas* on www.paginasamarillas.es (Spanish Yellow Pages) will produce lists of schools in the places you search, some with email and internet addresses. Most of the regional British Council offices in Spain maintain lists of language schools in their region apart from Madrid which does not keep a register of schools. The offices in Valencia, Bilbao, Barcelona and Palma de Mallorca also produce useful lists.

British or Irish nationals with a TEFL qualification or PGCE might want to make use of a recruitment agency, whether a general one or one which specialises in Spain such as English Educational Services (Alcalá 202°, 28014 Madrid; ☎91532 9734/531 4783/fax 91531 5298; movingparts@excite.com). The owner recommends that candidates with just a degree and CELTA come to Spain in early September and contact his agency on arrival. He works in conjunction with schools all over Spain.

Most teaching jobs in Spain are found on the spot. With increasing competition from candidates with the Cambridge or Trinity Certificate (now considered by many language school owners a minimum requirement), it is more and more difficult for the underqualified to succeed. The best time to look is between the end of the summer holidays and the start of term, normally October 1st. November is also promising, since that is when teachers hand in their notice for a Christmas departure. Since a considerable number of teachers do not return to their jobs after the Christmas break and schools are often left in the lurch, early January is also possible.

The beginning of summer is the worst time to travel out to Spain to look for work since schools will be closed and their owners unobtainable. There are some language teaching jobs in the summer at residential English camps for children and teenagers, but these are usually more for young people looking for a working holiday as camp monitors than for EFL teachers.

Although the majority of jobseekers head for Madrid or Barcelona, other towns may answer your requirements better. Language academies can be found all along the north coast and a door-to-door job hunt in September might pay off. This is the time when tourists are departing so accommodation may be available at a reasonable rent on a nine-month lease.

Private tutoring pays better than contract teaching because there is no middle man. But it is difficult to get started without a network of contacts and a good knowledge of the language; and when you do get started it is difficult to earn a stable income due to the frequency with which pupils cancel. The problem is particularly acute in May when school pupils concentrate on preparing for exams and other activities fall by the wayside. Finding private pupils is a marketing exercise and you will have to explore all the avenues which seem appropriate to your circumstances. Obviously you can advertise on notice boards at universities, public libraries, corner shops and wherever you think there is a market. A neat notice in Spanish along the lines of *'Profesora Nativa da clases particulares a domicilió'* might elicit a favourable response. Compile a list of addresses of professionals (e.g. lawyers, architects, air traffic controllers, etc.) as they may need English for their work and have the wherewithal to pay for it.

Salaries are not high in Spain and have not increased significantly over the past decade. A further problem for teachers in Madrid and Barcelona is that there is not much difference between salaries in the big cities where the cost of living has escalated enormously and salaries in the small towns. The standard negotiated contract is about €800 per month for a 21-hour week fulltime teacher, though gross salaries tend to fluctuate between €750 and €900 depending on number of hours worked. Rates are usually higher in Madrid and Barcelona. The best paid hourly wage is paid to teachers who are sent out to firms or those teaching short courses which are funded by the European Union.

Useful Addresses

TEFL Recruitment Organisations in Spain:

Berlitz Language Centre: Gran Via 80, 4°, E28013 Madrid; ☎915416103.

inlingua: Calle Arenal 24, 28013 Madrid; ☎915413246/7; fax 915428296. 40 centres in Spain.

Open English International Group: Rambla Catalunya 38, 08007 Barcelona; ☎934883601. 42 branches in Spain.

Opening School Spain: Central Offices, via Augusta 238, 08021 Barcelona; ☎932418900; fax 932418910; cwesterman@openingschool.com. Employs 450 teachers at its schools in Spain.

Wall Street Institutes: Rambla de Catalunya 24, 08007 Barcelona; ☎934120014/4125736/fax 934123803; www.wsi.es. 140 academies in Spain.

Training Centres:

British Language Centre: Calle Bravo Murillo 3772°, 28020 Madrid; ☎917330739; fax 913145009. CELTA centre.

Campbell College: Teacher Training Centre, Calle Pascual y Genis, 144a, 46002 Valencia; tel/fax 963524217; campbell@cpsl.com. CELTA centre.

CLIC International House Seville: Teacher Training Department, Méndez Núñez 7, 41001 Seville; ☎954500316; fax 954500836; www.clic.es. CELTA courses year round.

International House Barcelona, Calle Trafalgar 14, 08010 Barcelona; ☎932684511; fax 932680239; www.ihes.com/bcn. Regularly offers CELTA courses.

International House Madrid: C/ Zurbano 8, 28010 Madrid; ☎913101314; fax 913085321; www.ihmadrid.es. Fulltime and part-time CELTA courses.

Next Training: Rocafort 241243, 6°5a, E08029 Barcelona; ☎933220200; fax 933223495; www.teflteaching.com. Trinity TESOL centre. If qualified and looking for a job, you might be able to teach for Next (www.nexttraining.es). *Oxford House College,* Training centre offering the Trinity College TESOL Certificate at its partner school in Barcelona: Avinguda Diagonal 402, 08037 Barcelona (☎934580111). *Windsor Schools* info@windsorschools.co.uk.

TEFL Recruitment Organisations in the UK:
International House: Recruitment Services, 106 Piccadilly, London W1J 7NL; ☎020-7518 6970; fax 020-7518 6971; worldrecruit@ihlondon.co.uk; www.ihworld.com/recruitment. *inlingua Teacher Training and Recruitment:* Rodney Lodge, Rodney Road,

Cheltenham GL50 1HX; ☎01242-253171; recruitment@inlinguachelte nham.co.uk.
Berlitz (UK) Ltd: 913 Grosvenor Street, London W1A 3BZ; ☎020-7915 0909; fax 020-7915 0222; www.berlitz.com. Does not recruit directly, but website lists school addresses in Spain (several in Madrid, Barcelona, Seville, Valencia and Palma de Mallorca).

For many more addresses of recruitment organisations, training centres and individual language institutes in Spain, consult the most recent edition of *Teaching English Abroad* by Susan Griffith (VacationWork Publications, £12.95).

AU PAIR WORK

Spain's demand for au pairs and mother's helps is booming. The number of agencies inside Spain and of UK and European agencies which have added Spain to their list of destination countries has increased significantly over the past few years. Many Spanish families want more than an au pair; they want a young English speaker to interact with their children on a daily basis. The emphasis on conversational English means that a certain number of families are happy to consider young men for live-in positions.

Hours tend to be on average longer than in other countries. Some au pairs report that they have ended up working the same hours as a mother's help but for au pair pocket money (which is normally paid on a monthly basis in Spain). The minimum pay at present is €54 per week, though agencies urge families who live in suburbs some distance from the city centre to pay €60. No perks are built into the arrangement, so au pairs can't count on getting any paid holidays, subsidised fares or a contribution towards their tuition fees except at the discretion of their employers.

One of the biggest au pair and student exchange agencies with partner agencies around the world is *Club de Relaciones Culturales Internacionales,* a member of the International Au Pair Association (www.iapa.org). Although more a cultural exchange organisation than an au pair agency, *Castrum* makes family placements in Castille and Leon. The arrangement involves participants spending three or four hours a day teaching English to members of the family and enrolling in a Spanish course for at least five hours a week. The placement fee is €160.

Useful Addresses

Au Pair Agencies in Spain:

ABB Au Pair Family Service: Via Alemania 2, 5°A, 07003 Palma de Mallorca; ☎971752027; fax 971298001; abbaupair@ono.com.

Castrum: Ctra. Ruedas 33, 47008 Valladolid; ☎983222213; www.terra.es/personal2/castrumspain.

Centros Europeos Galve: Calle Principe 126°A, 28012 Madrid; ☎915327230; ccprincipe@inicia.es. Mainly places au pairs in the Madrid, Valencia and Alicante areas.

Club de Relaciones Culturales Internacionales (RCI): Calle Ferraz 82, 28008 Madrid; ☎915417103; fax 915591181; www.clubrci.es.

Compos Lingua: Urbanización San Sadurnino c/ A43, 15886 Teo, A Coruna, Galicia; ☎981801761; comp osli@composlingua.com. €300 fee for a stay of 312 months, €210 for shorter stays.

GIC: Pintor Sorolla 29, 46901 Monte VedatValencia; tel/fax 961565837; gic@eresmas.net. Founding member of the International Au Pair Association.

Helping Hands Agency Marbella: Edf. Fuengirola Centro 2/8, Avda. Matias Saenz de Tejada s/n, 29640 Fuengirola; ☎95266 6515/fax 95266 4003; info@helpinghands123.com/ www.helpinghands123.com. English-speaking au pairs placed on the Costa del Sol, mainly with expat families.

Kingsbrook Au Pairs: Kingsbrook Idiomas Barcelona, Travessera de Gràcia 60 1° 3a, 08006 Barcelona; ☎93209 3763; kingsb@teleline.es/ www.kingsbrookbcn.com. Registration fee of US$100 for Europeans, Americans and Canadians.

S&C Asociados, Avda. Eduardo Dato 46, 2°B, 41005 Seville; tel/fax 954642447; idiomas@supercable.es. Families mainly in Andalusia and sometimes Madrid, Barcelona and East Coast of Spain.

Au Pair Agencies in the UK:

Note that UK agencies are at present permitted to charge successfully placed au pairs £40 plus VAT, though this fee may be abolished in 2002/3.

Angels International Au Pair Agency: 31 Bushfield Crescent, Edgware, Middlesex HA8 8XQ; ☎020-8958 7002; admin@angelsint.demon.co.uk. Member of the Spanish-based International Organisation for Quality in Au Pair Services (IOQAPS).

Au Pair Connections: 39 Tamarisk Road, Hedge End, Southampton, Hampshire SO30 4TN; ☎01489780438; w ww.aupairconnections.co.uk. Agency started as Spanish Connections.

Home Concern: 105 Leighton Gardens, London NW10 3PS; tel/fax 020-8968 6871; gjc@onetel.net.uk. Au pairs sent to all regions of Spain.

SECRETARIAL WORK

Opportunities are both widely available and lucrative for bilingual secretaries in Spain. For anyone thinking of doing this kind of work it is often worth trying the Spanish Tourist Authority (Torre de Madrid, 6/7 Plaza de España, E28008 Madrid) which employs a multitude of linguistically-able secretaries. Additionally a few London agencies place bi-lingual secretaries abroad such as Merrow Employment Agency (23 Bentick St, London W1U 2EZ; ☎020-79355050) and Appointments BiLanguage (☎020-73551975). Many of the Spanish recruitment agencies listed above also recruit secretarial and office staff and may be contacted.

TOURISM

Large British tour operators like *Thomson Holidays* and *First Choice* employ hundreds of representatives to work abroad as managers, sports instructors, chefs, bar and chamber staff, etc. each summer. Although it is sometimes easier to arrange a job with an organisation such as Thomson or Mark Warner if you have a proven commitment to a career in tourism, this is not essential. Although you won't make a fortune (and will have to work hard), and although you may see decidedly little of real Spanish culture and life while working very long hours, these kinds of openings provide some potential for getting a job later on in tourism or related areas; and if for nothing else, then for a long, hot and enjoyable Spanish summer.

It is always worth checking the English language press (for instance *SUR in English* mentioned above). Ideally, you should arrange to visit the resorts you are considering, in advance of the tourist season which usually begins about Easter, and ask at all hotels, restaurants and tourist shops. If you are heading for the Canary Islands, the high season for British package tourists is November to March. Bear in mind that while working in these environments you will barely get a glimpse of genuine Spanish culture. Tradespeople, mechanics, handymen and gardeners can often find work inside the expatriate community in any resort.

Year-round resorts like Tenerife, Gran Canaria, Lanzarote and Ibiza afford a range of casual work as bar staff, DJs, beach party ticket sellers, timeshare sales people, etc. The website www.gapwork.com has information about working in Ibiza and provides the web addresses for some of the clubs which may be hiring such as www.manumission.com and www.slinky.co.uk. About 6,000 Britons try to find work on Ibiza each year so it is important to offer a relevant skill.

British tour companies such as *Canvas Holidays, Eurocamp, Keycamp Holidays, Haven Europe* and *Solaire Holidays* need Spanish-speaking couriers and children's staff to work at mobile home and tent parks from early May to the end of September. *Open Holidays* specialises in Balearic resorts in Menorca and Majorca.

Many specialist tour operators in the UK like *Acorn Venture* and *Pavilion Tours* need seasonal staff for their watersports and activity centres. Qualified windsurfing and sailing, kayak and climbing instructors are in demand for the season April/May to September.

Useful Addresses

Acorn Adventure: 22 Worcester St, Stourbridge, West Midlands DY8 1AN; ☎01384-446057; topstaff@acornadventures.co.uk. Staff needed for a watersports and multi activity centre near the resort of Tossa de Mar on the Costa Brava.

Airtours Holidays Ltd: Holiday House, Sandbrook Park, Sandbrook Way, Rochdale, Lancs. OL11 5SA; ☎08702-412642.

Canvas Holidays: East Port House, 12 East Port, Dunfermline, Fife KY12 7JG; ☎01383-629018; www.canvasholidays.com.

Club Cantabrica Holidays Ltd: 146148 London Road, St Albans, Herts. AL1 1PQ; ☎01727-833141; www.cantabrica.co.uk.

Eurocamp: Overseas Recruitment Department, ☎01606-787522.

First Choice Holidays: London Road, Crawley, W Sussex RH10 2GX; ☎01293-588528.

Haven Europe: 1 Park Lane, Hemel Hempstead, Herts.

HP2   4YL;   ☎0144-2203287;
www.haveneurope.com.
Keycamp Holidays: Overseas Recruitment Department, Hartford Manor, Greenbank Lane, Northwich, CV8 1HW; ☎01606-787522.
Open Holidays: Guildbourne Centre, Worthing, W. Sussex BN11 1LZ; ☎01903-201864; www.openholidays.co.uk.
Pavilion Tours: Lynnem House, 1 Victoria Way, Burgess Hill, W Sussex

RH15   9NF;   ☎08702-410425;
www.paviliontours.co.uk.
Solaire Holidays: 1158 Stratford Road, Hall Green, Birmingham B28 8AF; 0121-778 5061; www.solaire.co.uk.
Thomson Holidays: Human Resources Overseas, Greater London House, Hampstead Road, London NW1 7SD; ☎020-73879321; www.thomsonholidays.com/jobs.

AGRICULTURE

Reports of people finding harvesting work in Spain are very uncommon mainly because of the huge pool of immigrant labour from North Africa and of landless Spanish workers. Occasional opportunities do present themselves on organic farms especially those owned by back-to-the-land expats looking for congenial company as well as hard workers. These arrangements are normally taken on a work-for-keep basis.

Tomatoes and many other crops are grown on Tenerife. The Canaries are normally valued by working travellers only for their potential in the tourist industry, but there is a thriving agricultural life outside the resorts. Just a bus ride away from Los Cristianos, the farms around Granadilla, Buzanada, San Isidro and San Lorenzo may take on extra help between September and June. Most harvest workers camp and work on three-month contracts.

The organic farming movement *(Coordinadora d'Agricultura Ecològica)* in Spain has ceased its involvement in helping prospective volunteers. A list of farms which accept people to work in exchange for board and lodging (at present there are 18 addresses on it) can be obtained by email only from AEAM (Amics de l'Escola Agrària de Manresa): aeam@agrariamanresa.org. They stress that member farmers want to hear only from people whose main interest is organic farming, not learning Spanish.

The Sunseed Trust, an arid land recovery trust, has a remote research centre in southeast Spain where new ways are explored of reclaiming deserts. The centre is run by both full-time volunteers (minimum five weeks) and working visitors (minimum one week) who spend half the day working. Weekly charges vary from £45 to £96. Typical work for volunteers might involve germination procedures, forestry trials, hydroponic growing, organic gardening, designing and building solar ovens and stills, and building and maintenance. Living conditions are basic and the cooking is vegetarian. Occasionally workers with a relevant qualification in appropriate technology, etc. are needed who are paid a small stipend. The address of the centre is Apdo. 9, 04270 Sorbas, Almeria (tel/fax 950552770; www.sunseed.org.uk) or send £1 or 3 IRCs to PO Box 2000, Cambridge CB4 3UJ.

VOLUNTARY WORK

International workcamp organisations recruit for environmental and other projects in Spain for programmes as various as carrying out an archaeological dig of a Roman settlement in Tarragona to traditional stone quarrying in Menorca. The co-ordinating workcamp organisation in Spain is the Instituto de la Juventud (José Ortega y Gasset 71, 28006 Madrid; fax 913093066) which oversees 150 camps every year. You can approach them independently as well as through a partner organisation in your own country (see below). Note that many camps are restricted to volunteers aged 18-26 with a few accepting volunteers up to the age of 30.

Proyecto Ambiental Tenerife runs hands-on whale and dolphin conservation projects in Tenerife which accept about 150 volunteers from the UK who join the project for 26 weeks from a number of start dates between June and October. A contribution of £95 a week must be made towards expenses. For details send a 31p s.a.e. to Proyecto at 59 St Martins Lane, Covent Garden, London WC2 (www.interbook.net/personal/delfinc). The project's Tenerife office is at Calle Jose Antonio 13, Arafo, Tenerife (tel/fax 922510535).

Useful Addresses

International Voluntary Service (IVS Field Office): Old Hall, East Bergholt, Colchester, Essex CO7 6TQ (01206 298215/fax 01206 299043; ivsgbn@ivsgbn.demon.co.uk/ www.ivsgbn.demon.co.uk). The cost of registration on workcamps outside the UK is £120 (£95 for students and low-waged) which includes £25 membership in IVS.

Concordia Youth Service Volunteers Ltd: Heversham House, 2022 Boundary Road, Hove, East Sussex BN3 4ET (tel/fax 01273 422218; info@concor diaiye.org.uk/ www.concordiaiye.org .uk). Programme of workcamps costs £3. Registration costs £85.

Quaker Voluntary Action: Friends Meeting House, 6 Mount St, Manchester M2 5NS (0161819 1634; qva@quake rvolaction.freeserve.co.uk). Registration fee of £80 (£60 students/low-waged; £45 un-waged).

UNA Exchange: United Nations Association, Temple of Peace, Cathays Park, Cardiff CF10 3AP (0292022 3088; unaiys@btinternet.com).

Youth Action for Peace/YAP: 8 Golden Ridge, Freshwater, Isle of Wight PO40 9LE; 01983 752577/fax 01983 756900; www.yapuk.org). Registration fee £50 plus £25 for some camps.

ASPECTS OF EMPLOYMENT

Salaries

In unfortunate contrast with the always escalating cost of living, wages have tended to remain static over the last few years. However, it is fair to say that although Spain does not presently offer instant riches, it does have one of the most rapidly developing economies in Europe; and as the struggle to keep inflation down and to develop Spanish industry eventually succeeds, opportunities for industrial growth and financial success will be even greater.

There is a minimum wage for young people; the minimum rate for each professional category is usually negotiated in collective labour agreements, and will thus vary from industry to industry. One difference from the British system is the practice of employers distributing two extra payrolls each year: one at Christmas and another at the date stipulated in the collective labour agreement (generally before the summer). These bonuses are known as *pagas extraordinarias* and, unsurprisingly, comprise one of the greatest perks for UK nationals planning to work abroad.

Working Conditions

Spanish labour legislation is codified in the *Estatuto de los Trabajadores* (Workers' Statute), which has been in force since 1980. This covers most basic aspects of conditions of work, employee representation in companies, strikes etc. Pay and conditions of work are normally governed by collective agreements, negotiated either nationally or regionally in each sector.

The standard working week in Spain is 40 hours. Overtime cannot be forced, cannot exceed 80 hours per year and must, by law, be paid at a rate of not less than 175% of the normal hourly rate. According to Spanish law, workers are not entitled to paid holiday until they have been working for 12 months (hence the popularity in some lines of work, such as English teaching, of nine-month contracts). An annual paid holiday of thirty calendar days is then obligatory and this does not include the fourteen national public holidays which are celebrated each year, and one or two regional holidays as well. Paid absences are mandatory in certain circumstances such as marriage (15 days) and maternity or paternity leave.

The traditional long lunch-time siesta break is now being replaced by a shorter, one-hour lunch break in the larger companies and businesses of Spain. However, in line with the shorter lunch hour the working day is finishing earlier and instead of the traditional 9am-2pm and then 4.30pm-8.30pm day (still maintained, particularly in the summer, by smaller businesses) most Spaniards now work what is a comparatively relaxed 9am-6pm day with one hour for lunch.

Trade Unions

Out of a total population of just under 40 million people, there are approximately 15 million registered workers in Spain, of whom only two million belong to trade unions (*sindicatos*). The two major unions are the Socialist Union, the UGT (*Unión General de Trabajadores*) and the communist-leaning CCOO (*Comisiones Obreras*). Of less importance are the USO (*Unión Sindical Obrera*) and other markedly nationalist unions such as the Basque nationalist union, ELASTV.

Unlike some European workers' councils, the local union is not considered a joint management-employee structure; and neither unions nor employees as a rule have a direct voice in management decisions. The idea of co-determination which is found in Germany, does not really exist in Spain. Instead, unions are concerned with negotiations for base salary and standard salary rates (the latter is invariably higher than the state legal minimum salary) and for salary payments (most agreements require 14 monthly payments but some can demand up to 16 payments during the year, with the base salary split accordingly). Unions also deal with social aspects of work, technical training and fringe and retirement benefits, etc. Despite the low overall union membership in Spain, the two main trades union confederations play a key role in these industrial negotiations. Generally, industrial relations are relatively stable with few unauthorised strikes.

Agreements with Unions. Agreements made with unions are legally binding as the minimum working conditions for the organisation in question. No employee is obliged to join a union, but all business entities with fifty or more employees are required to have some kind of workforce representation.

Social Security Deductions. Although employers are not legally required to provide any pension scheme for their employees, they do have to pay high rates of social security (up to 28% of the gross wage). There are no requirements for an employer to provide fringe benefits; and these are generally of limited importance. Many retirement benefit schemes are designed largely to induce personnel to retire on a specified date (usually 65) although there is no law which determines a retirement age for men and women as in the some countries.

Training Schemes. Almost all employers in industry do provide training schemes for their employees. Training contracts for employees are subsidised by government funds and grant a reduction in the employer's social security contributions. Also significant is the government's promotion of industrial training through technical colleges, coordinated education and training programmes, and arrangements with various business enterprises.

Breaches of Contract. If the terms of a contract are being breached and the employer does not respond to reasonable representations from you, recourse can be taken to a *denuncio*, which involves informing the authorities (either in person or via a union, such as the Comisiones Obreros) that your employer is not complying with tax and social security rules or fire regulations or whatever. The *denuncio* can effectively close a small business if it is taken seriously (and if the employer does not have the proverbial friends in high places). In fact the procedure is complicated and time consuming but the mere mention of it might improve working conditions.

Women in Work

Around 40% of Spanish women under 40 work. This phenomenon has been developing over recent years and is partly a result of the increasing and high percentage of female university graduates. Female lawyers and doctors are particularly in evidence; and despite the traditional image of the macho and chauvinistic Spanish male there generally tends to be less sexism in the professions there than in other Latin countries. Having said this, the great majority of Spanish working women still occupy the less senior and less powerful levels of their professions; and a kind of self-deprecatory attitude is still in evidence in day-to-day office life as female professionals often introduce themselves in a business context by their Christian names, while Spanish business men would never dream of encouraging the same kind of liberty.

A working female is entitled to 16 weeks leave for childbearing; and the Spanish social security system will pay a large portion of her salary during this time; a new father gets two days off work and the mother can choose to transfer up to two weeks of her maternity leave to her partner. Women are protected from discrimination by the Workers' Statute of 1980 which prohibits discrimination on the grounds of sex, marital status, age, race, social status, religious belief, political opinion or trade union membership. Discrimination in the case of physical or mental disability is also illegal, so long as the work being performed will not be negatively affected by the disability. Legislation has also been introduced which further protects pregnant womens' rights at work.

BUSINESS AND INDUSTRY REPORT

After joining the European Union in 1986, the Spanish economy underwent a period or rapid growth. In the late 1980's the annual growth rate of 5% was the highest in Europe; a slump followed. In 1993 economic activity actually fell by 1.2%; but Spain has bounced back and is now experiencing low inflation (under 3%) and has reduced is public sector deficit to the target required by European monetary union. Interest rates have also fallen to a new low similar to those of the United Kingdom and the USA.

Under the Aznar government, privatisation has been the watchword. Although Spain has developed greatly in economic terms over the last decade there is still much ground to be covered before it is able to raise its competitiveness to the level of other EU economies. Inefficiencies due to structural fragmentation and a shortage of the latest technologies and machinery in the agriculture, textiles, food and leather sectors mean that radical restructuring is essential if these industries are to realistically compete with their EU rivals when the single currency finally arrives. Technological development in sectors such as electronics, data processing, aerospace and motor vehicles is also essential in order to achieve the same end.

The government plans to achieve this updating of the various industrial and high-tech sectors by the fiscal methods currently favoured in other industrial countries. Spanish industry has also been busy importing and researching modern technologies from abroad. So, anyone with mechanical, electrical or telecommunications engineering expertise may well find themselves in the right place for this kind of 'high-flying' job. There is radical change ahead in the power supply industry, for example, with plans for deregulation now under way in the electricity sector. Power generation and distribution are being liberalised. The national telecommunications company Telefónica is now wholly privatised; and the government has sold its share of the Repsol oil, gas and chemicals group, attracting attention from international investors. This is making it easier for these companies to work with partners abroad (one of whom, in the case of Telefónica, is BT). The internationalisation of these companies will also bring more foreign workers from the UK and elsewhere to Spain. The growth in information technology and the hightech sectors should provide opportunities for many other suitably qualified professionals.

There is a move towards liberalisation and the breaking up of the public sector monoliths left over from Franco's time; but also a powerful tendency towards the concentration of business activity; and away from the many small or medium-sized businesses which have traditionally been a feature of Spanish life. Mergers and acquisitions are frequent; and this has caused some disruption in traditional ways of working, and largescale redundancies in some areas.

For the job seeker, the principal growth areas in the Spanish economy are presently tourism, insurance, property, electronics and financial institutions. From an employer's point of view, the tendency is for the Spanish work force to be better trained. Nowadays, qualified workers tend to be highly motivated and disciplined. And the Spanish trade union movement has also achieved an impressive degree of protection for employees (which it is currently renegotiating with the government). On their part, the unions oppose what they see as the growth of a twotier employment market. Both sides are agreed that a situation where 35% of the workforce is employed on a temporary basis and only fulltime workers have job protection is unsatisfactory.

Some expatriates will have been posted to Spain by their company, which is collaborating with a Spanish partner or subsidiary. Management consultancy skills will be relevant here. For those seeking work, and the more entrepreneurial, gaps in the market exist for those with handson experience in the relevant sector in their own country (examples being the sale of agricultural machinery, or franchising – which is only now coming into its own in Spain). Many of the multinational companies which dominate Spanish industry also provide good potential for UK job hunters. These are to be found predominantly in the motor vehicles, chemicals and pharmaceuticals, industrial design, distribution and food industries. Traditional heavy industries (along with agriculture and fishing) are declining. Where possible, the largest companies in each industry – and many with UK connections – have been listed under the appropriate heading in the business and industry report below.

Although it will take perseverance to find a job – and indeed for businesspeople hoping to establish a presence in the Spanish market – those who wait may well miss the boat. The Spanish economic and business scene is changing rapidly. The time to act is now.

REGIONAL GUIDE TO INDUSTRY

The following list gives the principal cities in Spain with some of the main industries in that area. This may be used as a general guide when considering the business and industry report below.

Madrid (Madrid): pharmaceuticals, banking, transportation, chemicals, hightech industry, light engineering, computing, telecommunications.

Alicante (Valencia): shoes, carpets, agricultural exports.

Barcelona (Catalonia): automotive, electrical, chemicals, plastics, paints, fertilizers, textiles, pharmaceuticals, mechanical engineering and computing.

Bilbao (Asturias): shipbuilding, heavy engineering, steelworks, pulp and paper, glass works, oil refinery, automotive, construction.

Cartagena (Andalusia): petrochemicals and chemicals.

Huelva (Andalusia): shipbuilding, petrochemicals, nonferrous metals, agricultural.

Oviedo (Asturias): steel, heavy engineering, mining, light metal industries, power generation, coal.

San Sebastian (The Basque Country): foundries, machine tools, pulp and paper, electronics, chemicals.

Seville (Andalusia): shipbuilding, aerospace, nonferrous metals, mining, agricultural exports.

Valencia (Valencia): automotive, steel, furniture, ceramics, agriculture.

Vigo (Galacia): port, fishing/canning, food processing, ceramics, glass and automotive, plastics, rubber, pharmaceuticals.

Zaragoza (Aragon): automotive, mining, machinery, light engineering.

Please note that many addresses and phone numbers for the main companies operating in Spain are listed in the *Directory of Employers* in the following chapter. The *Spanish Chamber of Commerce in Great Britain* (5 Cavendish Square, London W1M 0DP; ☎020-7637 9061; fax 020-7436 7188)) has information on 500,000 companies in Spain and the UK and can offer details including directors' names, volume of sales, import/export etc. with a full Member List, Import/Export Companies list, Spanish Companies in the UK, Legal Services, Translation/Interpreting Services, Companies listed by Sector, and Main UK Investors in Spain. For details of these and other services (which are free only to members) please contact the Chamber at the above address.

Aerospace

Construcciones Aeronauticas SA has been the core of Spain's relatively small aircraft sector. CASA employs 8,000 workers and is Spain's only manufacturer of complete aircraft. Other major companies in the aerospace sector include, AISA (Aeronautica Industrial SA), EESA (Equipos Electronicos SA) and EISA (Experiences Industrioles SA).

Agriculture

Agriculture is one of the largest and most important of Spanish industries, employing ten percent of the national work force (if the other industries which service it – like food processing – are taken into account). This is compared to an average of 6% in the other EU countries. Spain is the largest exporter of agricultural products to the rest of the EU as well; and the world's largest producer of olive oil; the fourth largest of dried fruit; and the sixth largest producer of citrus fruit.

However, despite the importance of agriculture in terms of number of employees and value of exports, unfortunately, with the exception of the modern and efficient citrus fruit farms, Spanish farming methods are still lagging behind the rest of western Europe (with the exception of its neighbour Portugal) in terms of organisation, mechanical technology and efficiency. Recently it is true that EU investment and modernisation have made some difference to this; and farmers have been able to take advantage of EU trade protection where they are competing with producers from outside this area (citrus fruit production being one example). Cereals and vegetables are also important in the country's agricultural production.

There is still a severe shortage of agricultural and horticultural machinery, though, and that which is in use is often out of date. This is a definite gap in the market for anyone who wishes to import agricultural equipment of all kinds. The establishment of grain stores and seed conditioning centres are also officially encouraged and often funded by the EU.

The climatic difference between the temperate south and the wet north of Spain is reflected in the different land use; the north (especially Galicia) specialises in rearing cattle for beef and dairy farming while the south concentrates on fruit, wine, olives and cereal crops. Much of Spain's traditional small scale agriculture has declined (as mentioned above). Visitors to the tourist resorts will see a pattern of deserted fields and overgrown farms which is repeated all over Spain. Tourism is usually a more profitable activity, at least in the short term; but in some areas it has damaged farming.

Chemicals and Petrochemicals

Spain's chemical industry relies heavily on the capital and expertise of multinational companies. About half of the business is in the hands of multinationals, including Michelin, Pirelli, ICI, Unilever, RhônePoulenc and Shell; while the smaller firms face an uncertain future or have merged with larger ones. More optimistically, there is no shortage of raw materials for these industries; Spain possesses an abundance of pyrites, sodium and potassium salts, although coal deposits are generally low quality; almost all oil (the basis of petrochemicals) has to be imported. The principal production areas are the Basque country, Catalonia and the Madrid region, as well as Huelva, Cartagena and Puertollano.

The market leader in the petrochemicals industry is the formerly state-owned company, Pepsol, which produces 50% of the total national output of ethylene, propylene, butane and benzene and owns (or owned) a sprawling amalgam of petrochemical subsidiaries.

Defence

Spain boasts the position of the eleventh largest exporter and twenty-first largest importer of military equipment in the world. The defence industry consists of around thirty major companies which presently employ a total of approximately 80,000 people. However, the government has been making more of its defence purchases at home, providing a boost for the industry; and aims to make Spain 90% self sufficient for defence requirements. There are still problems; some of these firms are still state-owned and many run at a loss. Principal manufacturers include Construcciones Aeronauticas (CASA), Empresa Nacional Santa Barbara and Bazan. Other important companies include Explosivos Rio Tinto, ELBASA and Esperanza. Production items range from light weapons to armoured vehicles, tanks, missiles, fighter aircraft, navigation and electronic systems.

Electronics

The electronics industry is subdivided into three groups: consumer products, electronic components and professional components i.e. computer hardware, communications equipment, etc. The industry employs upwards of 70,000 people of which 1,800 are in research and development; and it is still largely located in the Madrid and Barcelona city regions. The electronics sector is dominated by foreign firms which are managed locally in wholly or partly owned subsidiaries. The Burroughs Group (UNISYS) produces peripheral units and terminals compatible with IBM equipment and occupies one fifth of the computer market, while Sanyo, BASF, Philips and Nixdorf are all also active in the Spanish electronics industry.

Although Spanish high-technology industries, of which electronics is one, are as yet severely under developed, they are being actively promoted by both the government and by the business sector and as such constitute a potential growth area.

Engineering

DBM *Engineering Management Services (Scotland) Ltd.* (7a South Gyle Broadway, South Gyle Industrial Estate, Edinburgh EH12 9EH) has contacted *Live and Work in Spain and Portugal* to say it has a sister company in Spain; and may be worth contacting for more information.

Fishery

Fish is a major feature of the Spanish national diet; and the country itself has one of the largest fishing fleets in the world with the largest world market for fish after Japan. This industry is very important to Spain, providing jobs for nearly 100,000 people directly and another 600,000 indirectly (almost as many jobs as in all the other EU countries put together, although these numbers are now declining). It is worrying then that Spain's own fishing grounds are nearly exhausted. The Spanish fishing fleet is also taking advantage of fisheries in international waters around the UK and Ireland, and further afield, and its often aggressive approach has led it into a number of disputes both within and outside the EU. The main fishing centre is the northern port of Vigo in Galicia. Along the northern Atlantic coast, the catches are chiefly hake, sardines, anchovy and shellfish, while sardine, tuna and striped tunny (*bonito*) are the principal catches along the Mediterranean coast.

Food and Beverages

The Spanish food industry supplies nearly 80% of domestic consumption. Recent years have been bad for the industry as prices escalated, demand fell and inflation rose higher than predicted. Most of the 40,000 or so companies in the industry are one-man businesses of which about 20,000 are bakeries and 5,000 wine-making concerns. Many of these smaller companies are disappearing as a result of Spain's full accession to the EU as fruit, vegetables and cereals (which were previously subject to import licences from the other European countries) have been freed from all restrictions. This has made it easier for the foreign market to fulfil the considerable potential which exists for importing selected UK and US-brand foods, especially cereal products and confectionary to Spain. Some of the major international companies presently in the Spanish food industry include Cadbury-Schweppes, Nestlé, Unilever and United Biscuits.

Spanish vineyards are the most extensive in the world, 60% larger than those of France, although output is roughly half that of its northern neighbour; the yield per hectare being comparatively low. Wine represents, on average, 5% of the value of total agricultural production, as compared to 10% in both France and Italy. The main wine-producing regions are la Mancha, Castille, Extremadura and Andalusia, although probably better known to the British palate are the wine and sherry-producing areas of Rioja, Jumilla, Jerez and Málaga. Beer is becoming ever more popular, with a consequent negative impact on the wine market.

Heineken and United Breweries have brought a much-needed injection of capital to Spanish breweries as well as much new technology and marketing techniques. However, breweries elsewhere in the EU still tend to be more competitive and to produce better beverages more cheaply, which means exports are small. Until recently, transport costs and Spanish tariff barriers had succeeded in alienating the foreign beverage market from Spain but now all the famous international brands are represented, with many being produced under licence in Spain. As health consciousness spreads worldwide, so does the popularity of mineral water; and this is definitely a lucrative market to enter. Currently, approximately 100 companies exploit 170 or so springs which have been discovered in Spain and two thirds of sales of mineral water are shared by only five local brand names.

Mining

The main mining areas of Spain are the north (Asturias) for hard coal and anthracite; and Catalonia, Aragon and Andalusia for lignite. The quality of Spanish coal is poor (low in calorific value) and production costs are relatively high so better quality coal is imported from Poland, Australia and the USA. However, Spain is expanding its home mining industry as the demand for coal has risen (growing by 47% between 1985 and 1991) and research and exploration operations have discovered new coal sources in Arenas de Rey, Padul, Mallorca and León. The industry is planning to improve the quality of its coal with new coalfired power stations and to encourage greater coal consumption by internal transport (Spain has a relatively low proportion of electrified railways). Nuclear energy (and oil imported from Algeria) also makes its contribution to Spain's energy sector. Despite the expansion of home production in coal, Spain will continue to import high quality coal and also to provide a good, on-going market for advanced mining machinery and equipment imported from abroad.

Motor Vehicles and Components

The Spanish motor industry, which employs 60,000 people directly and 300,000 indirectly, is almost entirely controlled by multi-national companies. Since the early 1970s Spain has been a major production and export base for such companies. The German-owned SEAT has works in Barcelona, Ford has its main base in Valencia while Renault are based in Seulte and Citroëns are manufactured in Orense and Vigo. The Japanese motor company, Nissan, has plants in Avila, Barcelona and Madrid and General Motors opened its own plant in Zaragoza.

The Spanish motor industry had traditionally been one of the most protected in Western Europe. Although all import duties have now been removed for other EU-manufactured vehicles, other imported foreign vehicles are still subject to a 35% tax on small cars and 60% on luxury cars. However, the minimum local content requirement for Spanish cars has been reduced to 55%, thus further improving the future prospects for imported vehicle components and parts.

Pharmaceuticals

As many as 300 firms (many of which are small concerns) employing roughly 35,000 people comprise the Spanish pharmaceuticals industry which is highly concentrated in the Madrid and Barcelona city regions. The pharmaceuticals industry, once prosperous, has slumped; and now only half the number of companies which existed 15 years ago remain. However, a lot of money is currently being spent and jobs are being created in research and development within the industry.

Foreign companies manufacturing in Spain include Beecham, Boots, Wellcome and Glaxo. Boots in particular has been very successful in Spain since it acquired a 50% share in Laboratorios Liade in 1979.

Retailing

Small, family-run shops still dominate the retailing scene – in numbers of outlets at least – in most areas of Spain. However, these small, privately-run family businesses are meeting increased competition from selfservice stores. Along with hyper and supermarkets, selfservice shops now command approximately 70% of all food sales in Spain. Additionally, fast food restaurants have become ever more popular since the first Wendy restaurant opened in Madrid in 1980. However, fast food services still being developed outside the major cities and tourist areas, providing an attractive opening for anyone with fastfood or franchising expertise who wants either to set up their own business or to run a franchise on behalf of one of the large US food companies outside some of the main Spanish city areas. Burger King, McDonalds, Wendy, Wimpy and Kentucky Fried Chicken all have local franchise agreements in Spain.

New boutiques catering for a more affluent, younger clientele and specialising in designer and brandname merchandise have begun to spring up around the major department stores; there is now a growing highfashion market in Barcelona and Madrid; and potential investors should note that the market for this kind of retail service is far from saturated. Another area of retailing to consider is the tourist retail trade which forms a substantial section of the industry's income. The needs of tourists, however, are not always adequately catered for away from the busy and commercial tourist areas. A shop in such an up-and-coming area for tourism containing all of those indispensable items which the British seem unable to live without, e.g. English-language newspapers, novels, videos, chocolate bars, etc. may turn out to be a very shrewd investment.

The two major department store chains in Spain are Galerias Preciadus which has 20 branches nationwide and El Corte Inglés which has 25. Although retailing slumped in the 1980's as domestic demand dropped with the rise of unemployment, the retail trade is now well on the road to recovery and provides a promising source of employment for appropriately qualified professionals.

Tourism

At the turn of the 21st century, the number of visitors to Spain continues to increase (and is currently about 12 million British visitors each year). Britain accounts for between a third and a quarter of all incoming tourism to the country. Spain occupies 9% of the international tourist market, the second most powerful position after France (11%). The Spanish tourist industry represents more than 10% of GDP and employs upwards of 700,000 people directly and another 500,000 indirectly – 11% of the total Spanish workforce.

Over the past decade, arrivals by sea and rail to Spain have declined while those by chartered aircraft and coach have risen. Chartered coach tourism in particular is very important for the hotel industry in the Costa Brava and the adjoining Costa Dorada. Group tourist travel has been continually growing and now represents nearly two thirds of the overall demand. While visitors of all nationalities flock to Spain over the summer months, in both the Canaries and the Balearic Islands, over 45% of holidaymakers are from two countries alone – the UK and Germany. The main areas visited by British tourists are: Catalonia (23%); the Balearic Islands (18.2%); Valencia (15.7%); and Andalusia (13.2%).

Surprisingly, unexplored potential in Spanish tourism does still exist, especially in the areas of winter sports, sailing, mineral spas, hunting and fishing. It may be worthwhile for anyone thinking of buying an existing hotel or club in Spain to contact the tourist ministry to investigate the possibility of drawing on loans given to enhance existing hotels and clubs with amenities such as swimming pools, golf courses or roads. But there is already a lot of competition from the 300 water sports installations, 136 golf courses, 128 spas, and more than 22 casinos. Success in future for travel agents, tour operators and others involved with this tourist infrastructure will involve identifying new, and probably niche markets, rather than trying to compete with existing concerns; and Spanish culture and its extensive national parks are two areas where there may be scope for further development. Latterly, Russia and the eastern European countries have become more important as a source of tourists to Spain.

Spanish tourism is presently implementing a strategy designed to increase the quality of its offers and services, and 'to modernise and innovate the service' according to the Ministry.

Transport

The largescale road development of Spain over the last few years has provided a reasonable amount of business for many British companies linked with transportation materials, machinery, industry vehicles and equipment. Road development is planned to continue for at least the next five or so years, causing inconvenience for some and creating opportunities for others; and during this time at least, the industry offers strong potential for suitably qualified British personnel.

DIRECTORY OF MAJOR EMPLOYERS AND FIRMS WITH UK OFFICES

Accountancy

BDO Binder: Calle Serrano 85, 28006 Madrid; ☎915636773; fax 915645336.

Deloitte & Touche: Plaza Pablo Ruiz Picasso, Torre Picasso 38°, 28020 Madrid; ☎915550252; fax 915567430.

Ernst & Young: Plaza Pablo Ruiz Picasso, Torre Picasso 38°, E28020 Madrid; ☎915727200. Also at 1 Lambeth Palace Road, London SE1 7EU; fax 020-7928 1345; www.ey.com.

Grant Thornton España SA: Centro Colon, Marqués de la Ensenada 16, 28004 Madrid; ☎913198300.

Jordan & Son: (head office) 2022 Bedford Row, London WC1R 4JS; ☎020-7400 3304/3301.

KPMG: Edificio Torre Europa, Paseo

de la Castellana 95, 28046 Madrid; and 8 Salisbury Square, London EC4Y 8BB; www.kpmg.com. *PriceWaterhouseCoopers:* Edificio Price-WaterhouseCoopers, Paseo de la Castellena 43, 28046 Madrid; ☎915684400; fax 913083566. Southwark Towers, 32 London Bridge Street, London SE1 9SY; ☎020-7583 5000; www.pwcglobal.com.

Agriculture and Food Processing

Agricola Mar Menor SL: Avenida Torre Pacheco Km 2, Los Alcazares, 30710 Murcia; ☎968574025/37; fax 968575358.

Bodegas Age SA: Barrio de la Estacion, sn 2326360, Fuenmajor; ☎941293500; fax 941293501.

Carbonell (UK) Ltd: 34 York Street, Twickenham, Middlesex TW1 3LJ; fax 020-8744 1172.

Conservas Napal SA: Carretera Zaragoza S/N, Valtierra, 31514 Navarra; ☎948867125/6; fax 948867356.

Cooperativa Agricola de Alginet: Valencia 13, Alginet, 46783 Valencia; ☎961751311.

Frutas Delicias SAL: Avenida Rio Segura S/N, Blanca, 30540 Murcia; ☎968778461; fax 968778461.

Industrias Agricolas de Mallorca: Avenida Antonio Maura 65, Pont D'Inca, Marratxi, 07009 Balearic Islands; ☎971600277; fax 971795070.

Kellogg España SA: Polígono Industrial de Valls, Apartado de Correos 40, Valls, 43800; ☎977603114; fax 977605431.

Miguel García e Hijos: Játiva S/N, Sagunto, 46500 Valencia; ☎962660600; fax 962665445.

Montesierra SA: Avenida Nazaret S/N, Jeréz de la Frontera, 11406 Cádiz; ☎956343295; fax 956340498.

Pescanova SA: PO 424 Vigo, 36280; ☎986818168; fax 986818200.

Riverbend España SA: Carretera de Abanilla Km 1.5, Santomera, 30140 Murcia; ☎968861111; fax 968865538.

San Miguel SA: Apartado 67, 25080 La Lerida; ☎973200600; fax 973205751.

Sucessores de Arturo Carbonell SL: Carretera N 301 MadridCartagena Km 384, PO Box 4, Molina de Segura, 30500 Murcia; ☎968643745; fax 968643774.

Asociación Nacional de Fabricantes de Cerveza (NationalAssociation of Brewers): Calle Fernandez de la Hoz, 28010 Madrid;☎915932813.

Federación Española de La Industria y El Comercio Exportador de Vinos y Licor (Distillers and Vintners): Martires Concepcionistas 18, 28006 Madrid; ☎914012191/4024096; fax 914023387.

Banking

Banco Bilbao Vizcaya (BBA): Paseo de la Castellana 81, 28046 Madrid; ☎913743000/5000; fax 913744665; 100 Cannon Street, London EC4N 6EH; ☎020-7623 3060; fax 020-7929 4718.

Banco Exterior (UK): 1 Great Tower Street, London EC3 5AH; ☎020-7623 3404; fax 020-7623 3235.*Banco Pastor SA:* Paseo de Recoletos 19, 28004 Madrid; ☎915245100. London information020-72333043.

Banco Santander: Paseo de la Castellana 32, 28046 Madrid; ☎915209000; fax 91575 5153. Also, DSN Banis.

Barclays Bank: Plaza de Colon 1, 28046 Madrid; ☎913361000.UK head office ☎01202671212.

Caixa de Galicia: Oficina de Representación, 125 3rd Floor Suite, Egyptian House, 170 Piccadilly, London W1 V0JL; ☎020-74913020.

Caja de Ahorros del Mediterráneo: Avenida Oscar Esplá 37, 03007 Alicante.

CECA (Confederación Española de Cajas de Ahorros): 16 Waterloo Place, London SW1Y 4AR; ☎020-71925 2560; fax 020-71925 2554.

Lloyds TSB Bank: Calle Serrano 90,

28006   Madrid;   ☎915209900;
London ☎020-76261500.
HSBC: Torre Picasso 33, Plaza Pablo,
Ruiz, Madrid; ; ☎914310613; 27 Poul-
try St, London, EC2P 2BX; ☎020-
7260 6000; fax 020-7260 5970.

Banks which Specialise in Mergers and Acquisitions

Banco de Sabadell SA: Placa Cataluña 1,
Sabadell (Barcelona); ☎937289289;
Sabadell House, 120 Pall Mall,
London SW1Y 5EA; ☎020-7321
0020; fax 020-7321 0075.

B W Corporate Finance: Hamilton House,
1 Temple Avenue, London EC4Y
0HA; ☎020-7353 0649; fax 020-
7353 9237.

Link International Brokers: Avda Republica Argentina 47, entlo 1, 08023
Barcelona.

Market Office Group SA: Valencia 288,
08007 Barcelona; ☎932160446; fax
932151701.

Pallas Finanzas SA: Calle Monte,
Esquinza 14, 3 Derecha, 28010
Madrid;   ☎91308   6330;   fax
913198481.

Business Consultancy Firms:

American Appraisal España SA: Principe
de Vergara 9, Planta 3, 28001 Madrid;
☎915783762.

Charles Calamaro: Lagasca 90, 28006
Madrid; ☎915756728.

Gumersindo Nebot Monne Lawyers: Via
Agusta 125, 5nd Floor , 08006 Barcelona; ☎932096799; fax 934141273.

Hamilton Bartram Asociados: Casa del
Nogal, Bubion, 18412 Granada;
☎958763028; fax 958763365.

Iberian Management Consultants: Plaza
de la Lealtad 26, 28014 Madrid;
☎915326639.

Isidro López Molina: Avenida de Sarria
38, 7th Floor 3, 08029 Barcelona;
☎933220443.

José L. Sánchez Izquierdo: 96 The Avenue,
Sunbury on Thames, Middlesex
TW16 5EX; ☎01932-781651; fax

01932-789795.
*PA Consultores de Direccion (PA Manage-
ment Consultants Ltd):* Castellana 1144,
28046 Madrid.

Chartered Surveyors

CB Hillier Parker SA: Edificio la
Caixa, Paseo de la Castellana 516a,
28046 Madrid; ☎913804242; fax
913194080 / Edificio Neron Barcelona, Avenida Diagonal 60586,
08028 Barcelona; ☎934193641; fax
934190285.

Concepción López: Cartagena 77, 3rd
Floor A, 28028 Madrid.

HamptonsFielding International: Urbaniza-
tion, Puerto Golf, Plaza de la Maes-
tranza, 29660, Nueva, Andalucia,
Marbella;   ☎952827754/6754   or
902399500; fax 902399501.

Goddard & Lloyd: Velasquez 85, 28006
Madrid; ☎915225414.

Healey & Baker: Torres de Colon
II, V Floor, Plaza de Colon 2,
28046 Madrid; ☎913084135; fax
913195483.

John H Rendle: Avenida del Golfe 29,
Penablanca, Aloha Golf, Marbella;
☎952812734.

Jones Lang Lasal España SA: Calle Serano
215, 28001 Madrid; ☎915770956;
fax 914310660 / Calle Pau Claris 162,
08037 Barcelona; ☎934331086; fax
934872122.

Knight Frank & Rutley España SA:
Velasquez   24,   28001   Madrid;
☎914314244.

Rutland Financial SA: Calle Cov-
arrubias 3, 1 Dcha 28010, Madrid
☎914482253;   fax   914463935
UK   Office: (Insignia   Richard
Ellis)Berkeley Square House, Berke-
ley Square, London W1 6AN; ☎020-
7629 6290; fax 020-7493 3734.

Contact the *Royal Institute of Chartered
Surveyors,* 12 Great George Street,
Parliament Square, London SW1
3AD; ☎020-7222 7000 for further
information.

Construction and Property Services

AWS Reality Investments, Carolina Park, Edifilio Aries, 40 Ctra de Cadiz, Km 178.5 Marbella, Malaga, 24600; ☎952827705; fax 582900436; www.awsreality.com.

Benneck Investments: Arrecise 1, E03180, Torrevieja; ☎966709629.

Chesterton y Asociados SA: Zurbano 51, 2 izqda 28010 Madrid; ☎913085367; fax 913085310.

Gran Sol Properties: Summerville House, Heatley Street, Preston, Lancashire; ☎01772-825587; fax 01772-251902; email:gran.sol.europe@zetnet.co.u k. Spanish office: Edificio Apolo 1, Calle Corbeta, Calpe, E03710 Alicante; tel/fax 965835468.

G & L Wambeek: Edificio Habanerar III Calle Vicente, Balsco Idanez, Trada 12/4B, 03180 Torrevieja; ☎965719393; fax 965719394; www.spanishpropertysales.co.uk.

Gil del Palacio & Associates: 15 Evelyn Mansions, Carlisle Place, London SW1P 1NH; ☎020-7630 6166; fax 020-7630 9152.

Grupo Infinorsa: Paseo de la Castellana 95, Plaza de Piso 19 28046 Madrid; ☎914359393; fax 915762874.

Healey & Baker: Torres de Colon II, 5B, 28046 Madrid; ☎913084135; fax 913195483.

Immobilaria Turistica de Cala d'Or SA: Carretera Sorta Selanitx 5 07669 de Sorta (Mallorca) Balearic Islands; ☎971167088/9; fax 971167155.

Jones Lang Lasal España SA: Paseo de la Castellana, Numero 33, Planta 14, 28046, Madrid; ☎915770956; fax 917180200.

Juan Porsellanes SA: Avenida Pais Valencia 6, Benisa, 03720 Alicante; ☎965730200/0704; fax 965730407.

Knight Frank: Paseo de la Habana numero 1, Madrid, 28036; ☎915773993; fax 914310830.

McCallum SL UK: ☎Spain 971866615; www.ihh.com. Specialists in Mallorca.

Nyrae Propeties (Overseas): Old Bank House, 1 High Street, Arundel, West Sussex BN18 9AD; ☎01903884663; fax 01903-732554. Deals with agencies throughout the world including Spain.

Solymar Estates S.L: Urb. El Saladillo, Oficina Solymar Estates S.L., Estepona 29680, Malaga; ☎95290 4020; solymarestates@hotmail.com

Richard Ellis SA: Paseo Castellena 51Sexta, Edificio Caixa, 28046 Madrid; ☎913084242; fax 913194080.

Wimpey Española SA: Orense 20, Madrid 20.

Y J Lovell (España) SA: Conjunto White Pearl Beach, Carretera Cádiz Km 192, Marbella, 29600 Málaga; ☎952830955; fax 952831781.

Names of other agents dealing in Spanish property can be obtained from the *National Association of Estate Agents,* Arbon House, 21 Jury Street, Warwick CV34 4EH; ☎01926-496800; wwwnaea.co.uk (select the international section. They can send a list (ask for their 'Homelink' department) of members specialising in Spain.

Insurance

Axa Arora: Paseo de La Castellana 79, 28046, Madrid; ☎915551700. Mortgages and insurance.

Commercial Union Assurance Co: Via Augusta 281285, 08017 Barcelona; ☎932534700. Mortgages and insurance.

Direct Seguros: Ronda Poniente 14, 28760, Tres Cantos; ☎918069500. Insurance.

Eagle Star Insurance Company: Oficina de Santiago, Erraez, Calle de Vasquez, Madrid; ☎915062860.

Guardian Assurance: Numero 158, Piso 1A, 28002, Madrid; ☎934053344.

Plus Ultra, Anonima de Seguras y Resuguras: Plaza de Cortes 8, 28014, Madrid; ☎915899292.

Royal Insurance España: Paseo de la Castellana 60, E28046 Madrid.

Union Española de Entidades Aseuradoras, Reascuradoras y de Capitalizacion[ac]n: (Association of Spanish insurance companies) Calle Nunez de Balboa 101, E28006 Madrid.

In the UK, contact *Towergate Sharp Brokers Ltd.* Towergate House, St. Edwards Court, London Road, Romford, Essex RM7 90D; ☎01708-745196; fax 01708-742524.

Law Firms

Antonio Roca Puig: Avenida Diagonal 506, 5th Floor 2, 08006 Barcelona; ☎934158116; fax 934151762.

Asesoria Juridica Baker & McKenzie: Paseo de la Castellana 33, Edificio Fenix Planta 6, 28046, Madrid; 913915950. UK Office: 100 New Bridge Street, London EC4V 6JA; ☎020-7919 1000; fax 020-79191999.

Asesores Legales Asociados: Paseo de la Castellana 121, 3 Planta A Izqda, 28046 Madrid; ☎915552959; fax 915562731.

Bufete Bano Léon: Pintor Lorenzo Casanova 66, 1st Floor, Alicante; ☎965921853; fax 965921854.

Bufete Bruna: Provenza 318, Planta 2 1, 08037 Barcelona; ☎932154561; fax 932156147.

Bufete Climente, Minguell & Martin Solicitors: Pau Claris 154, 2nd Floor, 08009 Barcelona; ☎934871084; fax 934871680.

CA Consulting Asociados: Bishopsgate House, 57 Folgate Street, London E1 6BX; ☎020-72231116; fax 020-7247 3982.

Octavio Veira: Las Palmas ☎928493010; 928493011.

De Cotta McKenna y Santafé Abogados: Madrid: Nuñez de Balboa 30, 3rd Floor B, 28001 Madrid; ☎914319525; fax 915762139. London: ☎020-7353 0998.

Cornish & Co. ☎ 9 5 2 8 6 6 8 3 0 ; c o r n i s h @ m e r c u r y i n . e s in Spain; and 41800; email c o r n i s h @ g i b n e t . g i in Gibraltar.

De Pinna Notaries: 35 Piccadilly, London W1J 0LJ; ☎020-7208 2900; fax 020-7208 0066.

Instituto de Proprietarios Extranjeros (Institute of Foreign Property Owners), Calle La Mar, 19303590, Altea, Alicante; ☎96584 2312; www.fipe.org. They examine Spanish-written contracts which are brought in.

Jesús Bello Albertos: N/Sra de García 24, 5B, Marbella, 29600 Málaga; ☎952772487; fax 952829329.

Mariscal, Monero, Meyer & Marinello CB: Calle Barbara de Braganza 11, Planta Segunda, 28004 Madrid; ☎913199686; fax 913085368.

Santiago Aguilar Canosa I Castella: Avenida Diagonal 529, Pral, 2nd Floor, 08029 Barcelona; ☎934053881/934308493.

Tomas Buxeda Nadal: Rambla de Catalunya 5355, Planta 6, Puerta A, 08007 Barcelona; ☎934880250; fax 934881656.

Tomas Lamarca Abello: Muntaner 400, Principal Planta, 08006 Barcelona; ☎932012444; fax 932003558.

M Vega Penichet: Alcalá 115, Primera Planta 28009 Madrid; ☎914315500; fax 914315938.

Ventura Garces Solicitors: Calle Freixa 2628 bajos, 08021 Barcelona; ☎932019444; fax 932098391. *Consejo General de la Abogacia Española:* Calle de Serano 9, 28001 Madrid; ☎915227711; fax 914319365.

A list of English-speaking lawyers may be provided by the *Law Society* (113 Chancery Lane, London WC2A 1PL; ☎020-7242 1222; www.lawsociety.org.uk)

Manufacturing and Marketing

Antonio Pernas S.A: Avenida de la Prensa Parcela 55 bis, Polígono Industrial de Sabon, Arteixo, 15143 La Coruña; ☎981641082.

BASF España SA: Apartado de Correos 762, 08800 Barcelona; ☎932151354.

Beecham Labatorios SA: Travera de Gradia 9, 08021 Barcelona; ☎932097200.

Beecham Products: Calle José Anfelm, Clave 92112, 08950 Esplugas de Llobregat, Barcelona; ☎933713262.

BIE Enterprise SL: Calle Constancia 9, Castellou, 081719 Barcelona; ☎938084153.

Biocosmetics SL: Arcos de la Frontera 15, 28023 Madrid; ☎913571583.

CadburySchweppes España SA: Sor Angela de la Cruz 3, 28020 Madrid; ☎915564664.

Carmen Marcos SL: Pintor Joaquin Vamonde 2, 15005 La Coruña; ☎981121365.

Confecciones Carmen Melero SL: López Mora 70 bajo, Vigo, 36211 Pontevedra; ☎986292949.

Central FM English Radio: Centro Commercial Peyca 11, Oficina B2, Arroyo de La Miel, 29631, Benalmadena, Malaga; ☎952566256; fax 952566367; www.centralfm.com.

Deulofeu Hermanos: Plaza San Jaime 3, 08002 Barcelona; ☎933187886.

Empresa Nacional Siderurgica SA (ENSIDESA): Velázquez 134, 28006 Madrid.

Fansa (Fansa Fabrica Alfarera Navarette SA): Carretera Entrena 38, Navarrete, 26370 La Rioja; ☎941440000.

Flexibox de España SA: Ronda de los Tejares 19, 14008 Cordoba.

Formica Española SA: Txomin Egileor 54, 48960 Galdakaol (Bilbao).

Alcala FarmaSA: Apartado de Correos 37, 28800 Alcala de Henares, Madrid; ☎918890600/0408.

ICI España SA: Gran Via Sur, km 2.2, 0898 Hostilet de Llovregat, Barcelona; ☎933356014/932640087. Ctra HostalricTosa, 08490 Fogars de Tordera.

Industrias Roko SA: Rua Dos Regos 27, 15173 Oleiros, La Coruña; ☎981631159.

José Moreno Martos: Camino de las Fuentes 1, Caravaca, 30400 Murcia; ☎968707441.

Lingotes Especiales SA: Calle Colmenares 5, Apartado 504, 47004 Valladolid; ☎983305249.

Luso Española de Porcelanas SA: Avenida Eliatxo 60, Irún, 20303 Guipúzcoa; ☎943627199.

Malta SA: Apartado 2, Guernica, 48300 Vizcaya; ☎946250050.

Materials Manufacturing: Avenida de Fuentemar 20, Polígono Industria de Coslada, 28820 CosladaMadrid; ☎916273628.

Michelin SA: Sase de Neumatico Michelin, Caloe Calle de Doctor Esqueido 157, 28007 Madrid; ☎914090940.

Nestlé: Sociedad Nestlé, Avenida de Paises Catalanes 3349, 08950 Esplugas de Llobregat, Barcelona; ☎933717100.

Oribo Calzado Deportivo: Zapatillas Ribo, Galceran Marquet 6, 08005 Barcelona; ☎933090632.

Plasticos Faca SA: Traversia Indusrtial Numero 87 08 08907 Barcelona; ☎933779812.

Plessey Semiconductors: Plaza de Colon 2, Torres de Colon, Torre 18b, 28046 Madrid.

Productos Pirelli SA: Domicillio Social y Sede, Avenida Diagonal 662, Planta 4A, 08034 Barcelona; ☎932053966.

Rank Video Services Iberia: Polígono Industriell, El Rasol, San Agustin, 28750 Madrid.

Repsol Quimica SA (UK): Kensington Centre, 66 Hammersmith Road, London W14 8UD.

Rover Espäna SA: Mar Mediterráneo 2, San Fernando de Henares, 28850 Madrid.

Sanyo España SA: Caseo de Santa, Santa Coloma 6, 08210 Polígono Industrial Santiga, Barbara del Valles, Barcelona; ☎937182000.

Shell Española SA: Rio Bullaque 2, 28034 Madrid.

Sur in English Newspaper: Avenida

Dr Marañon, 48, 29009, Malaga; ☎952649636; fax 952611256.
Unilever España: Apartado 36156, 28080 Madrid; ☎914572000.
United Biscuits: Productos Ortiz., Calle Alberto, Albocer 465B, 28016 Madrid; ☎914587844.
UQUIFA SA (Union Quimico Farmaceutica SA): Mallorca 262, 3 Planta, 08008 Barcelona; ☎934879477.

Shipping, Transport and Freight
Arthur Pierre, Calle Urogallo 12, Pol. Ind. Matagallegos, E28940 Fuenlabrada (Madrid); ☎91642 2080; fax 91642 2538.
Construcciones Delicias SA: Paseo Santa María de la Cabeza 73, 28045 Madrid; ☎914739111.
Dayfer SL: Veigadana 73, Mos, 36415 Pontevedra; ☎986330927; fax 986330434.
Cory Hermanosos SA: León Castillo 421, 35008 Las Palmas, Canary Islands.

Christian Salvesen Serposa SA: Barrio San Martin, 39011, Santander; ☎942352352; fax 942333496.
Hijo de Alfredo Rodríguez Ltd: Alvarez de Castro 34, Primero, 04002 Almeria; ☎950243044/238; fax 950234906.
Papi Transitos SL: Calle San Fernando 33 Entlo, 03001 Alicante; ☎965206233; fax 965207905.

Travel and Tourism
British Airways SA: Serrano 605°, 28001 Madrid.
British Tourist Authority: Torre de Madrid, Planta 6a, Plaza de España, 28008 Madrid. *Asosiación Empresarias de Agencies de Viajes Españoles:* Plaza de Castilla 3 9A 28046 Madrid; ☎913141830; fax 913141877.
Sol Melia Hotels: Melia White House Hotel, Albany Street, Regents Park, London NW1 3UP; ☎020-73871200; fax 020-73880091; www.solmelia.com.

STARTING A BUSINESS

CHAPTER SUMMARY

○ A business licence (opening licence) is required to start up a business in Spain.

○ Entrepreneurs are required by law to have at least one Spanish worker in their company.

○ The more likely it is that your enterprise will benefit the local community and provide work for locals, the more positive the response will be.

○ **Self employment.** Anyone who is self-employed in Spain has to register with the social security organisation soon after arrival.

○ **Employing Staff.** Employers are offered reduced social security contributions for young workers, workers over 45 years and disabled workers.

○ The majority of businesses started in Spain by foreigners are small concerns in the catering or beverages sector, special interest holidays and property rentals.

○ Spanish employers pay special bonuses (known as *pagas extraordinarias*) in the summer and at Christmas; in effect they are paying for 14 months' work per 12 months.

○ **Trade Unions.** Barely one sixth of Spain's twelve million workers belong to trade unions.

○ Notwithstanding low membership, wage agreements made with unions are binding.

○ **High Costs of Redundancy.** It used to be very difficult to dismiss workers in Spain, even for gross negligence.

○ It is now easier to lay off staff, but Spanish employers have to pay some of the highest redundancy fees in Europe.

Although Spain may seem to present a maze of complex procedures and formalities to those wishing to start their own business in the country, the situation as far as bureaucracy is concerned is one which has improved immeasurably over recent years. Procedures have been simplified and channels of information opened up to make the British expatriate's task a far easier one than ever before. Although a few difficulties remain for the prospective entrepreneur (some legal, and some existing, it still seems, to deter foreigners from entering a work force which is affected by unemployment), this is an undertaking which is becoming ever more manageable. Partly this has to do with the creation of the socalled 'Eurozone' with its shared currency, and the global nature of today's markets.

Furthermore, anyone setting up a business in Spain will get a far more positive response if they have something to offer the area, whether it be a needed facility which is so far unavailable or a business which will create much-needed jobs for local people. Parts of Spain are still relatively undeveloped; and the ability to spot a gap in the market could lead to success, which could bring positive benefits to your Spanish neighbours. For instance, the dramatically improved road infrastructure has had the effect of opening up the once little-known interior of the country to conventional tourism; and a natural follow-up to this is an increased demand for tourist facilities (hotels, bars and cafés) inland. All this creates employment; and benefits the local economy. The introduction of a single European currency has been hailed as a truly level playing field for eager entrepreneurs and professionals. It is necessary for some further dissolution of the bureaucratic barriers, but generally things are progressing. The difficulties new businesses are up against can be as much technical as economic and bureaucratic.

To find your way around the maze of rules and regulations, the information below will serve as a guide to anyone planning to start up a business in Spain.

Basic Requirements

Anyone intending to set up their own business must first of all follow a few basic but essential procedures. First of all, you will need a business licence (*licencia de apertura*) from the town hall (*ayuntamiento*); this will be granted once the authorities are satisfied that the premises are suitable for the proposed business, that they comply with planning permission and are safe and hygienic. Note that as an employer you will be required by law to have at least one Spanish worker in the new company; and you will need to observe Spanish labour laws in connection with minimum salaries, social security payments, etc. (see below).

After obtaining the licencia de apertura, you will have to register with the Spanish social security service for income tax and IVA (VAT). There is an IVA registration permit; and you need your fiscal licence, which relates to any taxable activity in Spain, as well as the opening licence (above) which allows you to start trading and open your premises for business. You should also make an application for registration with the Spanish National Health Service if you have not already done this; and for a suitable medical permit.

If you plan to practise your own trade or profession in Spain, whether you are a doctor or an accountant, a lawyer or a qualified electrician, you will have to become a member of the appropriate professional association and to have the right, agreed UK qualification. Your own trade or professional association can help; or LECs and other local business advice centres as well as the Euro-adviser at your local Job Centre (if you are still in the UK) can provide the relevant leaflet. EU directives have now implemented the reciprocal recognition of a wide variety of trade and professional qualifications between all EU countries; for further information see the section *Professional Mobility* below., *Poniente Properties* (an estate agency on the Costa del Sol) also draws attention to some of the pitfalls and problems in its brochure, available from *Poniente Properties*, Avenida Juan Gomez 'Juanmito', Edf las Yucas, E29640 Fuengirola; ☎952582785; fax 952461878.

Residence Regulations

As explained in Chapter Two on *Residence and Entry Regulations*, anyone who plans to be self employed in Spain is spared a lot of bureaucratic hassle which EU immigrants of different status are subjected to. However, the process is one which can still take time to complete; and there are many potential pitfalls along the way. Those who are thinking of opening a small business (e.g. a shop, bar, or restaurant) will need the abovementioned business licence which is often time-consuming to obtain, as well as the *trajeta comunitaria*, an EU document which removes the need for a residence/work permit. As mentioned above, anyone who is self-employed in Spain must be sure to register with the social security services soon after arrival. For full details of all entry regulations, see Chapter Two.

PROCEDURES INVOLVED IN BUYING OR START-ING A NEW BUSINESS

Creating a New Business

The Department of Trade and Industry used to run a nationwide campaign, entitled 'Spotlight Spain', the aim of which was to encourage more Brits to exploit the business potential which exists there, and from time to time initiates new campaigns like these. With the changes envisaged by the current government for Job Centres, these may also become useful advice centres for those who wish to start a business abroad, as well as those who are looking for work in Spain and elsewhere. For details of current DTI initiatives you can contact the Spain desk of the *DTI* (Business in Europe Branch), Bay 854, Kingsgate House, 6674 Victoria Street, London SW1E 6SW; ☎020-72155444; www.tradepartners.gov.uk. The DTI has an extensive website with major profiles on Spain and other major countries. Full of useful information and updates for anyone planning to set up or do business in Spain. Some of the areas identified by the DTI as expanding in Spain include aerospace and airport development, automotive components, clothing, computer software, food and drink, pollution control and the environment, food processing and packaging, railway equipment, telecommunications and data communications' as well as 'water and water-treatment' as the areas of greatest interest to UK exporters and business-people.

Readers of *Live and Work in Spain and Portugal* may have more modest targets; and most people who set up a business in Spain – whether this be a language school or a shop will be part of the service sector (see above); and probably in the part of this connected with tourism. Starting a business from scratch in these service industries usually requires less investment. But you should be aware that setting up a completely new business may require more capital than buying a going concern, and probably constitutes a greater risk. In an excellent series of articles on the subject, the editor of *Spanish Property News* offers some caveats, the main one being to get some experience in the area in which your business is operating; for example, if you are thinking of buying and running a bar. Get some hands on experience first if you can, he says. Proper financial backing is another key element. And 'there are probably more opportunities for setting up or buying a business in Spain and making, if not a fortune, then a reasonable living, than there are in Britain.' Prospects, in other words, are good. Anyone planning to do this will either need some knowledge of a business which already operates in Spain or be able to spot a gap in the Spanish market which they feel they could competently fill. Any new ideas will need to be practical and achievable; and most business owners must be prepared to wait at least a year or two for their concern to break even, and then to start making a profit.

Buying an Existing Business

Buying a business is often a cheaper and less risky venture than starting a new one. One problem with buying in Spain is that there is often not a wide choice of businesses for sale in any given area, as family enterprises tend to remain within the family or to be sold by word of mouth, rather than to be advertised. Also, many small businesses exist at subsistence level, rather than at a profitable one; many owners regard their businesses as a way of life, rather than as a profit centre. If the business provides the means to support a casual, relaxed way of life it is deemed a success by some. This may be no bad thing in the case of those who are moving to Spain to get away from the rat race at home; and are looking for a change in lifestyle as much as to make money. This type of concern may suit those who are looking for a sideline or semi-retirement business, but obviously not those who have more ambitious plans. The concept of a more profitable business enterprise is not unknown among expatriates in Spain as well, although it is true to say that, among Spaniards, 'getting rich quick' has not yet become as common a goal or ambition as in the UK or the USA.

Obviously, the final choice between creating or buying a business rests with you; and must be based on what you are prepared to invest in the way of time and money. You should weigh up both of these elements if you are thinking of launching any new enterprise of course; and consider whether you will need to become an employer (which brings with it other challenges which should be carefully considered beforehand). One-person businesses (and self-employment) are becoming more and more common in Spain, as they are in the UK. Also, if you are even contemplating starting a business, it is advisable to look at some other Spanish businesses for sale or which are operating in the same area by way of comparison.

Business Structures

A Spanish business may assume any one of several legal entities. But most small business concerns will be better with sole trader status (*empresa individual*), which involves limited liability. The trader must register with the appropriate trade association, e.g. for commercial agents it is the *Colegio Oficial de Agentes Comerciales* in Madrid (☎912204098), with branches in other areas. For this honour, the trader must pay a small entrance fee plus an equally nominal monthly subscription; oneperson retailers would follow the same procedure.

Large limited liability companies are usually formed as public companies, SA's (*Sociedad Anónimas*) which are the Spanish equivalent of the French, *société anonyme* (SA). Small concerns take on the status of private companies, SL's (*Sociedad de Reponsabilidad Limĺtada*), the equivalent of the French *société à responsibilité limitée* (SARL). A wealth of choice exists however, and those who plan to set up a partnership (Sociedad Colectiva) or a joint venture with a Spanish company (*Associacion de Empresas en Participacion*) may do so, but would be well advised to take specialist legal advice first.

SA. To form an SA, a minimum capital of about three and a half million pounds and at least three initial shareholders are required. The organisation must employ 50 or more workers and must have a committee on which workers are represented (*Comité de Empressa*). There is no maximum capital limit and the requirement that half of the share capital must be held by Spanish nationals was abolished in the 1970's. The directors need not be Spanish or even be resident in Spain. A deed of incorporation (*escritura de constitución*) must be drafted for the company to attain legal status, which should include a range of information about the proposed company: the structure of management, the amount of capital being invested, the number of shares, etc. Official formation is achieved by public deed (*escritura publica*) before a notary. The deed must be entered in the Mercantile Registry within two months of its being signed; thereupon the corporation is a separate legal entity.

This procedure will take about two months; and along the way you are bound to need some professional legal and tax advice (see *Accountancy Advice* and *Legal Advice* below). Registration costs include a 1% transfer tax on the registered and paidup capital, plus notary's and Mercantile Registry fees at scale rates. This amount does not include professional fees for submitting applications to government ministries, drafting bylaws and general assistance in preliminary negotiation, obtaining tax and legal advice, etc. As a general rule, initial investment can be repatriated, including any profit made, although this sum will be subject to tax clearance.

SL. In contrast to the SA, an SL does not have public shares; the capital is divided among the stockholders (of whom there should be no more than 50) in accordance with their agreed participation as set out in the public deed under which the company is formed. The minimum capital required is about £18,000 ($25,000). Obviously this is the form which the majority of smaller companies in Spain will assume. Anyone who requires detailed advice on business structures can contact one of the business consultancy firms in Madrid which offer advice on direct investments, company formation, etc. A list of such firms in Madrid is given below; similar lists for the Barcelona and Bilbao regions can be obtained from the Consulates in these areas.

Useful Addresses

American Appraisal España SA: Principe de Vergara 9, Planta 3, E28001 Madrid; ☎915783762.

Bove Montero and Cia: Mariano Cubi 79, Atico 2, E08006 Barcelona; ☎932180708; fax 932375925. Tax

advisers and management consult-
ants. Publishes *Doing Business in Spain*
and newsletters on tax matters.
Charles Calamaro: Lagasca 90, E28006
Madrid; ☎915756728.
De Pinna Notaries: 35 Piccadilly, London
W1V 0PJ; ☎020-7208 2900; fax
020-7208 0066. (Advisers on prop-
erty transfers, private and commer-
cial investment and probate work in
Spain).
Gumersindo Nemot Monne Lawyers: Via
Agusta 125, 5th Floor, E08006
Barcelona;   ☎932096799;   fax
934141273.
Hamilton Bartram Asociados: Casa del
Nogal, Bubion, E18412 Granada;

☎958763028; fax 958763365; emaill
info@andaluciahousehunters.com.
Primarily help expatriates find and
set up homes in Granada (Alpujarras
Mountains).
International   Venture   Consultants:
Felix Boix 181, E28036 Madrid;
☎912506905. Home search and
relocation consultants.
PERCO   Consultores   de   Empresa   SA:
Castellana   135,   E28046   Madrid;
☎912796503.
Spanish Labour Office: 20 Peel Street,
London W8 7PD; ☎020-7221 0098;
fax 020-7229 7270. Spanlabo@globa
lnet.co.uk. Publishes a useful intro-
ductory leaflet *Setting Up a Business.*

EEIG. In 1989. a new type of business entity was innaugurated throughout the
European Community, known as the European Economic Interest Grouping
(EEIG). An EEIG can be conducted by individuals and companies and is
designed to facilitate cross-border cooperation between businesses in different
parts of the EU. The EEIG is governed by EU regulations rather than the
sometimes narrow and diverse constraints of individual countries' company laws.
The aim has been that EEIG's will be subject to identical legal and tax regimes
regardless of the country of operation.

Each EEIG may have a maximum of 20 members and no more than 500
employees within the grouping. The rules governing the EEIG's activities are
designed to protect third parties as much as possible and incorporate some of the
features of a partnership and some of a company.

In order to form a EEIG, the prospective members must conclude a contract to be
filed at the appropriate registry in the member state where it is based. An EEIG may
deal with companies outside the EU but must itself remain within the boundaries of
the EU, although it is totally free to move around between member states.

Professional Mobility

On April 17 1991, regulations were passed through Parliament enforcing the
EU directive on the mutual recognition of professional qualifications. Today,
nearly 200 professions and trades are included in the terms of the directive.
This was the first ruling to establish a general system of mutual recognition
for the professions throughout the EU, as opposed to the earlier approach of
harmonising professional requirements profession by profession. The aim of the
directive is to allow freedom of movement within the EU across a wide range of
occupations. Thus, fully qualified professionals from one EU country (whether
doctors, surveyors, accountants, electricians, etc.) are entitled to membership of
the equivalent profession in Spain without having to requalify. It means access
to regulated professions is provided through home country qualifications. There
are currently a range of these professions in the UK regulated by law, or public

authority or professional bodies, which are included in this ruling. A list of the main professional associations and groups which carry out the same role in Spain is given below. To check qualifications, you can contact (for a guidance pack and application form) the *British Chamber of Commerce Certification Unit* (Oak Tree Court, Binley Business Park, Harry Weston Road, Coventry CV3 2UN; ☎02476654321).

There are some safeguards which are allowed by the legislation mentioned above including allowing the regulating authorities to require the individual in question to undertake an adaption period or to take an aptitude test. Some professions (such as teaching) may be difficult to enter in Spain, where teachers are considered to be civil servants working for the state; and where the individual's professional qualification period is shorter than that in the host country, evidence of professional experience can be required (obtainable from the DTI, see above).

Despite the implementation of this directive in both Britain and Spain – in fact throughout the EU – UK nationals moving to Spain with the intention of continuing in their own profession may encounter some animosity from the equivalent professional body. This will largely be the result of an understandable lack of enthusiasm on the part of the Spanish body to admit foreign competition within its own ranks. However, with the law on your side, any such attitudes should not prove to be a deterrent to enthusiasm and determination. Some of the main professional bodies are included here. The address of the equivalent professional body in Spain can be also be contacted through your UK trade union or regulatory body.

The *UK National Academic Recognition Information Centre* (NARIC) provides information on the comparability of overseas qualifications and can be contacted at *ECCTIS Ltd*, Oriel House, Oriel Road, Cheltenham, Glos. GL50 1XP; ☎01242260010; fax 01242258600.

Professional Bodies in Spain

Architects: Consejo Superior de los Colegios de Arquitectos de España, Paseo de la Castellaba 1012, E28001 Madrid; ☎914351859.

Commercial Agents: Consejo General de los Colegios Oficiales de Agentes Comerciales de España, Goya 55, E28001 Madrid.

Doctors and Dentists: Consejo General de los Colegios Médicos de España, Calle Villanueva 11, E28001 Madrid; ☎914317780.

Estate Agents: Consejo General de los Colegios Oficiales de Agentes de la Propiedad Inmobiliaria, Gran Vía 70, E28013 Madrid.

Lawyers: Consejo General de la Abogacía Española, Calle General Castoños 4, E28004 Madrid.

Nurses: Consejo General de Ayudantes Técnicos Sanitarios y Diplomados de Enfermería, Buen Suceso 6, E28008 Madrid.

Pharmacists: Consejo general de los Colegios Oficiales de Farmacéuticos, Villanueva 11, Planta 6, E28001 Madrid; ☎914312560.

Raising Finance

You will need a certain amount of ready capital to start any business in Spain. Some people raise this capital by selling their UK property and buying a cheaper home, using the profit as business capital. Most Spanish banks will look favourably on applications for business loans from Britons wishing to set up business in Spain and these may be contacted at either their UK or Spanish offices (see the *Banks and Finance* section in Chapter Four, *Daily Life*). In order to secure a Spanish loan to start a business in Spain, you would have to demonstrate some business ability, have a well thoughtout business plan and cash flow forecast; and be able to offer some financial security. In addition, you should consider not only the purchase or setting-up costs of your new business but the expenses for stock, wages, repairs, services, improvements, depreciation of capital items, and so on, which you will meet further down the line, when considering how much finance you need to raise. It is unlikely that a bank will provide a loan for a sum in excess of the amount which you yourself are able to inject in cash: such a loan would usually need to be repaid over a period of between five and seven years. One alternative worth considering as a means of raising business finance is to mortgage the new Spanish property to provide business start-up or purchase capital, as this will allow for a longer repayment period from the bank.

Government Investment Incentives

Foreign investment in Spain, by virtue of boosting the country's economic and industrial growth and reducing unemployment, is generally welcomed by the government. Over recent years, Spain has eased the regulations which once made it so difficult for foreigners wishing to invest within the country. Foreign investment regulations have been liberalised significantly, even from countries outside the EU; increased credit facilities have been made available to foreign businesses; and the banking system has been opened up to foreign banks, of which there are an ever-increasing number. Certain government-owned sectors are still closed to private enterprise; but Spain is currently privatising much of its nationally owned industry. In practice, certain of these industries (e.g. gas, electricity and water) are still substantially government regulated (as they are in Britain) but these areas all offer great scope for foreign investment. Opportunities in other areas are also diverse and numerous (see the DTI's *Spain Trade Brief* and he section *Ideas for New Businesses* below).

The government particularly encourages investment in certain regions of the country which have not benefited from industrial expansion and which are experiencing economic difficulties. These regions are known as promotional areas (*zonas de promoción económica* or ZPE's) and include all of the autonomous regions with the exception of Madrid, Rioja, Catalonia and Valencia. Domestic and foreign investors in these areas qualify for substantial tax and non-tax investment concessions; these may include a reduction on social security payments or on the local taxes on the business premises or even a waiving of the business licence tax during the construction and startup period. The other category to benefit from government-directed regional incentive schemes are the *zonas industrializadas en declive* (ZID's), which include specific areas of Galicia, Asturias, Cantabria and the Basque Country. However, as a result of recent political changes, the various incentives for foreign investment are under review at the time of writing; prospective business people and investors will have to check with the relevant local authorities as to which incentives are available for their projected venture. (The Spanish Embassy can also provide further information and contacts concerning these schemes).

Various other incentives have been introduced by the labour authority to promote the employment of young people. In general, a reduction of between 75% and 100% in the employer's social security payroll contribution per person is offered once an unemployed person has been hired. You may also be liable for a subsidy for each day of training for taking on young workers employed under training programmes. There is an additional reduction of 50% of the employer's social security contributions for personnel hired over the age of 45. Finally, in the case of the employment of a handicapped person, a reduction of 70% of the employer's social security contribution still obtains.

Finding a Business

Businesses for sale can be found at both specialist business agents and estate agents. The easiest way to locate these is through the Spanish *Yellow Pages*, available at major city libraries in the UK, e.g. the DTI Trade Partners UK department, (6674 Victoria Street, London SW1E 6SW; ☎020-7215 5444/5; fax 020-7215 4231); www.tradepartners.gov.uk. Major Spanish newspapers eg. *El País* (Miguel Juste 40, E28037 Madrid) and *ABC* (Serrano 61, E28006 Madrid) also include some 'Business for Sale' type advertising. These newspapers are listed along with relevant English-language publications in Spain under *Media and Communications* in the *Daily Life* chapter. Some businesses for sale, like bars and hotels, are advertised in the useful English-language magazine *Lookout*.

Although some preliminary research and investigation can be done from outside Spain, in order to prepare any sort of valid shortlist it is essential to visit the country on at least one inspection trip. It will also be necessary to consider such matters as location, local competition, previous results and profits, very much as one would do in the UK.

For those considering the purchase of any business connected with tourism or leisure, as many expatriate businesses tend to be, it is particularly important to see how the business varies seasonally as the extent of the trading season varies considerably in different parts of the country – is there any out-of-season trade at all? Also be careful to ensure that the area you plan to set up in is still in tourist vogue. For example, Marbella, once the dream destination for second home buyers, has fallen from favour over recent years, while Majorca is becoming the Eden to which those who can afford the escalating property prices flock. So although hotels, cafés, etc. in Marbella are being sold for substantially less than equivalent businesses were a few years ago, there is no point in having a hotel or a café anywhere if there isn't enough of a client base.

Be sure to obtain an independent evaluation of any business for sale to ensure that the price asked is fair. When buying in Spain it is better to take professional advice both on the viability of the business and the purchase procedure. To do this one can employ an accountant, a lawyer and one's own estate agent as a consultant. It is possible to find a UK firm with suitable experience by contacting the Law Society (113 Chancery Lane, London WC2A 1PL; ☎020-7320 5876;www.lawsoc.org.uk). They have a search facility on www.solicitorsonline.com for finding an appropriate solicitor. Alternatively, lists of English-speaking accountants and lawyers are given in the sections *Accountancy Advice* and *Legal Advice* below.

Business Purchase – Rent or Buy?

Plans for building business premises must be approved by the town hall to obtain the necessary building permit. For rented business property, make sure that you have a contract which specifies clearly the obligations of both parties, tenant and landlord/lady; and one which is clear on matters of deposit, charges, contract duration, etc. Tenancies are either governed by the Law of Industrial Leases (for an existing business which is being taken over) or the Law of Urban Leases (for a new business). The main difference between the two is that there is no statutory security of tenure under the Law of Industrial Leases; renewal is a matter of negotiation between the landlord and the tenant; and the landlord is not under any obligation to renew. This potentially problematic point can be mitigated by an appropriate contract with the landlord when the agreement is first made. However, for a new business, the Law of Urban Leases gives the tenant security of tenure provided he or she has paid the rent and kept to the terms of the lease; the landlord may only increase the rent annually and only by the amount specified in the state-issued release, *Boletin Official*. The Law of Urban Leases allows tenants to sell their businesses. The tenant must notify the landlord of the proposed transaction and of the sum asked by the vendor. The landlord may then exercise what is known as the right of redemption and pay the purchase cost to the tenant to recover the premises. However, if this right is not exercised then the landlord must agree to the transaction and is entitled to a percentage of the purchase price. If the business has been established since 1942 the landlord is entitled to 10% of the purchase price, through some quirk of history however, before 1942 it can be as high as 30%. The percentage applies only to the premises, not to the sum paid for fixtures, fittings or stock.

IDEAS FOR NEW BUSINESSES

Although it is impossible to cite the exact number of British expatriates who have started up their own businesses in Spain, the evidence to prove that this is becoming an increasingly popular hobby horse can be seen clearly from the number of new expatriate businesses springing up all over the country. A wide range of businesses exist along the popular resort areas, mostly restaurants, bars and cafés, while slightly unexpected businesses, such as photocopying franchises and building contractors are also flourishing in less touristy areas.

Hotels, Restaurants and Cafés

Recent statistics from the Ministry of Commerce and Tourism in Spain show that tourism in Spain is steadily on the up, especially away from the more 'touristy' Costas. These figures also support one theory, that the Spanish coast, although still teeming with tourism, has passed its peak of popularity and that the polluted, concrete cities and their perennial, drunken visitors will in future years become a phenomenon of the past. Regardless of whether this prediction will be realised, as mentioned earlier in this chapter, tourism in the interior of Spain is now becoming a viable concept. The reason for the sudden surge in popularity of these little-known areas, rich in history, culture and atmosphere, is greatly due to the radically improved road system in the interior of the country. Now that it is the turn of the backwaters of Spain to enter the limelight, so the demand for hotels for visitors to stay in, restaurants for them to eat at and bars for them to drink at will surge in many areas. This kind of opening is one opportunity for any business-minded person or couple, as especially in demand are reasonably-priced, familyrun hotel businesses along the main roads of newly accessible Spain.

Renting Out Property

This is one of the most obvious ways for second-home owners to exploit their infrequent but recurring visits to Spain. Terms and conditions of rent agreements and the tax implications of renting out second homes are discussed in full in Chapter Three, *Setting Up Home*. One word of general advice, however, is that anyone considering buying property, largely in order to rent it out, should note that property in the north will only be viable as a holiday home through July and August; June can actually be quite cold in this part of the country. In contrast, however, the holiday season in the south extends from spring through to the end of autumn, by virtue of the weather, which consequently involves higher property prices.

Franchises

Anyone who is tempted by the idea of running their own business, but who is deterred by the high failure rate, may consider taking on a franchise – the number of which are currently increasing rapidly throughout Spain. Under this system, a company authorises the franchiser to sell its goods or services in a particular area, usually exclusively. Franchising brings with it several advantages. Normally in the first year of business, many small business concerns experience difficulties while establishing a reputation and building up a clientele. With a franchise, the franchiser is selling a name that already has a reputation, and whose products are in demand through national advertising. The company offering the franchise will also help the franchiser obtain, equip and stock the premises, and will handle the accounting. In exchange, the franchiser pays royalties to the parent company which are proportional to the sales.

Since franchise terms vary greatly amongst companies, and some may not be favourable (to put it politely), it is essential for anyone considering this option to go into the details extremely carefully before making any kind of commitment.

Exporters

The Spain desk of the Business in Europe Branch of Trade Partners UK (DTI, Bay 854, Kingsgate House, 6671 Victoria Street, London SW1E 6SW; ☎020-7215 5000 (general enquiries; fax 020-7222 2629; also ☎020-7215 4274 for Southern Europe Enquiries) as well as their regional offices (see below), provides help and information specifically for exporters in a number of ways. They are able to provide basic market information, commission status reports on specific companies and find suitable representatives for UK firms, as well as giving current information on tariff rates and import procedures. Fees are charged for most of these services. Although this service will mainly be of use to those considering exporting to Spain, the DTI also publishes several booklets focused on the EU, and on starting new businesses, which are potentially useful to anyone considering setting up business abroad. Additionally, their free quarterly magazine *Single Market News* is a good source for the most current business news and regulations concerning the ever more imminent advent of the single market. All of these publications are available free of charge from the DTI. Additionally, the DTI's Export and Market Information Centre Library (also based at 6671 Victoria Street, London SW1E 6SW) is worth a visit for anyone researching into business opportunities in Spain. The library boasts a mine of statistical information and business and industry reports as well as an extensive supply of the Spanish *Yellow Pages*. It is open from 9am-8pm Monday to Friday, and 9am-5.30pm on Saturday. Visitors may use the library at any time within these hours (you will have to sign in with a business address), although students and researchers are required to make appointments in advance.

RUNNING A BUSINESS

As in the UK, it is necessary to have licences to operate certain businesses in Spain, or to sell or provide specific products and services. This applies especially to businesses which sell or serve alcohol, and to catering businesses which require health licences. The best course of action is to enquire at the local town hall. If the proposed business involves complex licensing requirements, you should enlist the expertise of a lawyer to help you through the application procedure.

Employing Staff

In Spain, all workers, by law, must be covered by social security, although particularly in the case of domestic staff (maids, cooks, etc.) this regulation is often conveniently overlooked. The local employment office (*agencia de colocaciones*) will usually be pleased to help with staffing requirements and to advertise these free of charge. All employers must abide by the regulations regarding working conditions as set out in full in Chapter Six, *Employment*. These conditions include a minimum hourly wage, a standard working week of 40 hours on an annual basis and a provision that overtime cannot be forced, cannot exceed 80 hours a year and must be paid at a rate of not less than 175% of the standard hourly rate. All the provisions of the European Union's Social Chapter concerning the rights of employees also apply in Spain. An annual holiday of thirty calendar days is obligatory; remember also that Spain has its many national public holidays and usually one local public holiday each year. Paid absences are mandatory in certain circumstances such as marriage and maternity leave, although the Spanish social security system will pay a large proportion of the wages during this time.

One of the principal problems involved in employing workers in both Spain and Portugal, namely that of firing them, is gradually changing. Traditionally, Spanish law strongly protects the worker's right to job security and continues to do so in many cases. Legally, it has been almost impossible in the past to dismiss a worker for any other reason than gross incompetence without paying a large redundancy sum. Although legal reform in 1984 served to provide the employer with more let-out clauses than ever before (continual lateness, being drunk at work, and failing to follow orders are cited as just causes for terminating employment), the costs of redundancy in Spain are still among the highest in Europe; and the maximum an employer can be forced to pay out for unfair dismissal is the highest: fortyfive days per year worked up to a total of 42 months. It is an issue which continues to cause much controversy and a lot of ill feeling in Spain (who usually choose to settle out of court in such cases). Legislation is currently in the pipeline to reduce the costs to employers of hiring and firing staff, with the intention of reducing this maximum unfair dismissal figure to 33 days per year worked, up to a maximum of 24 months' salary.

The unusual Spanish custom of companies making special payments to employees in July and at Christmas also continues to apply. These extra pay rolls are known as *pagas extraordinarias* – and may well seem extraordinary to UK employers, or those taking on staff in Spain for the first time, who are not used to this concept of a 14-month year. Their original purpose was to ensure that workers had some extra funds in hand for the Christmas and summer holidays. Thus an employee's salary is apportioned each year in 14 payrolls.

The Spanish trade union movement barely exists, some would say; of Spain's 12 million workers, less than two million belong to trade unions. However, agreements with unions are legally binding, as are the minimum working conditions. The employer does not have to provide any private pension scheme, but has to pay high rates of social security. There are no requirements for an employer to provide fringe benefits; and these are generally of limited importance. Many retirement benefit schemes are designed largely to induce personnel to retire on a specified date (usually 65) and this has now been included in Spanish legislation as a result of the Social Chapter.

Taxation

All legal entities must register with the Ministry of Finance immediately following their incorporation and will be assigned a Fiscal Identity Number (NIF) which is used for all tax purposes. Foreign businesses which operate but which are not based in Spain are subject to the normal corporation tax rate on profit arising in Spain (see below); this includes Capital Gains Tax.

Tax Returns. All Spanish businesses must file corporate tax returns to be submitted to the provincial tax headquarters (*Delegacíon de Hacienda*) of the area corresponding to the registered addresss (*domicilio fiscal*) of the taxpayer. The return is made on forms provided by the authorities and must include all taxable profits. When filing a return you must attach a label with the taxpayer's addresss and fiscal identity number on it which can be obtained from the Ministry of Economy and Finance (Ministerio de Economia y Hacienda, Paseo de la Castellana 162, E28046 Madrid; ☎914682000; fax 915226935). Returns should be made on all of the following taxes: corporate tax, witholdings on account of personal income tax, income tax of sole proprietors, and VAT. All the company's financial statements and accounting records are needed to support the tax return. As in the UK, necessary business expenses are tax deductible, if they are properly recorded and supported with receipts.

Procrastination regarding tax payment, whether intended or unintended, is not looked upon kindly by the Spanish tax authorities and delayed payment of taxes is subject to interest at a minimum of 10% while delayed filing of returns is liable to a surcharge of 20% plus interest from the time of filing. Major tax infringements can carry fines from anything between 50% and 300% of the tax. The rate of interest applicable on delayed payment of taxes is established by the government in the annual budget, usually a few percentage points above the legal rate of interest (8% currently).

Corporate Tax. This is levied at 35% on the profit which the business generates. Taxable income includes all the profits from operations, income from investments not relating to the regular business purpose and capital gains. Tax is withheld on dividends distributed to any shareholders and the dividends must then be grossed up in the taxable income of the company, although the withholding may be taken as a tax credit for company dividends. Sole traders are subject to personal taxation on their profits and also Capital Gains Tax if appropriate.

Accountancy Advice

The majority of small businesses may present what is a simplified version of the statutory audit required annually by all companies. Businesses qualify for this simplified form of audit if their total assets do not exceed a sum currently equivalent to around £1,500,000; and also if the average number of employees during the financial year does not exceed 50. Auditors who are qualified professionals and are officially recognised by the Institute of Accountancy and Auditing must be appointed to carry out the audit.

Every business, regardless of size, is required to keep certain records. These include a journal (*diario*), balance sheet, profit and loss account and minutes of important (i.e. directors' and shareholders') meetings (*actas*). All these records should be kept in bound volumes and each page must be prestamped by the municipal authorities. Entries, in Spanish, should be made in chronological order and show amounts in pesetas. Only records which comply will these standards will be accepted by the authorities. It is worth noting that Spanish company law allows shareholders to inspect accounting records, with professional assistance, if necessary.

The main accountancy body in Spain is the *Instituto de Censores Jurados de Cuentas in Madrid* (☎914460354) which is responsible for drafting accounting and auditing standards there. The second accountancy body, formed by the country's leading economists, is the *Insituto de Contabilidad y de Auditoria de Cuentas*, also based in Madrid (☎912544906) which is responsible for coordinating the profession and formulating national accounting charts and principles.

A list of the leading international firms of chartered accountants which have offices in Spain is provided below; Similar lists for the various regions (such as Barcelona, Bilbao and Madrid) can be obtained from the Consulates in these areas.

Useful Addresses

BDO Binder: Calle Serrano 85, E28006 Madrid; ☎15636773; fax 15645336. *Deloitte & Touche:* Plaza Pablo Ruiz Picasso, Torre Picasso 38°, E28020 Madrid; ☎915550252; fax 915567430. *Ernst & Young:* Alberto Alcocer 247, 28036 Madrid; ☎912508000; fax 914578917. Also, Becket House, 1 Lambeth Palace Road, London SE1

7EU; ☎020-795 2000; fax 020-7928 1345.

Grant Thornton España SA: Centro Colon, Marqués de la Ensenada 16, E28004 Madrid; ☎913198300.

Jordan & Son: (head office) 2022 Bedford Row, London WC1R 4JS; ☎020-7400 3304.

KPMG: Edificio Torre Europa, Paseo de la Castellana 95, E28046 Madrid and 8 Salisbury Square, London EC4Y 8BB www.kpmg.com.

PricewaterhouseCoopers: Edificio PricewaterhouseCoopers, Paseo de la Castellena 43, E28046 Madrid; fax 913083566. Southwark Towers, 32 London Bridge Street, London SE1 9SY; ☎020-7583 5000.

Legal Advice

The prospective businessman in Spain is almost certainly going to need specialist legal advice, both in the setting up or purchase of the business and in future operations. This applies no matter how small or large the business is. Although there are some UK law practices with knowledge of Spanish law, as well as some international law firms with offices in Spain, most small businesses will be best served by a local Spanish practice. Although these are numerous, English-speaking lawyers are fairly rare. Listed below are Spanish law firms in Spain which employ one or more English-speaking lawyers and many of which employ British lawyers with Spanish law expertise; as above, a similar list for your local area can be obtained from the British Consulate.

Useful Addresses – Spanish Lawyers

Antonio Roca Puig: Avenida Diagonal 506, 5th Floor 2, E08006 Barcelona; ☎934158116; fax 934151762.

Asesoria Juridica Baker & McKenzie: Paseo de la Castellana, Edificio Senix, Planta 6, 28046 Madrid; ☎91391 59 50. UK Office: 100 New Bridge Street, London EC4V 6JA; ☎020-7919 1000; fax 020-79191999.

Asesores Legales Asociados: Paseo de la Castellana 123, 6th Floor, A Left, E28046 Madrid; ☎915552959; fax 915552921.

Bufete Bano Léon: Pintor Lorenzo Casanova 66, 1st Floor, Alicante; ☎965921853; fax 965921854.

Bufete Bruna: Provenza 318, 2nd Floor 1, E08037 Barcelona; ☎932154561; fax 932156147.

Bufete Climente, Minguell & Martin Solicitors: Pau Claris 154, 2nd Floor, E08009 Barcelona; ☎934871084; fax 934871680.

Canary Trust Co. SL: José Franchy Roca 5, Office 308, Las Palmas, Gran Canaria, E35007 Canary Islands; ☎928267632; fax 928222343.

De Pinna Notaries: 35 Piccadilly, London W1V 0PJ; ☎020-7208 2900; fax 020-7208 0066.

Enrique Rauet Guinau Solicitor: Via Augusta 59, 6th Floor, Desp 602, E08006 Barcelona; ☎934150407; fax 934193944.

Jesús Bello Albertos: N/Sra de García 24, 5th Floor B, Marbella, E29600 Málaga; ☎95282426/2772487; fax 952829329.

Mariscal, Monero, Meyer & Marinello CB: Calle Barbara de Braganza 11, 2nd Floor Right, E28004 Madrid; ☎913199686; fax 913085368.

Rosa L Machi Pérez Solicitor: Prol Rámon Y Cajal, Edificio Nortysur 2,1, Santa Cruz de Tenerife, E38003 Canary Islands; ☎922249137; fax 922273567.

Santiago Aguilar Canosa I Castella: Avenida Diagonal 529, Pral, 2nd Floor, E08029 Barcelona; ☎934053881; fax 934308493.

Tomas Buxeda Nadal: Rambla de Catalunya 5355, 6th Floor, E08007 Barcelona; ☎934880250; fax 934881656.

J. Polanco: Flat 208, Goulden House, Bull Street, London SW11 3HQ; ☎020-7223 1116; 020-7350 0282.

Tomas Lamarca Abello: Muntaner 400, Pral 1st Floor, E08034 Barcelona; ☎932012444; fax 932003558.

M Vega Penichet: Alcalá 115, 2 dcha, E28009 Madrid; ☎914315500; fax 914315938.

Ventura Garces Solicitors: Calle Freixa 2628 bajos, E08021 Barcelona; ☎932019444; fax 932098391.

Consejo General de la Abogacia Española: Calle de Serano 9, E28001 Madrid; ☎915227711; fax 914319365.

Useful Publications

Many of the major accountancy firms in London produce booklets which focus on different aspects of business in Spain, e.g. tax, finance and banking laws from the potential investor's point of view. Also recommended are the series of articles by Roger Faulks in *Spanish Property News* 'Getting Down to Business' (SPN, 2 Paragon Place, Blackheath, London SE3 0SP). Write to SPN for a subscription and request some copies. The business pages of the UK press also occasionally feature articles of interest to those thinking of setting up in business, at home or abroad.

All of the following publications deal directly with all or some of the issues which face small businesses in Spain discussed above; but as they are updated periodically it is useful to contact each organisation in order to find the most current edition.

Doing Business with Spain (ISBN 07494 31393) is endorsed by the Spanish Chamber of Commerce and offers an overview of opportunities, and all aspects of business practice there. The second edition costs £40 and is available in most bookshops; or direct from FREEPOST 1, Kogan Page, 120 Pentonville Road, London N1 9BR; ☎020-7278 0433; fax 020-7837 6348.

Also available from Kogan Page, as well as the Spanish Chamber of Commerce in London (1 Harley Street, London W1G 9QD; ☎020-76379061; fax 020-7436 7188), is the Spanish Chamber of Commerce's *AngloSpanish Trade Directory* and they have extremely useful website at www.spanishchamber.co.uk. They can also provide a list of their members both in Spain and in the UK. Their bimonthly *Trade Opportunities Bulletin* (free for members, £10 for non-members) contains commercial opportunities offered by UK and Spanish importers and exporters. Members and non-members of the Chamber can also commission commercial reports on specific Spanish companies themselves and receive company listings from their extensive database.

Overseas Trade is the DTI (and Foreign Office) publication for news, advice and information for UK exporters throughout the world (published by the Brass Tacks Publishing Company Ltd., 102 Sydney Street, London SW3 6NJ; ☎020-7368 9600; www.amdgroup.com).

Trade Partners UK (DTI/Business in Europe, Kingsgate House, 66/74 Victoria Street, London SW1E 6SW; ☎020-7214 5444), www.tradepartners.gov.uk have an extensive website with major profiles on Spain and other countries. Very useful for anyone planning to set up or do business in Spain.

Portugal

SECTION 1

LIVING IN PORTUGAL

GENERAL INTRODUCTION

RESIDENCE AND ENTRY REGULATIONS

SETTING UP HOME

DAILY LIFE

RETIREMENT

Provinces & Main Towns of Portugal

R. Minho
Melgaço
Valença
R. Lima
Chaves
Bragança
R. Tâmega

Minho
Viana do Castelo
Braga
Guimarães
Trás-os-Montes

Vila Real

Douro Litoral
Oporto
R. Douro

Atlantic Ocean

Beira Alta
R. Vouga
Viseu
Guarda
Covilhá
R. Mondego
R. Zêzere
Aveiro
Coimbra

Figueira da Foz
Beira Litoral
Beira Baixa
Castelo Branco

Leiria
Batalha
Fátima
Nazaré
Tomar
Caldas da Rainha
Alcobaça
Torres Novas
Obidos
R. Tagus
Portalegre

SPAIN

Santarém
Ribatejo

Matra
Mora
Élvas
Sintra
Éstremoz
Estoril
LISBON
Alto Alentejo

N

Setúbal
Évora
Sesimbra

0   50   100 Kms
0   25   50 Miles

R. Sado
Houra

Beja
R. Guadiana
Sines
Baixo

Alentejo
R. Mira

Vila Real de Santo Antonio
Silves
Tavira
Portimão
Lagos
Faro
Sagres
Albufeira
Olhão
Algarve

Azores
Corvo
Flores
São Jorge
Graciosa
Terceira
Faial
Pico
Porto Santo
São Miguel
Santa Maria
Funchal
Madeira

General Introduction

CHAPTER SUMMARY

○ **The Portuguese.** Portugal is a mix of influences including Celtic, Roman and Moorish.

  ○ The Portuguese north and south of the Rio Tejo are of Celtic and Moorish ethnic origins respectively.

  ○ Foreigners are struck by the slightly oldfashioned feel, the relaxed attitute of the locals and the byzantine bureaucracy.

  ○ Most of the modern developments in Portugal are concentrated in the Algarve.

○ **The Capital.** Lisbon is more in the mainstream of cosmopolitan Europe than the rest of the country and has been transformed in the last decade by renovation and prestige building projects.

  ○ Lisbon has great nightlife, steep hills, cheap restaurants and an excellent tram system like San Francisco's.

  ○ The original city was destroyed by an earthquake which killed 30,000 in 1755.

○ **Motoring.** Portugal has the highest fatal accident rate per head of the population than any other European country.

○ **Demography.** Over half the Portuguese population is still rurally based.

○ **Politics.** For nearly forty years, Portugal was ruled by a military dictator, Antonio de Oliviera Salazar.

  ○ A bloodless military coup in 1974 ended the dictatorship and led to the establishment of democratic government.

○ **Language.** Portuguese is spoken by an estimated 200 million people (mainly Brazilians) worldwide.

○ **Historical.** Historically, Portugal is renowned for its shipbuilding and navigation skills.

  ○ Vasco da Gama and Columbus both studied at the famous Portuguese shool of navigation in Sagres.

Destination Portugal

The pace of life in the small country of Portugal is slow compared to its neighbour Spain. The inexorable march of tourism has made its impact, largely in the southernmost region, the Algarve, and the coast around Lisbon. As in Spain, where the tourists go, the foreign residents usually follow. There are estimated to be 30,000 Britons living and working in Portugal, with many other retired people and other residents. For years before mass tourism came in the 60's, there were expatriate colonies in Lisbon (Lisboa) and Oporto (Porto) involved mainly in trade. Portugal was never particularly fashionable. Artistic and literary types went to Mallorca, or the South of France, to North Africa, Paris or the Greek islands, but almost never to Portugal, and so for a time the idyllic calm was preserved.

Nowadays, nearly every fishing village in the Algarve has a tourist development, but there is as yet no comparison to the jetset resorts of the Spanish Costa del Sol. Some may prefer it this way and although this southern region is among the most developed, with good (if congested) roads and an abundance of cardphones, cashpoints and other modern items, visitors and foreign residents (*estrangeiros*) are still struck by the slightly oldfashioned feel, the relaxed attitude of the locals... and the bureaucracy. The latter tends to be more accentuated outside the main tourist and city areas. Lisbon nowadays is more in the mainstream of cosmopolitan Europe, with a lively fashion and nightlife scene as well as its picturesque old Moorish quarter. There was a building boom in Lisbon as it upgraded the urban infrastructure for Expo '98, which attracted international focus on the city and increased the numbers of tourists.

The hope is that all this building work will leave behind a more modern infrastructure. This premillennial exhibition was based, like much of Portuguese history, on the theme of the oceans of the world, past, present and future: and was backed by over one billion pounds of government and private sector finance. Development of the site in Lisbon has continued after the exhibition.

Portugal's history as an independent country can be traced back to the medieval kingdom of Portuçale (see below); and its roots are in the mingling of the Celtic and then the Roman people who came here. To the south, a Moorish influence is still evident. More recently (and importantly, for Britons wishing to work there) Portugal joined the then Common Market in 1986, the same year as Spain and Greece. Membership of the European Union has accelerated the modernisation of town and country life, with the increased mechanisation of agriculture; and aid and investment coming from Brussels for projects like the expansion of the underground railway in Lisbon (the *Metropolitano de Lisboa*) and new motorways which are being driven through the tranquil countryside by the state-owned Brisa company.

These new roads are visual proof of change and the gradual reduction of the numbers of donkeycarts in the countryside, which are still a common form of transport in the more rural areas, like the Minho region, lying between Oporto and the Spanish border in the north. But development has seen the tracks worn and plodded by these familiar quadrupeds, widened, asphalted and then motorised with a vengeance.

Its heritage and traditions are sometimes under threat. There was an international outcry recently when a £200 million project to build a new dam and reservoir in the Côa Valley turned out to be threatening the site of Europe's largest Stone Age 'art gallery'. Engravings of animals dating back to the last Ice Age were discovered; and the project was stopped (by the incoming socialist government) before too much damage was done.

Visitors to this remote valley are now welcome; and it may become another feature of Portugal's burgeoning tourist trade. The Portuguese are quite keen to encourage tourists to move away from the Algarve, and to see some of the less well-known parts of the country. As a result there are many places in Portugal which still have potential for tourism development, which it is hoped will be carried out in a less environmentally damaging way than it has sometimes been in the past. To the east and north, there are still many villages connected to the outside world only by dirt tracks trodden by donkeys, an attraction for some visitors with the transport to get there. In Portugal, there are still places to get away from it all and over 60% of the population is still rurally based.

Not everything is changing for the better, though, despite the great strides the country has made in recent years. As more imported goods fill the shops, and services and facilities are upgraded, the cost of living is also rising, especially in Lisbon. Although Portugal is no longer a bargain Eden of retreat, it is still has the cheapest living costs in western Europe; and an equable climate (rainier in the north). It is also a more relaxed country in which to live and work than some of its Mediterranean neighbours.

Pros and Cons of Moving to Portugal

The strong historical links between Britain and Portugal have long made it a popular and welcoming country for citizens of the UK to retire to. Relations between England and the ancient medieval kingdom of Portuçale go back to at least the time of the Crusades, when a party of English knights bound for the Holy Land stopped off to help King Alfonso Henriques drive out the Moors, and took part in the capture of Lisbon. This was the first action of what is probably England's oldest continental alliance; and trade has ebbed and flowed between the two countries ever since. (It is unusual that UK imports and exports in Portugal are more or less in balance; today the country is said to be 'a relatively easy market for first time exporters').

Friendly relations are only one of the advantages. While property prices have shot up in the past ten years, there are still bargains to be found, even in the Algarve, if one is prepared to go a little inland. Unfortunately for those not yet contemplating retirement, there are still far fewer employment opportunities for foreigners in Portugal than in many other countries.

In spite of a steadily improving economy, and low unemployment, it is extremely difficult for non-Portuguese speakers to find work; and since immigration and work restrictions were eased after its joining the EEC or European Union, the main limitations seem to be first of all the language. English is not so widely spoken here. Second, there are the low wages paid to Portuguese employees with which the British find it hard to compete. On the plus side, prospects for seasonal jobs, for holiday company personnel, entertainers, and in bars and hotels, are better than you might expect; while self-employed foreigners generally do extremely well in the Algarve, running businesses catering for their fellow northern Europeans.

Remarkably, 80% of the UK investment in Portugal has gone to the Algarve, mostly into real estate; and UK companies see further propects here for expansion.

This may bring more jobs for those, like lawyers and accountants, involved with these new investments and companies. There is expansion, too, in the engineering and consumer goods sectors.

The business capital of Portugal is Porto, not least because of the port wine trade which began in the Middle Ages. The English exported in return wool from the South Coast to Portugal. Dried fruit, salt, honey and wax – as well as wine – were also traditional imports into England from Portugal. Porto has, since those days, attracted a range of British and other foreign commercial investments, particularly from American and German companies. Siemens, the German electronics and engineering giant recently completed a £300 million memory chip plant near Porto. Other multinationals established there are Opel Portugal, Ford, Volkswagen, Texas Instruments, Alcatel, Yasaki, Borealis, Continental, Bendix, Mitsubishi, Samsung, Pepsico, Nestlé and Pioneer. The financial service sector changes in areas like banking which have helped to bring Portugal into the European Monetary Union and the adoption of a single currency may also provide useful openings for anyone considering developing business connections with the country.

One of the attractions of Portugal for business is a positive disadvantage for international workers. Although minimum wages are fixed by law, they are dismally low compared with Britain: for example a state school teacher earns about £600 per month while casual workers can easily find themselves working simply for bed, board and pocket money. Such a disadvantage has to be weighed against the traditional hospitality of the Portuguese people and the comparatively low cost of living.

Another disadvantage is the legendary Portuguese bureaucracy. It can take a minimum of six months to get a residence permit (if you come from outside the EU that is). But the problems don't end there. Even if you are a Portuguese citizen, it can take up to two years to get a licence to run a business in Portugal. The same applies to expatriate Britons and others. Further details on residence and permits can be found in the chapter which follows on *Residence and Entry Regulations*.

As a result of Portugal's membership of the EU, however, for British and Irish citizens, quite a few of these regulations have been simplified. But it is certain that all kinds of bureaucracy still exists in Portugal for locals and immigrants alike; and foreign workers and residents will often have the added disadvantage of not being able to speak the language well.

Despite being spoken by an estimated 200 million people worldwide, it would be a mistake to assume, unless one is a talented linguist, that Portuguese is an easy language to pick up. In written form, it bears more than a passing resemblance to Spanish but in pronunciation it resembles other tongues. Although a knowledge of Latin, or Romance languages like French and Spanish, will help with word recognition, the difficulty of learning to speak Portuguese may be a drawback for those wishing to live and work there.

PROS AND CONS OF LIVING IN PORTUGAL

Pros

O Portugal is an extremely hospitable country with a long historical association with the UK.

O Procedures for house and property-buying have become well-established over several decades and there is plenty of professional advice to help the uninitiated avoid the pitfalls.

O Portugual has a mild climate all year round, as do the Portuguese islands of the Azores and Madeira.

O Services are well-developed in the areas popular with tourists and expatriates.

O Portugal is fast catching up with its more sophisticated EU neighbours, but its unspoiled picturesque charm is one of the many attractions it still has over them.

O Although prices, especially property taxes, have increased dramatically over the past few years, the cost of living generally and most property prices (except in the most sought after areas) are lower than in many northern European countries.

O New investment also means there are now a wider range of job opportunities.

O Tourism has meant that travel between Britain and Portugal is relatively inexpensive.

O The Portuguese generally are relaxed and easy-going.

Cons

O Despite a thriving economy and low unemployment, openings for foreigners in Portuguese industry are often limited.

O Housing conditions often do not meet Western standards.

O Wages in Portugal are low compared with the rest of the EU.

O Dealing with bureaucracy in Portugal constitutes a test of forbearance and fortitude.

O In remoter regions communications, the roads and utilities are often still poor.

O The climate in the north can be cold and rainy.

O Those expecting a faster pace of life may be disappointed.

O Portuguese life, especially family life, can be closed and inward-looking.

O Development, especially in the Algarve, has made it a less attractive place for those wishing to get away from it all.

O Essential services like hospitals have room for improvement.

O Prices are rising, and imported goods can be expensive.

HISTORY AND POLITICAL AND ECONOMIC STRUCTURE

History

Under the Romans, Portugal was part of the province of Lusitania and populated by Celtic tribes who became Romanised and adopted the Latin language. Following the break-up of the Roman Empire the barbarian hordes swept unimpeded through the Iberian Peninsula. Then, conversion to Christianity came (as in Britain) in the sixth century. In the eighth century virtually the whole of the Peninsula was taken over by the Moors. Until the eighth century, in fact, the history of Portugal vitually mirrors that of Spain; but the Moslem occupation of the area later to become known as Portugal lasted two and a half centuries less than in the rest of the Peninsula, a fact that was to have an important effect on its development as a separate political entity later on.

From the twelfth century, Portugal was an independent kingdom; and King Alfonso Henriques fought his way down the coast with the help of his Crusader allies to recapture the modern capital Lisbon from the Moors. By the midfourteenth century, the country had expanded to approximately its present boundaries; and in 1386 the Portuguese signed the Treaty of Windsor with the English against their mutual enemies at the time in Spain; and so was born a long history of Anglo-Portuguese friendship and cooperation.

To consolidate this treaty, Phillipa, the daughter of John of Gaunt, was given in marriage to King John of Portugal. The third son of this marriage was later to become known as Henry the Navigator. So begins Portugal's history of maritime expansion.

A man of vision and learning, Henry secreted himself on Cape Sagres, the southwest extremity of Portugal, where he founded a school of navigation attended by both Vasco de Gama and Christopher Columbus. Prince Henry also refined the process of boat building which resulted in the Portuguese *caravel*, a vessel designed to withstand lengthy sea voyages and adverse weather conditions.

The most significant result of his navigational researches, though, was the realisation that the route to India and the Spice Islands lay not to the west, as Columbus stubbornly believed until his death, but around the Cape of Good Hope and eastwards, which is where the main focus of Portuguese expansion lay. The Portuguese had long been fishermen and traders. Now they were becoming a world power.

In 1488, Bartholomew Dias set sail from Portugal, rounded the Cape of Good Hope, and sailed into the Indian Ocean. In 1497, Vasco de Gama sailed the same route and landed first in what became Portuguese Mozambique; and then continued to India and the Spice Islands. By the end of the fifteenth century the Spaniards and Portuguese had also become rival colonists in the New World, a problem which exercised world leaders at the time.

The rough east-west division between Portuguese and Spanish territories prompted the Pope's pragmatic solution (over-mighty even by Papal standards). The Treaty of Tordesillas which he devised in 1494 divided the world vertically between Spain and Portugal; and each would claim any land as yet undiscovered in their respective hemispheres. Portugal's half included by chance the yet-to-be-discovered country of Brazil, stumbled upon by Pedro Alves Cabral in 1500.

By the midsixteenth century this tiny nation on the western shores of Europe (with a population of only about one million at most) had become the first world power, acquiring a vast empire which included Morocco, parts of East Africa and the islands along its coast, the enormously rich prize of Brazil, and the East Indies. Thus over-extended, Portugal found it impossible to protect her overseas interests from the ravening English and Dutch navies, or, on her own doorstep, to protect herself from the designs of Philip II of Spain. He seized the Portuguese throne in 1580 and thus initiated sixty years of Spanish rule. During this period the disintegration of overseas Portuguese interests continued, including the loss of the East Indies to the Dutch.

In 1807, during the Napoleonic wars, the Portuguese royal family were saved by the British from impending capture by the French, and borne off to Brazil with an escort provided by a British naval squadron. Brazil declared her own independence in 1821.

The intended unification by Portugal of her two African colonies of Mozambique and Angola (which was successfully prevented by Cecil Rhodes in Rhodesia) was a sticking point in late nineteenth-century relations between Britain and Portugal – one of the rare disagreements between the two countries. Following the declaration of the Portuguese Republic in 1910, the British navy provided its customary rescue service for beleaguered Portuguese royalty, this time removing Manuel II to Gibraltar.

Relations between Britain and Portugal prospered once again when Portuguese soldiers fought on the Allied side in the First World War. In the Second World War, Portugal remained neutral; but the British invoked the fourteenth century Treaty of Windsor to enable the Americans to build bases on the Azores. From here they pursued German submarines which were attacking the Atlantic convoys.

Government

The monarchy was abolished in 1910; and the First Republic lasted from 1910 to 1926. Portugal had emerged from the First World War in economic and political chaos. During 1920 alone seven consecutive governments were formed and dissolved. This was followed by a period of changing military governments in 1925. In 1926, a right-wing military coup led by General Gomes da Costa overthrew the republic; and established a military dictatorship which was itself overturned by General Carmona in 1928. Carmona survived as president of Portugal until 1951.

Like Portugese bullfighting, Portuguese coups have tended to be bloodless. In 1928, President Carmona appointed a young law professor from Coimbra university as minister of finance. The name of the new minister was António de Oliveira Salazar. By 1933, Salazar had become prime minister and instigated a new constitution, the New State (*Novo Stado*), under the guise of which the democratic rights of the Portuguese were slowly whittled away. Political opposition was neutralised and workers' rights were nullified by the introduction of statecontrolled union organisations.

By 1956, there were penal colonies for dissidents and arrests of citizens for an unlimited period in the interests of national security were commonplace. In short, the apparatus of dictatorship was firmly in place. Salazar retained his post for nearly forty years by rigging the various presidential elections so that only candidates who supported him achieved office: they then naturally reappointed him prime minister.

Cracks appeared in Salazar's regime when the 'winds of change' that were stirring the African colonies of western nations to strive for their independence were resisted by the Salazar regime. The deeply unpopular Colonial Wars, launched in 1961, were to be one of the main contributory factors to the eventual downfall of the regime.

Salazar was forced to retire in 1968, following a fall on the head that incapacitated him permanently. He was succeeded as prime minister by Marcello Caetano, who had no intention of relinquishing the colonies of Angola, Guinea-Bissau and Mozambique. The main guerrilla liberation movements of these lands were UNITA, PAIGC and FRELIMO who, between them, took up a good deal of foreign news space during the thirteen years that Portugal waged war in Africa. The refusal of Caetano to make a settlement with the rebels in Angola caused deep resentment in the ranks of the military. General António Spínola, the governor general of the colony who had prepared the ground for a settlement, had argued that the only way forward was for the colonies to be formed into a Portuguese-speaking federation with a measure of self-autonomy. He was subsequently sacked for expressing such views.

Following the increasing politicisation of the military and a split in ideology between the upper and lower ranks (effectively the older and younger officers) the seeds for a military coup were sown. The younger officers rallied around the figure of Spínola, who was later jettisoned in favour of Major Otelo Saraiva de Carvalho, who took charge of the Movement of the Armed Forces which eventually staged a coup on April 25th 1974, thus ending fifty years of dictatorship. The first constitutional parliament was elected democratically on 25th April 1976.

Under the constitution, a president is elected by popular vote every five years, and the parliament, the Assembly of the Republic, every four years.

Political Parties

By 1976, power had been returned to civilians and four main political parties had emerged: the PCP, the PS, the PPD/PSD and the CDS. The oldest is the PCP, the Portuguese Communist Party. Founded in 1921, it went underground during the dictatorship. Its main areas of influence are amongst the industrial working class and the farmers of the Alentejo region. The PS (Socialist Party) was founded in 1974 with Mário Soares as its general secretary. Vigorously anticommunist, it has strong links with the German Social Democratic Party. The PPD/PSD was the right-wing party whose leader, Sâ Carneiro, became prime minister in 1979 and 1980. Supported by the professional and managerial cadres of Portuguese society it also finds favour with the lesser bourgeoisie and is roughly comparable with the Liberal Democrats in Britain.

The CDS is a conservative party founded by Freitas do Amaral. Its influence is strongest in the north of the country, where its support is based amongst the professional and property-owning upper middle classes and right-wing Catholics.

After the 1985 elections, President Ramalho Eanes asked Dr Anibal Cavaco Silva to form a government when Mário Soares stood down as prime minister. Mário Soares took over the presidency in 1986. In 1995 Portugal elected the PS (Socialist Party) into government headed by Dr Antonio Guterres a Christian Socialist and 'moderniser' in the mould of Tony Blair. For many years he enjoyed high popularity at home and international respect. He even adopted the British Prime Minister's law and order prescription 'Tough on crime, tough on the causes of crime'. The Guterres government combined higher public spending in some areas (like education) with a rigorous fiscal and economic policies which favour deregulation and privatisation.

Since winning a large re-election victory in 1999, the Guterras government gradually lost its popularity. Despite overcoming economic problems to bring Portugal into the Euro, in December 2001 Dr Guterres resigned. A heavy defeat for his party in local elections aggravated a perception of drift and errors. Seventy people had earlier lost their lives when a bridge over the River Douro in northern Portugal collapsed, reinforcing a belief that the government had failed to address the country's declining infrastructure.

Following national elections in March 2002, Portugal's new government reflected a move to the right when the centre-right Social Democrats, led by Durao Barroso formed a coalition with the smaller conservative Popular party.

Economics

Until the 1950's the majority of Portuguese led a lowly and largely agrarian existence. Wealth was enjoyed by a small minority of the population; and the rest lived in conditions reminiscent of eighteenth century (i.e. pre-revolutionary) France. The Salazar regime ran the economy hand-in-glove with a small circle of magnates whose riches were largely accrued through massive colonial exploitation. Basically five families were involved: Champalimaud, Mello, Quina, Queiroz, Pereira and Espiríto Santo. The unions in Portugal having been rendered toothless by the regime, a plentiful supply of cheap, subdued labour ensured that industrial wheels ran smoothly for the benefit of this small section of society.

Additionally, and with equal complicity of the industrial barons, the regime practised protectionist policies which precluded the setting up of any rival companies to upset the monopolies of the five leading families. The effect of this was to ensure the Portuguese nation remained in the economic dark ages, by preventing much needed modernisation and industrialisation.

A belated spurt of industrial development in the fifties caused the exodus of rural populations to the towns in search of jobs, leaving behind in the villages only the old and the very young, which resulted in severe agricultural decline.

In 1975, the Agrarian Reform Law was passed with the aim of breaking up the large estates south of the river Tagus, whose ownership had been maintained by the same social stratum through exploitation of the mass of miserably paid farm workers. By restricting the size of estates, expropriating the surplus land, and encouraging its occupation by these workers, the Agrarian Reform achieved a redistribution of ownership which resulted in a rush of people attempting to earn a living through agriculture. However, the achievements of the reform were diminished when Barreto's Law of 1976 partially reversed the earlier legislation by increasing the permitted size of estates, thus enabling former landowners to claw back some of their former property. This resulted in thousands of farm workers being thrown off the land they had been occupying; and caused mass unemployment in the countryside. The effects of Barreto's law can still be seen today, although Portuguese agriculture is now moving out of the dark ages with the help of EU subsidies and the Common Agricultural Policy.

1974, the year of the coup (which was otherwise known as the Carnation

Revolution) was not an auspicious one for the economy. Faced with the dual horror of revolution and a world recession, many Portuguese businessmen fled the country (having first emptied their bank accounts) leaving their factories rudderless behind them. To aggravate matters, tourism and foreign investment both slumped. In an effort to stabilise the economy the government nationalised the banks, insurance companies and transport; and some major industries including petrochemicals and brewing. They also began to dismantle the old industrial monopolies.

It is probably a measure of the state of the economy that nine constitutional governments came, wrestled with the economy, and went, in the six years between 1976 and 1984. Economic austerity became the watchword of the late seventies; and negotiations for IMF and European bank loans were continuously on the agenda. In addition, negotiations for entry into the Common Market began, although it was to be ten years before they came to fruition.

In 1983, the budget included a 28% retrospective increase in income tax; and an exit tax was levied on anyone leaving the country, a means of raising cash more often encountered in third world countries. The situation since the late 1980's has been improving though. The years between 1895-95 have been called the 'Prodigious Decade'. This was when Portugal began to catch up with its European neighbours.

Prime Minister Gutieres successfully engineered Portugal's official entry to the Euro in 1999, partly by privatising 22 companies and so reducing the public deficit. Income from tourism has been steadily increasing: no less than two hundred and fifty tour operators currently feature Portugal (including Madeira and the Azores) amongst their destinations. American investment has also been significant.

In step with many developed economies Portugal began to experience a slowdown in economic activity during 2001 and inflation rose to a rate over 4%. For the year 2002 the Portuguese economy is projected to grow at a rate of 1.5%, picking up to 3% in 2003.

Portugal deftly used the Expo '98 exhibition in Lisbon to attract foreign investment and improve facilities (see above), much as Barcelona achieved when that city made urban inprovements to hold the Olympic Games in 1992. In future, generous subsidies may decline as other, even poorer countries to the east join the European Union. However membership of the EU has brought Portugal many economic benefits and the institution is still seen as a guarantor of the country's relatively recent democratic institutions.

GEOGRAPHICAL INFORMATION

Mainland and Offshore Portugal

Portugal occupies the southwestern extremity of Europe and covers an area of 34,340 sq miles/88,941 sq kms or approximately 15% of the Iberian Peninsular. Around the the west and south of Portugal stretches 500 miles/804 kms of Atlantic coastline, while in the north and east is the border with Spain. The Minho river, which rises in the Spanish province of Galicia and flows across

Portugal to the sea, forms the northern boundary. The other great Portuguese rivers are the Douro, which forms part of the eastern Spanish border and flows through the port wine region on its westward course to Oporto, and the Tejo river which cuts Portugal in half; and effectively divides the more mountainous north from the plain of the south.

The Tejo river flows into the Atlantic at Lisbon. The plains are again interrupted in the south by the Monchique and Caldèirão Mountains which provide the backdrop for the Algarve.

Madeira, made up of two inhabited islands Madeira and Porto Santo, and two groups of uninhabited islands – all of volcanic origin – lies west of Morocco and 535 miles/861 kms southwest of Lisbon. The total land area of the Madeira Islands is 307 sq miles/796 sq kms. The island of Madeira itself is steep, rising at its highest point to a height of 6106 feet/1861 metres.

The Azores, located about 900 miles/1,448 kms due west of Portugal, comprise nine islands also of volcanic origin (last eruption on Faial 1973), and are divided into three groups, with a total area of 902 sq miles/2,335 square kms. The central group of islands consist of Terceira, Graciosa, São Jorge, Pico and Faial. To the east of these lie São Miguel and Santa Maria; and to the west Corvo and Flores. The largest is São Miguel; and the smallest, Corvo is only ten miles square.

Regional Divisions and Main Towns
Portugal is composed of eleven provinces. North to south these are:

```
MINHO – Braga
TRÁS-OS-MONTES – Braganca, Vila Real
DOURO LITORAL – Oporto
BEIRA ALTA – Viseu, Guarda
BEIRA LITORAL – Aveiro, Coimbra, Leiria
BEIRA BAIXA – Castelo Branco
ESTRAMADURA – Lisbon, Sétubal
RIBATEJO – Santarém
ALTO ALENTEJO – Portalegre, Evora
BAIXO ALENTEJO – Beja
ALGARVE – Faro
```

Population

The current population of Portugal is approximately 10,300,000 with an annual growth rate of about 0.2%. The average density of inhabitants is around 300 per sq mile; in some areas it is as low as 60. The most densely populated regions are unsurprisingly Estramadura, Douro and Minho, since they embrace the main industrial and business centres: Lisbon, Sétubal and Oporto. The north is more populated than the south, the Algarve being one of the least inhabited regions with an indigenous populace (excluding expatriates) of around 350,000.

It is said that the Portuguese north and south of the Rio Tejo are of different ethnic origins: the people of the north are descended from Celtic and Germanic tribes, while the southerners are known as *moreno* (dark skinned) not because of the hotter climate, but as a legacy of their Roman and Moorish antecedents (the south being the area most resolutely occupied by these respective invaders).

During the 1960s and early seventies, when the colonial wars were in process,

TABLE 7		TEMPERATURE CHART						
Area		Jan/Mar Air Sea		Apr/June Air Sea		July/Sept Air Sea		Oct/Dec Air Sea
Monte Estoril	C	17°	15°	22°	17°	26°	19°	17°	16°
(Lisbon Coast)	F	63°	59°	71°	63°	79°	67°	63°	60°
Quarteira	C	17°	16°	22°	19°	27°	23°	18°	17°
(Algarve)	F	63°	61°	72°	67°	81°	73°	64°	63°
Santa Maria	C	17°	17°	20°	19°	24°	22°	919°	20°
(Azores)	F	63°	63°	67°	66°	75°	72°[	67°	69°
Funchal	C	19°	]9°	22°	20°	25°	23°	21°	21°
(Madeira)	F	67°	65°	71°	68°	77°	73°	70°	70°

it is estimated that over a million Portuguese left the country, most of them illegally, to escape army conscription. Many of them made new lives in North America and Venezuela. The departure of such a large number of able-bodied workers contributed to the decline of Portuguese agriculture by aggravating the depopulation of the countryside. Today it is estimated that over four million Portuguese are emigrants, spread throughout Western Europe, Brazil, Australia and South Africa as well as the countries listed above.

Climatic Zones

Portugal is well-known for its mild climate, which is of the Mediterranean-type on the southern coasts, and is influenced by the Atlantic and the Gulf Stream on the northern ones. The littorals, whether south (the Algarve), or west (Costa Prata and Costa Verde) have similar summer temperatures, which rarely exceed the low 70s Fahrenheit (22°C). However there is a considerable difference in the amount of rainfall between north and south, the latter having a dry Mediterranean climate all year round. Winters become progressively cooler and wetter towards the north.

Greater extremes of temperature are found inland: in the mountains of the northeast, the regions of the Trás-os-Montes and Beira Alta are either blitzed by cold or hammered by sun depending on the season. In the south the temperatures of the plains (roughly the area south of the inland town of Évora) are also ranged at opposite ends of the temperature scale, depending on the season.

In the far south there is a noticeable difference in climate between the most westerly and the eastern part of the Algarve coast. Cape St Vincent, which juts into the Atlantic, understandably takes the brunt of the winter gales. The fact that from Lagos eastwards is packagetouristland is indicative of the fact that this is the balmiest climatic zone with Mediterranean warmth and dryness.

Madeira and the Azores, which the Portuguese refer to rather inappropriately as the *Adjacente* (Adjacent Isles), have their own exotic climates. Madeira is subtropical, which means it is has a pleasant climate year through. It also claims an average of 2,000 hours of sunshine annually. The rainy season is from October to March and the misty season (*capacete*) lasts through most of August. Dry winds from Africa (*leste*) intermittently deposit a small part of the Sahara on Madeira. The pleasures of the Madeiran climate however vastly outweigh the minor irritations of the capacete, leste and the odd tropical cloudburst.

The Azores have a surprisingly mild climate considering their location. Their position on the map is vaguely unexpected: isolated in the Atlantic they are reminiscent of a convoy which dropped anchor on the way to America, and decided to stay put. Some of its people did. Temperatures in this exposed archipelago are mild in summer and rarely go below 58°F/14°C in winter.

REGIONAL GUIDE

Asked to perform a word association exercise, the chances are that the average Briton will say Algarve, (or possibly sardines), as a response to 'Portugal' (with port wine a close third). The Algarve is undoubtedly the spot that most foreign would-be residents would choose to buy a home, attracted by the mild climate and the relatively good facilities and infrastructure that have already grown up around the expatriate communities. It is also likely to be the most obvious place for jobseekers to pick up temporary work related to the tourist industry. Summer tourism monopolises large chunks of the coast from Lagos to Faro. The western and eastern extremities are, however, surprisingly empty.

Other expatriates, perhaps wishing to escape the intrusion of holidaymakers into their idyll, have made their homes in and around Lisbon. The Estoril coast north of Lisbon, and the Lisbon coast south of the city, both have their champions (the peripatetic Lord Byron among them) who rate the combination of a superb climate and the attractions of the capital as unbeatable. Byron put it more picturesquely, and added that one cannot expect comfort to be always attendant on pleasure. Perhaps, however, in modern Portugal, it is possible to attain both simultaneously.

Other foreign residents, in particular business people of various types, not just those in the port wine trade, have made their homes in Oporto. Porto, as it is called locally, is probably the only city in Portugal where one is likely to encounter the frenetic atmosphere characteristic of big business centres everywhere. The commercial life of Oporto has received a boost since Portugal joined the single currency. Thus the remaining trade and employment restrictions with the rest of the EU are ended.

Beyond the main tourist and urban areas, Portugal offers remarkable scenic variety. If the character of the Portuguese has been shaped by the sea, then its landscape must have been moulded by rivers, a multitude of which crisscross the length of the land. The result of such a watery abundance, is a pastoral landscape of great beauty and variety. This ranges, northwards, from lush vine-covered valleys, vast pine forests and fields of corn and root crops, to the baked plain of the south, where citrus groves, cork forests and fig plantations give a more Mediterranean aspect to the scenery.

Some adventurous foreign residents have bought properties at knockdown prices in the remoter regions of Portugal. For reasons best known to themselves they are prepared to live without mod cons, including plumbing and mains electricity, in what has been called, without exaggeration, the 'third world of Europe'. Nowhere, in western Europe at least, do such extremes of poverty and relative prosperity exist side by side. For this kind of existence not only is a Byronic attitude to comfort essential; a pioneering streak and an ability to mix with locals will help.

Information Facilities

Before departing for Portugal, basic information can be obtained from the Portuguese Tourist Office in your own country. In London this is 225 Sackville Street (2nd Floor), London W1X 1DE; ☎020-7494 1441; fax 020-7494 1868; www.portugal.org). This is the head office of ICEP (Investment Trade and Tourism of Portugal), an unusual organisation which combines the functions of promoting trade, tourism and investment in the country. The Tourist Office provides fact sheets and leaflets on the different regions (as well as much trade and commercial information). The head office of ICEP/Turismo is: Icep Portugal, Investimento, Comúrcio e Turismo, Avenida 5 de Outubro, 101, 1050051 Lisbon; ☎21-790 9500; fax 21-793 5028. Maps of Portugal are usually combined with Spain and are often out-of-date. You will almost certainly find more recent ones on sale in Portugal itself. Also invaluable, once you are there, are the Tourist Offices (Turismo), located in all the main tourist towns.

Finally, to arrange flights (and for some special offers for villa owners and those managing property there, contact *Clubs Abroad* (Guildbourne Centre, Chapel Road, Worthing, West Sussex BN11 1LZ; reservations ☎01903-201864; fax 01903-201225) which can send its *Flight Club* leaflet offering charter flights to Portugal. The booking telephone number for this is 01903-231857. If you ('or any of your friends') own or manage an overseas apartment or villa they also offer substantial incentives and a free information pack: ☎01903-215123.

THE SOUTH

The Algarve

Main city: Faro
Main tourist office: Rua da Misericordia, 912 8000 Faro; ☎289-803604.
British Consulate: Largo Francisco A. Maurício 71 Portimão 8500 ☎282-417800.

The Algarve takes its name from the Moorish word *algharb* which means west. The famous sandy Algarve coast is a familiar one to tourists and foreign residents alike. At the southwestern point of the Algarve is Cape St Vincent whose illustrious maritime associations include not only Prince Henry the Navigator's fifteenth century school of seamanship, founded at the tiny port of Sagres on the Cape's east side, but also several naval battles including Nelson's daring victory against the Spanish in 1797.

Faro is the administrative centre of the province. The airport, situated four miles/six km from the city centre, operates around the clock during the summer to shuttle sunseekers to the resorts west of Faro including Quarteira, Albufeira, Carvoeri and Praia da Rocha. East of Faro, the coast with its offshore sandbanks has remained, literally, a place where 'sheep may safely graze' (and fishermen and farmers still make a modest living).

The tourists tend to home in on the ancient town of Tavira, which, with its castle, Roman bridge and dozens of churches, is one of the region's picturepostcard sights. So attractive is the town that a couple of smart housing developments have materialised in the vicinity. These developments apart, property prices drop dramatically once you are in the eastern Algarve. It is highly likely that anyone who buys a desirable property here, or preferably land with advance building permission (see Chapter Three), will be able to make a handsome profit in a few years' time.

Another picturesque inland town is Silves, once the hilltop capital of the Moors, and with an impregnable-looking fortress at the summit. Both the castle and the thirteenth-century cathedral, built on the site of a former mosque, survived the terrible earthquake of 1755 which caused widespread devastation. It is possible to rent apartments in Silves, a useful base to prospect the region away from the hubbub of the coast. Further inland from Silves is the beautiful mountainous area of Serra de Monchique based around the spa town of Caldas de Monchique.

Baixho Alentejo & Alto Alentejo (The Plains)

Main towns: Beja, Evora, Portalegre.

These two provinces, lower and upper Alentejo respectively, account for over 25% of the surface area of Portugal. Sparsely populated and mainly agricultural, most of the region is taken up by a vast tableland which begins south of Evora and reaches to the borders of the Algarve. Lower Alentejo is the less scenic, offering virtually no visual variant from sunbaked wheat fields. The coast of Baixho Alentejo which gets pummelled by the Atlantic (unlike the more pampered Algarve coast), nonetheless has the beginnings of tourism. The southern part between Sines and Cape St Vincent may become a modest tourist centre of the future.

The northern half from just below the industrial port of Sétubal, is virtually deserted and is likely to remain so now that a giant oil terminal has been built at Sines. The one bright spot in this otherwise bleak province, is the hilltop city of Beja, a UNESCO-designated area of special cultural interest. Unfortunately this accolade has made Beja a tourist honeypot. Founded by Julius Caesar as a resting place for pensioned-off legionnaires, it was later occupied by the Moorish invaders. In the thirteenth century, a castle was built by Dom (King) Dinis, directly over the Roman site. Beja's convent of the Immaculate Conception is renowned in Portugal for the seventeenth-century nun, Mariana Alcoferado, whose un-nunlike letters to the Chevalier de Camily who passed her window each day were published in translation in Paris in 1669. Tame by contemporary standards, they were nevertheless a sensational bestseller in their day.

The province of Alto Alentejo is more rewarding, with its vestiges of Roman architecture and fortified towns like Elvas and Estremoz; the latter is also known as the 'marble town', from the source of its prosperity quarried nearby. The province is also full of prehistoric sites including standing stones and stone circles. Évora is the main town, formerly invaded by Moors and now by tourists. Évora's population of 40,000 is double that of Beja.

The other main town of the Alto Alentejo is Portalegre, set amongst rolling countryside and famous for its old tapestry factory, where it is said 5,000 shades of wool are used by the peasant women employed there to reproduce centuries old designs.

Ribatejo

Main town: Santarém

On the northwest edge of the plains region Ribatejo, meaning beside the Tagus, is a fertile province where large estates produce figs, olives and citrus fruits in great abundance. Another agricultural speciality is rice which is grown in specially flooded meadows along the banks of the River Tagus. Ribatejo is also cattle country, where you can see the Portuguese cowboys (*campinos*) wearing traditional dress and carrying lances. Their charges are the grazing bulls and horses, as yet blissfully unaware of their fate in the bullrings of Portugal. The Portuguese version of this sport does not match the barbarity of its Spanish counterpart: in deference to the sensibilities of a former royal patron who saw his son gored to death before his eyes, the bulls are not killed in the bullring, but outside afterwards.

The capital of the province is Santarém, which was one of the the six great Moorish strongholds of Portugal. Set high above the Tagus river, it makes an impressive sight from the surrounding countryside. The best view from the city itself is from the Moorish tower, the Portas do Sol. Throughout the fourteenth and fifteenth centuries it was the meeting place of the royal parliaments. Nowadays, perhaps the most famous meeting is the two-week fair which starts on the fourth Sunday in May.

Estremadura

Main towns: Lisbon, Setúbal.
Main tourist office: Lisbon: Palacio Foz, Praça dos Restauradores; ☎21-346 3658 **British Embassy:** Rua de São Bernardo 33, 1249082 Lisbon; ☎21-392 40 00; www.ukembassy.pt.

The narrow coastal province of Estremadura takes in the southern part of the Costa Prata in the north, and reaches to the estuary of the Sado river in the south. The province's great attraction for the large expatriate community is in part the excellent coastline around Lisbon, known as the Lisbon coast (southwards) and the Estoril coast (northwards), and also the bright lights of Lisbon itself. A thriving port since Roman times, its importance grew under the Moors who called it Lishbuna, and again during the time of the great Portuguese colonial expansion of the late fifteenth and sixteenth centuries. Largely destroyed by the earthquake of 1755, it was rebuilt on the grid pattern in less than ten years, under the frenetic direction of the Marquess of Pombal. Some quarters of the city survived the earthquake, notably Belem and Alfama. In more modern times, Lisbon has acquired a huddle of rundown suburbs. Housing became a major problem when the excolonials flooded home following the liberation of Portugal's African colonies shortly after the 1974 Portuguese Revolution.

A cosmopolitan and lively place, Lisbon is built on a series of hills, most of which can be negotiated by some ancient wooden trams which are one of the city's hallmarks. The *Alfama* is the old Moorish quarter of the city.

The towns and villages around Lisbon are another highlight of this region: Sintra, singled out for praise by Lord Byron amongst others, has many buildings of architectural merit, including the fourteenth-century palace, (*Palacio Nacional de Sintra*). Beautiful sub-tropical vegetation provides the backdrop.

The walled city of Óbidos was once a Moorish stronghold. In the twelfth century, the bride of King Dinis was so enamoured of the place that he promptly gave it to her as marriage gift. From that time until the overthrow of the monarchy six centuries later, Óbidos was the customary wedding gift of the Portuguese kings.

A few miles west of Óbidos is the spit of land on which the large fishing port of Peniche is situated. From there a ferry leaves for the nearby islands Ilhas Berlengas.

Setúbal, 31miles/50km from Lisbon, is Portugal's most industrialised and also its third largest city. The magnificent suspension bridge, the Ponte do 25 Abril, one of the longest in Europe, was built by the Americans and opened in 1966. It spans the Tagus estuary leading to Setúbal and the south of Portugal.

THE NORTH

Beira Litoral

Main towns: Leira, Coimbra, Aveiro.
Main tourist office: Largo da Portagem, P3000 Coimbra.

The coast of Beira Litoral is a continuation of the Costa de Prata, which is untroubled by tourism except for a few minor resorts; and therein lies its charm. The outstanding centre of the province is inland – the ancient, cobblestoned city of Coimbra, the former capital of Portugal in the twelfth and thirteenth centuries. Piled high above the right bank of the Mondego, its crowning point is the tower of the historic university, one of the oldest in Europe and referred to in the tourist literature as 'the Oxford of Portugal'. It was founded in 1290; and one of its major later additions is a magnificent Baroque library containing over a million volumes. There is no doubt that it would be delightful place to live, with its ancient atmosphere, scholarly traditions and reputation for poetry and music. Local industry in the port of Aveiro was traditionally based around seaweed harvesting and sea salt production.

Beira Baixa

Main town: Castelo Branco

The parched landscape of the plain of Beira Baixa is on the whole as unproductive as it looks, though it manages to produce a modicum of cork and fruits; you can drive for miles through this rolling and sometimes mountainous landscape without seeing another car or person, before reaching the whitewashed walls of the next sleepy village. The main town of Castelo Branco has a population of 15,000 souls. The neglected remains of its castle are a reminder of its frontiertown origins. From Castelo Branco it is possible to visit mountain villages barely touched by modernity, including Monsanto and Idanha-a-Velha. The latter was once an important Roman town, parts of which have not greatly changed from that time: the walls are still standing; the Roman bridge is still viable; and the more durable vestiges of daily Roman life, including inscribed and sculpted marble, are just lying casually about the place.

Beira Alta

Main towns: Viseu, Guarda.

The province of Beira Alta embraces the wooded and largely unfertile valleys of the lower Douro in the north, and a stretch of the granite mountains (the highest in Portugal) of the Sierra da Estrela in the south. Viseu, which from its high plateau dominates the surrounding landscape, was once the heart of Roman Lusitania. The remains of the Roman garrison camp, built at a crossroads, are still visible on the outskirts of the mediaeval city. Viriatus, the Iberian rebel, and symbol of Lusitanian independence, supposedly made his last stand against the Romans at Viseu. The other main town of the region, the aptly named Guarda, is pitched high in the north east of the Estrela mountains at 3,400 feet/1057 metres and commands outstanding views into Spain. As you would expect from its location Guarda was instrinsic to defence against Spanish acquisitiveness.

Largely unexplored, this region is suitable for walkers and those of an adventurous bent.

Douro Litoral

Main town: Oporto (Porto)
Main tourist office: Praça Dom João 1 4000; ☎22-3393470.
British Consulate: Avenida da Boavista 3072, P4100 Oporto; ☎22-6184789; fax 22-6100438.

The smallest province of Portugal is also the most bustling and industrial. The scenery of the Douro Litoral is dominated by the valley of the Rio Douro (Golden River) which rises in western Spain and once foamed and frothed its way across northern Portugal. Its wilder excesses now curbed by damming, it nevertheless remains an impressive sight as it cuts a swathe through a series of spectacular gorges. Atop the northern bank of the final gorge, where the Douro meets the Atlantic, is piled Portugal's second largest conurbation, Oporto (Porto to the Portuguese), population 400,000. Prosperity here has agricultural and trading origins; and dates back to the beginnings of the port wine trade. In the eighteenth century, the king's minister, the all-powerful Marquess of Pombal, strictly delineated the zone in which the grapes for port wine could be grown. In effect this became a strip which varies from ten to thirty miles in width either side of the Douro. As with all wines of character, it is the fortuitous combination of soil qualities, climate, grape and centuries of expertise, which produce the unique and much-prized end result.

The filled casks are transported from the valley to Vila Nova de Gaia, the port wine dealing suburb of Oporto, on the opposite side of the Douro from the main city. Surprisingly, the British have dropped to second place, after the French, in the league table of port tipplers, while American demand is growing at the luxury end of the market. Porto was also the birthplace of Henry the Navigator.

In tourist office parlance, the coast of Douro Litoral is the southern half of the Costa Verde (Green Coast). North of Porto is Póvoa de Varzim, an elegant sea resort where traditional industries such as fisheries and silversmiths coexist with tourism. There are also natural spas in this areas, as well as beaches, and a native pine forest which stretches along the coast.

Minho

Main town: Braga

For those who appreciate remote escapes, there are no crowds in Minho. A province of wooded river valleys, vineyards and wild coastline Minho has remained isolated, and mistrustful of change. In the north of the province the Rio Minho forms a watery frontier with Galicia in northern Spain. The main city, Braga, was originally the Roman Bracera Augusta. Destroyed by the Moors, it rose again from rubble under the auspices of King Ferdinand of León who liberated it in 1040. It became an important archbishopric and ultimately the religious centre of Portugal; its archbishop's palace and cathedral are of monumental proportions and considerable interest. Outside the city is the Bom Jesus, a highly ornate granite and marble staircase with resting places dedicated to Christ, the five senses, and the virtues, in ascending order. Although a marvellous Baroque concoction, the site itself has no religious (i.e. miraculous) associations but this does not prevent the devout from climbing it on their knees.

The province possesses a number of unbelievably romantic-looking towns: Guimarães was the first capital of Portuçale, the land between the Lima and Douro rivers which was the starting point for its reconquest of the lands occupied by the Moors. Viana do Castelo on the estuary of the Lima river has some fine elegant buildings of the renaissance period. The Minho's other great attraction is the 70,000-hectare Parc National da Peneda-Gerês in the northeast of the province. Although popular with campers it is large enough not to seem crowded.

Trás-os-Montes

Main towns: Vila Real, Bragança.

The poorest and most backward province is the northeastern one of Trás-os-Montes (Behind the Mountains). It has half the number of inhabitants of the Minho in twice the area. The lower part embraces the upper reaches of the Douro, whose fertile valleys are synonymous with wine production; in addition to vines, citrus and succulent fruits flourish here. The upper part of the province is a complete contrast; the most inhospitable mountain terrain and harshest climate of Portugal can be found here. Left more or less to itself the region has evolved its own traditions and dialects and provided a refuge in harder times for those fleeing religious persecution.

The largest industrial town of the region, Vila Real, is situated amidst the foothills of the Serra do Marão. The building depicted on Mateus Rosé wine labels is the Solar de Mateus situated a couple of miles from Vila Real.

Bragança, the remote, brooding capital of the province is the royal seat of the family of that name who ruled Portugal from 1640 to 1910. Rising from the splendid mediaeval citadel, set above the new town, is a massive keep, the Torre de Menagem, symbol of the city's impregnability in days gone by.

An architectural curiosity within the citadel is the Domus Municipalis in the shape of an irregular pentagon. Anyone in the citadel on Ash Wednesday will see a sinister, caped figure representing death stalking the narrow streets. The children of the town throw stones at him as part of this traditional but macabre ritual. Others no doubt prefer to watch Batman on television.

OFFSHORE PORTUGAL

Madeira

Main town: Funchal
Main tourist office: Avenida Arriaga 18, P9004 Funchal; ☎291 225658.
British Consulate: Apartado 417EC Zarco, 9001956 Funchal; tel: 291-221221.

Although it is certain that the Phoenicians knew of its existence, the 'discovery' of Madeira in 1419 is attributed to Zarco and Vax Teixeira, young adventurers from Prince Henry the Navigator's entourage. Named from the Portuguese for wood, the main island, steep and uninhabited was first colonised by emigrants from the Algarve and the inmates of Lisbon prisons. The beginnings of first the sugar, and then the wine trades were established, and the Flor do Oceano (Flower of the Ocean) with its beautiful vegetation and climate has never looked back. Over the centuries the painstaking construction of hillside terraces has helped to make the island *farta* (richly productive) in grapes for the famous Madeira wine, sugar, and fruits, especially bananas.

The island's airport is at Santa Cruz, 12 miles/19 km from the capital, Funchal. Nearly a half of the island's inhabitants live in and around Funchal, a sheltered town which has long been a discreetly elegant resort probably best epitomised by the worldrenowned Reid's Hotel which stands amidst twelve acres of glorious gardens. A large number of swimming pools on the island compensates for the fact that steepsided Madeira has no sandy beaches. On the other hand, the neighbouring island of Porto Santo, 25 miles away, has an abundance of beaches and is a popular holiday place for sandstarved Madeirans amongst others. It can be reached by air from Madeira in fifteen minutes, or three hours by boat. The six other islands in the Madeiran archipelago are inhabited only by goats. Although the internal combustion engine has long reached Madeira, there are other varieties of local transport, including oxcarts, wickerwork toboggans, and, for the the unashamedly slothful, there is the hammock, slung between two bearers.

Anyone wishing to live and work on Madeira would probably find tour companies the best starting point.

The Azores (Açores)

Main Tourist Office: Rua Comendador Emesto Rebelo, 14 9900 Horta Faial.
British Consulate: Quinta do Bom Jesus, Rua das Almas, 23 Pica da Pedra, 9600 Ribeira Grande, Azores; ☎296-498115.

Unfortunately the charming notion that the Azores are the vestiges of the lost continent of Atlantis is highly improbable. This midAtlantic archipelago of nine islands was formed gradually by seething volcanoes which, like Atlantis, are now considered defunct. The name unromantically enough comes from the word for vultures, which the Portuguese discoverers thought they saw circling the islands. In fact they were hawks, but the name stuck. The islands' estimated 250,000 inhabitants include a large proportion of fair-haired, blue-eyed Azoreans, descended from the Flemish Knights of Tomar who were among the original settlers in the fifteenth century. A traditional stoppingoff point for transatlantic sea traffic, the Azores are not the easiest chunks of land to get to: one can fly from Portugal to Ponta Delgada airport on the largest island São Miguel. Inter-island air services are run by SATA (*Servicio Açoreano de Transportes Aeros*). Corvo, the only island without an airstrip, can be reached by helicopter.

Just beginning to be visited by tour operators, the Azores are a tranquil haven. It is hard to see what work possibilities might be available beyond a little yacht maintenance and some tourism work. Living on the islands may be an option for the truly self-sufficient who have discovered its unspoilt scenery and subtropical climate, but they are not the most likely port of call for British emigrants.

Useful websites

www.portugal.com: provides travel resources and booking for visitors to Portugal and the islands.

www.portugal.org: a comprehensive guide to Portugal published by ICEP, the national tourist and investment agency.

www.portugaltravelguide.com: accommodation, culture, gastronomy, shopping, sport and travellers' tips.

www.portugal-info.net: who, what, where and when in Portugal – from jobs and property to food and films.

www.portugalvirtual.pt – A directory of contacts.

RESIDENCE AND ENTRY REGULATIONS

The Current Position

Portugal, along with its neighbour Spain, is a full member of the EU and one of the founding members of the Euro. Consequently, many of the complications regarding visas and work permits which affect American and other non-EU entrants do not apply in the case of British and Irish citizens. For the former, unfortunately, the Hispanic love of paperwork is as strongly in evidence in Portugal as in Spain and can exacerbate some of the painfully slow and plentiful bureaucratic demands involved in your application for a work or residence permit. EU citizens will need a residence permit too: applications should be made at the *Serviço de Estrangeiros e Fronteiras* Foreigners and Frontiers Service (Avenida António Augusto Aguiar 20; ☎21-314 3112.) Apart from a residence permit (*Autorização de Residência*) and a fiscal number (*Cartão de Contribuinte*) prospective residents will also require an identity card (*Bilhete de Identidad*) which must, by law, be carried at all times by Portuguese nationals as well as by foreigners resident in the country. Application forms for these should be available at the nearest British Consulate; and then you should submit these to the local district council (*Junta de Freguesia*).

Visas

British visitors do not need one; but others entering Portugal who do require a visa should make their application to the nearest Portuguese Consulate. Visits can then be extended for up to six months by applying to the *Serviço de Estrangeiros e Fronteiras* (the Foreigners' Department of the Ministry of Internal Affairs, address above) once you are in Portugal; branch offices can be found in most major cities (including Coimbra, Faro, Oporto, Madeira and the Azores). Remember, if you are planning to extend your visit and you do need a visa, that your passport will have to be stamped on entry to Portugal so that the authorities will be able to determine the date of entry. This does not apply to Britons and other EU nationals.

Applying for a residence visa for Portugal directly from the UK is possible; but this is both complex and time-consuming. To work there, Britons will simply need a residence visa; no other work permit is required. If possible, find someone already resident in Portugal (a national or foreign resident) who is willing to act as your referee. You will also need a pile of passport-sized photos, your passport, proof that you have some kind of housing arranged in Portugal, evidence of good financial standing, and a medical certificate.

It is useful, though, not to delay getting the residence visa until you are actually in Portugal, especially if you are a non-UK or non-EU national, as you will avoid becoming embroiled in Portuguese bureaucracy on arrival; and it is not unknown for non-EU nationals be forced to return to their own country to apply from there, or to have to travel to the nearest Portuguese Consulate (which will be in Spain) to do this.

Applying for a Residence Permit

Once safely ensconced in Portugal, EU citizens (and others) who have not already made their residence permit arrangments must apply immediately to the Serviço de Estrangeiros for the *Autorização de Residência*, the vital document which confers residence status on the holder.

Although some non-EU residents manage to avoid applying for the residence permit by simply leaving the country every few months and getting their passport stamped on reentry for a further visit, this is not really advisable; and anyone who intends to live permanently in Portugal will find that it is virtually impossible to do this without this Autorização de Residência and the privileges which it brings. The best way for UK citizens to apply for it is to go to the local British Consulate first; for a small fee they will certify that you are a British citizen and, if you have no prison record, that this is the case.

Next, take your passport, the consular certificate, three passport photos, a copy of your most recent bank statement to the Serviço de Estrangeiros and they will process the Autorização de Residência in just a few weeks. It is a red and green card bearing the applicant's photograph and signature (and sometimes thumbprint) which must be carried with the holder at all times for possible inspection. The authorities warn that all foreigners must also apply to their nearest *Arquivo de Identificacão* for an identity card after six months in Portugal, which must be presented to the police on demand.

For visitors, of course, another EU ID card or your passport will do just as well. The police may give you 12 hours to present your ID card at the police station if you do not have it to hand and may detain anyone who does not have this card or suitable passport etc. indefinitely, or until they can obtain one (although this rarely happens).

When the times comes to renew the card you will need to give proof that you can support yourself for the coming year, e.g. current bank statements showing a regular income. After following this process for five years, the non-EU resident is entitled, like Britons and others from within the European Union, to the five-year Autorização de Residência, and which also saves a phenomenal amount of annual hassle.

Work Permits

These are not required by British and other European Union citizens. Otherwise, anyone planning to work in Portugal for a temporary period of less than 30 days is not required to have a work permit, but must gain written consent from the Ministry of Labour (*Ministerio do Trabalho*) in the area in which he or she wishes to work. The head office of the Ministerio do Trabalho in Lisbon (Praça de Londres, P-1091 Lisbon) will be able to provide a list of all of the regional offices for anyone who has difficulty in locating their nearest Ministerio de Trabalho office. Others who intend to work in Portugal on a long-term basis will need their work permit; and for this they must be able to present proof of having a job, e.g. a contract of

employment from the prospective employer and the approval of the Portuguese
Ministry of Labour.

Similarly to the procedure described for Spanish work permits in the part of
this book on Spain, this process can be long and laborious for non-EU citizens.
Applications are made to your country's nearest Consulate at the same time as
the request for the initial residence visa; the contract of employment will be
sent to the Portuguese employer, who must then submit this to the Ministry of
Labour for approval. The entire procedure is likely to take a few months; and so
preparations should be made well in advance.

Although some more reckless travellers who only want to work in Portugal
temporarily (but for longer than the 30-day exemption period) go there first, find
a job, and then apply for the work permit later, this is not recommended as the
Portuguese authorities are clamping down on such cart-before-the-horse tactics.

Applications for work permits in Portugal tend to be fraught with difficulties;
and a labour market which is more open to British and other EU workers is now
quite difficult for Americans and others to enter. Basically, the local Ministry of
Labour in Portugal must be convinced that the job for which you are applying
could not be done equally well by a Portuguese (or EU) national; and this
decision will depend heavily on the amount of unemployment in the particular
area. Furthermore, any employer resident in Portugal is restricted by law to an
intake of one foreign (i.e. non-European Union) employee in every ten. The only
groups which are exempt from having such a work permit are au pairs, academics
employed by Portuguese universities and private English tutors.

The permit for long-term employment is usually granted for six months, after
which time it can be renewed at halfyearly intervals. It should be emphasised that
British and other EU citizens coming to work in Portugal do not need a work
permit and do not need to go through these procedures.

Entering to Start a Business

No work permit, only a residence permit, is required for those who enter Portugal
to set up their own business. However, professionals (e.g. doctors, lawyers) must
first have their qualifications checked by the relevant Portuguese body which will
grant permission to practise based on the authenticity of these qualifications (and
whether they are considered equivalent to Portuguese qualifications). Although
the need for a work permit is waived for the self employed, many of those who fall
within this group will be forced to obtain a licence before setting up business; this
includes any concern which deals with food, the maritime industries, or renting
out property in Portugal.

Entering with Retirement Status

Anyone who intends to retire to Portugal will have to provide pension details and
proof that they have 'sufficient funds' with which to support themselves without
working while resident in Portugal. This information must be provided when
applying in the UK for your residence authorisation in the UK; or after your arrival;
and produced when applying for the Autorização de Residência in Portugal.

Identity Cards

Although to many of us the mention of identity cards evokes sinister images of totalitarianism, the Portuguese version of these is useful (though not compulsory) for foreign residents. The identity card works in much the same way as in France and other European countries. The ID card entitles the holder to apply for a Portuguese driving licence and can be used in lieu of a passport when registering at hotels and for identification purposes, even for travel to Spain and elsewhere. Applications for the card by UK citizens should be made to the local British Consulate. You will need to produce your passport, a few photos, and the Autorização de Residência. Once you have completed the application form available from the British Consulate, take this, along with the above mentioned documents, to the President of the local district council (the *Junta de Freguesia* mentioned above) whose responsibility it is to certify the authenticity of your address and to certify the card. After this, your application is in the hands of the Portuguese authorities; and will take anything between one day and one month to process.

Fiscal Numbers

A fiscal number is essential for work, to do business, or to buy anything substantial in Portugal, e.g. a house, land, or a car. The *Cartão de Contribuinte* is available to tourists or residents on presentation of a current valid passport at the local tax office. You will be given a temporary fiscal number which will be replaced by a permanent number and card after a few months. The fiscal number will then appear on all your tax returns and on any formal documentation involved in the buying or selling of property or on any business transactions.

Portuguese Residency

Remember to register your arrival and to give your current address to the local British Consulate as soon as you arrive. Once a UK national has obtained the residence permit, he or she is entitled to the same rights as a Portuguese national, with the exception that he or she is not allowed to vote in Portuguese elections. However, UK nationals living abroad still retain the right to vote in UK elections and remain British citizens even though they are resident in a foreign country.

If at any time you decide to leave Portugal permanently, then simply hand in your Autorização de Residência at the local police station before your departure.

Non-EU Nationals

Holders of Canadian or American passports may reside in Portugal for 60 days without a visa; mysteriously those holding Australian passports are allowed an extra 30 days, to make a 90-day stay. However, Canadian and US passport holders do still require a visa to visit the Azores. For longer stays, apply to the district police headquarters, in Lisbon to the Serviço de Estrangeiros (address above). The Portuguese Embassy addresses in the USA and Canada are included under *Useful Addresses* below. Some travellers have been turned away through lack of funds; the minimum amount seems to be 15 Euros (about £10) per day. Alternatively – and probably better – non-EU nationals can apply for a visa to the Portuguese Embassy or Consulate in their home country before leaving for Portugal.

Useful Addresses

Portuguese Embassy: 11 Belgrave Square, London SW1X 8PP; ☎020-7235 5331; fax 020-7245 1287; email Port embassyLondon@dialin.net.

Portuguese Consulate: Silver City House, 62 Brompton Road, London SW3 1BJ; ☎020-7581 8722

Portuguese Consulate: Alexandra Court, 93A Princess Street, Manchester M1 4HT; ☎0161-834 1821.

Portuguese Consulate: 25 Bernard Street, Leith, Edinburgh EH6 6SH; ☎0131-555 2080.

ICEP (Investment Trade and Tourism of Portugal): 2nd Floor, 22-25A Sackville Street, London W1X 2LY; ☎020-7494 5720 (tourism)/ 020-7494 1517 (trade).This is the Por-

tuguese national tourist and trade office in London.

Abroad:

Portuguese Embassy: 2125 Kalorama Road NW, Washington, DC 20008, USA; ☎202-3288610; fax 202-4623726.

ICEP (Portuguese National Tourist Office): 590 Fifth Avenue, New York, NY 10036, USA; ☎212-354 4658; fax 212575 4737

Portuguese Embassy: 645 Island Park Drive, Ottawa, Ontario K1Y OB8, Canada; ☎613-729 2270.

ICEP (Portuguese National Tourist Office): Suite 1005, 60 Bloor Street W, Toronto, Ontario M4W 3B8; ☎416-921 4925; fax 416-9211353.

A leaflet entitled *Some Hints on Taking Up Residence and Living Conditions in Portugal* is available from the British Embassy in Lisbon (address above). The government's employment service (www.jobcentreplus.gov.uk) also provides a full range of information online for people wanting to work in Portugal. Subjects covered include immigration, health, job searching, taxation and education.

SETTING UP HOME

It may seem ironic to the Portuguese that thousands of foreigners have cheerfully set up home on their doorsteps, or where their doorsteps would be if they could afford them, around Lisbon and the Algarve. Only about 40% of Portuguese own their own home; and in Lisbon, Oporto and Funchal (Madeira) the percentage is little more than 20%. In fact, Portugal faces an acute housing shortage, particularly in the main industrial areas, where property prices and rents are excessive for those on Portuguese salaries. The foreign resident population (for whom such considerations are often remote) may salve their consciences by reflecting that they make a contribution to the prosperity of the country and provide work for Portuguese builders, handymen, caretakers and domestic employees. In the case of domestic employees, incidentally, Portugal is one of the few European countries where house servants are commonly employed. Usually these staff expect free accommodation and salaries of around £250-£300 monthly.

Owing to the continuing influx of foreign residents (as well as holidaymakers) to the Algarve, property prices are upwardly mobile. It is a vendor's market; and the British nowadays are feeling more confident about house buying generally, with even interest latterly from an unlikely expatriate source: Hong Kong. In Quinta, to give one example, it is estimated that only 10% of properties are for sale at any one time. 'Most people here buy because of the clean air and the lack of highrise development', according to an estate agent; and good communications are another important factor.

The airport at Faro has brought the Algarve within easy reach of most foreigners who go on holiday there; and also for those who want to keep in touch with friends and family at home after moving to Portugal.

The coastline west of Faro is the most built up, but already, in the quieter eastern half, coastal development is well underway. A property here is likely to appreciate in value as the demand increases in this area. The Lisbon coasts, north and south, are the most expensive areas, and the most sought after amongst the Portuguese themselves. There are some signs that foreigners are increasingly moving northwards, largely in order to escape the holiday hordes. As a consequence, prices have rocketed. Houses in fashionable areas like Estoril can start at £450,000 rising to £1 million plus for villas with four/five bedrooms with a swimming pool etc. However, the majority of properties cost much less than this.

As in France, you should be able to find inland homes costing far less than their equivalent in the UK. Up in the hills prices drop; but even here a two-bedroom house ten miles or so inland from the Algarve, or inland from the Costa de Lisboa, can set you back at least £90,000. There are still some unrenovated farmhouses about, starting at around £50,000. After renovation and other expenses (like installing a swimming pool) this would not necessarily prove any less expensive though. Renovation costs can prove much greater than the price of the property itself, upwards of £60,000.

There are not so many rural and rundown properties like this in Portugal as in France, say, or in neighbouring Spain; Portugal is only one sixth the size of France, and with a burgeoning expatriate population this means that the price of land for building, particularly in the most sought-after areas, has also risen astronomically in recent years. Consequently, many British housebuyers are taking matters into their own hands, looking for properties in need of renovation, and doing it all themselves, as an alternative to buying the land to build on. There are still some bargains like this to be had. and if you can avoid estate agents' fees of 57% all the better.

You should beware of possible future road and building developments if you are intending to buy. In one recent case a British couple lost their life savings after buying a property whose garden, they subsequently found, was due to be bisected by a major road. Remember that renovation is still a formidable expense for the prospective resident, even if you decide to do most of it yourself; this is hard work, and you really do have to speak the language and know the country well to get by.

In the south, the signs that the Algarve is becoming increasingly popular with tourists – and the mass tourism which brought prosperity to this region of poor farmers and fishermen some thirty years ago – are a mixed blessing for those thinking of setting up home today. Yes, the place is a welcoming one for British visitors (for all the historical reasons mentioned earlier). But some may regret not buying when the tourist boom started, all those years ago. Ironically, tourism is making this a less desirable area to live; and some of those who settled there a few years ago are themselves now trying to move further north, especially to the Estoril and Sintra coasts in the Lisbon area, thus pushing up Lisbon area property prices further still (as mentioned above). According to an *Independent* newspaper report, these are at least 30% higher than the south.

Until 1963, the year that tourism in Portugal took off, it is hard to believe that the Algarve was a thinly populated and largely neglected area. This means that most of the coastal developments (e.g. villas and condominiums) have been purpose-built. Initially, a cheap area to live and retire to, increasing demand has pushed up prices to the following average levels: one-bed apartments start at about £85,000; a terraced two-bed villa upwards of £120,000, a three-bedroomed detached villa with swimming pool costs upwards of £180,000.

As already stated, property in Portugal is no longer cheap; and any rental income to be gained also may not be high. Weigh up the suitability of the property for renovation if you are going to do it this way; but for the persistent and adaptable – who do not insist on having a *vista mar* (view of the sea) – bargains can be found. This used to mean farmhouses costing around £1,000. Nowadays even a dilapidated ruin would cost £40,000 or more; and prices mainly depend on how much land is attached. If you can do your own restoration work, so much the better.

Mention should also be made, in this brief survey of the Portuguese property scene, of the purposebuilt golf resorts. As in Spain, this kind of development, with leisure facilities attached, or special provision for the elderly, is proving more and more popular (and will also be correspondingly expensive). A property built as part of a golf course development will cost approximately £200,000.

The rest of this chapter aims to guide the prospective resident through some other issues relating to housebuying or renting in Portugal, and through some of the steps necessary to complete the various buying or renting formalities and procedures. It is not however a substitute for professional and local advice, which is easily obtainable both from property agents and in the UK and in Portugal; or from lawyers (you can find a list in the *Directory of British Employers in Portugal* in the *Employment* chapter); or from those who have already set up home in Portugal and have their own tales to tell, cautionary or otherwise. One starting point is to consult FOPDAC (The Federation of Overseas Property Developers, Agents and Consultants) who can advise you about purchasing property in Portugal and recommend a sales agent: 3rd Floor, 95 Aldwych, London WC2B 4JF; ☎020-8941 5588.

A firm of solicitors specialising in Portugal is *John Howell & Co*, 17 Maiden Lane, Covent Garden, London WC2E 7NL; ☎020-7420 0400; fax 020-7836 3626; email info@europelaw.com. They are the only firm of English solicitors to do nothing but work involving Spain, France, Portugal and Italy. They will answer your enquiries on all aspects of buying property in Portugal and send you a free information pack.

Rent or Buy

On the whole, if you can afford it, it is better to buy your home rather than renting if you intend to stay long-term. Not only is this likely to prove a sound investment, but renting in the main towns and cities can be as expensive as rents in Britain, if not more so. The paradox of renting in Portugal (and one which is not fully understood even by the locals) is that doing this on your own account is becoming more expensive every year; but the income to be derived from renting your property out is somehow not so lucrative. You could earn £350-£475 per month from your renovated farmhouse or villa in the Algarve, for instance, but you may only be able to rely on this in the summer months. Lisbon remains one of the cheapest cities in Western Europe in which to rent property, but it is no longer a bargain. A three-bedroom flat might cost £1,350 per month. The absolute minimum anywhere is about £250.

It is usual for foreigners working for large companies or in the international schools (of which there are many in Portugal) to have their accommodation provided free. However, those doing shorterterm jobs (e.g. English-language teaching) or who have temporary or summer jobs, or who, for some other reason, are unable to afford the above rents, may prefer to bypass their local estate agents and look in the *alugamse* (to rent) columns of newspapers like the *Diário de Notícias*, where it is possible to find something cheaper, either in the suburbs or perhaps in one of Lisbon's picturesque but crumbling eighteenthcentury buildings. One central Lisbon resident explained his surroundings thus:

> *Every one of these old buildings has a UNESCO preservation order on it. You cannot even install a new lift without a committee approving it. The landlords can't be bothered to go through all the procedures necessary to get permission for the repairs and they can't charge high rents, so the buildings are falling down.*

Terms likely to be used in newspaper rental advertisements include *quarto* (room), *cozinha* (kitchen), *bahno* bathroom, *terraço* (terrace). As there is such a shortage of accommodation in Lisbon, Oporto and the Algarve anyone landing a job there should try to get their housing provided if possible, or at least help with finding accommodation at a price they can afford. The minimum rental is usually six months. It may also be possible to rent part of a house – look for *Partes de Casa* advertisements. In the Algarve, holiday accommodation is rented out by the foreign owners at exorbitant prices in summer. It is not usually feasible to rent a villa for a year as the owners will probably want to inhabit their property for some summer weeks, and Christmas, Easter etc. It may be possible to find a country property for rent but own transport will be essential. Sometimes those working in the tourist industry manage to rent flats in the large apartment blocks inhabited by the Portuguese in the main Algarve towns. Such accommodation is best found by asking on the spot, in bars and restaurants, or consulting the advertisements in the *Anglo-Portuguese News*. Those who have building or handyman/woman skills should not neglect the possibility of negotiating lower rentals as a quid pro quo for maintenance work. This method of finding accommodation may also suit those who eventually intend to buy their own property and do it up, as it gives them a chance to look around and not pay through the nose while they are doing so.

How Do the Portuguese Live?

In response to this question, one Portuguese replied 'beyond their means'. This is understandable, in view of the high cost of housing and rents relative to the generally low Portuguese wages and the rising cost of living, which means that Portugal is not a prosperous country in the same sense as its western European neighbours. Because of the general housing shortage, there is a tendency for offspring to live with their parents until they get married. Even after marriage, newlyweds will often live with one or other set of inlaws; a situation that gives rise to its own set of problems. In country areas especially, several generations of one family will live under the same roof and even go on Sunday outings together.

In common with their European counterparts, many urban Portuguese tend to live in apartments in suburbs from which they can commute to work. Life in the cities is much more like that in London, Paris or Rome. Traditional Portuguese architecture includes gracious nineteenth century porticoed villas, terraced town houses with tile decorations on the outside walls, and thickwalled rustic farm dwellings with either no windows, or very small ones, designed to protect the inhabitants from the molten summers and icy winters.

Owing to the tendency of the Portuguese to try to make a better living in the two main cities, or to move where job prospects are likely to be better, country properties are often abandoned; and can make interesting homes for foreign buyers keen on restoration and conversion work, and who have the time and money necessary (see above). At present, the Algarve accounts for 90% of all sales in Portugal to foreigners; and 50-60% of these are estimated to be to the British (although it is not known quite how many there are, as some buy through offshore companies set up to avoid the 10% Sisa tax they would otherwise have to pay). The Portuguese themselves are moving away from the country and into towns, meaning that the bargains are to be found outside the built-up areas.

Thus, there are all types of property available in Portugal. The only foreseeable problem is that a country as small and as much in demand with foreign residents may reach saturation point in certain areas, if immigration continues at current levels. Development is another factor. The government of Portugal is seeking, with the aid of EU initiatives, to attract business development to even the remotest province of Trás-os-Montes, which may make even this northeastern corner of Portugal more conveniently inhabitable in the future. Maybe remote districts like this will become the Algarve of the future, for those presentday expats still in search of property bargains, and a life away from the tourist crowds.

Owing to their distance from Europe, both Madeira and the Azores tend to attract more timeshare residents than permanent ones. One estimate puts the number of expatriates living permanently in the Azores at less than one hundred: these have certainly yet to become Portugal's answer to the Canary Islands. Setting up home in mainland Portugal, though, is far less of an adventure than it used to be.

Prices

Obviously, Portuguese property prices like any others are subject to the laws of supply and demand.

Prices are inexorably rising, which means the ones given in this section, although correct at the time of going to press are likely to be quickly exceeded. Any UK-based estate agent dealing in Portuguese property will be able to supply a prospective buyer with a list of current prices of various types of property around the favoured areas, as will British and Portuguese estate agents in Portugal. Overall, according to their estimates, property prices in Portugal are equivalent to if not higher than those in the UK. There are still prospective British residents who arrive in Portugal expecting to buy a home by the sea for £25,000.

An alternative to going to an estate agent is to consult the property columns of the *Diário de Notícias* or other Portuguese newspapers. There is always a variety of properties advertised. The drawbacks are first that it is rare for prices to be given; secondly, one can be almost certain that if a foreigner were to answer the advert, the price would double; thirdly, that an interpreter would be required for the negotiations. If the prospective buyer were to have Portuguese friends who could make enquiries on his/her behalf, so much the better.

Naturally, there are always stories of bargains to be had, especially in isolated areas. The national press in Britain (and especially the property pages of the Sunday newspapers) also occasionally carries stories of the latest trends in the Portuguese property market. However, you should think twice about bargain properties without mains electricity and piped water. Installation of these amenities can be a longdrawn out process; and you should think of restoration also in terms of the time it will take (often several years), when building and other costs are also likely to go up. These properties away from the coast (and to the east of Faro) are as likely to be located through exploration and wordofmouth as through an estate agent; and there are charges for the management of your property to consider as well, if you are only going to be there for part of the year; and for letting it out (which can be up to 20% of the income you receive). Those who make offers for these properties should ensure that they carry out the recognised buying procedure and register the property in their name at the Land Registry Office etc. Full details of these processes are given later in this chapter.

TABLE 8	PROPERTY PRICES	
Property	**Area**	**Price**
Farmhouse for restoration	Northern Algarve	£60,000
2 bed appartment with garage	Quinta do Lago	£90,000
2 bed village house	Sintra	£90,000
3 bed house	on the Silver Coast near Lisbon	£190,000
4 bed villas	Penha Longa	£420,000

Sources of Property Information. There are two main English language publications in Portugal in which properties both for sale and to let as holiday accommodation are advertised (and which carry uptodate information on events and other matters of interest to the British expatriate community there). They are available from newsstands which sell foreign newspapers in Portugal. Such newspapers are not generally available in the UK but may be ordered direct by writing to the following addresses.

APN (Anglo-Portuguese News): Av. De Sao Pedro 14 dp 2756 Monte Estoril, Lisboa; ☎21-466 1423; fax 21-1466 0358. It is published weekly on Thursdays and includes a Property supplement with every issue.

The Algarve News: Algarve Resident, Apartado 131, 8401902 Lagoa (tel: 282-342936). It is published fortnightly every other Friday and is available in hotels as well as newsstands and places like pubs and clubs in the Algarve which are frequented by expatriates.

The Madeira Island Bulletin, Apartado 621, 9001907 Funchal.

In addition to the above, the overseas property columns of the British press in the UK (e.g. the *Sunday Times,* the *Independent on Sunday, The Observer,* and the *Mail on Sunday*) can be a useful source of information on property prices.

It is worth looking for property adverts in the specialist publications like *Homes Overseas* (www.homesoverseas.co.uk; ☎020-7939 9888), one of the UK's leading magazines for people seeking a second or holiday home abroad. It includes informative and entertaining features covering where and what to buy in Europe and beyond, as well as a wealth of legal and financial information. In early March there is a major *Homes Overseas* exhibition at Olympia in London organised in association with the magazine. It presents an opportunity to meet agents, developers, and to attend seminars on the legal and financial aspects of buying abroad (www.homesoverseas.co.uk). Blendon Communications organise thirty further exhibitions per year throughout Europe.

A list of UK property agents who collaborate with property developers and estate agents in Portugal can be obtained from the Portuguese-UK Chamber of Commerce in London which is located at the ICEP address:

Portuguese-UK Chamber of Commerce, 4th Floor, 22-25A Sackville Street, London W1X 1DE; ☎020-74941844; fax 020-74941822.

Estate Agents in Portugal

Whether one chooses to buy property through a British estate agent based in Portugal or a Portuguese agent, one should ensure that it is licensed by the

Portuguese government as a *Mediador Autorizado*. This official status will be indicated on their stationary; and the licence will be displayed in their premises. The licence is the prospective buyer's assurance of the qualifications of the agent, but unfortunately not always the quality of the service. There is only one really sound method of finding the best agent in your area: the prospective buyer should ask local foreign residents for their recommendations. However, even amongst licensed agents the commission rate is not fixed and can vary from four to ten per cent, but usually averages around five to seven per cent.

Portuguese-based lawyers will be best to ensure the transaction goes smoothly, but these will not usually do planning searches unless asked. See the *Directory of British Employers in Portugal* in the *Employment* chapter, which also contains a list of Portuguese based lawyers with UK connections. There are also UK surveyors on the Algarve. A typical charge for a valuation and general condition survey would be £350-£500 for a £300,000 house.

FINANCE

Mortgages

There are various mortgage possibilities including offshore mortgages, open to those who wish to buy property in Portugal. The offshore type of mortgage is increasingly used by Britons wishing to avoid the 10% 'Sisa' tax purchasers would otherwise have to pay on top; and also to simplify questions of death and inheritance. Conti Financial Services, 204 Church Road, Hove, Sussex BN3 2DJ; ☎01273-772811; fax 01273-321269; www.overseasandukfinance.com and Philip Lockwood (71 Coventry Street, Kidderminster DY10 2BS; ☎01562-745082; fax 01562-740202) both arrange mortgages from both UK and Portuguese lenders (see below).

Portuguese Mortgages. There is no Portuguese equivalent to building societies. It is difficult and expensive for foreigners (and incidentally Portuguese) to take out mortgages with Portuguese banks in Portugal: such banks are not usually keen to lend money, besides which the relatively high interest rates are something of a deterrent. Although a comparison should be made with the British rate you will usually find this is more expensive in Portugal. However, for someone already based there and earning a salary in escudos it could be a viable option; and would avoid the exchange risk (see below) which looks likely to continue as Britain stays out of the single currency. Also, for anyone thinking of buying from a local developer it would be advisable to approach a bank in the same region, as they are most likely to know the developer; and assuming he or she is reliable, they may well be willing to offer a mortgage. Some of the bigger banks include: Banco Pinto and Sotto Mayor, Banco Commercial Portugues and Banco Espirito Santo e Comercial de Lisboa.

The central bank in Portugal is *Banco de Portugal:* R. do Ouro 27, 1100150 Lisboa; ☎21-321 3200; fax 21-346 4843

UK Mortgages with Portuguese Banks. If one is organising the purchase of Portuguese property from the UK it is possible to take out a mortgage with one of the Portuguese banks in London which offer this service. This is easier and cheaper than taking out a mortgage in Portugal with a Portuguese bank. When telephoning the banks one should ask for the overseas mortgage or credit departments:

Banco Totta & Açores: 68 Cannon Street, London EC4N 6AQ; ☎020-7236 1515; fax 020-7236 7717.

Banco Espirito Santo: 33 Queen Street, London EC4R 1ES; ☎020-7332 4300.

On the whole Portuguese banks in the UK deal with clients who already own a home in Britain and are in the process of buying a second home in Portugal. However they will consider other situations on an individual basis. Credit is advanced at about 2% above the UK base lending rate.

TABLE 9	MORTGAGE COMPARISON TABLE	
	With UK Property As Security	**With Portuguese Property As Security**
Types available:	Repayment or Endowment or pension mortgages etc.	Same but foreign currency mortgages also available
Maximum % of value advanced:	95% (can remortgage, i.e. clear existing loan and the new advance becomes a 1st charge or 2nd mortgage	75%
Maximum compared to income:	3 times salary	3 times salary
Period of mortgage:	5 to 25 years	5 to 15 years
Interest rate: than using UK property as security	fixed or variable	variable and higher
Repayments made:	monthly	1,3 or 6 monthly

Offshore Mortgages with Channel Island and Gibraltar Companies.
An increasingly popular alternative to a bank mortgage is property purchase through an offshore company, mostly those situated in Gibraltar and the Channel Islands. The principle involves turning the property into a company, the shares of which are held by the offshore company as collateral against a mortgage of up to 75%. The property owner's name is kept confidential and the property company is administered on his or her behalf by the offshore trustees. The idea is to reduce tax liability in the country of purchase as, if and when the property is resold, it merely becomes a question of transferring the shares confidentially to a new owner.

The advantage of offshore mortgages for buying Portuguese properties is that the Sisa (property transfer tax), usually levied at 10%, and conveyancing costs payable in Portugal are both avoided. A former British building society which recently became a bank, namely Abbey National, has moved into offshore mortgaging from its offices in Gibraltar and Jersey. Information is available from any of its high street branches. Similar information is now available through many British building societies/banks which often offer similar services: your local high street branch should be your first port of call. One is the *Halifax Building Society. Halifax International (Isle of Man) Ltd.*

PO Box 30, 67 Strand Street, Douglas, Isle of Man IM99 1TA; ☎ 01534-613500. The Halifax has leaflets on offshore mortgages and other financial matters like international payments which will be worth consulting. *Lloyds Bank Overseas Club* also offers a range of services; and is based at the Offshore Centre, PO Box 12, Peveril Buildings, Peveril Square, Douglas, Isle of Man IM99 1SS; ☎ 0870-5 301641; fax 01624-638181; www.lloydstsboffshore.com/.

Exchange Risks. Owing to the fluctuation of currency rates, the sterling equivalent of one's liability under a foreign currency mortgage may be increased, or decreased, depending on the rates.

REGULATIONS GOVERNING OWNERSHIP OF PROPERTY AND LAND

Once official residency has been established, a foreigner may own more than one property. If the foreigner is resident for five years and obtains a permit for permanent residency, there are no restrictions on the amount of land and property ownership.

Ensuring the Property is registered in the Vendor's Name

There is one pitfall that may await the unprepared and that is the question of property ownership in Portugal. Prospective buyers are strongly advised to ascertain whether the vendor has a legal entitlement to the property he or she is trying to sell you. This is necessary as many Portuguese do not bother to make a will in which case all their relatives are then entitled to claim a portion of the estate. If the land is not registered in the vendor's name at the land registry office *Conservatório do Registo Predial*, there is the distinct possibility that the deceased's long lost relatives will turn up sooner or later to claim their rights.

Obtaining Building Permission

For some the prospect of buying land and having a house built on it to their own specifications has enormous appeal. However there are certain factors to be taken into consideration.

Buying a plot of land is relatively simple and purchasers can approach the usual sources ie UK property agents and estate agents in Portugal, or use advertisements in the Portuguese press. If possible you should only buy land for which planning permission has already been granted, or alternatively land which has previously been built on. If this is not possible, then the purchaser has to apply for planning permission; a lengthy procedure which involves the usual mountain of paperwork in Portuguese. In case permission is not ultimately granted, it is advisable to try to get the agent/lawyer to draw up a contract on which your commitment to purchase the land is dependent on whether building permission is forthcoming. This has to done by a legal expert. The prospective purchaser will have to decide whether he or she has found the dream plot for which all obstacles are worth overcoming, or if it would be better to look elsewhere.

There are various reasons why an objection to building may be upheld: the land may be designated for agricultural purposes, or the objection may be aesthetic (make sure your architect is not too avant garde). The basic steps involved in obtaining planning permission are as follows:

○ Apply to the local *Câmara* (Town Hall) for a large scale map of the land on which you wish to build. You will also need an area map showing the infrastructure of the area (roads, railways and district boundaries etc). It is advisable to obtain at least three copies of each map. On each map you, your agent, architect, etc. will have to mark in red the exact boundaries of the land on which you propose to build, and the precise location of the proposed building project and its dimensions. Send a copy of the map, accompanied by a recognised architect's letter in Portuguese to the *Direcção Regional de Agricultura* (Department of Agriculture) in the local district capital, and be prepared to wait up to two months (the statutory period) for a reply which you hope will give approval.

○ The letter of approval from the Agriculture Department and an identical map must then be submitted to the *Câmara* (town hall). This application must be accompanied by a letter in Portuguese specifying the use to which the building will be put. At this stage the purchaser is of non-resident status so he or she should specify that the building is for use as a holiday home.

Assuming that permission has been granted the purchaser may need to commission his or her legal advisor to draw up a contract with the builders. However if the purchaser is buying through an agent it is likely that the handling of all the formalities will be included in a package deal, making the process relatively painless for the purchaser. If the purchaser is operating independently, and does not plan to be on site during the construction period, it will be necessary to appoint a surveyor. Names and addresses of British surveyors in Portugal, companies that offer land and construction package deals, British lawyers etc. may be found in the various English-language newspapers and magazines published in Portugal. It is advisable however to check all credentials and even better to have them personally recommended by previous satisfied customers.

To summarise the points mentioned above: it is easier to purchase land for which building permission has already been granted, i.e. the proposed building is at least on the drawing board, or to buy land which has a building on it, i.e. a property that can be reconstructed, or knocked down and rebuilt, in similar form.

THE PURCHASING AND CONVEYANCING PROCEDURES

The Portuguese procedure for purchasing property is subject to constant changes and therefore it is essential to appoint a company or individual qualified to handle all the necessary legal formalities. Some estate agents employ staff who are competent to handle all the procedures. In other cases the purchaser will require a legal advisor with specialist knowledge of conveyancing, usually a British lawer based in Portugal or Portuguese lawyer there with English-speaking staff. The PortugueseUK Chamber of Commerce can provide a list of Portuguese lawyers in the UK.

Generally speaking, there are two stages involved in property purchase in Portugal: the promissory contract (*Contrato Promessa de Compra e Venda*) and the title deeds (*Escritura*).

Contrato Promessa de Compra e Venda

The promissory contract legally binds both the vendor and the purchaser. It contains a precise description of the property and its boundaries, the land registry file number (*artigo matrical*), and the terms of payment. A deposit is immediately payable by the purchaser. Usually, this is in the region of 10%, but can be as much as 50%. The initial deposit is usually paid into a Portuguese savings account, rather than a bank. Under Portuguese law if the buyer defaults he cannot reclaim the deposit. However, in the case of the vendor defaulting, he or she must pay the buyer twice the original deposit. On the face of it, this arrangement seems sound; however, there is a giant loophole for the vendor which permits him to renege on the contract if he or she gets a better offer that still leaves him or her better off after paying back twice the deposit. This is unlikely to occur, especially where a single property is concerned but in the past it has allowed greedy and unscrupulous developers engaged in long-term building projects during the property boom, to leave clients without a roof over their heads and no redress.

Importing Foreign Funds to Buy a Property

Having completed the promissory contract stage the vendor then has to import funds from abroad to pay for the Portuguese property. Usually, funds imported by a non-resident of Portugal may either be in a foreign currency or preconverted into euros. Forget any ideas of bypassing the banking system with suitcases of cash as, if there is no original record of the transaction, there is no legal way to resell the property!

SISA

Paying the *SISA* (Property Transfer Tax) is the final formality before the land belongs to the purchaser. This is not necessary if the purchaser has an offshore mortgage (see previous section) in which case the property is exempt. The rate of SISA may be levied on a sliding scale depending on the value of the property. The Sisa is paid at the local tax office.

Escritura

The *Escritura* is the final stage of purchase and constitutes the drawing up of the title deeds to the property. This is done by a *notário* . To do this he or she must see a receipt for the Sisa and the habitation licence of the purchaser. The notary records all the details of the property, and the names of the parties concerned in the transaction, or those acting for them; and reads it aloud to both parties before their signatures on the document are witnessed. It may be necessary to have copies of the Escritura made for future transactions; and it is a good idea to ask the notary to make a few of these, for which a small fee is charged.

Registering the Property

There are two final formalities to complete which are the responsibility of the purchaser:

> O *Conservatória do Registo Predial (Land Registry Office):* A notarised copy of the Escritura should be submitted to the Land Registry Office.
> O *Repartição de Finanças (Inland Revenue Office):* The purchaser must register the property with the local tax office for eventual payment of annual rates.

Maintenance and Improvements

Having acquired a Portuguese property, one also takes on a whole host of responsibilites to do with its upkeep. Maintaining and improving the bricks, mortar and fittings, especially if one is in residence intermittently, is not an easy exercise. Taxes must be paid, bills settled and the garden flora has to be restrained from its natural ambition to assume the density and proportions of a tropical rainforest. One way to avoid the whole problem is to buy into a development that has its own management service, for which the owners usually pay a fixed fee. The next easiest way is to appoint a professional property manager, located through the usual sources or by word of mouth. Property management companies offer contracts and a scale of fees depending on the amount of work involved, and the area and value of the property. The property manager may offer a combined service, both renting out and ensuring regular maintenance is carried out.

Even if the owner is basically an allyear resident, maintenance and improvement projects taken on in a foreign country can assume entirely novel aspects. Not the least of these is that southern Portugal is in an earthquake zone; and methods of construction used are designed to withstand force seven on the Richter Scale. This basically means that in case of disaster some walls may fall down but the structure will not. Earthquakes (one hopes) are not as likely to cause maintenance problems as the damp and indoor condensation in winter. Many Portuguese houses do not have damp courses; and so this and cavity wall insulation are advisable improvements that may be carried out at reasonable cost.

Other desirable improvements, which are however costly, include a swimming pool and solar heating panels. However the former should add thousands to the value of the property. The latter should ultimately pay for itself several times over; and moreover the Portuguese government is so keen to save energy that low-interest loans are available for solar panel installation – local architects will know the details.

Some improvements are unquestionably essential. Heating comes into this category. The coastal regions, even in the Algarve, can be extremely chilly in winter. As wood is the only readily available fuel, the most popular form of heating among the foreign residents is woodburning stoves. If need be these can be adapted to provide hot water and central heating. The rural Portuguese seem able to manage somehow without heating, and so few Portuguese houses in the Algarve have fireplaces; installing one is a major structural improvement and thus requires architectural, if not scientific, consulation as to the width of flues and positioning of the fireplace to extract maximum heating benefit.

INSURANCE AND WILLS

Any responsible owner of a Portuguese home will want to arrange appropriate insurance for home and property. Apart from being a sensible precaution it is also a legal requirement that one has third party insurance for property. Most insurers will also feel happier with a multirisk policy that covers theft, damage by fire etc. If the insurer has bought into a development it may well turn out that the building as a whole is already covered. It is advisable to check this before taking out an individual policy. In any event it is unlikely that the existing cover will include the private property of individual inhabitants.

Anyone who has purchased a property from a previous owner may find the seller's insurance can be carried on to the next owner. However the new owner will have to check whether the policy is transferable, or indeed, whether they wish to cancel it in order to take out a new policy. There are several British insurance companies operating in Portugal including Sun Alliance and Royal Exchange Insurance.

One company which does work with property and wills etc. in both Portugal and Spain is *Bennett & Co. Solicitors*, (144 Knutsford Road, Wilmslow, Cheshire, SK9 6JP; ☎01625-586937; fax 01625-585362; www.bennettandco.com)

Useful Addresses

American Life Insurance Av. da Liberdade 364, 1250 Lisbon; ☎21-347 5031
   Axa Av. Barbosa Bocage 54, 1000 , Lisbon; ☎21-790 4460.
Commercial Union Assurance Co: Av da Liberdade 384°, 1250145 Lisbon; ☎21-347 5570.
General Accident: R. de Malaca 30, 4150 Oporto; ☎22-610 4388.
Royal Exchange Assurance: Av Marquês de Tomar 2, P1050 Lisbon; ☎21-315 5235.

Wills

One extremely important task that should be carried out by the purchaser as soon as all the purchase procedures have been enacted, is to make a Portuguese will with a Portuguese lawyer. This is essential as under Portuguese law if the foreign resident dies without having left his or her Portuguese property to legally specified heirs, the estate is automatically claimed by the Portuguese state. However, when making a Portuguese will it is unwise to mention any property held in Britain (or elsewhere) as this could lead to further complications. In other words British and Portuguese property should be kept entirely separate.

RENTING OUT PROPERTY

Once a Portuguese property has been acquired, one way of recouping some of the expense is to rent it out, particularly if it is in a desirable area where optimum rents can be charged for short lets, especially in summer. In parts of the Algarve the average villa can gross over £1,800 a week during the summer, although this varies depending on the area, facilities and the degree of luxury provided. £3,000 is a normal rate at the luxury end of the spectrum. Allowances should be made also for the letting agent, if you decide to rent your property this way, who will deduct 10%-15% of the gross. In the Lisbon and Oporto areas, prospective owners are more likely to be able to let accommodation to the employees of international companies who receive large housing subsidies and who wish to stay for a year or longer.

An owner wishing to rent out property has several alternative ways of going about it. Many owners simply hand over the responsibility to a managing or letting agent. This is usually done by agreeing with the agent to set aside times for owner occupation and also agreeing the rental rates with the agent. Any agent worthy of the name will be able to suggest the correct level of rent for a given property. The agent then pays the owner as and when the rental is effected. Although most agents will have a standard agreement to cover their terms for handling rentals it is advisable for the owner to have this checked by a lawyer, as there are a number of hazards in renting out which are dealt with later in this section.

Agents can be found by consulting the English-language newspapers published in Portugal. It is best to select the well-established ones with plenty of experience in this field. It is also worth contacting British villa holiday operators, particularly if your property is in the Algarve. The Portuguese National Tourist Office's booklet *Tour Operators' Guide* is a useful source of addresses. Two of the main companies are Villa Retreats Ltd., 8/10 Trafford Road, Alderley Edge, Cheshire SK9 7NT; ☎01625-586586; fax 01625-586481; www.villaretreats.co.uk and First Choice, First Choice House, Peel Cross Road, Salford, Manchester M5 2AN; ☎0870 750 0465; www.firstchoice.co.uk.

The most lucrative way of renting out a property, because it cuts out the middleman, is to advertise it yourself in *The News, Anglo-Portuguese News*, or a similar newspaper or newsletter in Portugal; or in the British national press. Alternatively you can advertise in the glossy property magazines like *Villa Abroad*.

Once the owner has selected a tenant, the next step is to draw up a tenancy contract. This is essential as Portuguese law comes down heavily in favour of the tenant, who can behave outrageously and still be extremely difficult to dislodge if he, she or they have a mind not to vacate the property after a year's occupation. A contract should normally be for a year and thereafter renewable by mutual agreement between landlord and tenant. There is an increasing tendancy for owners to let only to foreigners who are semipermanent residents of Portugal (i.e. on job contracts) as it is practically certain that they will not claim squatters' rights indefinitely and are considered perhaps as being more reliable.

The one drawback for many owners who intend to offer their property for long-term rental is that they are obliged to declare the income for tax purposes. Many owners are reluctant to fulfil this obligation as even though there are double taxation agreements between Portugal and the UK, there may be some taxes not included in this. It is advisable to consult a financial expert on the current taxation situation. Failure to declare income from rentals will almost certainly invalidate any tenancy contracts should problems with tenants arise. However the owner decides to handle the tax situation, it is in any case advisable to have a written agreement with the tenant, if only as a way of making clear to both parties what the rental charge includes, i.e. electricity and water (which are metered in Portugal). Many owners abide by the tax laws and consult a Portuguese lawyer and have the tenancy contract endorsed by a notary.

UTILITIES

Electricity

If compared to average national earnings, Portugal's electricity is expensive. A typical Portuguese salary can be as little as £400 per month, of which a substantial percentage could easily be spent on winter heating. The voltage is 220 AC and plugs are of the continental two-pin type. Appliances from the UK (where the voltage is 240), will work quite satisfactorily, if a little sluggishly, once they have been replugged. Alternatively adaptors can be used. The national electricity company is the EDP (*Electricidade de Portugal*). In some regions the power is given to tidallike fluctuations which can damage expensive electronic equipment, so it is worth contemplating the purchase of a voltage stabilizer – costly but probably less so than replacing damaged equipment. Electricity meters should if possible be installed outside the building, where they can easily be read whether or not the owners are at home. It is advisable to pay bills promptly as, unlike the UK, where a couple of warnings are issued before the electricity is cut off, in Portugal it happens with alacrity once the payby date is passed. All this assumes that the property is connected to the electricity supply in the first place: outside the regions of Lisbon, Oporto and the main towns and villages of the Algarve, there are still some areas which are not yet electrified. How easy it is to be connected to the main power supply depends entirely on whether the inexorable march of the pylons has reached the area.

Eventually mains electricity will be available anywhere in Portugal. Until this happens one can install a private generator, or do without. Many Portuguese are accustomed to not having electricity. Even foreign residents can function without. In the summer relatively little hardship is involved. In the winter when it is cold and damp, it could be grim. Electricity is rarely used for cooking because it is expensive. Bottled gas is the usual alternative. Water can be heated by gas and there are even gaspowered refrigerators. Smelly petrol stoves, log fires and tilly lamps are other ways of providing heating and light.

Gas

Piped gas is scarce in Portugal, and is limited to the main connurbations. There are plans afoot to extend the gas network, but it will take several years. However bottled gas (propane and butane) is widely available owing to its popularity for cooking. Both types come in domestic-sized containers of 45 kilograms. Most householders place a regular order with a local supplier who collects a deposit for the first cannister and thereafter charges only for the contents. Normally one has to collect the cannisters, but it may be possible to arrange delivery.

Water

Even if a property is connected to the mains, a continuous output is not necessarily the result. The normally baking summers dictate that the supply will be periodically cut off as a water conservation measure. This is especially likely in the south, which means that properties should have an emergency cistern installed to cover such contingencies.

Those without any form of water supply, even a well, will have to have a water deposit (*cisterna*) built and arrange for a water tanker to make regular visits. The local fire brigade often provides this service. Undoubtedly it is less hassle to ensure that the property does have its own water supply. In some instances it is not unheard of to summon the services of a dowser. The ancient art of water-divining is alive and well in Portugal; and there are expert practitioners who can locate a source with pinpoint accuracy. The next step is to have a well sunk to the depth of the water table in that area. Water diviners can be found more easily by word of mouth than by consulting the yellow pages. Those who prefer to be linked to the main water supply should ascertain at the time of purchase how easy this is likely to be. It is advisable to employ a local agent to handle the formalities of application which usually include presenting a Certificate of Habitation and copies of documents proving ownership of the property.

Water is metered and usually payable on a monthly basis. Bills can be paid when the meter reader calls or in person at the Câmara (Town Hall).

Owing to the hardness of the water it is essential to have filters installed preferably within the system (as opposed to just on the outlets), to prevent the furring up of pipes, radiators etc.

Telephones

The good news about applying for a telephone in Portugal is that over the past few years a tremendous reduction has been made in the waiting time for installment, which is now down from ten years to just a month or less. However, the bad news is that those in the remoter areas will probably have to do without, or get a mobile phone. Mobiles are in use where there are no telephone lines in country districts as well as in downtown Lisbon. Although the Portuguese telephone system has been steadily modernised over recent years, there is at present an extreme reluctance to erect a line of telegraph poles to anywhere that is considered to be off the beaten track. The telephone system has also retained some idiosyncrasies, including giving a ringing tone even when the line at the other end has been disconnected or is out of order. Faults on the line, however, are most likely to occur during bad weather.

Applications for telephones should be made to the local telephone company. As the process could still be of long duration, applications should be made as early as possible and the equipment required (extensions etc.) should be thought out well in advance; any changes required after installation are likely to engender the same waiting period as the arrival of the original telephone (still an unpredictable matter). After a long or short gestation period, a representative from the telephone company will eventually materialise to collect an installation fee of about £60. Shortly afterwards the equipment will be installed. It is quite a good idea to have an automatic meter as the neighbours will probably be so impressed by such an invaluable gadget that they will all want to use it.

LOCAL TAXES

Annual Property Tax.

There was a time in Portugal when the property tax (*Contribuição Predial*) was miniscule, with rates based on an unrealistically low estimate of the rentable value of the property, rather than the actual saleable value. Unfortunately such largesse was too good to last; and in 1990 the system was scrapped and replaced with a tax based on the value of the property combined with the desirability of the location and the standards of local services. Individual municipalities became responsible for the assessments in their area. Thus came into being the *Contribuição Autárquica* which translates roughly as economicself sufficiency contribution, which is much more in line with rates on property charged by other EU countries. For nonurban property (*prédios urbanos*) this is currently levied at an annual rate of 0.8% and for urban property the rate varies between 0.7% and 1.3% depending on the municipality. Requests for payment (*aviso para pagamento*) are despatched in January with payment falling due in April. It is usually possible to pay in two instalments, April and September.

REMOVALS

The amount of moveable possessions that any prospective foreign resident will take with them will vary considerably. But generally speaking anyone moving to Portugal on a long-term basis to take up a job, or to take up a leisurely expatriate existence will need the professional services of a removal firm to transport their most treasured possessions and basic necessities to Portugal.

Ideally anyone setting up home in a foreign country should take as little as possible as transport charges are high; for the larger items like wardrobes and beds the costs can be hundreds of pounds per item. Besides which, depending on the design, they may look ridiculous in a Portuguese setting. Before asking a removal firm to visit your home to give an estimate of removal costs, it is a good idea to have a thorough turn out of all the personal or family possessions and try to reduce the mountain as much as possible. Also think through carefully which items really are essential; if you are an inexperienced mover, try to find out from others who have previously moved there, and learn from their mistakes! You may bear in mind that the less furniture you take to Portugal the more interesting it can be to furnish your new home with items acquired locally with their exact setting in mind.

General Conditions of Import

The conditions for importing personal effects into Portugal are in line with regulations in force in other EU countries, namely that citizens of the EU countries (including Britain and Ireland) may apply to take any household goods and effects, which they have owned for at least three months into Portugal tax and duty free, provided that they have obtained right of residence or purchased unfurnished property in Portugal. They must also have had their usual domicile for at least a year outside Portugal. Unfortunately, the basis on which personal goods and household goods may be imported into Portugal change frequently; so before embarking on the procedure it is strongly recommended that you contact a knowledgeable and experienced international removals firm for advice (see below); the Portuguese Consulate can also supply a checklist of information.

THE IMPORT PROCEDURE

○ The basic all-important document for importing personal goods into Portugal, Madeira or the Azores is the *Certificado de Bagagem* (Baggage Certificate). Initially one should contact the Portuguese Consulate in London (address below) to make the application. The Consulate charges a small administration fee and will require the following documents:

○ Either a copy of the Escritura (title deeds) of the Portuguese property purchased, or if the applicant has had a house built, a copy of the applicant's residence certificate (*Atestado de Residencia*) issued by the *Junta de Frequesia* or local authority which also grants planning permission for building; and proof of your application for residence in Portugal.

○ Two copies in Portuguese of an inventory of all the belongings that you intend to import including the makes serial numbers of all electrical items.

○ Two copies of a declaration of ownership of goods and personal effects in Portuguese.

○ A full passport.

From the moment of being granted residence in Portugal an individual is allowed up to one year to import all household goods in as many trips as are needed. For those who have bought a second home or holiday residence the procedure for importing personal effects and furnishings is similar to that for more long-term and permanent residents, except that the documents required by the Portuguese Consulate can also include a photocopy of the deeds, or *Caderneta Predial* (Property Register), or *Título de Registo de Propriede*.

On arrival in Portugal the individual must draw up a notarised declaration that he or she will not sell, hire out or otherwise transfer ownership of the property or personal goods within the twelve months following importation.

It is extremely difficult to import goods not on the manifest after the expiry of the one-year period allowed for importation. It can take up to a year to get a separate import licence from the *Ministéro de Finanças* for an individual item, and the duty can be high.

Although it is obviously more economical to transport all of your possessions in one go, you are allowed to import all household goods in as many trips as are required.

It is possible to buy most electrical goods in Portugal. Televisions bought in the UK will have to be retuned to receive Portuguese channels; and in the end it is probably less trouble to buy or rent one there. In every European country these days, Sky, the BBC, and other satellite channels are also fairly easy to receive; and this arrangement can be made on arrival by those who cannot do without English-language television programmes.

If you are buying anything to take with you before you go, such as a fridge or stereo, it can also by supplied VAT free if the goods are delivered direct to the remover for export; but VAT cannot subsequently claimed back when in Portugal.

CHECKLIST BEFORE MOVING

- ○ Confirm dates with mover
- ○ Sign and return contract together with payment
- ○ Book insurance at declared value
- ○ Arrange a contact number
- ○ Arrange transport for pets
- ○ Dispose of anything you don't want
- ○ Start running down freezer contents
- ○ Contact carpet fitters if needed
- ○ Book mains service for disconnection
- ○ Cancel all rental agreements
- ○ Notify dentist, doctor, optician, vet
- ○ Tell your bank and savings/share accounts
- ○ Inform telephone company
- ○ Ask PO to reroute mail
- ○ Tell TV licence, car registration, passport offices
- ○ Notify HP and credit firms
- ○ Make local map for friends/removal company
- ○ Clear the loft
- ○ Organise your own transport to new home
- ○ Plan where new things go
- ○ Cancel the milk/newspapers
- ○ Clean out the freezer/fridge
- ○ Find and label keys
- ○ Address cards to friends and relatives
- ○ Separate trinkets, jewellery and small items
- ○ Sort out linen and clothes
- ○ Put garage/garden tools together
- ○ Take down curtains/blinds
- ○ Collect children's toys
- ○ Put together basic catering for family at new house

The British Association of Removers (3 Churchill Court, 58 Station Road, North Harrow, Middlesex; ☎020-8861 3331; www.barmovers.com.) can provide advice on choosing a suitable company. Write to *BAR Overseas* at the address above. The Financial Times publishes a niche magazine called FT Expat for overseas residents with information relating to personal finance, investment services and other practical information. Subscriptions for one year are £59 (☎020-8606 7545; www.ftexpat.com).

Removal Companies

You should remember also to do all the planning which is necessary; and check on the import/customs procedures mentioned above with the Portuguese Consulate. The *British Association of Removers* publishes a useful leaflet *Now that you're ready to move...* which is recommended reading before you go; and it is probably better to use a removal company specialising in exports to the Iberian Peninsula (which includes most of those listed below; these can give you a quote, but should also be able to give information on the relevant procedures as well). At the time of writing, the approximate charge from the UK to Portugal is around #150 per cubic metre, plus a fixed fee for administration and paperwork.

Finally, it is worth taking out comprehensive insurance against damage to your possessions incurred while in transit. Your removals company can advise you about cover and make arrangements on your behalf.

On arrival in Portugal the entire consignment of household goods has to be cleared through customs. Although the imports are freed from duty there will be clearance charges calculated on the value and tonnage of the consignment. As these can run into hundreds of pounds it may be advisable when making the inventory to list the lowest (but not suspiciously low) estimate of the value of each item. It is recommended that one selects a removal company who will provide a customs clearance service through their local agent in Portugal. Although there is a charge for this, it will almost certainly be worth it just to escape some of the time-consuming paperwork involved in the import procedure.

Useful Addresses

Overseas Removal Companies:

Allied Pickfords: Heritage House, 345 Southbury Road, Enfield, Middlesex, EN1 1UP; ☎0800-289229. A world-wide network with many branches in Britain.

Andrich Removals: ☎020-8561 3386; www.andrichinternationalremovals. com. Based in Hayes, Middlesex, and offers a regular service to Spain and Portugal with full and part loads.

ARTS International: Ditchling Common Industrial Estate, Hassocks, West Sussex BN6 8SL; ☎01444-247551; fax 01444-870072. Spain and Por-tugal.

Avalon Overseas: Drury Way, Brent Park, London NW10 0JN; ☎020-8451 6336; fax 020-8451 6419 www.transeuro.com. The private removals division of the large firm Transeuro.

Britannia Bradshaw International: Units 2 and 3 Tilson Road, Roundthorn Industrial Estate, Manchester. M23 9PH.; ☎ 0161-946 0809; fax 0161-946 0442; www.bradshawinternatio nal.com.

Cargo Forwarding: International Forwarding Agents, Transit 1 1 Westbank Way, Belfast, Northern

Ireland, BT3 9LB; ☎028-90373700; fax 028-90373736; www.cargoforw arding.co.uk. A worldwide service including Spain and Portugal with doortodoor or doortodepot rates on request and storage facilities.

Clark & Rose Ltd: Barclayhill Place, Portlethen, Aberdeen AB12 4LH; ☎01224-782800; fax 01224-782822; www.clarkandrose.co.uk.

Cotswold Carriers: Unit 9, Worcester Road Industrial Estate, Chipping Norton, Oxon OX7 5NX; ☎01608-642856; fax 01608-645295.

Crocker International Removals: Unit 3, Cornishway South, Galmington Trading Estate, Taunton, Somerset TA1 5NQ; ☎01823-259406 or 277404; fax 01823-334091.

Crown Worldwide Movers: Birmingham (01827-26 4100); Glasgow (0123-6449666); Heathrow (020-897 1288); Leeds (0113-2771000); London (020-85913388); Manchester (0161-273 5337); www.crownworldwide.com. A large multinational removals and relocations company.

Four Winds International Group: Georgian House, Wycombe End Beaconsfields, Bucks, HP 9 7LX, England; ☎01494-675588; fax 01494-675699; www.fourwinds.com.hk.

Harrison & Rowley: 3436 Foster Hill Road, Bedford MK40 2ER; ☎01234-272272.

Harrow Green International: Merganser House, Cooks Road, London E15 2PW; tel: 020-85519188; fax: 020-85519199; www.harrowgreen.com. Full removals service, but they can also make arrangements for pets.

Interpack Worldwide Plc: I n t e r p a c k House, Great Central Way, London NW10 0UX; ☎020-83242000; fax 020-83242048;www.interpack.co.uk. International company offering pet shipping, full / part house contents, motor vehicles, air freight and storage.

Luker Bros (Removals & Storage) Ltd: Shelley Close, Headington, Oxford OX3 8HB; ☎01865-762206.

Pink & Jones Ltd: Britannia House, Riley Road, Telford Way, Kettering, Northants. NN16 8NN; ☎01536-512019.

Robinsons International Moving and Storage: Nuffield Way, Abingdon, Oxon OX14 1TN; ☎01235-552255. They can send a brochure on *International Moving.*

Branches in London: ☎020-8208 8484; fax 020-8208 8488; Basingstoke: ☎01256-465533; fax 01256-324959; Birmingham: ☎01527-830860; fax 01527-526812; Bristol: ☎0117-9805800; fax 0117-9805828; Manchester: ☎0161-766 8414; fax 0161-7679057; and Southampton: ☎023-220069; fax 023-331274; www.robinsonsintl.com.

TransPortugal European Ltd: 59 St Thomas Street, London SE1 3UW; ☎020-74031440; fax 020-7403 0093.

Portuguese Consulate: Silver City House, 62 Brompton Road, London SW3 1BJ; ☎020-7581 8722.

Lisbon Customs and Excise (Direcção Geral das Alfândegas): Rua da Alfandega 5, P1194 Lisbon; ☎21-881 3990.

Cars

Anyone thinking of importing a foreign-registered car into Portugal should consider carefully the drawbacks: the inconvenience of having a righthand drive car in a country which drives on the right and the inevitable tortuous red tape that the import procedure gives rise to. Although in rural areas a car is a virtual necessity, Portuguese driving standards leave a lot to be desired. Portugal has the highest accident rate in the EU and there are certain times of night (mainly the small hours) when the police appear comatose and the night clubs are shutting down when it is simply not safe to be on some coastal roads.

It is relatively simple for both tourists and temporary residents to drive a foreign registered vehicle in Portugal for up to six months. Temporary residents may include those who are awaiting a residence permit. For permanent foreign residents the regulations are decidedly complicated: a foreign resident who is permanently domiciled in Portugal, must either reexport a foreign registered car as soon as he or she receives a residence visa or import the said vehicle permanently within the sixth month temporary stay period. He or she must also have owned and used the vehicle in the UK for a minimum of six months. Once a resident has received the residence permit he or she will not be permitted to drive the vehicle until the importation process is completed. Once the procedure has been completed the owner is not permitted to hire out, sell or lend the vehicle for two years, nor is it permitted to import another vehicle for five years. Import duty is calculated on the basis of cylinder capacity (cc), and purchase value. Initial advice on the import procedure and the duties payable can be sought from the automobile associations of both Britain and Portugal (see useful addresses below). As with all Portuguese bureaucratic processes it is a question of months rather than weeks before anything happens, so it is essential that anyone contemplating importing a car should begin the procedure on arrival in Portugal, rather than wait until the end of the temporary (i.e. six-month) import period.

Owing to the complexity of the procedure it is strongly recommended by the British Embassy in Lisbon, that one appoints a local, accredited import/export agent to handle the whole business. In order to obtain a Portuguese licence plate, the agent will require a declaration from the British Consulate that the applicant's UK residency has been cancelled and a certificate from the district or local council (*Junta de Freguesia*) where the applicant is resident; also a copy of the vehicle log book.

It is worth pointing out that secondhand cars are available locally without difficulty. Japanese, American and British car manufacturers have assembly plants in Portugal. All in all it makes sense to buy a Portuguese-registered car in Portugal.

Buying a Car in Portugal

The process of buying a car in Portugal is fairly similar to buying one in the UK. One places an order with a dealer and waits for the car to arrive. Generally speaking it is advisable to buy new. For further details of driving, rules of the road and regulations, see Chapter 4 on *Daily Life*.

Importing Pets

The introduction of the pet passport scheme has made life much easier for owners of pets wanting to travel abroad without putting animals into a sixmonth quarantine if they want to bring them to the UK. The scheme solely applies to cats and dogs. Portugal (includes the Azores and Madeira) is one of several countries that qualifies for the scheme. For an animal to participate it must have an identifying microchip implanted, be vaccinated against rabies, take a blood test at an approved laboratory, receive a certificate, and be treated for ticks and tapeworm with certification, all in this order.

It is certainly much easier to import the family pets into Portugal than the family car. The regulations apply equally to Portugal, Madeira and the Azores. Dogs and cats may be imported with the following documentation:

1. Any animal being brought into Portugal from another EU country must have a health certificate (Atestado Sanitario). In the UK an Export Health Certificate can be issued by a British veterinary surgeon who is registered as an inspector of the Department of the Environment, Food and Rural Affairs (DEFRA). A list of vets who have this designation, may be obtained from the Portuguese Consulate or DEFRA. The health certificate must then be sent to one of the regional Animal Health Division offices around the country for authentication of the vet's signature. (See www.defra.gov.uk for contacts and details.)

2. An Import Permit for which application must be made to the Director General of Livestock, Ministerio da Agricultura, Secretaria de Estado da Produção, Praça do Comúrcio, 1149010 Lisboa; ☎ 21 3234600.

The authorised vet (known as an LVI, or Local Veterinary Inspector) must examine the pet for export not less than 48 hours before departure and the export health certificate must accompany the animal there. All dogs in Portugal over four months old must also be vaccinated against rabies, a procedure which should be carried out beforehand in the UK; and the owner will also have to sign a declaration that the animal has not been imported into the UK over the last six months.

There are also some agencies which offer help with importing or exporting your pet including the following (and some of the removals firms above). For general travel insurance, and also insurance for your pet, contact *Inter Assurance Ltd:* The Courtyard, 16 West Street, Farnham, Surrey GU9 7DR; ☎01252-747747; fax 01252-717788.

Airpets Oceanic: Willowslea Farm Kennels, Spout Lane North, Stanwell Moor, Staines, Middlesex TW19 6BW; freephone 0800 371554, ☎01753-685571; fax 01753681655; www.airpets.com.

Animal Airlines, Manchester, England; ☎0161-9800601; fax 0161-9800602; www.animalairlines.com.uk.

Par Air Services: Warren Lane, Stanway, Colchester, Essex CO3 5LN; ☎01206-330332; fax 01206-331277; www.parair.co.uk. Specialists dealing with all pets and livestock, and with kenelling facilities in Colchester. As already stated in the *Spain* section of this book, they can also send a leaflet on request with instructions on 'How to measure your dog'.

DAILY LIFE

CHAPTER SUMMARY

○ In Portugal the pace is much slower and there are more marked differences between town and country than most western Europeans are used to.

○ **The Language.** Portuguese is more difficult to learn than Spanish because the way it sounds diverges from the written form.

○ **Open Markets.** Portugal has hundreds of specialist open markets for birds to handicrafts. It is worth checking with locals where to go for what.

  ○ Hand thrown and decorated ceramics are good value and very attractive.

  ○ Fish markets are held at dawn on quaysides and you have to get there early and haggle.

○ **Clothes Shopping.** Portugal has home grown designer fashions, also cotton clothes, and shoes, but they are all very pricey.

○ **Motoring.** Portugal's road system has been transformed into a modern motorway network linking north and south. Unfortunately, driving skills are way behind the technology.

  ○ It is illegal to carry an emergency petrol supply in the car.

○ **Transport.** Travel by rail is inexpensive and the trains run on time.

○ **Banks.** Portugal has too many banks and this has led to many takeovers and mergers.

○ **Public Health System.** Public hospital standards are uneven.

  ○ A&E departments tend to have patients lined up in the corridors awaiting treatment.

  ○ Most Portuguese and foreigners take out private health insurance.

Anyone who decides to become a resident in a foreign country will find that everyday rituals acquire new and in some cases daunting aspects. In the case of Portugal they will find that life moves at a slower pace and that the differences between the town and country are more marked than they are in Britain. Portugal is fast catching up with its more industrialised partners in the EU; but this process is not happening overnight. While the combination of a certain backwardness and high tech may seem to be part of its charm, it should be remembered that Portugal certainly has its own traditions and customs; these often revolve more around family life and the immediate locality. For some, these can be a source of frustration, particularly the tendency to take a more relaxed approach to the minor irritations of everyday life and to getting things done. In some respects Portugal is even more relaxed than the other Latin countries.

Efficiency, however, is becoming more important, as well as customer service. In the workplace, formality in dress and behaviour are often greater than in Britain or the USA and so are traditions of hospitality and courtesy among the Portuguese, who are seen as being more 'laidback' by their more talkative Spanish neighbours. One source of frustration for expats who live there is the tedious paperwork that seems to be generated around everything to do with managing one's daytoday affairs. These everyday tasks are best delegated, wherever possible, to someone else; and assistance should be sought. In Portugal, for emigrants and locals alike, patience is not simply a virtue, it is a necessity. It will take time to adapt to this new way of life and culture, which may however be familiar to some who have already visted the country.

Many expats discover Portugal as a holiday destination before they decide to live there permanently. As mentioned in the Spanish part of this book, this is only one reason for moving to any country and the day-to-day life we discover on holiday is rarely, if ever, the same as that which is lived by the locals. One way of looking at retirement is as a holiday from work. But you will need something to do! As well as the affluent middle classes, and teachers and temporary workers, Portugal is mainly popular among those who decide to retire there; or to enjoy some rest and relaxation away from cold winters. It is a country which Britons, over the years, have found congenial and welcoming.

The details in this chapter provide basic information on how to deal with the various demands of everyday life. Where opening times and other factual information have been given it is important to note that there are likely to be local variations, to which one should be alert. Those who have written to us with their experiences of living and working in Portugal all agree that there is one crucial preparation which can ease the transition to a new way of life (and is often a test of your true desire to live there).

This is to endeavour to speak, however badly, the Portuguese language.

IS IT ESSENTIAL TO LEARN PORTUGUESE?

Although it is possible to get by without speaking the language, especially in the Algarve and in the cities, where there are sizeable numbers of foreigners and international visitors, it seems only a matter of courtesy to be able to converse in Portuguese, however badly, even if your work and daily life is mainly conducted in English. It is also important to understand the written form. English is becoming more widely spoken in business circles, and among the young; but not always by the legendary bureaucracy with which, at some time or another, you will have to deal. So, although this may not seem the highest priority among the many other preparations which are involved, if you do not already speak the language you should certainly try to learn some elements of it before departure.

As well as proving an invaluable accomplishment when the next bureaucratic notice announcing an amendment to one of the endless regulations appears in your letterbox, or the national press, you will discover that speaking the language helps in other ways; and can open a whole new window on the country and its people; it will help you settle in, and smoothe the process known as 'culture shock'. Speaking the language will help you to come to terms with life in another country and help you to feel more at home.

Of course, language learning – and adapting to life abroad – will take time; but when a bill arrives you can actually make enough sense of it to know whether or not it requires urgent attention; you will be able to understand job advertisements; even to meet and talk with your neighbours. In the end, it will be worth it.

Who does this apply to? Nearly everyone involved in trade with the Portuguese, or anything more complicated than a casual summer job, needs to speak the language: there may be some exceptions: for example, many doctors, dentists and lawyers with a mainly British or northern European clientele can often get by with just English, particularly if they have a bilingual staff and partners. So can English teachers. But generally, in the long run, this is unsuccessful. As regards shopping, you can also probably get by without speaking Portuguese in areas with self-service shops and supermarkets; tourists find they manage in the open-air markets with just sign-language. However for dealing with clients, or socialising, or getting things done and integrating yourself more than superficially into your surroundings, the effort you put into learning Portuguese will be rewarded. There are some signposts on how to do this below. What better way to understand a country and its culture than to speak its language?

The Language

Portuguese is spoken by an estimated two hundred million people worldwide, three quarters of whom are Brazilians. It is the national language of Portugal (including Madeira and the Azores) as well as Brazil; and is also spoken in parts of India and Sri Lanka, Angola, Mozambique and Macau. The Galician language of northwest Spain is more closely related to Portuguese than Spanish. As a result of the early Moorish occupation a number of Arabic words were also incorporated into Portuguese. But it is, like Spanish, one of the European languages which evolved from Latin as a result of the lengthy Roman occupation of the Iberian Peninsular. It is a Romance language, like French or Romanian.

Today, as a result of its colonial and imperial history, it has become a truly 'world' language, the next in line in terms of numbers of speakers after English and Spanish. It has more speakers than French.

Learning Portuguese

Unfortunately, though, it is not considered an easy language to master. The vowel sounds seem particularly complicated to native English speakers, and difficult to imitate, especially the dipthongs indicated by the tilde (wiggly mark) over ã and õ. Initially, Portuguese consonants appear even more bewildering than vowels, as the written and oral forms do not seem too closely related; but once the basic rules of their pronunciation have been learned, they will prove easier to cope with than the mouth-distorting vowels. In Portuguese *ch* is pronounced like English *sh*, while *s* is pronounced like English *sh* when it comes before a consonant and at the end of a word, thus Cascais is pronounced 'Kushkaish'. The letter *x* is pronounced a little like the English *sh*; thus *peixe* (fish), is pronounced 'paysh'. In written form one can see more easily the similarity with Spanish.

A knowledge of Latin, or Spanish, or French, can help you to recognise the roots of many Portuguese words and to understand them this way; this can be an encouraging start for anyone trying to learn the language. But the main difficulty in learning arises in understanding the spoken form, which sounds more Slavonic than Latinate and is further complicated by the fact that many sounds are slurred, or sound very indistinct until one has developed an ear for them. The secret is to assimilate the pronunciation (that is to say, the rules of its phonology or soundsystem) and then practise listening, then imitating or reproducing these sounds. Country dialects pose yet another another problem.

Here are some different ways of learning the language, before you go and when you are in the country.

Self-Study Courses. These generally consist of a combination of books and cassettes which are usually aimed at holidaymakers and business-people. Such courses include the BBC's *Get by in Portuguese*, a package of two cassettes and a book; also *Discovering Portuguese* consisting of a book and cassettes. *Colloquial Portuguese* is a similar and slightly more expensive 'interractive' bookwithcassette (Routledge, 11 New Fetter Lane, London EC4P 4EE). Useful for selfstudy, and also with a private teacher or in the classrom, is the excellent *Teach Yourself Portuguese* (Hugo), also comprising a book and cassette. These self-study courses are available in most larger bookshops at prices ranging from £20 to £35; or they can be taken out from the library: nowadays there is often a charge for this. The well-known *Linguaphone* (www.linguaphone.com)Portuguese course can be ordered by telephoning 0800-282417. In the cases of *Discovering Portuguese* and *Teach Yourself Portuguese* the cassettes are a necessary backup to the the books. Harraps also publish a very reasonably priced phrase book for Portuguese with a cassette: *Essential Portuguese*.

Language Courses in Britain.
There are various types of courses held all over the UK to suit different needs and pockets, from local education authority evening classes to the highpowered business person's onetoone intensive course. Details of some courses available around the UK are published in a leaflet obtainable from the Hispanic and Luso Brazilian Council. Although the majority of courses mentioned are Londonbased, there are Portuguese courses held in universities and colleges of further education from Belfast to Bristol. A leaflet on courses in London is available free from the *HLBC* (Canning House, 2 Belgrave Square, London SW1X 8PJ; ☎020-7235 2303. Contact the Education Department there.

One of the longest established UK language schools for Portuguese is the *Portuguese Language School*, EBC House, 235 Upper Richmond Road, London SW15 6SN; ☎020-8877 1738. The Hispano and Luso-Brazilian Council also arranges its own termlong evening courses at Canning House. Further details may be obtained from the address above. Some uptodate information on school or private courses may also be found on the HLBC library noticeboard downstairs; see also the *Anglo-Portuguese Society Newsletter* which has news for members and from time to time features information about learning Portuguese (Anglo Portuguese Society, c/o Canning House, 2 Belgrave Square, London SW1X 8PJ).

Private Tutors in the UK. This can be a pricey option – the going rate is anything from £20 to £30 per hour – but offers advantages for those who are lucky enough to find the right tutor. London especially has its floating population of Portuguese and Brazilian students who will be willing to eke out their existence by giving a few language lessons. The main source for this kind of tuition is the Canning House library noticeboard mentioned above. More officially, the *Institute of Linguists* (Saxon House, 48 Southwark Street, London SE1 1UN; ☎020-7940 3100; www.iol.org.uk) keeps a register of private language tutors all over the Britain and has about twenty Portuguese tutors on its list. A free database is operated on the Institute's website. If the Institute is unable to put you in touch with a tutor in your area, an alternative is to enquire at your local library or see your own local press or newsletters where you may be allowed to post a 'tutor-wanted' advertisement; or enquire at local universities or colleges which usually have departments of modern languages and noticeboards to find Portuguese students in your locality.

Portuguese people resident in the UK who are learning English may also be willing to 'exchange' conversation or lessons with a similarly minded English person; universities – or even your local language school – are the places to post such an ad (or the Hispano and Luso-Brazilian Council noticeboard – see above).

Language Courses in Portugal. If one wishes to improve one's Portuguese on arrival, there are a variety of courses in general or businessorientated Portuguese available through various organisations in the main cities and towns. The following is a list of language schools and organisations which offer such courses:

Centro Audio Visual de Linguas: Praça Luis de Camoes 36, P1200 Lisbon; ☎1394988.

Centro de Iniciacão e Aperfeicoamento de Linguas (CIAL): Avenida da Rep[ac]ublica 41, 8°, P1050 Lisbon; ☎21-794 0448.

CIAL – Centro de Linguas: Rua Passos Manuel 222, 5°, Porto; ☎22332 0269.

CIAL – Centro de Linguas: Rua Almeida Garrett 44 R/C, Faro; ☎89813211.

EuroAcademy Outbound: 77A George Street, Croydon CR0 1LD; ☎020-8681 2905; fax 020-8681 8850. Offers a number of courses in attractive locations in Portugal suiting both young people and adults. Executive courses at all levels are available beginning on any Monday throughout the year.

Instituto Camóes: Praça do Principe Real 141, P1200 Lisbon; ☎213464508.

inlingua School of Languages: 52 Charlotte Road, Edgebaston, Birmingham B16 9JL; ☎0121-446 6709; www.inlingua.com. Has schools in Porto and Lisbon and an extensive range of courses. Prospective participants may write in the first instance to the address above. Schools in Portugal: *inlingua Language Centre:* Rua Sa da Bandeira 607, PT4000 Porto; ☎22 339 44 00; www.inlinguaporto.com

Instituto de Lingua Portuguës: Letras do Porto, Rua do Campo Alegre 1055, P-4100 Porto.

Instituto de Linguas de Alges: R. dos Bam-

beiros Voluntarios Alges, P-1495 Lisbon; ☎212102910.
Universidade de Coimbra; Secretariado do Curso do Ferias, Cabinete de Relacoes Internacionais, Faculdade de Letras, P3049 Coimbra Codex;☎23934613.

SHOPPING

The quality, range and style of the local shopping depends on where you are in Portugal. There are relatively few high street chains, although large supermarkets (*supermercados*), unknown there twentyfive years ago, are very plentiful in the main cities, and the towns of the Algarve. Shop opening hours vary, but in smaller towns they are likely to close for two hours from 1pm to 3pm and remain open until about 7pm in the evening. Except for supermarkets and department stores, shops close at 1pm on Saturdays. Wherever you shop, the cost is not necessarily any less than it would be in the UK – see below for prices of some everyday items.

Food Shopping

Serious foodies are probably best catered for in Lisbon and Porto where there are dozens of enticing delicatessens (*Charcutaria*) where foreign and national produce including cheese, meats and wines are sold. However, delicatessens are also on the increase in the Algarve, where the range of available products until a few years ago was fairly basic. A *padaría* is a bakery and *talho* is a butcher. Portuguese meat can be disappointing, not to say tough, so it is advisable to ask for local recommendations. The big supermarkets (where they exist) are excellent; and prices are comparable to the UK. The frozen precooked meals, especially Portugueserecipe seafood and meat dishes are especially good; and it is worth investing in a freezer to stock up on such items. Dairy products, yoghurt, milk, cheeses etc. are sold in supermarkets or sometimes in openair markets (see below).

Those who have not become reliant on convenience foods will presumably not mind living in the remoter areas where the choice of items is dependent on the season and subject to other variables: transport strikes and crop damage being some of the more usual. Your shopping list will have to be flexible here. Many Portuguese as well as foreign residents lament the fact that although Portugal produces superb fruit, the best quality often goes for export. Others maintain that finding what you want is just a matter of shopping around, especially in the town centre and openair markets.

Many familiar international brand names are made under licence in Portugal which also imports many foreign food products. (UK firms have their own representatives there – see some of the *British Employers in Portugal* under *Marketing and Manufacturing*, in the following *Working in Portugal* section). Increasingly, however, the Portuguese are manufacturing their own brands of yoghurts, breakfast cereals, canned pet food and so on. Whichever version one buys they are often more expensive than one expects. Alcohol is usually good value, especially local wines (which can still be bought for less than £3 for a bottle of country wine) and cigarettes are less than half their UK price.

Shopping Centres. The main towns of the Algarve including Faro, Loulé,

Portimão, Albufeira, Tavira, and the main towns of the Estoril Coast like Cascais, all having traditional shopping centres located in their small pedestrianised streets. In addition to the famous old shopping area of the Baixa (lower town), the capital Lisbon has what is undoubtedly the most architecturally interesting shopping mall in Portugal: the Amoreiras, looking like a castle from the covers of a science-fiction novel; its immense sugarpink towers are a landmark for miles around.

Inside are several floors of shops including a giant supermarket. Other facilities within the Amoreiras include a tenscreen cinema, a post office, travel agent, dozens of restaurants and a hotel.

Open-air Markets. Open-air markets are held weekly in almost every sizeable town. Some can be a little drab and uninspiring, with their motley secondhand clothes stalls. Some expat residents may be able to sell craft and other products here. A licence is usually negotiated through the local town hall. Others specialise in live animals (chickens, songbirds, rabbits, lambs etc.) while others are full of life and colour, selling everything from porcelain to tomatoes in a mix familiar in many Mediterranean countries. Among the Portuguese, the best markets are reckoned to be in the fertile northern half of the country: two well-known ones include Barcelos in the Minho province and Caldas da Rainha in the Estramadura province near Lisbon. It is worth doing some research to find out where the best ones are for the provisions or handicrafts that you want (or would like to sell); and driving the extra miles for the best homegrown and cured hams and sausages, fresher fruit and vegetables than in the shops, and local cheeses, honey and cakes.

Fish markets are held on the quaysides at dawn in Cascais and other coastal towns; this is one itinerary for those wishing to explore the country by car. The Portuguese claim that there are over 200 kinds of fish and crustaceans available there, which go into specialities like the *caldeirada* a mixed fish stew, as well as soups. *Sopa de marisco* is a shellfish soup cooked and served with wine. Some of the commoner varieties includes the *peixa espada* (swordfish), *salmonete* (red mullet), and the *eiroz* (conger eel). To shop in fish markets you need an alarm clock, some courage, and the ability to haggle, preferably in Portuguese.

Non-Food Shopping

Clothes. Since Portugal joined the EU, imported goods are increasingly available in the shops, where they are often quite expensive. However, the country has for many years produced good quality shoes (which are exported around the world) and is working hard at upgrading its textiles and fashion industry for international markets. There are dozens of fashion boutiques in Lisbon's Baixa, and all the famous names, but Portugal's capital has some way to go before it compares with Rome or Paris as a place to shop for smart clothes. There is no home-grown equivalent of the international fashion chains like Benetton yet. The best known Portuguese shop for children aged 0-12 years is Cenoura, which has about sixty shops nationwide. High class Portuguese fashion designers are mostly found in Oporto; and include Ana Salazar, Olga Rego and the Nuno Morgado collection.

Chemist (Farmácia): As in France and Switzerland the pharmacist can be consulted on treatments for minor ailments. As pharmaceutical products are extremely expensive in Portugal, and the brand names are unfamiliar, it is advisable to bring a supply of your regular medicaments from the UK until you have identified the Portuguese equivalents.

Household: Kitchen gadgets and electric household appliances are only a little more expensive in Portugal; some may choose to bring these from the UK, though. Decorative tableware, including colourful glazed pottery and embroidered fine linen, are some of the traditional national wares to look out for. The best quality pottery (based on the complexity of its handpainted decoration) is not cheap. However it is possible to find lowerpriced versions in some of the openair markets. Table linen is of extremely fine quality. One famous shop for this and other houseware is a private house in Porto (Oporto) run by Beatris Perry Sampaio (Rua do Campo Alegre 713). One has to ring the doorbell to be admitted. Linen can also be found in the shop Alecrim, in the Amoreiras shopping centre in Lisbon.

Generally speaking, handcrafted items made in Portugal are much cheaper than they would be in the UK or the USA, including leather goods like belts and shoes, copper and ceramics items (decorative plates, vases, etc.), handmade silver and gold jewellery, embroidery and tapestry work, every kind of cork product, crystal and glassware, and porcelain, which souvenir sellers and outdoor markets all stock.

CARS AND MOTORING

Driving Licence

For temporary visits to Portugal a valid British, pink EU, or international driving licence may be used to drive there; and the driving licences of any country in the European Union are valid in any other member state. You may be required to produce an identity document with photograph (e.g. passport) with the licence. A Green Card or receipt issued by your insurers is also essential.

Non-EU citizens taking up residence in Portugal are required to exchange their licence for a Portuguese national licence. This does not apply to those holding pink EU driving licences issued in Britain or any other EU country. Anyone holding a licence issued in an EU country can now use it after obtaining a residence card.

To obtain a Portuguese driving licence in Portugal if you are a non-EU citizen, apply to the district office of the *Direcção de Via[ce]ção* where you will be issued with the Portuguese version of the EU licence.

In order to drive on a licence issued outside the EU one needs to obtain an International Driving Permit from the *Automóvel Club de Portugal* (ACP), Rua Rosa Araújo 24, P1250 Lisbon; ☎21-318 0100 fax 21-318 0237; www.acp.pt.

Portuguese licences must be renewed at the ages of 65 and 70, and every two years thereafter, for which purpose a medical certificate must be submitted. This used to be different for those who drove as part of their job; but 'there is now no difference between professional and nonprofessional drivers' according to the Direcção Geral de Viação.

EU-issued licences are valid in all member countries, regardless of the country of issue.

Running a Car

Petrol (*gasolina*) prices in Portugal sit in the middle of the European cost scale and cheaper than the UK. Unleaded petrol is roughly 53 pence (75 cents) per litre and diesel (*gasoleo*) is considerably cheaper at 40 pence per litre. Some petrol stations, as in the UK, will offer petrol at a discount, and these prices are given as a guide only to the current situation.

Many of the best known European car makes are now sold in Portugal, so you should be able to find an agent for spares in the Lisbon and Porto areas. Finding a reliable garage, or more usually a self-employed mechanic for servicing, is probably more a matter of trial and error (and there are some work opportunities here for qualified mechanics from the UK). The Automóvel Club de Portugal (see above), which has a reciprocal agreement with the AA, can advise.

Insurance: Third party insurance is compulsory. The minimum sums to be guaranteed are 100,000 euros per accident and 60,000 euros per person including material damage. Again, as with all prices quoted here this may be subject to change.

Registration and Road Tax: In order to register one's car, application should be made to the district office of the *Direcção Geral de Viação (Ministerio das Obras Publicas, Transportes e Communicações, i.e. the Ministry of Transport and Communications)*; and the appropriate registration tax must be paid. Road tax *(Imposto Sobre Veículos)* can be as much as 80% cheaper than in the UK. The amount of tax one pays is related to the cubic capacity and age of the car.

Roads: Until quite recently the roads in Portugal were of very poor quality. Entry into the European Union, and the need to have a proper road infrastructure for commercial and tourism purposes, gave the necessary impetus to a spate of road building that has upgraded existing roads and created new motorways; but the programme is not yet completed. Once off the principal routes the road surfaces deteriorate rapidly into potholes and are really only suitable for robust vehicles of the fourwheel drive variety. However, travelling around in Portugal is probably best by car. Some of its beautiful scenery and many of the sights are off the the main public transport routes.

Car travellers will discover four main road classifications:

Autoestrada*:* Motorway. There are at present 593.5 kms (about 350 miles) of motorway in Portugal running north and south of Lisbon and from Conimbriga to just north of Porto. Recently a plan was drawn up to extend the motorway network by 307 kms (190 miles), most of which are currently under construction or completed.   Motorway tolls are payable at various staging points on the motorways. A list of toll prices can be obtained from the very helpful Portuguese National Tourist Office in London.

Via rápida: Dual carriageway. The main northern dual carriageways are the west to east highway from Aveiro to the Spanish border and Porto to Vila Real. In the south, there is the Algarve Coast highway from Lagos to Vila Real de San António and the road northwards from Faro to just south of Lisbon.

Estrada principal: corresponds roughly to an A road in the UK.

Estrada secundária: corresponds roughly to a B road in the UK.
The main 'highways of death', as they have been called, are the notorious
Marginal (coast road) from Lisbon to Cacais, the Lisbon to Porto route and the
Algarve coast road. Care should be taken driving anywhere (see below).

Driving

The annual mortality rate from road accidents in Portugal is among the highest
in Europe. In 1999, 1800 people were killed on the country's roads. But the
Portuguese powers-that-be are sensitive about this appalling record; and have
introduced measures to improve road safety, including medical and psycho-
technical tests for drivers of commercial passenger vehicles in addition to the
regular written and practical driving test. There are also mechanical tests made
on commercial and private vehicles. Improved training and tests are making a
difference. In the first edition of this book it was stated that 'one of the main
problems is that transport has been transformed from donkey carts to high-speed
modern vehicles in the space of a few years, so that those who now sit behind the
wheel are generally first generation drivers. The result is that most Portuguese
car drivers have no concept of high speed danger either to themselves or to
pedestrians, not to mention the animal transport that still remains in country
areas'. Many UK residents used to a more sedate driving style would agree but
the authorities in Portugal inform us that 'this is a very subjective opinion and we
cannot agree with your sentence.'

Those living there will have to judge for themselves how far attitudes have
changed; and whether the Portuguese really are 'extremely hazardous road users
with a near fatalistic attitude to death!' Whatever your view, the Portuguese are by
no means the only culprits, especially in the Algarve, where a certain number of
the drivers are, after all, not Portuguese but foreigners. Groggy tourists arriving
in the midday heat and driving off in a hire car without so much as a glance at the
unfamiliar instrument panel are another danger; and can be just as lethal as any
'doordie' native inhabitant. Certainly, the watchword when you are driving – or
cycling – in Portugal is, go cautiously.

The Rules of the Road.

In common with most of Europe, Portugal drives on the right and overtakes
on the left, except when overtaking stationary trams (see below). Road markings
include: a broken white line which may be crossed when clear for overtaking;
and a continuous white line which must not be crossed. Traffic approaching from
the right has priority, except when entering a main highway from a side road
displaying a 'Stop' sign, or from a private driveway.

Speed limits: These have been reduced recently to 50kph (30mph) in builtup
areas (also 50kph if one is towing a trailer). Outside towns the limits are 90kph
(56mph), and for cars with trailers 70kph (44 mph). On motorways the minimum
and maximum speeds for cars are 40kph (25 mph) and 120kph (75mph). If you
have a trailer or caravan this maximum speed is reduced to 100 kph.
Seat belts and mudflaps: For some time it has been compulsory for both driver
and front seat passenger to wear a seat belt. This law has recently been extended
to include rear seat passengers, so all passengers now have to belt up, as in Britain.

More unusually, it is also compulsory for cars to have rear mudflaps *páralamas*).

Prohibitions: It is prohibited: to drive with undipped headlights in builtup areas; to carry children under 12 years and dogs in the front of the car; and to carry an emergency petrol supply. This last injunction is a particular nuisance as in some areas petrol stations (*bombas de gasolina*) are still few and far between.

Alcohol Limits: The legal limit is below 0.5 grammes per litre. Penalties include a fine and withdrawal of driving licence. Anyone found to have in excess of 1.2 grammes in their blood is prosecuted under criminal law and liable to a prison sentence.

Driving in Lisbon and Oporto: This is difficult if not hazardous: one must give way to cars and trams (*elétricos*) approaching from the right in squares, and at crossroads and junctions. At official tram stops (*paragem*) overtaking trams is forbidden until passengers have finished boarding and leaving the tram. Overtaking of stationary trams is permitted on the right (i.e. the opposite to usual) only when passengers have finished their external manoeuvres and the way is clear.

In built-up areas use of the horn is prohibited during hours of darkness, except in an emergency. In Lisbon there is a Blue Zone disc parking system in operation. Free discs are available from the Automóvel Club de Portugal or local police. No parking signs are the universal clearway sign: blue, with a red circle and diagonal red slash.

Cycling is not recommended; and the best way of getting around in cities is probably by public transport.

Police and Fines

If you are caught committing a traffic offence in Portugal you can receive a hefty onthespot fine; and unlike in the UK where you do not have to produce your insurance documents for immediate inspection, in Portugal the police will want to see all driving documents including an insurance receipt. If you are driving a vehicle which is not registered in your name it is essential to have the owner's written permission on a special authorisation form issued by the motoring organisations. Due care should be taken not to violate traffic regulations.

Breakdowns and Assistance

If one is unlucky enough to break down it is compulsory to display the universal warning triangle to indicate to other road users that something is wrong. Those who are members of the AA or RAC can call on the ACP (Automóvel Club de Portugal) for assistance. The ACP runs a 24hour towing and breakdown service from offices in Lisbon and Oporto (see below). If one calls these offices they will call the nearest ACP office to you and arrange assistance.

In cases of accident the police (*policia*) must be called. If necessary an ambulance (*ambulância*) should also be requested. Main highways are furnished with orange emergency SOS telephones. To use these one should press the SOS button and wait for an answer. If you do not know your exact location, give details of the emergency and the number of the SOS telephone. If one is reporting an accident from a private telephone the emergency number 112. After 1998, 112 became the only number for emergencies in Portugal.

Maps. The Michelin Map for Portugal is No. 940. ACP also produces a national road map periodically updated and published usually in July. A list of Portuguese maps (commercial and large scale OStypes) is available from Edward Stanford Ltd. (1214 Long Acre, London WC2E 9LP; ☎020-7836 1321; www.stanfords.co.uk)

Useful Addresses:
*ACP:*Rua Rosa Araújo 24, P1250 Lisbon; ☎21-318 0100
DirecçãoGeral das Alfandegas (DirectorGeneral of Customs): Rua da Alfandega, P-1100 Lisbon; ☎21-881 3776; www.dgaiec.minfinancas.pt.

TRANSPORT

Air

The national airline is TAP (Air Portugal) which operates regular flights to 40 cities in Europe, Africa and the Americas. TAP flights between the UK and Portugal are from Heathrow and Manchester direct to Lisbon and direct from Heathrow to Porto, Faro and Funchal (Madeira). From time to time there are 'special' flydrive and other offers which TAP will be able to tell you about; the UK reservation number is: 0845-6010932.

Also keep an eye open in the British newspapers for the expanding miniprice airlines Buzz, Ryanair, bmibaby, etc. as between them they go to dozens of main and smaller airports all over Europe and are always adding new ones.

The Portuguese internal airline is Portugália Airlines, a private company. It has regular flights between Lisbon, Oporto, Faro and also several towns in foreign countries, and charter flights to Madeira and abroad from mainland Portugal and elsewhere. There are charter companies and air taxis which can also provide transport to Portugal's regional airports like Bragança, Chaves, Vila Real, Coimbra, Covilhã, Portimão, and Viseu, as well as the international airports of Lisbon, Porto and Faro. Portugália also operates between Lisbon and Faro.

The Azores have their own airline, SATA, which operates regular connections between the islands and charter flights to Madeira, continental Portugal and several countries in Europe.

Useful Addresses:
TAP Air Portugal: 3844 Gillingham Street, 4th Floor, Gillingham House, London SW1V 1JW; ☎0845-6010932; www.tap.pt.
TAP Air Portugal: Praça Marquês de Pombal 3A, Lisbon; ☎21-8431100.

Rail

The network of the national rail company, Caminhos de Ferro Portuguese (CP), covers most of the country. Trains everywhere in Portugal are inexpensive. For instance the fast service that operates between Lisbon and Cascais (a twentyfive minute journey) costs £1.50 ($2) for a return ticket. Senior citizens (those over 65 years) pay even less – only 50% of most fares. Over 90% of trains are so called *Regional* slow trains which stop at every station en route. The medium-fast trains are the *Intercidades* (Intercities) and the fastest are the *Rápidos* which link Lisbon and Oporto. The ticket prices on the Intercidades are double that of the Regional. For the Rápidos there is a supplement. In Portugal it is obligatory to buy tickets in advance; unfortunately this often means queueing. There is no provision for paying after boarding the train.

Further information when in Portugal may be obtained from travel agencies or the CP, ☎808208208 (from 7am to 11pm).

Stations: International trains use the Estação Santá Apolónia station in Lisbon and the Estação de São Bento in Oporto. Trains from Lisbon to Sintra depart from Estação Rossio and trains for the Estoril Coast (north of Lisbon) from Estação Cais do Sodré. In the provinces stations can be several miles from town.

Bus

There are local and long-distance buses (*autocarros*).The old bus company, the Rodoviária Nacional (RN), has been disbanded and replaced by a number of smaller private operators. Fares are higher than on the railways. Unlike many provincial rail stations, bus stations are nearly always in town centres. There are a number of private companies running express services (e.g. Lisbon to the Algarve and Lisbon to Porto). Tickets for such buses should be bought in advance from bus stations or travel agents. The central bus station in Lisbon is on Avenida Casal Ribeiro (nearest metro Saldanha). In Lisbon, travellers and commuters may also use the underground railway, trams and the various elevators to get around.

In Madeira and the Azores, buses are the only form of public transport. For further information contact their respective tourist boards:
Madeira. Direcção Regional de Turismo de Madeira, Avenida Arriaga 18, P9000 Funchal; ☎291-229057; fax 232151.
Azores. Direccao Regional Do Turismo Dos Acores, Rua Ernesto Rebelo 14, P9900 Horta; ☎292-200500; fax 292200501.

Boats

Ferries. A ferry to northern Spain is the only way to get to Portugal by sea *Brittany Ferries* runs a service from Plymouth to Santander (☎023-9289 2200; www.brittanyferries.com) and P and O operates a service between Portsmouth and Bilbao (☎023-9230 1000; www.poportsmouth.com.) Within the country, boat transport is used particularly on the Rio Tejo (River Tagus) estuary around Lisbon where ferries depart from the Sul e Sueste river station (near the Praça do Comércio) and the river station at Cais do Sodré to Cacilhas/Almada, Trafaria, Barreiro (train station for the south), Seixal, Montijo etc.

South of Lisbon a car ferry crosses the Sado River from Setúbal to the Península de Tróia, a well known playground for the locals which projects into the Sado estuary. There are also ferries across the Rio Guadiana between Vila Real de San António and Spain, and across the Rio Minho from Vila Nova de Cerveira, Monção and Caminha to Spain.

Pleasure boats. From Oporto one can take boat trips up the Douro River past the port wine vineyards; minicruises are also available. The departure point is at Ribeira. Portugal specialist travel agent *Unicorn Holidays* offers short breaks in Oporto with a daylong cruise along the Douro River leaving from Oporto Quay; an oppportunity to sample some of the wine, port and local cuisine: (☎0173-7812255; www.unicornholidays.co.uk.)

Taxis

Taxis are plentiful in the main towns and are distinguishable by their black and green livery. It is, however, usually difficult to hail a taxi; normally one has to queue at a taxi rank (e.g. in front of the Cais do Sodre rail station in Lisbon) or to telephone. To summon a cab in Lisbon telephone one of these 24 hour radio taxi centres 21-811 9000/ 21-811 1100 / 21-793 2756; in Porto call 22-488061/ 482691/676093. Compared with other European countries Portuguese taxis are inexpensive. Hire is as per the taximeter in large towns or by the kilometre in more outoftheway places, From 10pm to 6am there is a 20% supplement to pay; and large and heavy suitcases may mean an additional 50% charged; tipping is as in the UK, i.e. about 10%, although this is not obligatory.The journey from Lisbon airport to the city centre, which takes about 25 minutes, costs around £10.00.

TAX

Moving Overseas

In the future it is expected that the tax systems will become standardised throughout Europe, thus making the business of moving overseas no more complicated than moving within one's own country so far as tax is concerned. However, this Utopian reform will not have been accomplished by the time the single currency zone (with or without Britain) comes into existence at the beginning of the next century. In the meantime, as a result of the widely differing tax systems still operated within the nations of the EU, moving overseas involves careful arrangements of one's affairs in order not to pay more tax than is necessary.

A list of UK chartered accountants who deal with personal taxation in Portugal can be obtained from the PortugueseUK Chamber of Commerce (1st Floor, 22-25 Sackville Street, London W1X 1DE; ☎020-74941844; fax 020-7494 1822.) in London. An individual is deemed to be resident in Portugal (i.e. liable for Portuguese tax) if he or she spends 183 days or more in Portugal in any calendar year.

Portuguese Income Tax

At the beginning of 1989 the Portuguese taxation system was completely overhauled, which put an end to Portugal's reputation as a land of minimal taxes. Today, tax rates are unfortunately comparable with those in any other EU country. Personal Income tax (*Imposto Sobre o Rendimento das Pessoas Singulares*, otherwise known as IRS) is a wideranging tax in four main bands levied on nine categories or classifications of income:

CLASSIFICATIONS OF INCOME FOR TAX

(A) From employment
(B) From self-employment
(C) Commercial/Industrial profits
(D) From farming
(E) From investment
(F) From rental of property
(G) Capital gains
(H) Pensions
(I) Other income

Residents are taxed on their worldwide income after deduction of the specific allowances (including medical and basic personal allowances) granted under most of the above categories. Whichever categories an individual's income falls into, will thereafter be added together, to arrive at the annual base from which income tax will be deducted at the appropriate rate: 15% is the marginal rate and income is taxfree up to the personal limit of 5,237 euros a year. This is then taxed at 25% on 5,237 euros and over up to 12,470; 35% on 12,470 euros up to 31,324 euros; and 40% thereafter. Note that non-resident individuals are only liable for IRS on their Portuguese income.

Main Allowances. Reductions of income tax may be claimed on the following: mortgage interest and housing loan repayment; life insurance; and medical and educational expenses. Personal income tax allowances are about 200 euros for single persons; and 150 euros for each partner of a married couple; also 100 euros for each dependent. Foreign taxes paid are deductible as expenses.

Assessment and Payment of IRS. Tax returns must be submitted to the tax authorities in the year following assessment either by the end of February in the case of those earning income only from employment and/or pensions, or by May 10th if other categories of income are involved. In the case of married couples income is divided into two for the purposes of assessment and the resulting tax liability is doubled. However, if the main earner is responsible for 95% of the total income, the splitting factor is reduced to 1.85, which effectively increases tax liability. After assessment, the tax authorities will make any adjustments, upwards or downwards, to the level of taxation; and an additional payment will be requested, or an overpayment refund will be issued (one hopes). There are some other wrinkles in the system. For example, 'acquisition of equipment using renewable energy' (to a limit of 150 euros for a single person) which is a taxdeductible expense (making the purchase of solar panels a reasonable option); and some additional deductions which can be made for the various specific categories of income (from 'A' to 'I' above) where the services of a Portuguesespeaking accountant will come into their own.

Other Taxes

There is a range of other taxes in Portugal most of which have a direct or near equivalent in the UK:

VAT. Known as IVA or *Imposto sobre o Valor Acrescentado* this tax was introduced again in 1986 when Portugal was joining the then European Community. IVA is levied on a wide range of goods and services transferred within Portuguese territory. In addition it is levied on imports. The standard rate is 17%, with a medium or intermediate rate of 12% and a lower rate of 5% which increasingly covers less, but still applies to some food products, food, medicine, educational material, medicine, water and electricity etc. Some food products, restaurants and similar activities as well as diesel for farming etc. are subject to the medium rate.

In the autonomous regions of Madeira and the Azores the IVA rates are levied in bands of 12% (*genérica*, standard), 8% (intermédia], medium), and 4% (*reduzida*, reduced) but otherwise operate in a similar way.

Inheritance and Gift Tax (Imposto de Sucessões e Doações). This gift and inheritance tax is levied on gifts and bequests above a low exemption limit (€3,500) in the case of a spouse or a minor offspring). The tax is progressive according to the closeness of the relationship of the recipent, proceeding from this spouse and decendant category through 'parents, grandparents or siblings', 'first cousins, aunts, uncles etc.' to 'any other person'; and the amount of taxation for the gift or bequest ranges from 7% (for a gift of less than €3,500 to a parent, grandparent or sibling) to 50% (for a gift or inheritance greater in value than €342,500 transferred to 'any other person').

Inheritance tax at the rate of 5% has also been extended to income arising from share dividends of companies with their head office in Portugal; and 'the transfer of shares and bonds is liable to Substitute Gift and Inheritance Tax at a rate of 5% on the income resulting from these securites, when its payment takes place and not when the securities are transferred.'

Municipal Tax (Contribuição Autárquica). Municipal tax is payable by all property owners on December 31st annually. The rates are 0.8% on country property; and varies from 0.7% to 1.3% on urban property, where rates are fixed locally. Here, the amount of municipal tax is reviewed annually by the municipal district in which the property is situated. For details of payment see the section *Property Tax* in Chapter Three *Setting Up Home.* An exemption for permanently owneroccupied or rented residential property should be applied for within 90 days after the initial use of the property, or six months of acquisition. This exemption applies an amount of up to €150,000 which is taken into account in the value of the property when the *Contribuição Autárquica* is assessed; and there is an exemption period lasting from four to up to ten years.

Capital Gains Tax (Imposto de Mais Valias). As part of the reform of the tax system in 1989 the application of Capital Gains Tax was widened from being purely a tax on businesses to profits made by individuals on various transactions: 10% on any profits from the sale of shares held for a period of less than two years; 20% on the sale of nonresidential property and 24% on the sale of land for development.

In common with France, capital gains tax is not charged on the sale of an individual's sole residence, provided the proceeds of such a sale are reinvested in another property (or land) within two years. The sale of urban land for development gives rise to real estate transfer tax (SISA) at 10% on the higher of the following: the purchase price, or the official rateable value of the property.

The rate is reduced to eight percent on rural land.

Generally speaking, companies may be subject to VAT (IVA) and all the above. In addition certain transactions may be liable to stamp tax (*imposto de selo*).

Useful Addresses

Portuguese-UK Chamber of Commerce: 4th Floor, 22/25A Sackville Street, London W1X 1DE; ☎020-7494 1844; fax 020-7494 1822; www.portu guesechamber.org.uk

Deloitte and Touche: London Hill House, 1 Little New St, London EC4A 3TR; ☎020-9363000; www.deloitte.com or www.deloitte.co.uk.

Deloitte and Touche: Libson Edificio Atrium Saldanha

Praca Duque de Saldanha: 17, 1050 Lisbon; ☎21-0345256; fax 21-0343343

Ernst and Young, London Rolls House, 7 Rolls Buildings, Fetter Lane, London EC4A 1NH; ☎020-7951 2000.; www.ey.com

KPMG: London, 1 Canada Square, Canary Wharf, London , E14 5AG; ☎020-7311 1000; www.kpmg.com/ or www.kpmg.com/uk

KPMG: Lisbon EdifÝcio Monumental, Avenida Praia da Vit¾ria, 71 A 115, 1069 Lisboa; ☎21-0110 000.

PricewaterhouseCoopers: London,

1 Embankment Place, London WC2N 6NN; ☎020-7583 5000; www.pwcglobal.com.

PriceWaterhouseCoopers: Lisbon: Avenida da Liberdade 245 81 A, 1269 Lisbon; ☎ 21-3197000.

PriceWaterhouseCoopers: publishes its detailed *Doing Business in Portugal* guide, with chapters on audit and accounting, and tax.

In the UK, you can also contact the two major accountancy bodies the ICAEW (Institute of Chartered Accountants in England and Wales) and ACCA (Chartered Association of Certified Accountants) for advice and professional contacts.

ICAEW, PO Box 433, Chartered Accountants Hall, Moorgate Place, London EC2P 2BJ; ☎020-7920 8100. (www.icaew.co.uk).

ACCA, 29 Lincolns Inn Fields, London WC2A 3EE; ☎020-7242 6855. (www.acca.co.uk).

BANKS AND FINANCE

The Banking System

The Portuguese banking system has come through a decade of privatisation and deregulation; but it is clear the transformation process is far from over. There used to be twenty or so national banks. Now, if smaller investments banks and branches of foreign banks are included, there are fortysix. Most observers say that for such a small economy Portugal has too many banks; and the governor of the central bank *Banco de Portugal* describes the sector as 'quite competitive.' At the last count, there were 3,337 bank branches throughout the country, chasing too few customers. So competition is leading to takeovers and the creation of larger banking groups.

The banking sector has six major banks; and three heavyweight financial groups controlling one or more of these. These are the BCP Group (Banco Comercial Portugues), which took over Banco Portugues do Atlantico (BPA) in 1995; the Champalimaud Group, with Banco Totta and Açores, and Banco Pinto and Sotto

Mayor; and the Espirito Santo Group, with Banco Espirito Santo e Comercial de Lisboa. Other banks, including German and US ones, have established branches in the main cities; and Spanish banks are making a considerable impact on the Portuguese banking system, notably the Banco de Bilbao. The equivalent of the Bank of England in Portugal, the Banco de Portugal, is the only bank authorised to issue bank notes and all credit institutions come under its control.

Bank Accounts

The type of bank account permitted under Portuguese regulations will depend on the individual's status (i.e. resident or non-resident).

Non-residents Accounts. Non-residents can open tourist accounts in euros to which they may transfer funds from UK banks. Such accounts are useful for paying bills, taxes and general domestic expenses. For those who may be absent at the time certain bills fall due (e.g. water, electricity, television licences etc.) it would be advisable to pay by direct debit. Overdrafts are not permitted on tourist accounts. The mininum opening capital varies between banks, but can be as little as £75 for a current account and considerably more for a deposit account. It is generally known that Portuguese banks are not keen to lend money at all.

Deposit accounts in foreign currency may also be opened in Portugal by Non-residents although there is a time limit, usually one year, that one may hold such an account. The interest rate is fixed by the banks and is taxed at source.

Once the coveted resident status has been conferred the individual is free to join the mainstream banking system and open a normal account. Portugal has a double taxation agreement with Britain which avoids income being taxed twice.

Opening an Account and Writing Cheques.

When opening an account one should ask for the manager (*gerente*) and fill in the forms appropriate to the type of account (e.g. joint/single, current/deposit). In due course you will be issued with a book of cheques which will appear unfamiliar to UK cheque users: the payer's signature (*assinatura* comes at the top, underneath which comes the payee's (*é ordem de*) name, and the amount (*a quantia de*) at the bottom. On Portuguese cheques you also have to write the place (*Local de emissão*) where the cheque is issued (e.g. Lisbon, Cascais etc.). When writing figures in Portugal, note that a fullstop is used rather than a comma to indicate thousands. As in France it is a criminal offence to write a cheque with insufficient funds to cover it.

Money

The old Portuguese unit of currency was the escudo (pronounced *eshkoodosh* in the plural) but of course this was replaced in January 2002 by the Euro. Each euro is worth 100 cents. The Euro is divided into notes of 5,10,20,50,100,200,500. Coins are available as 1 and 2 euros and as 1,2,5,10,20,50 cents. The notes are standard across the eurozone but each member country of the euro will produce coins bearing a standard picture of the European Union and one carrying national symbols or heads of state.

At the time of conversion from escudos to euros the rate was fixed at 200.482 escudos to one euro.

Exchange Controls

Inward investment from external sources (within the EU) has been unrestricted since 1990. With the creation of the Single European Market in 1993, there is now virtually free movement of capital between Portugal and its EU partners; and no limit in value on the entry of foreign currency and payments from the EU into Portugal.

Now Portuguese customs simply expect visitors to declare all money exceeding 12,470 euros whether it takes the form of notes, gold, travellers' cheques or securities. This is simply so the government can monitor cash flows and prevent potential money laundering.

One important point to remember is that anyone importing money into Portugal to buy property should do so legally (see Chapter Three, *Setting Up Home*) as, when or if they subsequently sell the Portuguese property and wish to transfer the proceeds out of Portugal, they will not be able to do so unless they can prove that the funds were legally imported in the first place.

Choosing a Bank

Selecting a bank in Portugal should be carried out in much the same way as one would do in UK, i.e. by obtaining the relevant information from a range of banks and comparing the charges, services offered, etc. It is worth asking one's UK bank for advice: Barclays for instance, has several branches in Portugal and will be able to tranfer accounts from their UK to Portuguese branches. Other UK banks such as Lloyds have representatives to whom they can refer you. The advantage of banking with Barclays International or a UK bank with correspondents in Portugal is that they will be used to dealing with the requirements of foreign clients. Alternatively one can enquire at Portuguese banks with UK branches who will give details of their nearest branch in Portugal. A list of Portuguese banks operating in the UK may be found in Chapter Three on *Setting up Home*.

Banking hours vary in the regions, but in the large cities banks open from 8.30am to 3pm. Monday to Friday. Banks are closed at weekends and on the numerous national holidays.

Offshore Banking

One great advantage of being an expatriate is the use of offshore banking facilities as a means of earning taxfree interest on deposit accounts and investment portfolios. There are many offshore banking centres (a.k.a. tax havens) worldwide and the publication *Tax Haven Encyclopedia* lists details of such centres where no or low taxation is available. The more exotic locations include Bermuda, the Bahamas, the British Virgin and the Cayman Islands, and Panama. There are also two main centres on the European mainland: Gibraltar and Luxembourg. However those most commonly used by UK expatriates are those in reassuring proximity to the UK, namely the Channel Islands and the Isle of Man. Companies offering offshore banking include High Street Banks (e.g. Nat West) and increasingly, subsidiaries of British building societies (e.g. Nationwide Overseas Ltd., a subsidiary of the Nationwide Building Society). More and more high street banks and building societies along with the merchant banks are setting up offshore banking facilities and the list given below offers only a handful of the most widelyknown which offer such services.

The minimum deposit required by each bank will vary; ranging from £600 to £12,000, with the norm being between £1,200 and £6,000. Usually, a minimum of £12,000 is needed for the yearlong deposit accounts while the lower end of the minimum deposit range applies to 90-day deposits; instant access accounts are also available. The deposit account interest rates work on the basis that the more inaccessible one's money the higher the rate of interest paid.

Useful Addresses

Abbey National Offshore: 56 Strand Street, Douglas, Isle of Man IM99 1NH; ☎0845-054 4000; www.anoffshore.com.

Abbey National (Gibraltar) Ltd: 237 Main Street, PO Box 824, Gibraltar; ☎350-76090; fax 350-72028.

Bradford and Bingley Ltd: 30 Ridgeway Street, Douglas, Isle of Man; ☎01624-695000; fax 01624-695001; www.bradfordbingleyint.co.im.

Brewin Dolphin Securities Ltd 5 Giltspur Street, London EC1A 9BD; ☎020-7248 4400; fax 020-7236 2034

Expat Tax Consultants Ltd: Suite 2, Shakespeare House, 18 Shakespeare Street, Newcastle-upon-Tyne, NE1 6AQ; ☎0191-230 3141; fax 0191-230 3142; www.expattax.co.uk.

Halifax International (Jersey) Ltd: PO Box 664, Halifax House, 31/33 New Street, St Helier, Jersey, Channel Islands JE4 8YW; ☎01534-613500; fax 01534-759280.

HSBC Group: International Branch, 6 Arthur Street, London, EC4R 9HR; ☎No. 020-7260 9568; fax 020-7260 0260

Jayga Ltd: Thornton House Business Centre, 16 Parkstone Road, Poole, Dorset BH15 2PG, United Kingdom; ☎07092 149775; fax 07092 259913; www.jaygaltd.co.uk. Financial services for British expatriates.

Lloyds Bank Plc: Isle of Man Offshore Centre. PO Box 12, Douglas, Isle of Man IM99 1SS; ☎0870-5301641; fax 01624-638181; www.lloydstsb.co.uk. One of the services offered is the Lloyds Bank Overseas Club.

Moores Rowland Chartered Accountants: Mitre House 177 Regent Street, London, W1B 4BB, UK; ☎020-7470 0000; www.mriworld.com/. With partners in 500 offices around the world providing home and host country tax compliance and tax minimisation services.

Wilfred T. Fry Limited:, Crescent House, Crescent Road, Worthing, Sussex BN11 1RN; ☎01903-231545; fax 01903-200868. A comprehensive tax and compliance service. They may send a copy of their useful free guide *The British Expatriate.*

Useful Publications

The British Expatriate: see above.

FT Expat magazine ☎020-8606 7545; www.Ftexpat.com. A monthly magazine for expatriates and offshore investors.

Expat Network Rose House109a, South End, Croydon CR0 1BG; 020-8760 5100; fax 020-8760 046; www.expatnetwork.com. The Network provides a 'home-base' for expatriates or those looking to work overseas. Membership is £72 in Europe and benefits include a monthly magazine, which can be accessed online, a jobsearch facility, tax advice, a directory of contacts, and a members' forum.

HEALTH INSURANCE AND HOSPITALS

The Health System

Treatment within the Portuguese public health system is free, as are essential medicines and general medical consultations or GP services. Health care is, as a rule, provided in the health centres (*Centros de Saúde*) and their local offices; and if treatment cannot be provided here you are entitled to consult a registered doctor. There is a range of charges from 40% to 100% for non-essential medicines; and contributions are made for items like spectacles, dentures, spa treatment etc.

Exemptions, where payment of these charges is waived include children under 12, pregnant women, pensioners and others receiving less than the national minimum wage, etc. In spite of the increasing number of hospitals and health centres the sometimes chaotic public-health system in Portugal makes the British NHS look efficient and affluent. It can take months to get an appointment and waiting times for hospital admission are on average more than three months. Facilities for emergency casualties are equally uneven: the corridors of some public hospitals are lined with those too ill to walk, who are kept there for observation or until their condition becomes too acute to ignore. Improvements are being made but it is hardly surprising that any Portuguese who can afford to, takes out health insurance to cover the cost of treatment at one of the many new private clinics and health centres where the doctors may be either Portuguese from the state sector or, increasingly, foreigners.

UK citizens visiting Portugal (including Madeira and the Azores) i.e. non-residents, are entitled to inpatient treatment in a general ward of an official hospital under EU reciprocal health agreements. The E111 form available from post offices (ask for the form T6 *Health Advice for Travellers* which contains the application form for the E111. You can also get the application form from the Inland Revenue (international services helpline 0845-915 4811; www.inlandrevenue.gov.uk/nic/intserv/ose.htm) is a must for people moving temporarily there. Permanent residents may apply for form E109 which provides for your family members who may be resident elsewhere in the EU by bringing the (dubious) advantage for them of entitling them to Portuguese healthcare. The regional social security office (CRSS) is where you go to apply for this. However, if treated by a doctor working in a state health centre (*Centro de Saúde*) mentioned above, you must expect to pay some fees; and charges for most prescibed medicines and for dental treatment etc.

An important point to bear in mind is that once you have taken up residence permanently in Portugal, you are no longer entitled to receive treatment on the British NHS unless you move back to the UK. In the light of all of the above, it is therefore extremely advisable to take out private medical insurance or alternatively to contribute to the Portuguese national insurance scheme, the *Caixa de Previdência*, normally referred to as just the *Caixa*.

Hospitals, Chemists and Emergencies

British Hospital. The British Hospital in Lisbon is a small one-ward institution. (British Hospital, Rua Saraiva de Carvalho 46, Estrela, 1250 Lisbon; ☎21-395 5067; fax 21-397 4066) Patients pay fees but the hospital is strictly nonprofit. Other funding comes from public subscription. Although it has a small operating theatre the hospital is not equipped to deal with serious emergencies. The British Hospital also runs an outpatient service of which details are available on request.

There is also the International Medical Centre for non-emergencies in Lisbon staffed by English speaking medical staff (Av. Antonio Augusto de Aguiar, 40, 1050 Lisbon; ☎ 21-353 0817.

Chemists: (Farmácias) Fortunately many Portuguese chemists speak English. Opening hours are generally from 9am to 1pm and 3pm to 7pm. In Lisbon and Oporto there are several 24hour chemists; in other areas there is a rota. The name of the chemist on duty is usually posted in all chemist windows and in the local press. In Lisbon a list of chemists may be found on the Agenda page of the newspaper *Diário de Notícias*.

Emergencies. (Urgências). If your condition is serious go to the casualty department of the nearest general hospital or *Cruz Vermelha Portuguesa* (Red Cross hospital). An ambulance can be summoned by dialling the emergency number (*Número Nacional de Socorro*) 112. Ambulances in Portugal are driven by *bombeiros* (firemen or women) often known as the *voluntários*, who are trained in firstaid. Their midwifery skills are also frequently in demand as owing to the state of the Portuguese roads mothers in labour often give birth long before the ambulance reaches the hospital.

Health Insurance Contributions

Anyone legally employed in Portugal will have health insurance contributions automatically deducted from their salary by their employer for payment to the Caixa. Anyone who is self-employed will have to make their own payments which are subject to change but which are currently around 30% of the official minimum wage. Useful leaflets setting out what one is entitled to when living in Portugal may be obtained from your local Jobcentre if you are unemployed and thinking of moving there. You may write to the Benefits Agency, Pensions and Overseas Benefits Directorate (International Office, Tyneview Park, Newcastle-upon-Tyne NE98 1BA; ☎0191-218 7777) with enquiries relating to health contributions and pensions etc. before moving to Portugal, giving your national insurance or pension number, and explaining your specific circumstances so that the relevant information can be sent to you.

Once in Portugal, if you are still in any doubt about your status or eligibility for subsidised health care, enquire at the local *Centro de Saúde* or International Clinic.

The E111

The form E111 (see above for how and where to obtain the application form) is necessary to receive medical treatment for accident or unexpected illness during short visits abroad. It is therefore useful when one is on holiday, or during the initial period of moving to Portugal. It is only valid as long as one is still living in the UK. In most countries the E111 does not cover all medical expenses. It is therefore advisable to have private medical insurance to cover the charges made. On the Portuguese mainland and the Azores a nominal charge is made for treatment at health centres (Centros de Saúde). In Madeira it is necessary to pay for a GP consultation and claim a refund from a bank appointed as an agent 'before leaving Madeira.' The charges for prescribed medicines are 40% to 100%; and X-rays and some other treatments like laboratory tests are also chargeable.

Private Health Insurance

Those who are employed by a British company in Portugal will most likely have health insurance schemes arranged for them. Those who have to arrange their own will find them fairly expensive. The rates vary depending on age and occupation from as little as £300 a year for an 18-29 year old up to £1,500 for a 60-64 year old. Executives of any age pay around 60% more. There are several insurance companies specialising in expatriate insurance. One of the leading providers is *BUPA International*:Russell Mews, Brighton, BN1 2NR; ☎01273-208181; fax 01273-866583; www.bupa-intl.com. *Derek Ketteridge & Associates* (1st floor 130a, Western Rd, Brighton East Sussex BN1 2LA; ☎01273-720222) offers a private healthcare scheme including general longstay insurance and non-UK residents insurance. Another leading company is *Expacare:* e-mail info@expacare.net or visit www.expacare.net. They are specialists in expatriate healthcare offering high quality health insurance cover for individuals and their families, including group cover for five or more employees. Cover is available for expatriates of all nationalities worldwide.

Those interested can set up the policy from the UK before moving to Portugal or on arrival in Portugal through a broking agency. One of the advantages of UK health insurance schemes is that their policies cover the claimants for treatment incurred anywhere in Europe.

Also, if you are transferring your Jobseeker's Allowance to Spain (see below) you are automatically entitled to free health care. Make sure you apply for the appropriate form, the E119, before you leave the UK (and take this along with the Jobseeker's Allowance form you need, the E303).

Doctors and Dentists

In the Algarve and other developed areas of Portugal there are an increasing number of smart new private medical and dental clinics, often run by foreigners, or Portuguese doctors with excellent English. Clinics usually specialise in one area of medicine so it is advisable to keep an address book of specialities – just in case. The usual method for finding a reliable doctor or dentist is by personal recommendation; alternatively most doctors and dentists advertise in the English-language publications.

SOCIAL LIFE

In common with other Latin countries, Portugal has a lively and colourful ambience and it is up to the foreign resident to make the most of it. Traditional beliefs play a greater part in the fabric of life in Portugal than in most other EU countries; and community life frequently revolves around centuries' old religious and secular festivals celebrated by the inhabitants of every town and village.

Expatriates tend to live in well-defined areas and have their own social networks organised around clubs and associations, many of which announce their forthcoming events in the English-language publications. Turning up at the bridge circle, drama society, bowling or archaeological club is an excellent way of meeting new faces. There are some useful addresses for expatriate clubs and organisations in the *Retirement* chapter which follows.

Making friends with fellow expatriates is a lot easier than meeting the Portuguese, who do not have an organised social life along the same lines as the foreign community and are not as 'clubbable' as, say, the Danes or Germans. Social life often revolves around meals with close friends and family at home or in a restaurant. For foreign residents living in country areas it will be essential to make contact with some Portuguese neighbours in order not to feel socially isolated. This requires a concentrated effort as the Portuguese, although extremely friendly and helpful, are naturally reserved; and it is not usual to be invited into their homes. If such an invitation were to be offered, it should be regarded as a privilege and a major step towards being accepted into the community.

The Portuguese Attitude to Expatriates

The Portuguese seem to have no difficulty in accepting the ever increasing number of expatriates who choose to live in their country. Perhaps this is not surprising in view of their history as maritime explorers, and their links with most of the world's peoples from Africa to South America. It is part of Portugal's inheritance as a trading nation that the country's prosperity and wellbeing has been traditionally associated with contacts with people from other countries; and the continuation of traditional ideas of hospitality in the countryside means that welcoming strangers is important here as well.

This applies especially to British visitors. The Anglo-Portuguese connection predates even Portugal's great era of maritime exploration; and there has been an English presence in Portugal for most of the millennium. There are British hospitals, schools, churches and even a British cemetery. In Oporto the ancestors of some of the famous families associated with port wine came from England six generations ago. Then the French arrived in the nineteenth century, principally to carry out engineering projects. More recently American culture has made an impact: American companies participated in the 1970's in the building of the magnificent suspension bridge over the Rio Tejo among other projects, and have since invested heavily in Portuguese industry, in this way cementing a bond that exists through the many Portuguese who settled in America at the turn of the century.

Perhaps as a result of their wide dealings with foreigners, the Portuguese – like the Dutch – are also often able linguists; and it is common to find educated locals speaking three or more languages fluently. However, due to the marked difference in the levels of sophistication in town and country, it would be virtually impossible to make social headway in English or other foreign languages in the remoter areas.

Whether one lives in the cities or in the countryside, one will find the Portuguese attitude to foreigners easygoing and remarkably tolerant.

Social Attitudes

For years Portugal lagged behind the rest of Europe in almost every respect. Forced into obedience by the Salazar regime, the people were kept in ignorance of the true state of the country and their deprivation compared badly with the rest of western Europe. Social attitudes in Portugal were shaped to a great extent by repression and hardship; and by the feudal divisions between rich and poor.

During the years of repression, corruption and nepotism were developed into an art; and loyalty to the family and one's immediate circle were stronger than interest in the fate of the country, let alone the outside world.

In the past, this concern with parochial affairs above national ones was due to the pessimism with which the majority of Portuguese viewed their lot: without powerful friends and connections they saw themselves as the hapless pawns of the ruling regime. Today, a passionate concern with local reform is seen in a more positive light, as a way to influence and improve one's prospects and environment.

Thanks to political upheaval and progressively better education, attitudes and aspirations are changing fast. Improved technical training for young people aged 18 to 25 has given them lucrative job prospects in an economy that is bounding forward to catch up with that of its EU partners. For the many Portuguese whose families have lived at subsistence level for generations, things are at last improving. But unfortunately, despite the changes bought about by the Revolution and the transition to democracy, old habits of nepotism die hard; even today it remains largely true that it is not what you know but who you know that counts.

These sometimes inward-looking attitudes affect even the foreigners living in Portugal, who claim that knowing the right people and having the right connections can have a startling, galvanising effect on some of the bureaucratic procedures. Attitudes to women can also sometimes be old-fashioned; but these have improved substantially from the dictatorship days when the female half of the population was firmly relegated to the home by legislation. Contemporary women have won the right to independence largely through academic ability: over half of all university graduates in Portugal are female and their increasing entry into the professions can no longer be ignored. Once again, however, there is a gap between the cities and the countryside, where the stereotype drinking, moustachioed machoman is unfortunately much in evidence.

Whatever their background and social status, all Portuguese share a love of family. Their consciousness of ancestry is acute, no matter how far away individual members of families may have strayed: the homing instinct is still strong enough to bring many back from the Americas, Australia etc. for long visits. On these occasions the red carpet is rolled out and reunions are celebrated in the most lavish style that can be afforded.

With such familial devotion, it comes as little surprise that families are traditionally large and extended in Portugal; and parents indulge their children (boys, more than girls) to excess. Some of these lucky offspring enjoy the adoration of both parents, but in country areas many have had to make do with one, as fathers traditionally left their wives and young children to roam the world in search of work, often staying away for years at a time.

Culture and Entertainment

For anyone living and working in Portugal, the rich and ancient culture and the lively entertainments are one of the main attractions. Apart from traditional art forms, particularly folk music and village festas, Portugal is increasingly on the international circuit for world-renowned musicians and singers as well as contemporary rock stars.

Architecture. To a lesser extent than Spain, Portugal inherited a legacy of architecture and design from the Arabs. This can be seen in the magnificent Moorish palace at Sintra and throughout the Algarve, where there are many ancient fortifications and houses built in the Moorish style. Also a legacy of the Moors are the tiles (*azulejos*) which ornament the doorways of churches and mansions, as well as the walls of countless houses. A uniquely Portuguese form of architecture, the Manueline, flourished during the early fifteenth century. In form, the Manueline also drew inspiration from Moorish architecture, but the decoration consists of maritime motifs: ships in full sail, armillary spheres (a representation of the globe constructed of metal rings), crossed anchors, and knotted ropes. This indigenous Manueline style was blended with the more classical Renaissance architecture which developed later here than in Italy or France, from around 1530.

Like Catalonia or the Basque country in neighbouring Spain, Portugal celebrates its maritime traditions in architecture as in many other areas of its life and culture.

Painting. During the Renaissance, a Portuguese school of painting also flourished. Among the Portuguese masters are Cristóvã de Figueirido, Francisco Henriques and António de Holanda. The main art musueums in Lisbon include the Museu Nacional de Arte Antiga in the Rua das Janelas Verdes and the Museu Nacional de Arte Contemporânea in Caldas da Rainha.

Literature. Portuguese literary culture is rich in novelists, poets and and historians; the more flowery and romantic the style the greater their popularity. The Portuguese equivalent of Shakespeare is probably Luís de Camões (1524-1579). Not only was he contemporaneous with Shakespeare and Cervantes but his works dealt with national history told in epic verse. In addition to his plays his most enduring work is the lyric poem *Os Lusíadas*. Much of Portuguese literature is devoted to the voyages of discovery: some of the best known works on this theme include *Peregrinação* (Pilgrimage). Some Portuguese books have been published in English, notably the nineteenth century writer Almeida Garrett's *Viagens na Minha Terra (Travels in my Homeland)*. There are are a number of avidly read modern writers whose names are little known outside Portugal, including Maria Velho, António Lobo, João de Melo and Clara Pinto Correia. Those wishing to find out more about literature in Portuguese can consult the *Babel Guide to the Fiction of Portugal, Brazil and Africa* (Boulevard Books; £9.95), which has reviews, excerpts and a database of all fiction translated into English from Portuguese since 1945. In Portugal, in common with many European countries, there is a wide range of translations of foreign writers available. Expatriates with limited Portuguese will be pleased to know that literature in English is not difficult to find in the bookshops of the capital and main towns, albeit at inflated prices.

Theatre. Although there is a long tradition of theatre in Portugal, drama outside Lisbon is far from being the most popular form of entertainment. Actors are not well paid, but subsidies and grants from the government keep a reasonable range of plays from Sophocles to Alan Bennett on offer. Gil Vicente is Portugal's most pre-eminent contemporary playwright. One of the best known theatres is the Teatro Nacional Dona Maria II in Praça Pedro IV in Lisbon.

Cinema. Portugal has its own famous film directors including the grand old master Manoel de Oliveira, who began his film career in 1931. However the biggest box office hit ever in Portugal enticed only a total audience of 150,000. In order to be commercially viable, therefore, Portuguese films have had to be international coproductions like the 1990 *Aqui d'El Rei* a PortugueseSpanishFrench production. Many foreign films are shown in the towns and cities; unfortunately they are usually dubbed into Portuguese. Both national and foreign films are shown in Lisbon at the Cinemateca Portuguesa, Rua Barata Salgueiro 39, Lisbon; ☎ 21 354 6085. Expatriates unable to locate a British or American film showing in the original language will have to make do with the television which puts out many old black and white movies as well as more recent films in the original language, with Portuguese subtitles.

Music. Portugal has its own unique folk music traditions about whose origins the scholars are still arguing. It can however be said with certainty that the mediaeval troubadors were a great early influence. The most famous Portuguese music is *Fado* which means fate or destiny. Its conception (but not sound) is probably similar to the American blues, i.e. both grew out of the laments of African slaves. Characterised by its haunting sound which is full of melancholy and yearning, fado has male and female exponents, although the latter are still controversial. The repertoire varies with the region. In Lisbon the best places to hear fado are in the restaurant-cafés of the Alfama and Mouraria districts of Lisbon where, as a travel journalist has put it, 'the chip lady and the waiters sing'. For a more academic approach – the (male) students of Coimbra university are also renowned for their performances.

International classical music is also widely listened to in Portugal: Opera seasons are brief and the most notable one is based at the São Carlos Theatre on Largo Picadeiro in Lisbon. Concerts are a real joy, not least because they are often held in magnificent historical settings including palaces and monastery cloisters. Music festivals are held in summer in the Lisbon area, Sintra and the Algarve. Details can be obtained from the local tourist offices. The mammoth Gulbenkian Foundation in Lisbon, although chiefly renowned worldwide for its art museum, also organizes, concerts and recitals in its three concert halls.

Bullfighting. As in Spain, bullfighting is not considered a sport but a cultural event. The season starts officially on Easter Sunday and finishes in October. In Spain the matador is the star; in Portugal it is the *Cavaleiro* a splendidly caparisoned rider complete with eighteenth century ruffles and a tricorne hat. This romantically dressed figure wears down the bull in a series of encounters which permit a dazzling display of dressage and other riding skills. Successful cavaleiros traditionally come from the same families (e.g. Caetano and Telles) whose names are familiar to generations of afficionados.

Ticket prices for bullfights start at about £8 and can rise to £45 for the best seats.

Nightlife. Apart from restaurants and impromptu and staged fado concerts there are numerous nightclubs in Lisbon and the Estoril and Lisbon coasts. The Algarve too has its share of hotspots where things only get going at 11pm and finish at dawn. For less brain-numbing entertainment there are a growing number of places to hear African and South American music, not only from local bands whose players' nationalities corresponding to Portugal's former colonies, but also touring bands particularly from West Africa. The tourist office can provide details. Portugal's most celebrated jazz nightclub which has been going for at least forty years, is the Hot Clube de Portugal, Praça da Alegria, off the Avenue da Liberdade in Lisbon.

Even though the Algarve is catching up as far as entertainment is concerned, Lisbon and Porto are still the best places as regards the range and excellence and quantity on offer.

Sport

One might be forgiven for thinking that the sole spectator sport in Portugal was *futebol* (football) which is also the national pastime with every small village having a team of its own. However there are plenty of other popular sports ranging from Formula One racing in the famous Autodrome in Estoril to golf tournaments in Oporto and the Algarve, and tennis at Roger Taylor's Tennis Centre at Vale do Lobo. The Portugal Golf and Portugal Tennis Opens are fixtures now on the international sporting calendar. Watersports along the coast are also popular, including offshore fishing, waterskiing, sailing and windsurfing.

Those for whom life is not complete without the crack of willow on leather will find plenty of fellow fanatics in Lisbon and Oporto where cricket is pursued with expatriate fervour. Sports clubs are common in the cities; and many of the smarter developments have their own shared facilities including swimming pools and tennis courts. Squash has not yet caught on, perhaps because indoor games are not a priority in a country with such a mild climate. Keen yachties will find a very smart marina at Vilamoura just west of Faro and other smaller boating facilities along the Algarve coast. Nearly all the main coastal towns have a yacht club. Portugal's best kept sporting secret is probably the ski resort at Malhão da Estrêla in the province of Beira Alta which is better known as a hiking area in summer.

Holidays

For a nation whose early voyagers pushed back the frontiers of the known world and whose menfolk travelled across the world and Europe in search of prosperity in the nineteenth and twentieth centuries, remarkably few Portuguese take holidays abroad. Those who do are from the main urban areas. The fact is that the Portuguese would rather accumulate household appliances than holiday memories. This is perhaps an understandable obsession for those who have gone without these things for so long. They can now afford them (mostly on hire purchase) and the rate of acquisition particularly of automobiles and satellite dishes is phenomenal.

Portugal, in common with France and Italy, tends to take August off. Factories close and the Portuguese sport themselves at local beaches, campsites, or at friends' homes.

SCHOOLS AND EDUCATION

Education in Portugal

Along with the public health system the education system is not working as it should. It is a horrifying fact that Portugal has an illiteracy rate of 10% amongst the population over fifteen years old. This is twice that of Greece and three times that of Spain. Many of the illiterate are elderly women from rural areas and youngsters who have dropped out of their schooling, which until recently was compulsory only to the age of fourteen (the minimum working age).

The illiteracy of the elderly can be blamed squarely on the Salazar regime which regarded education as the privilege of the upper and middle-classes. Academics who objected to this heresy were immediately dismissed from their posts on account of being dangerous liberals. Meanwhile, up to 1970, over 60% of urban and regional councils did not have facilities for providing secondary education. For the primary schools the situation was somewhat better with 10,000 primary schools built in the 40 years of the dictatorship and the new universities of Lisbon, Braga, Aveiro and Évora and Lisbon technical university founded. The 1974 Revolution made education the right of every individual.

The Structure of Education

Despite its uneven quality, the education system has improved immeasurably in the last few years thanks largely to the vision of the minister of education in the late 1980's Roberto Carneiro, whose generous budget was only exceeded by that of Portugal's number one priority, public works. Carneiro's programme of reforms was sweeping; and included opening hundreds of wellequipped new primary and secondary schools, and a revamped curriculum.

In addition to the state schools, which are free (although parents are charged for books and stationary) there are private schools partly funded by the state. Compulsory state primary education begins at six years old and lasts for four years. There is no state preprimary education, although there are many private kindergartens of varying quality in the main cities. Charges are upwards of £120 a month. Those working for large companies are usually provided with free crêches.

The equivalent exams to GCSE's are taken in the tenth year of schooling; and 'A' levels in the twelfth year. Children who are more technically than academically inclined can take technical or vocational training course *formação profissional*) instead.

Further Education

The first university in Portugal was Coimbra founded in 1290. Although this ancient university has a revered place in the university system it is not necessarily the best. Some consider the University of Lisbon superior.

In 1970 Portugal had only five universities, four public ones, two in Lisbon and one each in Oporto and Coimbra, and a private one run by the Catholics: Universidade Cat[ac]olica Portuguesa. By 1995 this number had increased to fourteen public, autonomously-run universities including Aveiro, Minho, Évora, Alto Douro, Trás-os-Montes, Beira Interior, Azores, Madeira and a very small

University of the Algarve. Portugal launched its version of the Open University in 1988. Other institutions of further education include fifteen technical colleges (*Politecnicas*) and specialised public and private institutes for dentistry, fine arts, management etc. The estimate of students in higher education was around 220,000 for 1995 with a target of 250,000 by the year 2000.

In 1995 there were nearly twice as many applicants as places available which indicates that the scramble for education is an increasingly competitive one. Any Portuguese who can afford it will probably choose to study abroad. The wellconnected traditionally attend the Catholic University which has faculties spread over several cities. University entrance is by an exam, the *Prova Geral*, a general test taken in addition to the Portuguese version of 'A' levels. Adults over 25 years without formal entrance qualifications may enter unversity subject to succeeding in an adhoc aptitude test.

The degrees awarded by Portuguese universities are: *licenciado, mestre* and *doutor* (BA, MA and doctorate respectively).

Foreigners interested in studying at a Portuguese university should consult *Study Abroad*, an annual publication available from UNESCO Publishing Promotion and Sales Division; 1, rue Miollis; 75732 Paris Cedex 15; France; fax: (33 1) 45.68.57.37; www.ibe.unesco.org, which gives details of courses for which grants are available. The Gulbenkian Foundation (The Education Department, Avenida de Berna 45, P-1067, Lisbon) also provides grants, for artists and those wishing to study the Portuguese culture and language (philology). The International Association for the Exchange of Students for Technical Experience (IAESTE) is a reciprocal training scheme providing student exchanges from one month to one year (10 Spring Gardens, London SW1A 2BN; ☎020-7389 4509).

Further information on Portuguese universities can be obtained from the Ministry of Education in Lisbon (Gabinete Relacoes Internacionais, A. 5 de Outubro 107, 1069 Lisbon ; ☎21-795 0330; www.minedu.pt).

Portuguese Schools

Expatriate parents living in Portugal have three main educational options: to send their children to boarding school in Britain; to send them to a Portuguese state or private school; or the most popular option, to an international school of which there are many in the greater Lisbon area and the Algarve.

The first option, boarding school in the UK, is probably the most expensive as it involves not only school fees but also the cost of flying children between Portugal and the UK during school holidays. By being separated from their parents children will also miss an exciting opportunity of integrating fully into an international or Portuguese community and the broader perspective and linguistic advantage that this brings.

State and private schools. Over recent years an increasing number of expatriates have been sending their children to private Portuguese schools, particularly in the Lisbon area. The best way to find out which are the most academically respectable is by asking for recommendations. One should however note that there are few Portuguese state or private schools where English is taught by a native speaker. Also important to bear in mind is that prospective pupils will need to speak Portuguese in order to follow the curriculum, so it is essential to ensure that they learn enough Portuguese before beginning school. If necessary private coaching should be arranged. The main disadvantage of going to a Portuguese school is that children will miss an Englishbased education and all that it entails from cultural values to historical background which many would regard as a loss.

Further information including lists of Portuguese state and private schools can be obtained from The Ministry of Education (see details above.)

International Schools

There is a range of international schools in the main expatriate areas. These are basically day schools but some of them will make boarding arrangements, usually on a weekly basis for children whose parents live inconveniently far away in the hinterland, or who for other reasons would prefer their offspring to board. Some schools operate a school bus service to collect children from local addresses. The age ranges accepted by international schools are various so it is up to the parent to decide which would be the most suitable, based on whether they are likely to be in Portugal for a year or two or for longer and on causing as little disruption as possible in their children's schooling. Some schools take children from four to thirteen years; others will take children up to sixteen years i.e. until they have done GCSE's. Yet others take pupils up to age eighteen and include preparation for university entrance in the curriculum. Amongst the international schools, syllabuses on offer include the British, American and the International Baccalaureate. Nearly all the international schools are coeducational.

Useful Addresses

International Kindergartens:

Boa Ventura Montessori School: Rua Nunes dos Santos 5, P2765 São Pedro do Estoril; ☎21-4688023. Ages 2-5 years.

Colégio Monte Santos: Quinta das Ameias, Monte Santos, P2710 Sintra; ☎21-9233764. Portuguese/English. Ages 2-11 years.

The Cascais International School: Rua das Faias. Lt.7 Torre. P2750 Cascais; ☎21-484 6260. Montessori based. Age bands: 1-3 years and 3-6 years.

International Preparatory School: Rua do Boror 12, Carcavelos, P2775 Parede Codex; ☎ 21-4570149. From age 3.

Miss Rita Croft da Moura Nursery School: Rua Arriaga 13, P1200 Lisbon; ☎ 21-3978603. 3-6 years. Mornings only.

Montessori International School: Estrada de Oeras 22, Porto Salvo, P2780 Oeiras; ☎21-443 2848.

Queen Elizabeth's School: Rua Filipe Magalhães 1, Alvalede, P1700 Lisbon; ☎21-8486928.

International Schools:

American Christian International Academy: Avenida de Sintra, Lote 1Cascais; ☎21-4861860. American curriculum. Takes ages 4 to 16 years.

American International School of Lisbon: Apartado 10, P2795 Carnaxide; ☎ 21-4171819.

Algarve International School: Apartado 80, Porches, P8400 Lagoa (Algarve); ☎282-342547/8. IGCSE's and 'A' levels.

The British School: Rua dis Ilheus 85, P9000 Funchal, Madeira; ☎63218.

Colégio International de Vilamoura: Apartado 856, P8125 Vilamoura (Algarve); ☎ 289-366585. British and Portuguese curricula. Ages: 4 to 16 years.

International Preparatory School: See above. British curriculum. Ages from 3 to 13 years.

The Oporto British School: Rua da Cerca 326, Foz de Douro, P4150 Porto; ☎22-6180092. Founded in 1894.

IGCSE's and Common Entrance.

Prince Henry School: Almansil, c/o Rua Tenente Valadim 36, Faro (Algarve). Mainly a preparatory school for the Algarve International School.

Queen Elizabeth's School: Rua Filipe Magalhães 1, Alvalade, P1700 Lisbon; ☎21-8486928. Primary school mainly for Portuguese but accepts British pupils. Emphasis on English educational system.

St Anthony's International Primary School: Avenida de Portugal 11, P2765 Estoril; ☎21-2688098. British primary school for children up to 12 years.

St Dominic's International School: Rua Out-eiro da PolimaArneiro, Sao Domingos da Rana, P2775 Parede (Lisbon); ☎ 21-4440434. Catholic school. Age range 4-16 years. American system and IGCSE's.

St George's School: Vila Gonçalves, Quinta das Loureiras, P2750 Cascais (near Lisbon), ☎21 4840555. Primary/preparatory for public schools.

St Julian's School: Quinta Nova Carcavelos, P2777 Parede (near Lisbon); ☎21-4570140. One of the oldest and best known schools. Takes pupils from 3 to 18 years. Offers International Baccalaureate.

THE MEDIA

Television

Television in Portugal is surprisingly good. The equivalent of the BBC is RTP (Radiotelevisão Portuguesa) which has three channels, RTP1, RTP2 and RTPI. Then there are SiC and TVI, each offering a combination of news and current affairs, films, series, and sport. The bill of fare includes lyrical Portuguese documentaries, an inordinate number of Brazilian soaps, recycled British series like *A Touch of Frost* and various sitcoms, homegrown costume dramas, American quiz shows, and on RTP1, 2 and TVI plenty of sports coverage, including English, Italian and Brazilian football as well as the national football league. Unfortunately, keeping to television schedules does not seem to be a Portuguese strongpoint and programmes are liable to change without notice. Fortunately for expatriates the many old and recent cinema films on the television are rarely dubbed.

Satellite television is the current craze with parabolic dishes which have sprouted across city skylines like mushrooms on an autumn night. Dishes cost around £200 to £300; there are various rental packages; and installation companies are cutting each others' throats to cash in on the demand. The television scene was transformed by the introduction of the two private channels in 1990; and the myriad of programmes beamed into Portugal as into other European countries by satellite (and now available in some areas by cable). This is the way for those expatriates who wish to keep in touch with events at home to receive the BBC, Sky, CNN, and other English language services. Television licences in Portugal were abolished in 1991.

Radio

The choice of radio stations in Portugal is extensive. Over 400 licences have been granted. Portuguese stations are useful if you are trying to learn the language and also for music. Some of these are T.S.F. (89.5 FM) for news, talk and current affairs; R.F.M. (93.2 FM) for news and music; Antena 3 (100.3 FM), mainly music; Nostalgia (104.3 FM), for tracks from the 60's, 70's and 80's; and Antena (94.4 FM) for classical music. Still, many expatriates find themselves drawn inexorably to the BBC World Service whose broadcasts continue 24 hours a day. Radio 4 can also be picked up on long wave in some areas. To obtain the World Service you need a good quality shortwave radio. The frequencies change during the day.

The *Anglo-Portuguese News* radio page carries an hourbyhour wavelength guide. Alternatively the BBC World Service's own monthly magazine keeps you uptodate with any changes in broadcasting frequencies. The British Consulate and the British Council in Portugal should have copies, or you can write to the World Service subscription department: c/o Bush House, London WC2 4PH.

The Press

Despite its small population, Portugal supports an astounding number of newspapers and journals. There are over a dozen daily papers and around eight weighty weeklies to satisfy the Portuguese passion for discussing politics, business and sport.

Daily papers include the recently published *Público* (which has become a reference for expatriate as well as Portuguese readers), *Diário de Notícias* and *Correio da Manhã*. Magazines include *Visão* and women's magazines like *Caras* and *Maria*.

To keep the expatriate community informed about their parochial concerns there are several excellent English-language newspapers, notably the *Anglo-Portuguese News*. (Av. De Sao Pedro 14 dp2756 Monte Estoril, Lisboa; ☎21-466 1423; fax 21-466 0358.) It is published weekly on Thursdays and includes a Property supplement with every issue. Generally, the Anglo-Portuguese News is sold at newsstands where foreign newspapers are also on sale.

The Algarve News (Algarve Resident, Apartado 131, 8401-902 Lagoa (tel: 282 342936) is published fortnightly every other Friday and is available in hotels as well as newsstands and places like pubs and clubs in the Algarve, which are frequented by expatriates. On Madeira you can purchase The Madeira Island Bulletin (Apartado 621, 9001-907 Funchal). If you wish to have either of these publications mailed to your Portuguese address you can take out a subscription.

For those who cannot do without newspapers from home it is possible to buy the main British dailies from international newspapers stands in the main towns. Also from the International Press Centres in Cascais and Lisbon.

Useful Addresses

The International Press Centre: Avenida Marginal, Bloco C-Loja D. P-2750 Cascais (between the main Post Office and the BNU bank).
The International Press Centre: Shop 2108, Amoreiras Shopping Centre, Avenida Eng Duarte Pachecho, P-1000 Lisbon.

Books

Bookclubs. Some UK bookclubs will send books overseas; and it is worth checking this out before leaving the UK. One extremely useful organisation in this respect is *The Good Book Guide* (24 Seward Street, London EC1V 3PB; ☎020-

7490 9901). They produce a monthly magazine containing reviews and a huge list of books which can be mailed to anywhere in the world. For information about subscriptions contact The Good Book Guide at the address above.

Bookshops. There are several English and international bookshops in Portugal, usually advertised in the English-language press. As well as books some also sell a range of newspapers and magazines:
Livraria Britanica: Rua de S Marçal 83, P-1200 Lisbon.
Livraria Britanica: Rua José Falcão 184, Oporto.
Livraria Internacional: Rua 31 de Janeiro 43, Porto.
Livraria Bertrand: Rua Garrett 75, Lisbon.
Livraria Buchholz: Rua Duque de Palmela 4, Lisbon.

Libraries. Expatriates who are not fluent enough in Portuguese to join a Portuguese library may like to know that the following English libraries are open to the public (although the role of British Council libraries is currently being reassessed this one is at present still in operation):
British Council: Rua de São Marçel 174, P-1294 Lisbon. Open Monday to Thursday from 10am to 5pm. Closed during August.
AngloAmerican Library: Hotel Atlântico, Monte Estoril. Open Mondays, Tuesdays, Thursdays and Saturdays; 10am to 12.30pm.

Post and Telephones

Post. CTT (*Correios e Telecomunicacoes*) is the national company which runs both post and telephones. Portugal's postal service has been considerably modernised in the last few years and the service is reasonably efficient. There are over 1,000 post offices (*correios*) so you do not have to go far to find one. Those living in rural solitude often find it convenient to collect their mail from the nearest Post Office. This is done by renting a box (*apartado*) on a sixmonthly or yearly basis. The fee is usually a few pounds. The application form for the apartado has to be verified by a notary.

The price of stamps (*selos*) is subject to continual increase; and post office opening hours vary. Many also offer a fax service. In the main towns and tourist areas they are from 8.30am to 6pm Monday to Friday and on Saturday mornings until 12.30 pm.

Telephone. The easiest way to use a public phone is in a post office where there are telephone booths. You ask at the counter where you will be directed to a booth. When you have finished you return to the counter and pay, much the same system as in Spain. Telephoning is cheaper from 8pm to 8am and at weekends. All telephone numbers should be prefixed with the area code, frequently omitted from advertisements and business cards. From within the country the codes given below are preceded by a zero, as in Britain. Some main towns and codes are:

International calls can be made from telephone kiosks in main towns and from Post Offices; and increasingly from highstreet shops offering cutprice calls. From Portugal to the UK dial 00 44 then the code and number. To Portugal from the UK dial 00 351. For general enquiries in Portugal dial 16.

TELEPHONE AREA CODES	
Lisbon 21	Portimão 282
Oporto 22	Praia da Rocha 82
Albufeira 89	Sagres 82
Armação de Pêra 82	Sesimbra 21
Coimbra 239	Sétubal 265
Faro 289	Sintra 21
Figueira da Foz 233	Viana do Castelo 258
Lagos 282	Estoril 21
Monte Gordo 81	Cascais 21
Obidos 62	Viseu 32

SOCIAL SECURITY

Portugal has a system of social security known as the *Caixa de Previdência*, similar to systems in other EU countries. It includes a range of benefits: healthcare and pensions, and sickness, unemployment, invalid and maternity/paternity benefits.

Social security contributions are payable by both employer and employee as a percentage of the gross salary earned: those who are self-employed must also contribute. At the time of writing, the general contribution is 34.75% of earnings of which 11% is payable by the employee. Self-employed people pay between 23% and 28% of their earnings. Certain categories of employment (e.g. agricultural) are subject to lower contributions. Nonemployed people may pay voluntary national insurance contributions if they so wish.

Social Security is dealt with through the National Pension Centre and the regional social security centres (*Centros Regional de Segurança Social*). Two useful addresses for those thinking of claiming pensions or social security abroad are:

National Pensions Centre: Campo Grande 6, P1771 Lisbon.

Department of International Relations and Social Security Conventions: Rua da Junqueira 112, P-1300 Lisbon.

There is a leaflet (SA 29) available from the Overseas Benefits Office, Newcastle-upon-Tyne NE98 1YX (☎0191-218 7777) and Job Centres which gives details of social security, health care and pension rights within the EU; and is also useful reading for anyone intending to live and work in Portugal. The above address can also send useful information about your health rights.

Healthcare. All those who pay into the *Caixa* and their dependants are entitled to use the scheme. However in some cases, even while on benefit, one may have to pay a substantial contribution towards medical consultations and diagnoses involving the use of sophisticated equipment. Generally speaking, expectant mothers, children and pensioners and emergency cases are exempt from all charges.

Anyone who is moving to Portugal permanently and who claims sickness or invalidity benefit in the UK is entitled to continue claiming this benefit once in Portugal. Strictly speaking, to claim either benefit, you must be physically incapable of all work, however, the interpretation of the words 'physically incapable' is frequently stretched just a little beyond literal truth. If the claimant has been paying National Insurance contributions in the UK for two tax years (this may be less depending on his or her level of income) then he or she is eligible to claim sickness benefit. After receiving sickness benefit for 28 weeks, you are entitled to invalidity benefit which is paid at a higher rate. Although it may seem something of a Catch 22 when you can only claim sickness benefit if you are incapable of working and yet you are only entitled to the benefit through the last two years of National Insurance payments deducted from your income, the benefit is primarily used by people who have had to stop work due to severe illness.

Anyone currently receiving either form of benefit should inform the Department of Work and Pensions (formerly the DSS) that they are moving to Spain. They will then send your forms to the DWP International Services department (Newcastle-upon-Tyne NE98 1YC) who will then make sure that a monthly sterling cheque is sent either to your new address or direct into your bank account. The only conditions involved are that all claimants submit themselves to a medical examination, either in Portugal or Britain, on request.

Child benefit may also be claimed if the child goes abroad for more than eight weeks. Ask for leaflet CH 6.

Sickness. Once you working in Portugal, sickness allowance is payable to workers except in case of an accident at work or occupational disease which should be covered by the employer's insurance. In order to qualify, the worker must have been paying contributions for at least six months and have made at least twelve days contributions in the four months preceding the month of illness. The allowance is payable for a maximum period of 1,095 days after which the worker may be eligible for invalidity benefit. In the case of self-employed workers the maximum period is one year.

The level of allowance is 65% of average earnings before illness occured. More details are available from your employer, or the Centro Regional de Segurança Social – CRSS.

Pensions. Retirement pensions are payable from the age of 65. In order to be eligible the beneficiary must provide evidence of at least 10 years' contributions.

Full details of all social security benefits are given in the booklet *Social Security for Migrant Workers – Portugal* published by the Office of Publications for the EU in Luxembourg. This booklet is also available on request from the DSS International Services department, Newcastle-upon-Tyne, NE98 1YX.

CRIME AND THE POLICE

Crime

Until recently violent crime was outside the experience of most Portuguese. Even in Lisbon and Oporto, except for certain areas, there was no feeling of menace on the streets. The list of typical offences: smuggling, fraud, rustling, robbery, drunken brawls (occasionally ending in death) etc. is still small beer compared with serial killings, sophisticated art thefts, assasinations and other headline-grabbing misdeeds common elsewhere.

Traditionally Portuguese criminals have gone in for fraud and deception and these and bribery and corruption still account for most of the criminal statistics. Unfortunately in recent years nefarious activities have become increasingly connected with the drug trade; Portugal is conveniently situated on the drug route from Latin America and drug taking and laundering of the proceeds have become a major headache for the Portuguese police forces. The problem could be said to begin at street level where the contrast between low police pay and huge profits to be made from illegal drugs often diverts the police from the pursuit of law and order.

Police

There are several law enforcing bodies in Portugal and in common with most European police forces they are often armed:

Policía de Segurança Publica: The PSP are the city police of whom there are around 20,000, one third of them in Lisbon. They wear grey uniforms and are responsible for dealing with visitors' registration cards, reprimanding and fining those who commit traffic offences (e.g. illegal parking), dud cheques, making out statements dealing with lost or stolen belongings, directing traffic and generally patrolling the streets.

Not so long ago, the PSP were demonstrating in Lisbon in support of a wage increase and danger money and demonstrating police officers had to be dispersed by the riot squad in the Praça do Comércio.

Brigada de Trânsito: The Brigada are the traffic police who apprehend speeding and erratic drivers, stop dubious looking vehicles and elicit on-the-spot fines for various contraventions of the traffic regulations (e.g. failure to wear a seat belt). During the main tourist season they are much in evidence in their white and orange cars. When road accidents occcur it is the Brigada who are usually first on the scene.

Guarda Fiscal: Those who belong to the yachting fraternity are more likely to encounter the Guarda Fiscal, who are the coastguards. Always on the look out for smugglers their jurisdiction can also extend to dry land in the small coastal villages.
Guarda Nacional Republicana: The GNR are the national troubleshooters who are called in whenever violence erupts. They are a paramilitary organisation and can be spotted all over the country in vans, on motorbikes and sometimes on horseback.

PETS

Dogs in Portugal are subject to annual licensing for which a certificate confirming rabies (*raiva*) vaccination has to be produced. In country areas it is customary for the municipality to post an annual notice giving the dates and times when a government veterinarian will arrive to innoculate all the canines of the village in one swoop. Each dog is then issued with the certificate required for the licence application.

Animal welfare in the main expatriate enclaves is admirably served by a band of veterinarians (*veterinários*) many of whom are foreigners. The easiest way to find one is through recommendation or by looking in the English-language publications including APN where some of them advertise. To avoid quarantine (of up to four months), you will have to vaccinate your pet against rabies well in advance of your departure.

RELIGION

Portugal is predominantly Catholic; and the signs of fervour are greater here than in many other Catholic countries. There are thousands of annual festas across the country celebrating a galaxy of saints, some of whom have ceased to be or who have never been recognised in Rome. Portugal's most celebrated place of devotion is Fátima, where the Virgin is alleged to have appeared several times between May and October 1917 to three shepherd children. She apparently made three prophecies known as the secrets of Fátima. The first appeared to prophesy the Second World War, the second the end of Communism and the third was locked away by the Vatican and is consulted only by each successive Pope thus giving rise to wild speculation that it relates to the forthcoming millenium, or is too portentous for lesser mortals to hear. The present Pope visited Fátima in May 1991, which lent some of these ideas credence; and the purpose of his visit was to give thanks for the end of Communist rule in Eastern Europe. Hundreds of thousands of the faithful gather there each year in pilgrimage.

The devotion of many Portuguese runs in tandem with older religions. Superstition has never really died out in the remote villages where pagan and Christian beliefs exist side by side.

TABLE 11	PUBLIC HOLIDAYS

Portugal has thirteen statutory public holidays (*Feriados Obrigatórios*) which are celebrated nationally. During public holidays all shops, banks, and offices are closed. The public holidays in Portugal are:

1 January	*Ano Novo* (New Year)
Shrove Tuesday	varies
Good Friday	varies
25 April	*Dia da Liberdade* (commemorates the 1974 revolution)
1 May	*Dia do Trabalho* (Labour Day)
10 June –	*Dia de Portugal* (National Day)
Corpus Christi	during June
15 August	*Assunção de Nossa Senhora* (Feast of the Assumption)
5 October	*Dia da República* (Commemoration of the founding of the First Republic in 1910)
1 November	*Festa de TodososSantos* (Feast of All Saints)
1 December	*Dia de Restaura[ce]c[ti]ao* (Commemoration of the restoration of the Portuguese crown from Spanish rule in 1640)
8 December	Feast of the Immaculate Conception
25 December	*Natal* (Nativity)

In addition to the national holidays every region has its own calendar of feasts (*festas*), fairs (*feiras*) and pilgrimages (*romarias*).

RETIREMENT

Background Information

Twenty years ago Portugal was still considered a European backwater. Picturesque but desperately backward, it lacked sufficient amenities and infrastructure to make it a comfortable place for retirement. Its main attraction in those days was the long historical association with Britain and the presence of a longstanding British community; also an exceptionally pleasant climate, and an unspoilt coastline. Property prices were extremely low as were taxes. Since then a political and economic revolution have taken place which have changed many aspects of life there beyond recognition. Portugal is no longer a cheap paradise: property prices in the most popular places have soared to levels that in many instances are higher than in the UK; and taxes are rapidly reaching parity with other EU countries. The cost of living is rising generally.

However, as a result of being rocketed into the twentieth century, roads and communications are now reasonably efficient; and the quality of life can be exceptional for those with sufficient means to keep pace with the rapidly rising cost of living. And away from the main expatriate areas you may still find places which seem untouched by most of the changes that have taken place elsewhere in Portugal.

The most popular areas for retirees are the greater Lisbon area, including the coasts north and south of the capital, and the Algarve. It is the Algarve above all that has been transformed from being a poor, underpopulated and remote province of Portugal to an area where the British can feel at home; its exceptional coastline is being rapidly lined with condominiums, resort complexes, villas, marinas, and other developments, all designed to entice those who wish to holiday or live in Portugal. Unfortunately for permanent and long-term residents, the holidaymakers are arriving in ever increasing numbers causing the kind of traffic problems and overcrowding that one is used to back in the UK. Furthermore, there are plans afoot to promote the Algarve as a winter destination, making the tourist invasion a year-round occurrence.

However anyone looking for somewhere to retire to will almost certainly find the advantages of Portugal outweigh the disadvantages. The excellent climate and the easygoing people, the upgrading of the infrastructure, the lively expatriate community, and the proximity to the UK (useful for family visits in both directions), are just some of the reasons why this is an increasingly popular country for retirement.

The Decision to Leave

There has been much written about the plight of retired people in Spain who, after moving there in the 1970's when it was cheap, found by the 1980's that their UK pensions could not keep pace with the ever higher cost of living. This left many of them in desperate financial straits, and with nowhere to turn for help. Although the situation in Portugal is unlikely to reach the same extreme as in Spain, it is as well to bear in mind that the cost of living is likely also to rise in the next few years, if not quite so fast as in the past. At present, the Portuguese pension is still a meagre £150 monthly, less than half what it is in the UK. However it is essential to take into consideration the projected rise in prosperity in Portugal before deciding to move there. If you have no financial reserves or assets other than your Portuguese property, you are taking the risk that, in a few years' time, prices will outstrip your pension. Should you then decide to come home, you may find that UK property prices are no longer affordable.

But enough of the caveats! Most people who decide to retire abroad have the enthusiasm and energy required to cope with the challenges ahead. For those whose interests can be pursued just as easily in Portugal as in the UK there is a range of possibilities from travelling around, by car or train, to studying Portuguese history, or enjoying the sports facilities, and the climate.

Preparation and Research

If one has friends who have already moved to Portugal, the temptation to join them is very great. But retiring abroad does not suit everyone. The emotional as well as physical upheaval of moving from the UK can be a great strain. Once there, additional stress will be imposed by the unfamiliarity of everything, at least initially, and the inevitable frustration of the necessary bureaucratic procedures.

Since there is a vast difference between visiting Portugal for a few weeks' holiday in summer and living there permanently, it is advisable to visit once, in the winter months, to see what things are like then. Even better would be to buy a timeshare, or rent a holiday home, and spend several months in 'residence' before deciding irredeemably in favour of moving to Portugal.

When it comes to buying property or deciding to live abroad a great many people do so without the faintest idea of what this process entails, from winding up their UK affairs to the problems of getting stung by the ever alert Inland Revenue for thousands of pounds of back taxes if you overstay on a visit to the UK. What's more, the same normally sober citizens frequently throw their caution, learned from hard experience, out of the window, when it comes to buying property and making financial deals with builders etc. abroad, thereby tumbling into all manner of obvious pitfalls. It is therefore essential to take expert financial and legal advice. There are no short ways to deal with the procedure for buying property in Portugal; and it is pointless trying to find one, whatever you may hear to the contrary. For details of buying property in Portugal see Chapter Three on *Setting up Home*.

Entry Requirements

Applications for permanent residence in Portugal should begin a few months in advance of the date on which you are planning to move there, as the process is convoluted and timeconsuming, despite the EU and the rest. Applications are processed through the Portuguese consulates in the UK. The basic regulations regarding applications for permanent residence, and a list of Portuguese consulates in the UK, can be found in Chapter Two on *Residence and Entry Regulations*. Chapter Two also contains details of the residence application procedure once you have arrived in Portugal, the other way of going about it.

Additional documents required by the Portuguese Consulate for pensioners/retired persons are as follows:

> O Proof of retirement or old age pension indicating the amount received monthly.
> O Proof from the bank that you are dealing with in Portugal that a bank account in Portugal has been opened. The monthly balance should not be inferior to minimum gross earnings index in the UK, per member of the family.

Finance and Taxation

Anyone considering retiring to a foreign country is strongly advised to take specialist financial advice regarding their personal situation. Many people who are in the happy position of being able to retire overseas have a certain amount of income to invest. For those with spare capital there is a strong incentive to move their investments offshore since they can legally avoiding paying some taxes and thereby receive interest gross instead of net. Some property buyers also buy property in Portugal through offshore companies. Unlike Spain which is clamping down on this practice, in Portugal it is still permissable. For further details on offshore property buying, see the chapter on *Setting up Home*.

For those who wish to maintain financial involvement in both the UK and Portugal, impartial advice on tax matters is essential. The UK Inland Revenue is not one's immediate choice of advisor as one suspects it is imprudent to awaken their interest in one's affairs before an accountant with experience of expatriate finance has been consulted.

For those who wish to sever all financial connection with the UK, except for the receipt of a UK pension and possible allowances, the situation is relatively straightforward in that they will only be liable for Portuguese taxes (see Chapter Three *Daily Life*).

Social Security and Pensions

British pensioners who are resident in Portugal on a permanent basis are entitled to free or subsidised healthcare under the Portuguese social security system, the (*Caixa de Previdência*). Some charges are made for routine medical consulatations and technical services but emergency treatment is free. Substantial discounts are made on prescribed medicines; but you can still pay up to 100% on some of these. Those who are retired or who are otherwise eligible for UK social security should apply in Britain as far in advance of departure as possible to the Overseas Benefits Directorate of the Department of Work and Pensions (formerly the DSS), Newcastle-upon-Tyne NE98 1YX (☎ 0191-218 7777) for form E121; and on arrival in Portugal should register in Portugal with their nearest government health centre (*Centro de Saúde*).

If you move from the UK to Portugal for employment, and then retire there, one may be eligible for a Portuguese pension. As the current pension is under half that of the UK pension this is not an inspiring prospect. Indeed with the cost of living in Portugal rising fast it is probably due to ingenuity alone that any Portuguese pensioner can manage on such a small amount.

Useful Addresses

Department of International Relations and Social Security Conventions: Rua da Junqueira 112, P-1300 Lisbon.
Department of Work and Pensions: Overseas Benefits Directorate, Newcastle-upon-Tyne, NE98 1YX; fax 0191-218 7147.
Benefits Agency: Pensions and Overseas Benefits Directorate, International Office, Newcastle-upon-Tyne, NE98 1BA; ☎0191-218 7652.
National Pensions Centre (Centro Nacional de Pensões): Campo Grande 6, P-1771 Lisbon.

Health and Insurance

Before leaving the UK to retire abroad it is a good idea to have a thorough medical check up and make sure that all your innoculations are uptodate (you will require no new ones) and that you take with you a supply of any regular medicaments to last until you find out what the Portuguese equivalents are. It is also advisable to have a dental and eye check up and take spare sets of dentures and spectacles/contact lenses with you.

Although it is to be hoped that the beneficial climate in Portugal will induce good health generally, the possibility of serious illness or accident requiring hospitalisation cannot be ruled out. The standards of state health care in Portugal are uneven and in some cases inadequate. There are however an increasing number of swish, new, private medical centres such as the modern Clínica Europa in Carcavelos which offers both medical and dental treatment. Most people in Portugal who can afford to, go to private hospitals for which the fees can be astronomic. For this reason it is extremely advisable to take out private medical insurance to cover the cost of private treatment. Insurance companies specialising in expatriate health cover normally offer special 'senior' policies for those over 55 years old. Such policies are normally taken out annually. Two leading providers of medical cover are *Expacare:* (email: info@expacare.net or visit www.expacare.net) who are pecialists in expatriate healthcare offering high quality health insurance cover for individuals and their families, including group cover for five or more employees. Cover is available for expatriates of all nationalities worldwide, and BUPA International; ☎01273-208181; fax 01273-866583; www.bupaintl.com. The policy should cover the insured for private medical expenses including hospital inpatient care, local ambulance services, home nursing for a limited period, consultants' fees and technical diagnostic procedures.

Hobbies and Interests

Apart from financial worries, the main problems facing retired people living abroad, especially those who have never lived in foreign parts, is adapting to the different lifestyle, difficulties with the language, and not finding interesting ways of occupying spare time. Especially hard hit are couples, who until they retired led busy lives and did not see much of each other during the week. If one is not going to start a business to keep amused then it is essential to have some mindstretching and therapeutic hobbies and interests in order to prevent lassitude or murderous frustration from taking over. Endless bridge and cocktail parties are not sufficiently stimulating for everyone; and you do not have to look far in the English-language press in Portugal to find out where the latter leads: sadly, meetings of Alcoholics Anonymous are held in profusion. It is therefore vital to have some enthusiasms. Many people in their seventies enjoy golf, swimming, walking and fishing; and these are just a few of the outdoor pleasures readily available in Portugal.

Research has shown that the primary reason that prompt people into retiring abroad are the need to have a completely different life after work. So for many people, retiring to Portugal is a chance to create and enjoy to the full a new lifestyle with all the challenges that this entails. Portugal has certainly much to offer, although if it's ultra sophistication that you seek you will have to look elsewhere. But for outdoor pursuits of every kind, and wellorganised, lively expatriate socialising there is no better place to come as many of the habitués will testify. Those who are contemplating moving to Portugal, but have so far only been there on holiday might like to join the Anglo-Portuguese Society (Canning House, 2 Belgrave Square, London SW1X 8PJ) before they move to Portugal, as a way of building up advance contacts.

Once you have arrived, an invaluable publication is the *Anglo-Portuguese News*, as well as the *British Community Handbook* they also publish: APN (Apartado 113, 2765253 Estoril; tel: 21 466 1423; fax: 21-466 0358).

Ideas for Hobbies and Interests

Once the business of settling in and all the relevant permits and documents have been obtained, thoughts will necessarily turn to socialising and the pursuit of hobbies and interests for which there are many possibilities;

Keen gardeners will find that plants need no encouragement; and the creation of an exotic garden provides endless pleasure for some. The Garden Studio of Sintra (see below) holds regular gardening classes.

Wherever in the world the British congregate it seems that animal charities proliferate; and Portugal is no exception. There are dogs' homes and animal sancturies run by Brits from Sintra to the Algarve and you will find out about them soon enough, if indeed you do not decide to start one of your own, like Mrs Hicks of the Monte Ruivo Sanctuary at Odiáxere.

For those of a sporting nature there are sports strenuous and gentle. Golf and bowling are popular and if you would rather be a spectator there are plenty of spectacles on offer, from rugby (e.g.the annual Lisbon Sevens tournament) to car racing.

Travelling around Portugal will give you a better perspective on the country in which you are living. Accommodation prices vary but simple pensions can cost as little as £6 ($9), three star hotels from £55 ($80). Camping is also becoming popular in Portugal. If you do not have your own transport, the trains are interesting, cheap and go to most places of interest. What is more, pensioners are entitled to halffares. Portugal also has some wonderful steam train journeys which the local Turismo (Tourist Office) will be happy to tell you about. Restaurant meals can cost from £6. No doubt other expatriates will give recommendations. For serious travellers there are a number of guidebooks on the market including *Fodors Guide to Portugal* and *The Rough Guide to Portugal* available in most general bookshops, as well as travel bookshops and public libraries.

Painting is one of the most soothing occupations and scenically Portugal is a painter's paradise. If you move to the Lisbon area, the Sintra Garden Studio (Quinta dos Quatro Ventos, Rua da Ribeira, Azoia 2710, Sintra; ☎ 21928 0042) offers painting courses both for beginners and experienced painters. The studio also lays on transport from Lisbon. Alternatively, photography is a hobby that can bring a lot of pleasure. A collection of pictures taken of a disappearing way of life in the remote places of Portugal could become a valuable record for future historians.

There has been a spate of successful books about living in France since Peter Mayle's opportune bestseller *A Year in Provence*, and the sequel *Toujours Provence*. As yet there is no equally fascinating and droll equivalent about a year in Portugal. Perhaps it is time someone wrote one.

Useful Addresses

The British expatriate tends to be a clubbable creature and there are various associations which retired people are welcome to join in Portugal, some of them familiar from the UK, like the Royal British Legion and the Women's Royal Voluntary Service. Some of them will change addresses as their representatives change or are reelected. The British Embassy Consular Section (Rua de São Bernado 33, P1200 Lisbon; ☎21-392 4159) can provide some useful *Hints on Taking up Residence and Living Conditions in Portugal* which includes a list of British institutions there. The main clubs and organisations are:

The British Historical Society of Portugal: c/o St Julian's School, Quinta Nova, Carcavelos, 2777 Parede Codex, Portugal; ☎21-3978603.

Lisbon Casuals: c/o St. Julian's School, Quinta Nova, Carcavelos, Nr. Lisbon. A good value sports club with a congenial bar.

Lisbon Sports Club; contact: the Secretary, Casal de Carregueria, Belas; ☎21-432 1474.

Royal British Club: Sala 9 EscritoEstoril, Rua da Lisboa 1C, Estoril; ☎21-468 1712. A private members club which organises social and networking events, and includes a golf section

Wills

Many people who are approaching retirement age have already made a will. However acquiring foreign property means that it becomes subject to that country's legal system. In the case of Portugal therefore it is essential to draw up a Portuguese will with a Portuguese lawyer to cover one's assets there. The names of English-speaking lawyers who can arrange for the drawing up of a Portuguese will, can be obtained from the British Embassy or Consulates in Portugal. Alternatively one can ask for recommendations or contact a British legal firm that has Portuguese associates. The Portuguese-UK Chamber of Commerce in London (☎020-7494 1844) can also provide a list of suitable law firms. A few

Britishbased lawyers have associates in Portugal and can arrange for a Portuguese will to be drawn up. One such firm is Bennett & Co Solicitors (144 Knutsford Road, Wilmslow, Cheshire, SK9 6JP, UK ; tel: 01625-586937; fax 01625-585362; www.bennett-and-co.com.)

Death

Morbid though it may seem, this book would be incomplete without mentioning death since it affects us all sooner or later. Dying abroad complicates matters slightly in that one's near relations are often not on the spot to deal with the formalities surrounding burial: they may not even know the wishes of the deceased as regards the place of burial, i.e. in Portugal or the UK. It is therefore advisable to make ones wishes concerning this matter known in advance. The British Embassy points out that the famous British Cemetery in Lisbon is short of space and only the regular worshippers at St. George's Church Lisbon, St. Paul's Church Estoril, St. Vicente's Church, Portimão or the United Church of Scotland are eligible for burial there. There is usually no problem arranging for the internment of Catholics or Protestants in a Portuguese Catholic cemetery. Cremation is another possibility, although Portugal still has only one crematorium which is located in Lisbon.

The British Embassy warns that airfreighting a coffin back to the UK is an expensive business. Freight charges depend on weight but the minimum cost is about £3,000. It is advisable to get some quotations from Portuguese undertakers who offer such a service.

Section II

WORKING IN PORTUGAL

EMPLOYMENT

BUSINESS AND INDUSTRY REPORT

STARTING A BUSINESS

EMPLOYMENT

CHAPTER SUMMARY

- **Wages & Cost of Living.** Portuguese workers are some of the lowest paid in the EU.

  - The cost of living in Portugal is the 6th highest in the EU.

  - Nearly three million Portuguese live below the poverty line.

  - As in Spain, employers pay an extra month's salary before the summer vacation and at Christmas.

- **Job Prospects:** It is not easy for foreigners to get unskilled jobs in Portugal because of homegrown competition.

  - Portuguese government and private job agencies are unlikely to help anyone who does not speak Portuguese.

  - The best prospects for work are in multinational, British or American companies, English language teaching, working for expatriates, or working in tourism.

- **Industry.** The most industrially developed areas of Portugal are Oporto and its hinterland in the north, and the area between Lisbon and Setubal going south.

  - The biggest industries are foodstuffs, beverages and tobacco, textiles, clothing and leather goods.

- **The Economy.** Portuguese labour costs are amongst the lowest in Europe. This, along with massive EU subsidies has created a prosperous economy.

  - The Portuguese economy may be adversely affected by the even cheaper supply of labour provided by eastern European countries.

Ten to twenty years ago, even those accustomed to working in European countries would probably have found themselves driven to distraction by the antiquated business methods and lack of amenities in Portugal. For thè various reasons outlined in Chapter One, *General Introduction*, Portugal was simply in the dark ages as far as working conditions and the economy were concerned. The chaotic state of national finances was having an extremely destabilising effect on the government which was changing every few months. There was a terrible time at the beginning of the 1980s when public-sector workers did not know when or how they would be paid and as late as 1990 there were still 12,000 workers awaiting settlements on wages delayed from this time. Since Portugal's entry into the EU, the prospects for international workers have happily improved; but the locals are still some of the poorest paid in the EU.

Since EU entry, the economy has stabilised and contemporary technology has made the country compatible with its other European partners. The *Business and Industry Report* below will give an idea of the main sectors of the Portuguese economy, including textiles, pottery, shipbuilding, agricultural products, paper, and glassware among its more traditional industrial activities; and then there is tourism which – along with public sector and infrastructure projects like the Expo '98 exhibition in Lisbon, the expansion of the capital's underground system, and of the national road network, as well as new dams and a new gas pipeline from Morocco – will provide most of the specific employment opportunities for international and UK workers. Minimim wages are fixed way below those of EU competitors though, meaning there is stiff competition at the lower and less skilled end of the jobs market. Quite simply, the locals will work for less; so skills and qualifications are at a premium, more so in Portugal than many other EU countries.

As the cost of living has risen, to the extent that Portugal is rated the sixth most expensive country in the EU, workers are justified in complaining that wages have lagged far behind prices, although recently inflation has been brought under control and is currently less than 3%. According to the President of the stateowned Brisa corporation (which is responsible for many of the infrastructure projects mentioned above, and is also currently in line for privatisation) 'our standard of living is very much below the average of the European Union;' and those looking for work there should bear in mind the advice of correspondents to *Live and Work in Spain and Portugal* that 'accommodation and services like electricity, water and the telephone can be very expensive, especially in Lisbon' when assessing the salary they can comfortably live on in Portugal. This will have to be similar to that in the UK if they are to survive, and have a reasonable standard of living.

It is remarkable, with the cost of living so high, that local salaries are so low, with an average per capita income less than half that currently in the UK, at around £8,000. In 2002, the unemployment figure was among the lowest in the European Union: 4.1% (compared to Spain's 12.8% and France's 9%). of the working age population.

The main problem for expatriates seeking work in Portugal is not the process of acquiring a residence permit. Now all UK citizens have the same rights to live and work there as the locals, at least in theory. The problem is the conditions of the Portuguese economy itself, where there is strong competition from local and other EU staff. A traditional way around this, as in many other countries, for those seeking employment there, is to find an area (like English language teaching) where your language or other skills will put you at an advantage. In financial services and banking, now that this sector has been modernised and brought more into line with other EU countries, as well as in the field of business advice, UK workers may often have expertise which is at a premium in this rapidly changing economy. Certainly, in most areas of work, you will require a high degree of specialised technical knowledge and probably Portuguese language skills as well.

Residence and Work Regulations

EU nationals do not need a work permit to work in Portugal, but a residence permit is obligatory for those working there (see the chapter on *Residence and Entry Regulations* where full details are given). There are at present certain categories of worker who may come from outside the EU and who are also exempt from work permits: au pairs, academics employed by Portuguese universities, teachers employed at international or American schools etc.

An exception to the above is that for jobs lasting up to 30 days, no permit is required; but the worker must have his or her passport stamped at the *Serviço de Estrangeiros e Fronteiras* (Avenida António Augusto Aguiar 20, Lisbon; ☎21-3143112; offices also in Oporto, Coimbra, Faro, Madeira and the Azores). This minimal regulation may be appropriate for construction workers etc. on short contracts.

For artists, freelance journalists, photographers and those who handmake things to sell, and other small business operations, the tax office (as in Britain) requires a record of payment. The usual way to do this is to obtain a book of receipts (*Cadernata de Recibos*) from the tax office. It is advisable to consult an accountant at the outset on the correct way to maintain records as regulations are liable to change.

The Employment Scene

As already mentioned, anyone wishing to work in Portugal is up against the competitive nature of the domestic jobs market, the need usually to speak the language, and a large supply of local labour ready to do the same job for less pay. Non-Portuguese workers should therefore concentrate on assets which their Portuguese competitors may not have; which usually means work with an international dimension, perhaps in trade or commerce; in English teaching or in a specialised area where their skills are at a premium. It should be stressed that Portugal is not a country where it is easy for foreign workers to get a job.

Possibilities for Self-Employment. Apart from setting up your own business (which will be dealt with in the next chapter) there are possibilities for self-employment (e.g. as a private tutor or in commerce); working for a multinational or a British bank in Portugal; for UK and international companies with a branch office in Portugal, including accountancy and business advice firms; working as a rep or similar in tourism; or in the related catering and hospitality fields (perhaps running a bar or restaurant); in construction, for trained engineers but not usually for foremen, electricians, or those who are less skilled; in computing and information technology (and the allied field of developing new business systems); dealing with international clients for Portuguese companies (if you have

Portuguese as well as English language skills); and in all the various areas of trade between the two countries.

Import/export. The future trade opportunities are listed by the Department of Trade and Industry as being in the fields of the environment, healthcare, telecommunications and transport. As the Portuguese standard of living continues to rise in the wake of EU grants and urban regeneration projects, so will the demand for quality consumer goods and services creating more businesses and prospects for employment.

For a list of British companies active in Portugal, see the *Directory of Employers* at the end of this chapter. There is also a market for the artistic and artisan wares of freelance painters, photographers, potters, etc; and some may take a less traditional approach to getting a job and end up selling the results of their artistic endeavours to expatriate Britons or the locals.

In the past few years there has been a dramatic increase in the number of foreign companies investing in largescale projects in Portugal in the following areas: chemicals, electric and electronic equipment, foodstuffs and beverages, mining and quarrying, dams, paper, glass, textiles, footwear, tourism, machinery and transport. This has done wonders for the Portuguese workforce but at present they remain the sole beneficiaries of this industrial boom and there is as yet no great demand for workers from outside the country who do not have specialist skills.

At the present time, job seekers who have made Portugal their destination but do not have work lined up there will have to content themselves with the possibilities already mentioned. Those currently unemployed in the UK may even be able to transfer their   or Job Seekers Allowance there for a period while they look for work, and should enquire at their local Job Centre for the relevant leaflets. Local chambers of commerce are also useful sources of information; and may have specific Portuguese contacts and news.

A list of international companies with projects in Portugal is contained in the free booklet, *Guide for Investors in Portugal*, photocopies of which are available from the Portuguese Trade Office in London (ICEP), 2nd Floor, 21-25A Sackville Street, London W1X 2LY; ☎020-7494 1441; fax 020-7494 1517trade). The ICEP address in the USA is: 2125 Kalorama Road, NW, Washington, DC 20008; ☎212-2354 4658; fax 212-575 4737. The Commercial Department of the British Embassy in Lisbon can also send a short list of local employment agencies; and the local Yellow Pages available in most larger libraries can be your source for some more of these.

Demand for Foreign Staff

Industry. So far, the demand for international workers in Portugal is mainly at the higher level of qualified, experienced workers with language skills, and those on short-term contracts who may be posted there by their company. As mentioned above, Portugal generally remains a poor prospect for those working in industry. Trade and commerce with the UK – and those companies with UK connections – remain the best bet for those making enquiries about employment and who are sending off their CV's. A UK or international connection – as well as your own qualifications – should be your main criterion when selecting companies to contact. Your own personal experience working with Portuguese partners will also be a major advantage.

Working for expatriate-run enterprises. Working in pubs, bars, clubs, bookshops, restaurants etc. which are owned by British nationals, offers more obvious prospects. The clientele of such establishments is likely to be mainly Englishspeaking, therefore anglophone staff will be in demand. The foreign resident population, especially those from Britain and other northern European countries, is still rising; and your EU status will help when it comes to practical arrangements for your residence and work. For North Americans and others, the restrictions on the quota of foreign or non-EU workers who may work for a Portuguese company does not apply to businesses employing up to five employees, so working for a small company may be your best bet. Since many expatriaterun businesses are small ones, it follows that there are not huge numbers of vacancies even though this is the source of jobs most likely to yield results.

Generally speaking, jobs in bars, restaurants etc. – and also for English language teachers – can most easily be found by making a reconnaissance trip to Portugal. The majority of expatriate businesses are located on the Algarve and the Lisbon coast from Setúbal north to Cascais. Alternatively, jobs may occasionally be advertised in the local English-language press (see *Sources of Jobs* below). To find expatriaterun hotels and restaurants which may employ UK staff in the summer, as good a source as any, if you are looking for work from outside the country is an utodate guidebook or hotel guide, for addresses for many of these establishments which can also be potential employers for catering and bar staff etc.

Academic Staff. Another area of employment in which British staff are likely to be indispensable, is in providing education based on the English curriculum. There are several British and international schools in Lisbon, Oporto and the Algarve which offer preparation for British common entrance, GCSE exams etc. Suitably qualified staff should make enquiries about possible vacancies direct to the schools concerned. Their addresses can be found in Chapter Four, *Daily Life*. Again, an applicant who already lives on the spot is likely to be favoured, making this kind of work popular with the spouses of those who are already living and working there, as is also often the case with English language teaching (see below).

English Language Teaching. The market for English tuition is as buoyant as anywhere in Europe, especially in the teaching of young children. The many Portuguese in who aspire to work in the tourist industry especially on the Algarve want to learn English. But the demand for English teachers is greatest in the north. Apart from in the main cities of Lisbon and Oporto, both of which have British Council offices, jobs crop up in historic provincial centres such as Coimbra (where there is also a British Council) and Braga and in small seaside towns like Aveiro and Póvoa do Varzim. The British Council has English language centres in Almada, Alverca, Cascais (the prosperous seaside suburb of Lisbon), Foz, Faia, Maia, Miraflores and Queluz. The Lisbon office (Rua Sao Marçal, 1249062 Lisbon; ☎21-3214500) can provide a list of approved English language schools in Portugal.

One of the most important employers of English teachers in Portugal is *International House* which has nine affiliated schools in the country. Two other wellestablished school groups are the *Bristol School Group* and *Cambridge Schools* which import dozens of nativespeaker teachers each year. Of the international chains, Wall Street Institutes are well represented with 38 centres throughout Portugal; their central telephone number is 80020 20 40 and email wsi.info@wsi.pt.

If you are looking for teaching vacancies onthespot, you should call at the British Council, check the English language weekly newspaper *Anglo-Portuguese News* which occasionally carries adverts for private tutors (Apartado 113, 2766902 Estoril; ☎21-466 1551; apn@mail.telepac.pt) and make a personal approach to all the language schools. The Cambridge CELTA is widely requested by schools and can be obtained at International House in Lisbon (or part-time in Oporto). At present the Trinity College Certificate course is not offered in Portugal.

Useful Addresses

Bristol School Group: Instituto de Línguas da Maia & Ermesinde, Trav. Dr. Carlos Pires Felgueiras, 123°, 4470158 Maia; ☎22-9488803; fax 22-9606460. 4 schools near Oporto, 2 in the Azores, 1 each at Castelo Branco and Fundão.

Cambridge Schools: Avenida da Liberdade 173, 1250141 Lisbon; ☎21-3124600; www.cambridge.pt. 8 schools employ about 100 teachers with TEFL certificates.

Encounter English: Av. Fernao de Magalhaes 604, 4350150 Oporto; ☎22-5367916.

International House Lisbon: Rua Marquês Sá da Bandeira 16, 1050148 Lisbon; ☎21-3151496; www.internationalhouse.com. Also in Oporto

(Rua Dr. Sousa Rosa 381°, 4150 Porto; ☎22-26177641 and other cities.

Lancaster College: Praceta 25 de Abril 351°, 4430257 Vila Nova de Gaia; tel/fax 22-3772030; www.lancastercollege.pt. 1020 teachers for 8 schools.

Linguacultura Instituto de Linguas de Santarem Lda: Apartado 37, 2001 Santarém Codex; ☎243-309140; Linguacultura@Linguacultura.pt. 50 teachers working in several schools.

Royal School of Languages: Av. Lourenco Peixinho 922° andar & Rua José Rabumba 2, 3810125 Aveiro; 234-429156. 30+ teachers for 8 schools.

Wall Street Institute: Av. da Liberdade 166 R/C. 1250146 Lisbon.

Working in the Tourist Industry. Working for a British tour operator may not be the ideal way to get to know a foreign country since employees are likely to spend most of their time catering for their own countrymen and women on holiday. However, it can be a useful route to a job in the sun. Those interested should apply to the bigger operators like Thomson Breakaway (www.thomsonholidays.com) which operates in Albufeira, Alvor, Lagos, Sao Joao and Vilamoura, and JMC part of the Thomas Cook group (overseas.jobs@jmc.com). Job seekers may also usefully visit their local travel agency to find out from the brochures which companies are currently operating there. Also see *Working in Tourism* or the relevant chapter in the *Directory of Jobs and Careers Abroad* for a list of UK-based tour operators and their recruitment needs, or the invaluable *Directory of Summer Jobs Abroad* (all published by Vacation Work).

A useful tour operators' guide of all the companies that operate in Portugal can be obtained from the Portuguese National Tourist Office (ICEP) in London (see address above). The types of jobs available with major tour operators include children's representatives (nanny experience/qualifications normally required), resort administrators/office staff and resort representatives. The minimum age for reps is usually 21 years and at least one foreign language, not necessarily Portuguese, is essential, as well as experience and a career interest in the hospitality industry.

Secretarial Staff: If you know some Portuguese and have computer skills, you might find an opening in an office; without a knowledge of the language, chances are remote. For agencies specialising in temporary work, look up the Yellow Pages *(Paginas Amarelas)* under the heading *Pessoal Temporário* and see contact details for temp agencies such as Manpower at the end of this chapter.

ASPECTS OF EMPLOYMENT

Salaries

Average Portuguese salaries are around two to two and a half times less than the richer EU countries (e.g. Germany or the UK). The average rate of pay provides barely enough to live on; and most workers expect to be paid more. The average salary is currently around £8,000 per annum. Even a top hospital doctor in the national health service earns under £12,000 per annum, which gives an idea of the limited opportunities for professionals who wish to work in Portugal. Portuguese doctors are much more likely to wish to work in the UK than the other way around).

Provided foreigners stick to buying Portuguese products in the supermarkets, as well as in the open air markets, Portugal still has quite a low cost of living, especially outside the tourist areas. It has been estimated that an inextravagent couple without children, with their own property paid for, could live reasonably on about £10,000-£12,000 per annum. This sum is based on living in the Algarve, which is the most expensive region. Costs in Lisbon are comparable; for instance an English language teacher working there or in a small Portuguese city would find his or her income quite adequate for modest living, but leaving little scope to save: this is a problem which applies to many expatriate workers in Portugal who are working for 'local' salaries.

Since Portugal has this legal minimum wage, anyone working for Portuguese-based companies cannot be paid less than this official rate. Legislation also entitles all fulltime employees to just over one month of paid holiday (22 week days); and, as in Spain, there are two 'extra' months' salary paid at Christmas and before the summer vacation, a kind of bonus to deal with these extra expenses, so that the annual salary is usually paid in fourteen 'monthly' instalments.

Working Hours and Holidays

In addition to the month or so of paid holiday (see above), usually taken in August, other nonworking days include the thirteen statutory national holidays plus (normally) one local one. Working hours are long in Portugal. A 48-hour week was common up to 1990 when it was reduced to 44, and then to 40.

Trade Unions

Under the Salazar regime, workers' unions (*sindicatos*) were controlled by the dictatorship, under which striking was illegal. Since the introduction of democracy they seem to have been making up for such a long deprivation of their rights: long hours, and comparatively low wages – except for politicians who award themselves regular phenomenal pay rises which have fuelled the sindicatos outrage to the extent that the past few years have seen hundreds of strikes amongst almost every kind of worker but especially in the public sector. The unions are also engaged in a longrunning dispute with the government over the unemployment figures which the unions claim do not include those on temporary government training schemes, which in the unions' view do not constitute bona fide employment. In Portugal, strikes tend not to drag on for weeks as they have a habit of doing elsewhere in Europe, but can be extremely disruptive, involving just a small section of the key staff within a company: for instance by bringing public transport, or the process of justice, to a grinding halt. The main instigator is the *CGT-Intersindical* (General Confederation of Portuguese Workers) which is a trade union federation of about 300 unions, comprising just over half the total trade union membership. This powerful federation is still dominated by the Communists. Also the *UGT* (General Union of Workers) which is moderate and mainly whitecollar led.

Women in Work

After a long history of discrimination, the status of women in the workplace is rising, although outside professional circles, Portuguese womanhood does not seem to have made much progress. As late as the nineteenth century it was legal for a husband to kill his wife for adultery, but not the other way around. With the rise of republicanism the opportunities for women began to improve: the first women to qualify as doctors in Portugal did so in the late nineteenth century. After the overthrow of the monarchy in 1910, the first woman university professor was appointed. The clock was however turned back by the Salazar regime as women were relegated to the home by retrogressive legislation. The end of the dictatorship brought a more enlightened approach, regarding the equality of women. However lofty the intentions, though, the reality is that many Portuguese women are still little better off than their repressed forbears; working like beasts of burden in fields and suffering the abuse, often violent, of their menfolk. Better education and increasing prosperity are probably the long-term solution to these problems. Until recently, schooling was only compulsory until the age of fourteen. The situation for women is exacerbated by the fact that over three million Portuguese live below the poverty line (as defined by the EU). The result is that many Portuguese men have traditionally become itinerant jobseekers leaving behind their women in childrearing isolation. Despite the fact that equal pay for women is part of current legislation this is not always adhered to in practice.

Many Portuguese women work as *criada* (maids) but the job title has been changed to *mulheradias* (daily woman) or *empregada doméstica* (domestic employee). Domestic service is still a relatively common form of employment for women.

Amongst the better off, full advantage has been taken of the opportunities on offer: over half of Portuguese university students are women, giving them a passport to all the professions from law to engineering. Careers in the army and the police force are open to them. Since 1989 the Portuguese air force has been training women as pilots, while one year previously in 1988, the first civilian woman pilot was taken on by the internal airline Linhas Aéreas Regionais (LAR). In addition there are opportunities for women entrepreneurs (e.g. in the fashion trade, as art gallery proprietors etc.). As yet there are only a handful of women in the government, but Portugal had a woman prime minister for six months in 1979, a circumstance which did not continue for as long as in the UK.

Still, it is a fact that however well women are doing in the professions and as directors and executives, the vast majority of the larger industrial concerns in Portugal are still run by men.

Working Conditions

Many people feel tempted to uproot themselves from Britain and live abroad, particularly when they have encountered unemployment at home; or to move on in their career; or to start a new one; or to experience a different way of life and culture. They may decide to move to Portugal on the basis of a marvellous twoweek holiday spent on the Algarve coast, or a longer connection with the country. However, unwinding and relaxing in Portugal is not at all the same as living and working there: working, especially, highlights quite another aspect of the country and potential employers in particular will not be impressed if your desire to live and work there is seen as a kind of extended holiday. A serious attitude to the job in hand is much more important for most than your wish to meet people and see the world, however much you enjoy travel, or living abroad. If you work in travel and tourism, though, it is better if this is one of your interests; and if you do not enjoy meeting people, English language teaching – which often involves getting to know your students, and sometimes the interpersonal skills of knowing which ones not to get to know – may also be not quite your thing. In these shorterterm areas, in particular, you can expect to work long hours for wages which are enough to live on, but usually not sufficient for a particularly high standard of living.

If working conditions in Portugal do not match up to British standards, then you can reflect that things – for the Portuguese at least – are getting better. It is true that in Portuguese-owned companies wages are generally low; but up until the year of Portugal's entry into the Common Market, even as the tourists cavorted happily in the resorts and on the golf courses of the Algarve, the economy was in such chaos that 150,000 Portuguese workers had no idea when, if at all, they would receive their wages; times were so bad that they were providing their labour free on the mere promise of payment at some unspecified future date (a situation which is echoed today in eastern Europe). Since then, changes have been made. For nearly twenty years employment contracts were the bugbear of Portuguese companies trying to adapt to the mechanisms of the market. These contracts had the force of state legislation in protecting the rights of employees, many of whom had security of tenure, regardless of the prevailing economic conditions. Although employers are marginally freer to dismiss and lay off workers, this is still an area that causes grave dissatisfaction to employers and economists. But there is nowadays some measure of protection for workers, in line with the social chapter of the Maastricht Treaty, which does not however always benefit foreign workers. For some years foreign companies have managed to get round fixed-employment contracts by introducing early retirement and voluntary redundancy as is often the case in other EU countries and Britain).

By the beginning of the 1990's, the economic situation had improved enormously, thanks to EU subsidies, industrial development and massive capital inflow. At the time of writing, even the present slowdown is unable to throw a damper over potentially exciting developments in Portuguese industry. The fact that Portugal's growth rate is better than most other EU countries, while its labour costs remain among the lowest, is being exploited successfully as an incentive to foreign companies to set up projects in Portugal. However, the entry of central and eastern European countries into the EU is likely to have a negative effect on inward investment in future; and low labour costs will have to be matched by increases in output and exports if Portugal is to compete successfully with these even lower-wage economies.

If the Portuguese government follows this path of improved efficiency, training and investment – and not just a lowwage economy – the prospects for international workers, and working conditions generally, will be good. Such considerations should of course be weighed against the local cost of living, but there are increasing signs that wages are keeping pace with inflation. In the shortterm, the situation vis-á-vis working conditions in Portugal is likely to improve in the next few years as the economy reaps the benefits of an expanded market, industrial modernisation and increased output, as well as continuing foreign investment and the arrival of more UK and international companies. But in the medium-term, competition from the central and eastern European countries could have a negative effect on growth and investment.

Skills and Qualifications

Anyone thinking of working in Portugal will find that excellent skills and qualifications obtained in their own country will be necessary to enhance their choice of employment, as there is little demand for unskilled UK workers (except in some tourism and seasonal work). We have already outlined the main areas for employment prospects; and the range of jobs available to foreigners may be wider in the future as Portugal's industrial base continues to develop. In the meantime, the main way for foreigners who are already living in Portugal to exploit their skills is to offer a technical or professional service (e.g. plumber, hairdresser, private tutor, nanny, dentist, doctor, lawyer, veterinary surgeon etc.) to members of the growing expatriate community. Professionals have to submit their qualifications to the relevant Portuguese body for approval; and many will be recognised on an EUwide basis under European directives. Contact the relevant professional body in the UK or Portugal for more information. Also recognised by the EU are Certificates of Experience for those who have completed three to five years' work in a particular area. Contact the DTI on 020-7215 5000 or, alternatively, the British Chambers of Commerce Certification Unit on 01203-695688 for more information about equivalence of qualifications across the EU. Some small businesses may not accept your UK certificate, even after you have gone through these procedures, though; and only after you have received the approval of the relevant professional body in Portugal will you be free to practise your trade or profession there; so it is worth finding out beforehand if qualifications like NVQs and GNVQs will be useful. Those with business skills should seek out a gap in the market which they can exploit, see the chapter on *Starting a Business* at the end of this section.

It is wise to assume that in whatever field you choose to work, a knowledge of Portuguese will be useful; and in many cases this will be the most helpful skill you can acquire. You may get by with just a few words if you are working in tourism for one season, but for the longer-term jobs, self-employment, and for any jobs that bring you constantly into contact with the Portuguese, at least the technical terms of your trade or profession and enough Portuguese to get by in the workplace will be necessary.

Also, many expatriates are driven to a state of despair by the numerous bureaucratic regulations concerning business and employment, many of which change constantly. This causes less consternation to those with a working knowledge of Portuguese. In the cosmopolitan business circles of Lisbon and Oporto, English and French are widely understood, but rarely well spoken. For details on language courses see Chapter Four on *Daily Life*.

SOURCES OF JOBS

As already mentioned, one of the most promising areas for jobs for those who have not been posted there by their company (and who may not speak Portuguese) is among the expatriates, or in teaching English as a foreign language (otherwise known as TEFL). Newspapers and magazines can be a useful wellspring of vacancies in these fields. One of the best ways of going about looking for a job is to make a speculative trip to make contacts, especially among the foreign residents and the language schools, who are likely to be the most useful source of information about jobs; and may even offer you employment on the spot.

The relative ease of air communications makes this a good approach to getting a job there; and will help you make some practical preparations for your move as well (finding somewhere to live, or familiarising yourself a little more with the country). Making a reconnaissance trip is not as extravagant as one might think: in summer 2002 return flights to Faro were as little as £129. This can also help you avoid making more expensive mistakes further down the line, and to find out more about Portuguese life and culture. Job prospectors, once there, can also consult the English-language press as another possible source of temporary or permanent employment; or visit the various highstreet employment or accommodation agencies, or the local British Council office. If you are unemployed in the UK and have been receiving contributionbased Jobseeker's Allowance it is also your right to go to Portugal, or the other EU countries, to look for work, and still receive your benefit while you are there. Contact your local Job Centre, or fax the Overseas Benefit Directorate on 0191-218 7652 or ☎0191-218 7777. They have a Factsheet No. 1 with information on how to do this.

Any UK citizen who has a sufficient level of Portuguese (or Portuguese friends who can help) can also consult the *emprego* (work) columns of Portuguese newspapers like the *Diário de Notícias* or *Público*.

Newspapers

Newspapers and directories published in Britain. It is most unlikely that you will find a great many general vacancies in Portugal advertised in major national UK newspapers, or even international ones. These do carry advertisements for specialists in law, accountancy, computing, and so on, and these will generally be found in the relevant issue or section, but very few of these will be based in Portugal, the exception being vacancies for English language teachers, which are advertised from time to time in the *Times Educational Supplement* and the Education pages of the *Guardian*. The summer is the best time to look for the latter, as language schools recruit staff for the next academic year. For jobs connected with tourism, the specialist newspaper *Overseas Jobs Express* (subscriptions from Randstad 221117, 1316 BW Almere, P.O. Box 60126, 1320 AC Almere, The Netherlands; ☎+31 036 547140; fax +31 036 5471451; www.overseasjobsexp ress.co.uk), occasionally carries advertisements for bar staff, chefs, couriers, entertainers etc. in the Algarve. There are also vacancies for specialists like engineers and in information technology, and the latest news on international work and jobseeking worldwide.

For anyone interested in working in a specialised area, the relevant trade magazine (*Caterer and Hotelkeeper* for catering, *Certified Accountant* for accountancy, and so on) will probably be you best bet; and a visit to your local library (before you decide to take out a subscription) will be a way of finding out how many vacancies in Portugal are offered. Newspapers and magazines, needless to say, can also keep you in touch with your chosen area of work or business. In the UK, *The Financial Times* carries the most European (and Portuguese) news, with occasional special reports on Portugal which will certainly be worth tracking down, again probably through your local library which should keep back copies.

Also, there are all the books published by Vacation Work, especially *Teaching English Abroad*, *Work Your Way Around the World*, and the annual *Summer Jobs Abroad*, each of which contain a range of information about Portugal and recruiters of English teachers, in temporary or summer jobs like hotel work and summer camps. Contact: Vacation Work, 9 Park End Street, Oxford OX1 1HJ; fax 01865-790885; www.vacationwork.co.uk.

English-language newspapers and magazines published in Portugal. Job vacancies (e.g. au pair, private English tutors) often appear in the weekly *Anglo-Portuguese News* published on Thursdays in Lisbon (Apartado 113, 2765 Estoril; ☎21-4661423/31; fax 21-4660358). In the Algarve, these are also to be found in *The News* (Apartado 13, 84021 Lagoa, Algarve; ☎28-2341100; fax 28-2341201). These are both on sale at most newsstands where foreign newspapers are to be found. You can also place job-wanted advertisements in either of these papers.

Portuguese Newspapers and Magazines. For a country with supposedly less than 7% unemployment Portugal has a surprisingly large selection of situations vacant in its national newspapers, (e.g. *Diário de Notícias, Público, Journal de Notícias,* and the weekly business and politics magazine *Expresso*). Evidently you will need some knowledge of the Portuguese language (although occasionally some of these ads appear in English); and a large degree of optimism is also required if you apply for many of these jobs, which include restaurant workers, cooks and other domestic staff, shop assistants etc. Competition with Portuguese nationals is an obstacle of some magnitude, so it is better to aim higher, or at the general vacancies where speaking English, or some other experience or skill which you have, is specified. Portuguese newspapers will probably have to be consulted on the spot as they are not easily obtainable outside Portugal; but may be available in some London newsagents, in specialised libraries, e.g. university and business libraries, and in the Canning House library in London (2 Belgrave Square, London SW1X 8PJ).

Professional Associations

Many professional associations do not provide official information on working overseas as such. However, many of them will have knowledge of their counterpart associations in other EU countries acquired during negotiations involving the recognition of qualifications, as required by the EU directives (see above). Such associations, when pushed, should provide some help to individuals.

Details of all professional associations are to be found in the directory, *Trade Associations and Professional Bodies of the United Kingdom*, available at most reference libraries. There is also a *European Directory of Trade and Business Associations* available in some business libraries. It is certainly worth trying to contact the Portuguese equivalent of UK professional associations: the UK body may be able to provide a contact. Some of the main associations are given below.

Additionally some trade unions have contacts with their counterparts in Portugal, so it is worth contacting them for information. A list of Portuguese trade unions can be found under *Sindicatos* in the Portuguese yellow pages (*Paginas Amarelas*).

Portuguese Professional Organisations:
Ordem dos Advogados (Lawyers): Largo s Domingos 14, second floor, 1100 Lisbon; ☎21-867152.
Ordem dos Medicos (Medical Staff): Avenida da Liberdade 65, first floor, 1200 Lisbon; ☎213462725.
Associa[ce]ão Arquitectos (Architects): Rua Barata Salgueiro 36, 1200 Lisbon; ☎21-3526445.

UK Employment Agencies/The EURES Scheme

Only a few UK-based international employment agencies will consider handling job vacancies in Portugal. Your best bet, somewhat surprisingly, for a speculative application, is likely to be your local Jobcentre which, under the EURES scheme, can help you complete an application form (if you have suitable language and other skills) to be forwarded to the employment service in Portugal. The Euroadviser at the Jobcentre will also have access to the useful *Eurofacts* leaflets on Portugal, and vacancies which UK Jobcentres have been notified of, through EURES, in Portugal. See the EURES website (http://europa.eu.int/jobs/eures) for contact details for the EURES Advisers in Portugal and for registered vacancies (only 16 in all of Portugal at the time of writing). The exceptions, so far as private agencies are concerned, are entertainment agencies which send dancers, magicians, disc jockeys and so on abroad on two or three month contracts and will arrange work permits; and also some au pair agencies. Some of these advertise in *Overseas Jobs Express* (see *Sources of Jobs* above).

Employment Organisations in Portugal

Private Portuguese Employment Agencies. These are probably not much use for finding an office or even a manual job unless one is proficient in Portuguese. However they are listed in the *Paginas Amarelas* under *Pessoal Temporário* (Temporary Personnel) and *Pessoal – Recrutamento e Selecção* (Personnel Recruitment and Selection). The majority are based in Lisbon and Oporto.

Addresses of Employment Organisations in Portugal

Agência de Transacções e Emprego de Cacais: Rua Nova de Algarrobeira 10A, 2750 Cascais; ☎2864204.

ATEJ: PO Box 4586, 4009 Oporto. Au pairs and volunteers.

Creyf Portugal: Travessa do Carmo 4 R/C, 1200 Lisbon; ☎13-472061/2/3; fax 213428327.

Ellen Broom American Secretarial School: Rua Castilho 38 – 1°, Lisbon; ☎21-539650.

Eurocede: Rua das Lusiadas 58A, 1300 Lisbon; ☎21-3630968; fax 21-3621543.

Hospedeiras de Portugal: Rua Borges Carneiro 411°Esq°, 1200 Lisbon; ☎21-3951372; fax 21-603975.

José Joaquim Calvo: Rua Marques da Silva, 461°, 1100 Lisbon; ☎213554665.

Manpower: Praça José Fontana 9C, 1050 Lisbon; ☎21-3134000; fax 213134070; sede@manpower.pt; www.manpower.pt.

Manpower: Rua Campinho 24, 4000 Oporto; ☎22-2002426.

Manpower: Braga; ☎253214374.

Manpower: 8200 Albufeira, Algarve; ☎289588113. Also in the Azores, ☎296636341.

Price Waterhouse: Edificio JN, Gonçalo Cristóvão 217, 13th Floor, 4000 Oporto; ☎2312614.

PricewaterhouseCoopers, Lisbon: Avenida da Liberdade 245 8° A, 1269 Lisbon; ☎21 319 7000; www.pwcglobal.com

PricewaterhouseCoopers, Oporto. Edificios do Lago, Rua S. Joã de Brito, 605EEsc 1.2, 4100 Oporto; ☎22-6107941.

SELGEC: Rua Alexandre Herculano, 39 1° Dt°, 1200 Lisbon; ☎21-543505.

SELMARK Marketing, Rua do Salitre, 1753°, 1200 Lisbon (☎21-3877100).

SEQUIL: Rua de Buenos Aires 5 c/vB, 1200 Lisbon; ☎21-3957242; fax 213978940.

One other possibility is the company *Personal Relocations* (Apartado 432, 8136 Almancil Codex, Algarve; ☎89399941; fax 89399625), which comprises a collection of services for those who are thinking of setting up in Portugal. The services include recruitment of executives.

Portuguese Government Job Centres. The Portuguese equivalent of the UK Jobcentres are the *Centros Emprego* of which there are about 84 countrywide. They are unlikely to help anyone who is unable to communicate in Portuguese. In addition to operating a placement service they also give assistance to entrepreneurs. Although primarily a service for Portuguese nationals, the job centres have an obligation, imposed by EU regulations to be of assistance to nationals of other EU countries. However, as in France, where the government employment offices are notoriously unhelpful to foreigners, do not expect them to bend over backwards to help you even if you do speak the language. Government job centres come under the *Ministério do Emprego e Segurança Social* (Ministry of Employment and Social Security) who publish a list of addresses and telephone numbers of the Centres in the *Anuário dos Serviços Públicos.* Their address is listed below.

Useful Addresses

Centro Emprego: Rua Batista Lopes 34, 8000 Faro; ☎8983765.
Centro Emprego: Rua Conde Redondo 129, 1100 Lisbon; ☎21-589024.
Centro Emprego: Avenida Eng Ezequiel Campos 488, Porto; ☎22-671344.
Centro Emprego: Avenida Fernão de Magalhães 648, Coimbra; ☎23-936561.
All state-run employment centres in Portugal are administered by the *Ministerio do Emprego e Segurança Social,* Praça de Londres, 1000 Lisbon. They have a public information service known as the blue line (*linha azul*), ☎21-801012.

Embassies and Consulates

Helping people to find jobs is not one of the functions undertaken by embassies and consulates. However they do provide prepared information: The British Embassy in Lisbon (Rua de São Bernardo 33, 1200 Lisbon; ☎21-3924000; fax 21-3924188) provides sheets entitled *Taking up Residence* and *Living in Portugal.*

Other Sources of Information

Chambers of Commerce: Chambers of Commerce exist to serve the interests of businesses trading in both Portugal and the UK; they do not act as employment agencies. Nevertheless, their repositaries of information about member companies could prove invaluable if one wanted to know which companies customarily employ UK nationals. It is possible they may even know which companies currently have vacancies. Thus it is worth consulting these chambers of commerce and business associations on the off chance that they can be of assistance:

Associação Industrial Portuguesa (Portuguese Industrial Association): 1300 Lisbon Codex; ☎21-360 1000.

Associação Luso-Británica do Porto: (Portuguese-British Association of Porto), Rua do Breinver 155/165, 4000 Porto.

Câmara do Comércio Luso-Británica: (Portuguese-British Chamber of Commerce), Rua Sá da Bandeira 784, 2nd Floor, 4000 Porto;

Câmara do Comércio Luso-Británica: (Portuguese-British Chamber of Commerce), Rua da Estrêla 8, 1200669 Lisbon; ☎21-394 2020. CVs may be sent by email to bpcc@mail.telepac.pt though the Chamber cannot respond unless they have already been notified of a relevant opportunity. They plan to set up a facility whereby people can post CV details on their website (www.bpcc.pt) which would be accessible to Chamber members. They envision a system whereby the jobseeker's name and address would be divulged to prospective employers after consent had been granted and upon payment of a fee by the company.

The Hispanic and Luso Brazilian Council (Canning House, 2 Belgrave Square, London SW1; ☎020-72352303; fax 020-72353587; www.canninghouse.com) publishes a wellresearched leaflet called *Portugal: A Guide to Employment and Opportunities for Young People* aimed primarily at the younger worker/traveller.

Advertising in Newspapers

It is sometimes possible to attract a job offer from an employer by placing an advertisement in either the Portuguese press or the English-language newspapers published in Portugal. Advertisements in the Portuguese press can be placed through the agents Powers International in London (100 Rochester Row, London SW1P 1JP; ☎020-7592 8325; fax 020-7592 8326) who deal with the following newspapers and magazines: *Diário de Notícias* (Lisbon daily), *Jornal de Notícias* (Oporto daily), *Expresso* (weekly newspaper), *Negocios* (biannual business magazine), and *Público* (a national daily published in Lisbon and Oporto). Similar advertisements are to be found in the English-language press (see below); and appear from time to time in international publications like the *International Herald Tribune*, and *Overseas Jobs Express*.

Useful Addresses & Website

Anglo-Portuguese News: Apartado 113, 2765253 Estoril; ☎214661423/31; fax 214660358).

Overseas Jobs Express: (www.overseasjobsexpress.co.uk). *Powers International:* see above.

The News: Apartado 13, 8400 Lagoa, Algarve; ☎282-1341100; fax 282-341201.

The Algarve Resident: Apartado 131, 84021902 Lagoa; ☎282-342936.

Voluntary and Au Pair

There isn't a strong voluntary movement in Portugal. The statesupported Instituto Portugues da Juventude (IPJ), Av. da Liberdade No. 194, 1269051 Lisbon (☎21-317 92 00/fax 317 9216; ipj.infor@mail.telepac.pt) oversees a programme of heritage protection and other short-term voluntary projects. Applications should normally be sent through a partner organisation in the applicant's own country, for example *Concordia* and *UNA (Wales)* in the UK which may also have links with other Portuguese voluntary agencies.

Au pairing is not at all common in Portugal, and very few placements are made by UK agencies to Portugal. A few positions may be advertised in *The Lady* magazine with expatriate families. Summer openings are most likely to occur in the school holidays between the end of July and end of September. The international peace organisation International Friendship League (R. Ruy de Sousa Vinagre 2, 2890 Alcochete (fax 21234 1082; ifl.por@mail.telepac.pt) may be able to arrange English tutoring placements in families. According to information from the Instituto Portugues da Juventude, several other organisations can help people looking for vacation au pair placements, though this information could not been corroborated recently:

Entreculturas, Rua Pereira e Sousa 76 R/C, 1300 Lisbon; ☎21-387 0509).

Intercultura, Rua de Santo António da Glória 6 A, 1250 Lisbon; ☎21-346 4126).

Tagus, Rua Camilo Castelo Branco 20, 1250 Lisbon; ☎21-352 55 009).

Casual Work on Spec

Thousands of Britons and other Europeans take their holidays on the Algarve creating many job opportunities in bars and restaurants particularly in and around Albufeira. In some cases, finding somewhere to stay can be more difficult than finding employment. Not surprisingly, accommodation is quite expensive during the high season. Ask around so you can avoid the dodgy landlords and expect to pay at least £30 a week in a shared flat in Albufeira.

A few other possibilities for casual jobs can be investigated on the spot and are mostly aimed at attracting the attention of holidaymakers. These jobs include: handing out flyers for nightclubs and discos, new restaurants etc., enticing holidaymakers off the street to view timeshare properties (paid on a commission basis), and doing the dirty jobs on yachts at marinas such as the one at Vilamoura in the Algarve. Of these possibilities, the first two are the least rewarding as one runs the risk of being ignored or insulted. As far as the yacht work goes, it needs persistence and a pleasant manner when approaching yacht owners for work: offer to wash down or do a little painting work. If you are seeking a working passage to the Azores, Caribbean etc. you will have to work hard to impress and let it be known around the local wateringholes of the yachting fraternity that such is your aim. Also, see *Work Your Way Around the World* (Vacation Work) for more casual work opportunities in tourism, agriculture and English teaching.

BUSINESS AND INDUSTRY REPORT

Up to the present both the number and type of vacancies, as well as the level of salaries in Portuguese businesses and industries, have proved a disincentive to those considering this as a place in which to live and work. But the situation is improving as the economy develops and trade with the UK and other EU countries grows; certainly the Portuguese are optimistic about their future as an industrially dynamic nation; and the recent liberalisation of the banking and financial services sector as well as the government's programme of privatisation and deregulation are signs of the country's progress towards a more modern economy, as is the relative decline in the importance of agriculture.

The Eurozone. This may make living and working in Spain and Portugal, and many of the other EU countries, a lot easier. Although a decision to join the euro single currency by Britain looks unlikely during 2002, both Portugal and Spain are part of the 'Eurozone' and the the euro currency is now the single currency in most EU countries. This completes process begun with the 1992 Maastricht Treaty bringing the EU countries (or the majority of them) into both a single market and a single currency zone: in domestic economic matters these countries will then effectively have pooled their sovereignty, not unlike the constituent states of the United States; although the EU and single currency member states remain independent in most matters outside monetary policy. The effect of EMU on the economy and job prospects will be positive according to its supporters and potentially catastrophic according to the sceptics; the effects will be felt for readers of this book several years after 2002 if Britain decided to go ahead and join; with many foreign exchange and ultimately taxation and social security issues becoming more straightforward if EMU is a success.

The Portuguese Economy. Anyone thinking of working in Portugal, in whatever field, ought to have some idea of the main industrial concerns, and the economic trends which may influence their development; this may help you decide where the best employment opportunities will be found. It is a good idea to know the locations of the main areas of economic activity which, it will become apparent, are mainly Lisbon and Oporto, with tourism the most important industry in the south. The following is an overview of the Portuguese economy today, the domestic market (which is boosted every year by the large number of tourists and other visitors to Portugal), and trends in some of the main sectors of industry, followed by a list of the main British concerns and companies in Portugal.

The most developed manufacturing areas of the country are Oporto in the north, which is the traditional centre of the port wine and textile industries, and the Oporto hinterland, where fish canning, oil refining, vehicle components, light engineering, paints, tyres, earthenware, shoes, cork and jewellery are the main types of industry. The other major industrial zone is the area extending 25 miles/40 kms south of Lisbon to Setubal which is a national development region containing steel, shipyards, engineering, textiles, cement, chemicals and automobile assembly plants. The main commercial and trade centre is also Oporto. Most UK and international companies are based in these areas.

As will be seen from the data below, Portugal is in the process of upgrading its products from mainly raw materials to finished goods, thus increasing their export value. This is a traditional activity too. The port wine industry and food processing have always been based on its primary agricultural products; food and beverages today are an important part of Portuguese exports as they have always been, with other secondary industries based on raw materials like wood and cork also playing an important role in Portuguese trade.

Over 60% of its exports go to EU countries; and the annual amount of direct investment in the Portuguese economy also doubled in each of the four years after its accession to the EU, with Britain playing an important role, alongside Spain, as its main trading partner. In Portugal, UK direct investment is nearly twice as much as that of France; and nearly three times that of Germany. Of the EU countries, Spain is still the most important partner. After centuries of imperial and colonial rivalry, the two countries of the Iberian peninsular are discovering that they have many common interests and objectives, the latest being to join the single currency in the first wave of entrants if the circumstances allow.

Other trading partners are the USA and Canada, and the former Portuguese colonies in Africa.

Although Portuguese industry is expanding, statistics show that among the active population of under five million, a smaller percentage (35%), is employed in industry than in services (44.5%). The economy is that of an industrialised country, but one where the service sector is ahead of industry as the major contributor to its Gross Domestic Product, not unlike that of Britain. A common history of trade around the world, as well as a centuries' old tradition of commerce between the two countries, is one of the things which unites the two countries. Both Portugal and Britain, with their former colonial interests, are international in their outlook as well as European. For Portugal, as for Britain nowadays, continued prosperity will depend on developing these international trading links alongside contacts with its European partners.

The Portuguese UK Chamber of Commerce in London was set up (only fifteen or so years ago) to encourage trade and investment in both directions; and is a useful source of information about trends in the Portuguese economy, and trade and investment prospects there, as well as for those wishing to find about more about the leading Anglo-Portuguese companies. It represents Portugal's leading business association (AIP) in Britain, the Bolsa de Valores de Lisboa (the country's expanding stock exchange), regional development organisations in Portugal, and a variety of other bodies, as well as having links with the Câmera de Comércio

Luso Britânnica. It also promotes seminars and networking meetings; and is a source of information about EU funding in Portugal: *Portuguese UK Chamber of Commerce*, Fourth Floor, 22/25a Sackville Street, London W1X 1DE; ☎020-7494 1844; fax 020-7494 1822.

Foodstuffs, Beverages and Tobacco

This sector is undoubtedly one of the two most important groups of industries which represent 20% of industrial production. The bulk of production is for the home market, but many of the wares are familiar outside Portugal, including fish and fish products, tomato concentrate, olive oil and wines. The latter is responsible for much of the £50 million or so of beverages from Portugal imported into the UK; and beverages are number seven in the top ten of UK/Portuguese traded products.

One area for foreign companies to exploit is in producing Portuguese equivalents of products familiar in other EU countries, (e.g. breakfast cereals and instant foods), which are not yet commonplace in Portugal and for which there is an increasing demand; British brands of food and drink (like tea) are popular in Portugal; but the imported products are expensive compared with homegrown versions. Marks and Spencer has recently opened a retail outlet in Lisbon; and there is also scope in the retail sector for UK supermarkets and retailers to develop larger scale operations.

Beer, not wine, is the main product of the beverages sector though. Production is shared by two companies which were privatised at the beginning of the 90's: Unicer and Central Cervejas. The main Unicer brewery is in the north and Central Cervejas is in Lisbon. UK companies in this food and drinks sector with interests in Portugal include Bass (importer); Allied Domecq (joint venture); Cadbury Schweppes (direct); Guinness (direct); and United Biscuits (joint venture).

Textiles and Clothing

The production of textiles and clothing is the other main secondary industry. These currently represent almost 20% of national industrial output. The main products are woollen yarns, cotton yarns and other textiles, as well as knitwear, lace and embroidery. About 90% of Portuguese exports are absorbed by the European Union.

These industries are mainly concentrated in the Oporto and Braga districts; the only exception is wool, about half of which is produced in the Castelo Branco region. The top three Portuguese exports to the UK are listed by the Department of Trade and Industry as clothing, footwear and fabrics, and so this is by far the most important sector for exports to Britain. As with food and beverages, cheaper production in the new central and eastern European EU members could damage Portuguese trade with EU partners in textile and clothing products in the longer term.

Leather Goods and Hides

Leather is a traditional Portuguese export. The main change is a shift into quality products, particularly in high fashion footwear. It is estimated that 90% of manufacture is exported.

Timber, Cork and Furniture

Over one third of Portugal is forested. The most important species of trees are the pine, cork-oak and eucalyptus. The pine trees are exported via the sawmills as timber for making pallets. Over the last few years however, there has been a growing tendency to produce more sophisticated wooden goods (e.g. furniture) with a higher export value.

Portugal produces over half the world's cork, which is no mean feat for so small a country. This is mainly exported in the form of bottle corks; but cork products and agglomerates also find a ready market. The bulk of exports go to the EU and a small proportion to the USA; and the main area for cork production is the Alentejo region, north of the Algarve.

An example of the diversity of the Portuguese economy, and of the development of many of its companies is Grupo Amorim, traditionally a cork producer, which expanded in the 1980's into real estate, tourism, telecommunications and even banking. 'In a small country, you have to be in three or four activities to get bigger,' its chairman says. And the company is also developing no less than 26 joint ventures with foreign partners.

Wood Pulp and Paper

These products represent a major growth area in Portuguese industry. Portugal has become a large producer of cellulose for paper production and specialises in bleached eucalyptus pulp. There is an increasing trend towards producing paper as the finished product for export. The Portuguese are well aware that they can considerably undercut the prices of traditional suppliers (e.g. the Nordic countries). These are the seventh most important export to the UK, currently worth around £70 million a year.

Base Chemicals

The base chemical industry at present represents about 5% of industrial production and is diversified in different forms, the main sectors being inorganic chemicals, petrochemicals and fertilizers. The inorganic sector suffers from high production costs and is currently undergoing rationalisation. The petrochemical sector is expanding, particularly in the field of polymers for the plastics industry. There are also good prospects in the production of synthetic resins for paints, varnishes, and wood adhesives. Chemical fibres for synthetic textiles are also likely to be an area of expansion.

Fertilizers are a relative innovation; and this industry is likely to expand in relation to increasing demand from Portuguese agriculture which is being developed in line with practices elsewhere in the EU. UK companies with operations in this base chemical sector represented in Portugal include British Petroleum, Glaxo, ICI, and Unilever.

Light Chemicals

Light chemicals account for 8.5% of industrial production. By far the largest part of the light chemical industry is concentrated on medicinal products. Other sectors include plastic goods, tyres and inner tubes, resinous goods (pitchderivatives), pharmeceutical raw materials, cosmetics, detergents and essential oils. Many of these are growth industries.

Porcelain and Faience (decorated, glazed earthenware), Glassware, Cement, Ornamental Stone

Between them, these industries represent about 6% of the industrial product. Items include the famous Portuguese tiles which are sought after abroad for kitchen and bathroom wall decorations. The porcelain sector includes industrial ceramics for the building trade. Glass includes not only receptacles for foodstuffs but plate glass. Expansion is likely to occur as production is shifted to windscreens for the car industry.

As these are quality products traditionally associated with Portugal, there is scope for UK importers with the right Portuguese contacts. Demand for Portuguese marble is increasing, also for granites and similar minerals. Carved, ornamental stone is produced by efficient, factory methods and there are a number of modern companies operating in this field.

One of the major companies that has recently been partly privatised is the leading cement producer Cimpor (Cimentos de Portugal), which has 60% of the home market, some interests in Spain, and is keen to expand overseas.

Basic Metallurgy

Base metals account for nearly 5% of industrial production. There are two main industrial components of this industry, ferrousmetals and nonferrous metals. The first sector produces iron and steel products mainly for home consumption. In the second sector Portugal has important natural resources particularly of copper deposits, tin and tungsten. All of these are important exports. The British have invested heavily in the Neves Corvo copper mines which are some of the richest in Europe.

NonElectrical Machinery

The main products of this industry include farm machinery, machine tools and wood working machinery. This is one of the areas with good growth potential: particularly in demand within Portugal are machinery for the wood industry, equipment for the building industry, some types of farm machinery, machinery for foodstuffs and beverages and the ceramics industry.

Electrics and Electronics

The demand in these industries has grown in recent years as Portugal accelerates somewhat belatedly into the twentieth century. National industries, namely electricity generation, telecommunications, building, and public works have all heavily influenced the electrics industry.

There is also a greater demand for household appliances and manufacture of refrigerators, freezers, washing machines and cookers has increased. Portugal is also producing consumer electronics for the home market and there is also considerable development in the production of computer components which is predicted to be an international export growth area.

The telecom sector is now number nine in Portugal's top ten exporting industries; and worth up to £50 million a year in exports to Britain alone. A leading company is Efacec-Empresa Fabril de Fabricas Electricas, which has only been exporting since 1987, but now exports about 30%, mainly to Europe and also SouthEast Asia; and sees further scope for expansion in telecommunications and new fields like robotics.

Transport Equipment

This industry includes ship building and repair. Repair work is done at Lisnave and construction at Viana do Castelo and Setenave.

In the automobile sector there has been heavy foreign investment (e.g. Ford, General Motors, Citroën, Renault, Mitsubishi and Toyota). A large part of the automobile industry is devoted to automobile components which are worth over 70 thousand million escudos in export value per annum. The largest manufacturing enterprise in the country is the Auto-Europa project, a joint venture between Ford and Volkswagen, which is producing Ford Galaxy and VW Sharan mini vans at its plant at Palmela, south of Lisbon.

One of the traditional sectors is in railway rolling stock for export, which is however at present in decline.

Tourism

Tourism is an industry which shows no sign of fatigue. There is enormous scope for development; and the Portuguese government is giving every encouragement by offering financial incentives to foreign companies to build new tourist developments. ICEP, the Portuguese Government Trade and Tourism Office in London, can provide further information (2nd Floor, 22-25a Sackville Street, London W1X 2LY). These various schemes are hemmed by various restrictions which mean in effect that they only provide grants for companies who will guarantee construction jobs for the Portuguese; the size of the incentive grant depends on the number of building jobs created. However the fact that the tourist industry is expanding means that the increasing number of tourists will need swelling ranks of workers to look after and entertain them; and this is certainly the most important industry from the point of view of British expatriates living and working in Portugal.

DIRECTORY OF BRITISH EMPLOYERS IN PORTUGAL

Accountants and Consultants.
Agriter, Consultores e Gesto, Agricola Lda: Apartado 106, 8600 Lagos; ☎8262060.
Deloitte Touche Ross: Rua Silva Carvalho 2344°, 1200 Lisbon; ☎21-685626.
Deloitte Touche Tohmatsu: Galarias Alto da Barra, Avenida Das Descobertas, Piso 3, 2780 Oeiras; ☎21-4411134.
Ernst & Young: Avenida António de Aguiar 213 Esq, 1000 Lisbon; ☎21-3528889.
Grant Thornton & Kennard: Avenida Miguel Bombarda 21, 3Esq, 1000 Lisbon; ☎21-544202.

Banking & Finance.
Barclays Bank plc: Av da República 502°, 1000 Lisbon; ☎21-7935020; Av da Boavista 1283°, 4100 Oporto.
Lloyds Bank plc: Avenida da Liberdad 222, 1200 Lisbon; ☎21-535171/ 563571; Av dos Aliados 22°, 4000 Oporto; Av da Liberdado 140, 4700 Braga.
Midland Montagu SA: Avenida Eng Duarte Pacheco, Torre 117 S2A, 1000 Lisbon; ☎21-3875782.
Royal Bank of Scotland: c/o Banco de Comércio e Indústria SA, Praça Marquês de Pombal 2, 1200 Lisbon; ☎21-3521935.

Insurance Companies and Agencies:
Commercial Union Assurance Co: Av da Liberdade 384°, 1200 Lisbon; ☎21-324351.
Companhia de Seguros Eagle Star: Av 5 de Outubro 706°/8°, 1000 Lisbon; ☎21-77931.
General Accident: Praceta Prof. Egas Moniz 162 r/c, 4100 Oporto; ☎22-6104388.
James Rawes & Cia Lda (Lloyds Agents): Rua Bernadino Costa 47, 1200 Lisbon; ☎21-370231.
Newstead and Porter Lda: Rua António José de Almeida 8, 1000 Lisbon; ☎21-800104.
Royal Exchange Assurance: Av Marquês de Tomar 2, 1000 Lisbon; ☎21-3155235.
Royal Insurance: Rua Castilho 503°, 1200 Lisbon; ☎21-3863634.
Sun Insurance Offices Ltd: Av 5 de Outubro 1467°, 1000 Lisbon; ☎21-7978819.

Legal Profession:
A.M.Pereira, Sáragga Leal, Oliveira Martins, Júdice e Associados: Rua Silva Carvalho 234, 1250 Portugal; ☎21-3800700.
Abreu & Marques e Associados: Rua Filipe Folque, no 24° andar, S Sebastião da Pedreira, 1050 Lisbon; ☎21-3528268.
António Marante e Associados: Edificio 'Altis' 3°Q, Lotes 10/11, Cerro Alagoa, 8200 Albufeira, Algarve; ☎89-586888.
Barros, Sobral, G.Gomes e Associados: Rua 31 De Janeiro 81A, 5°E, 9000 Funchal, Madeira; ☎291227744.
Beltico – Emprieendimentos Turisticos SA: Apartado 2, 2510 Obidos; ☎26290125.
David Sampson & Co: Apartado 180, 2750 Cascais; ☎21-4834516.
Edmonds Bowen & Co./JM's Associados: Calcada Marquêes De Abrantes 382°ESQ, 1200 Lisbon; ☎21-3969684.
Grupo Legal Português: Rua Castilho 329°, 1200 Lisbon; ☎21-3521318.
Hedleys/António Marante e Associados: see above. Also at: Rua Ferreira Borges 691 Frenta, 4000 Porto; ☎22-2080701; Rua Dr M Arriaga

1A, Apartado 33, 8400 Lagoa; ☎8252878; Avenida Antonio De Aguiar 27/2 Dto, 1000 Lisbon; ☎21-3150801.

Lita Gale Solicitors: Rua D Francisco Gomes 181°, 8000 Faro, Algarve; ☎89801571.

Maria Teresa Silva e Associados: Centro de Servicios Valverde, 8135 Almancil, Algarve; ☎289396489; Rua António Aleixo, Lote 28, Apartado 2142, 8200 Albufeira, Algarve; ☎289586255; Av Conde Valborn 826 Dto, 1000 Lisbon; ☎21-7977601.

Neville de Rougement e Associados: Rua Tomas Ribeiro 544°, 1000 Lisbon; ☎21-3527618.

Oporto Investment Office: Rua de Ceuta 1182° andar, 4050 Porto; ☎22-2004281.

Refega/Dr P A L G: Parque Empreserial do Algarve, Apartado 246, 8400 Lagoa; ☎282342601.

William S Oddy: Rua 5 de Outubro 174, 8135 Almancil, Algarve; ☎289399131.

Manufacturing and Marketing:

Arjo Wiggins APL/Soporcel SA: Avenida da Eng°. Duarte Pacheco 191°, 1000 Lisbon; ☎21-3876406.

Beecham Portuguese Produtos Quinicos e Farmaceuticos Lda: Rua Sebstio e Silva 56, 2745 Queluz; ☎4370014.

Berec Portuguesa Lda (Berec Europe Ltd): Rua Gonçalves Zarco 6 6/J, 1400 Lisbon; ☎21-611034.

BP Portuguesa SA: Praça Marqués de Pombal 13, 1200 Lisbon; ☎21-3111600.

Cadbury Schweppes SA: Av Marquês de Tomar 355°, 1050 Lisbon; ☎21-7952420.

CELCAT – Fábrica Nacional de Condutores Eléctricos SA: Avenida Marquês de Pombal 3638, Morelena, 2715 Pêro Pinheiro; ☎21-9279030.

Comnexo SA: Av da República 245°, 1000 Lisbon; ☎21-575560. (subsidiary of British Telecom).

Cookson Matthey Ceramics: Costeira, Alfeloas, Apartado 128, 3781 Anadia Codex; ☎231515505.

De La Rue Systems SA: Rua Prof. Fernando Fonseca 26, 1600 Lisbon; ☎21-7577523.

Eastécnica Lda: Rua Prof. Vitor Fontes 11B, Telheiras, 1600 Lisbon; ☎21-7589391. (subsidiary of Cable & Wireless).

Eurosteel Portugal Lda: Edíficio Concordia, Lt 1974 E, 2685 Sacavém; ☎21-9434118. (agent for Corus).

FastécnicaElectrónica e Técnica Lda (Cable and Wireless): Praça Prof. Santos Andréa 5, 1500 Lisbon; ☎21-7145568.

GEC Alsthom International Lda: Av Elias Garcia 1235°, 1000 Lisbon; ☎21-7930031.

Glaxo Wellcome Lda: Rua Dr. António L. Borges 3, Arquiparque, Algés, 1495 Lisbon; ☎21-4129500.

Hoover Eléctrica Portuguesa Lda: Rua D Estefánia 90A, 1000 Lisbon; ☎21-525349.

ICI: (now *Zeneca,* see below).

ICL Computadores Lda: Av Duque d'Avila 120, 1050 Lisbon; ☎21-527011.

Industrias de Alimentação Lda (Heinz): Av da Republica 527°; 1000 Lisbon; ☎21-766011.

Lucas Automotive Lda: Avenida 24 de Julho 62 e 64, 1200 Lisbon; ☎21-3910500.

Rank Xerox (Portugal) Ltd: Rua Pedro Nunes 16, 1050 Lisbon; ☎21--577110.

Reckitt Portuguesa Lda (Reckitt & Colman): Rua Sebastio da Pedreira 1221°, 1000 Lisbon; ☎21-548112.

The Rover Group Portugal: Rua Vasco da Gama, 2685 Sacavém; ☎21-9406000.

Shell Portuguesa SA: Av da Liberdade 249, 1250 Lisbon; ☎21-3559155.

Singer: Rua da Garagem 9/9A, 2795 Carnaxide; ☎21-4179300.

Smith & Nephew Healthcare Lda: Rua

Cotão Velho, S. Marcos, 2735 Cacém; ☎21-4260652.

SLI, Lda: Segunda Rua Particular 26, Alcantra, 1300 Lisbon; ☎21-3639252. (subsidiary of Burmah Castrol).

Smithkline Beecham Lda: Av das Forças Armadas 12512°, 1600 Lisbon; ☎21-7903500.

Soc. Industrial de Aperitivos SA: Além do Mourão, Tentugal, 3140 Coimbra; ☎39951116. (joint venture with United Biscuits).

Tate & Lyle/Alcantara SA: Av da Índia 10, 1300 Lisbon; ☎21-3637075.

Thorn Iluminação Lda: Edifício ABB, Estrada Casal Canas, 2720 Alfragide; ☎21-4174726.

Unilever/Fima Lda: Largo Monterroio Mascarenhas 1, 1000 Lisbon; ☎21-3889121.

ZenecaAgro: Av D. Carlos I 423°, 1200 Lisbon; ☎21-602870.

Port Wine:

Cockburn Smithes & Cia Lda: Rua Corados 13, 4400 Vila Nova de Gaia; ☎22-394031.

Croft & Co: Largo Joaquim Magalhes 23, 4400 Vila Nova de Gaia; ☎22-390181.

Delaforce Sons & Cia Vinhos SARL: Largo Joaquim Magalhes 23, 4400 Vila Nova de Gaia; ☎22-3303665.

Taylor Fladgate & Yeatman: Rua Choupelo 250, 4400 Vila Nova de Gaia; ☎22-390187.

Warre & Cia Lda: Rua do Br Forrester 10, 4400 Vila Nova de Gaia; ☎22-396063.

The Symington Group: Rua do Golgota 63, 6100 Oporto; ☎22-696695.

Property:

Bovis International Ltd: Qta do LagoAlmansil, 8100 Loulé, Algarve.

Bovis (UK); ☎01202-291906; *Hamptons* (UK), ☎020-78228822; *Vigia* (Portugal), ☎28265376; *Villas and Vacations* (Portugal), ☎289394807;

Quinteca (Portugal), ☎289395542; *KnightFrank* (Portugal), ☎217951906. All involved in residential developments on the Algarve.

Cliff Bay Resort Hotel: Estrada Monumental 147, 9000 Funchal, Madeira; ☎917070707.

Hotel Central: Praça da República 35, 2710 Sintra; ☎21-9243821.

Penina Golf Hotel: Apartado 146, 8502 Portimáo Codex, Algarve; ☎82415415. (subsidiary of Forte).

Ritz InterContinental: Rua Rodrigo Fonseca 88A/C, 1093 Lisbon Codex.

Shipping and Freight:

DHL International: Aeroporto de Lisboa, Rua de Edificio 121 R/C, 1700 Lisbon; ☎21-808520.

IML: Aeroporto de Lisboa, Rua de Edificio 121, 10D, 1700 Lisbon; ☎21-8140204/8122.

James Rawes & Cia Lda: Rua Bernadino Costa 47, 1200 Lisbon; ☎21-370231.

Lassen Transport Lda: Av D Carlos 1, 426°, 1200 Lisbon; ☎21-602233.

Lloyd's Register of Shipping: Av D Carlos 1, 446°, 1200 Lisbon; ☎21-664131.

P S Wainwright Marine Consultants & Surveyors: Rua Ant[ac]onio Nobre 13B, 2800 Almada; ☎2754641.

TransPortugal European Ltd: In Escritório and Armazém; tel/fax 212332611.

Trans Viriato: Office in Armazém. UK office: 274276 Queenstown Road, London SW8 3NP; ☎020-7733 5094.

Wall & Cia Lda: Rua do Instituto Industrial 182°Dto, 1200 Lisbon; ☎21-678520.

Willie Portuguesa Navegaçao Lda: Av Infante Santo 232°D, 1200 Lisbon; ☎21-606391.

Translation Service:

Communicate Language Institute: Praceta Loão Villaret 12B, Povoa de Sto. Adrião, 2675 Odivelas; ☎21-

9372635.

Travel and Tourism:
Agencia de Turismo Garland Laidley: Trav do Corpo Santo 102°, 1200 Lisbon; ☎21-363191.
Blandy Bros & Cia Lda: Av de Zarco 2, 9000 Funchal, Madeira; ☎20161.
British Airways: Av da Liberdade 237°, 1200 Lisbon; ☎21-3423118.
Sociedade Comercial Blandy Bros (Lisboa) Lda: Rua Vitor Cordon 311°, 1200 Lisbon; ☎21-36651.
Turisvaz Viagens & Turismo: Centro Comercial Avenida, 9200 Vila de Machico, Madeira; ☎291962872.
Viagens Rawes: Rua Bernadino Costa 47, 1200 Lisbon; ☎21-370231.

British Tour Operators.
Airtours Holidays Ltd: Holiday House, Sandbrook Park, Sandbrook Way, Rochdale, Lancs. OL11 5SA; ☎0870-2412642. Tours to Faro, Funchal, etc.
British Airways Holidays: Astral Towers, Betts Way, London Road, Crawley, West Sussex RH10 2XA; ☎01293-723100. To Lisbon and Faro.
Club Med: Kennedy House, 115 Hammersmith Road, London W14 0QH; ☎020-73483336.☎020-7581 1161.
CTC Cruise Lines: 1 Regent Street, London SW1Y 4NN; ☎020-7896 8899.
DA Study Tours: Williamton House, Low Causeway, Culross, Fife KY12 8HL; ☎01383-882200.
Destination Portugal: Madeira House, 37 Corn Street, Witney, Oxon OX8 7BW; ☎01993-773269. (also *EHS Travel*).
JMC Holidays: Overseas Personnel Department, 6 Midford Place, London W1T 5BF; ☎0870-6070309.
Magic of Portugal: 227 Shepherds Bush Road, London W6 7AS; ☎020-8741 1181.
Page and Moy Ltd: Operations Department, 136141 London Road, Leicester LE2 1EN; ☎0116-250 7000. Employs a number of personnel for Portugal as tour leaders and reps.
Palmair: 2 Albert Road, Bournemouth, Dorset BH1 1BY; ☎01202-299299. Charters to Faro.
Portugala Holidays Ltd: 94 Fortis Green, London N2 9EY; ☎020-8444 1857. To Lisbon, Oporto, Faro, Funchal, the Azores.
Shearings Holidays: European Product Department, Miry Lane, Wigan, Lancashire WN3 4AG; ☎01942-823416; fax 01942-829760.
Thomson Tour Operations Ltd: Overseas Personnel Department, Greater London House, Hampstead Road, London NW1 7SD; ☎020-7387932. Employs a range of staff based in the resorts.

Starting a Business

Many emigrants from the UK and other European countries who choose to live in Portugal will do so with the intention of starting a business there. Indeed many are already doing so. Generally this is only a realistic proposition for those with previous experience of running a business in the UK or elsewhere, and who have located a demand for a similar enterprise in Portugal. Those without any hands-on knowledge of business practices may be heading for disaster. It is all very well to have been nourishing a retiree's pipe dream of a little bar or restaurant in a sunny place but before embarking on such a project it would be advisable to get first hand accounts from those who are already running catering establishments in Portugal. The alternative is to go into business with someone whose business credentials are already well established. Advice from old hands will almost certainly counteract the idealistic tendencies of the uninitiated. Inevitably long hours and hard work are the lot of anyone in the catering business.

Anyone wishing to escape the professional rat race and use their qualifications (e.g. medical, architectural, legal etc.) to start a practice in Portugal can realistically expect a less pressured working atmosphere and a healthier lifestyle than working in the metropolises of the UK. There will of course always be some expats who have emigrated with a single notion: to live a life of ease with no stimulation except golf, sailing, and the pursuit of pleasure. After initially enjoying the relaxation, boredom might well set in and the need for a challenge arise. Setting up a business in Portugal is certainly that – an obstacle course crammed with trials in the form of endless red tape and regulations. Generally speaking, the bulk of the red tape is reserved for larger business structures requiring substantial startup capital. There are less elaborate procedures for those who are self-employed for which no permit is needed.

One is tempted to suppose that the mass of paperwork and the snail's pace bureaucracy that has to be endured exist to deter the ambitions of entrepreneurs. It is therefore good news that positive encouragement exists in the form of the Portuguese Trade Office (ICEP) and the Portuguese UK Chamber of Commerce (see below), which are both indefatiguable in their production of leaflets, booklets and in the case of the Chamber of Commmerce a useful newsletter (*Tradewinds*), which contain much information pertinent to business creation in Portugal. Another useful source of information is the British-Portuguese Chamber of Commerce, Rua da Estrêla 8, P1200 Lisbon; ☎21-3961586. The following sections detail the necessary procedures for setting up different kinds of businesses, namely:

- ○ Preparation and groundwork in order to select a type of business.
- ○ Raising finance and investigating the possibility of claiming grants and incentives.
- ○ Selecting the most appropriate legal/corporate business structure.
- ○ Submitting a prior declaration of intent to start business to the
- ○ Foreign Investment Institute.
- ○ Starting the company formation/branch registration procedure.
- ○ Registering the chosen entity for tax and social security purposes.

Preparation

Before launching into the formalities involved in starting a business, solid preparatory groundwork is essential. This undoubtedly means spending some time in Portugal. Prospective entrepreneurs can rent accommodation in the Algarve, Lisbon, Cascais and other expatriate playgrounds while they do their reconnaisance. The Portuguese National Tourist Office in London and the Portuguese-UK Chamber of Commerce (see previous chapters), can provide a list of UK-based propertyletting agencies,and other useful information. It is advisable to rent outside the main tourist areas, or out of the summer season, as seaside, summer rents tend to be astronomical (i.e. in the region of £600 per month). Whilst out in Portugal the aspiring businessman or woman should carry out a thorough survey of the areas in which they are interested. It is advisable to assess carefully the potential of any proposed business, and in particular the general viability of any scheme (e.g. supplies, supporting infrastructure) they have in mind. Demand is also a vital factor in the success of any business: for instance, can the area support another bar, restaurant, horticultural centre, bookshop etc.? Is income purely seasonal, or all year round?

Accountancy Firms. All prospective business persons intending to set up in Portugal are advised to consult British accountancy firms with branches there. These include PricewaterhouseCoopers, Deloitte Touche, and KPMG. PricewaterhouseCoopers produce an information guide (*Doing Business in Portugal*; ☎020-7583 5000). See the List of accountants in *Daily Life* for further contacts.

Corporate Relocation. Those who would like to transfer an existing business from the UK to Portugal can employ the services of a corporate relocation specialist. Relocation specialists are widely used in the USA but are a relatively new concept elsewhere. These will offer services similar to but more extensive than a lawyer or accountant. Smaller businesses will usually take the option of setting up a new business from scratch in Portugal; and it may be better then to seek your legal and accountancy advice on the spot.

Residence Regulations

As already mentioned, the self-employed do not require a work permit, only a residence permit. The procedure for obtaining this is detailed in Chapter Two, *Residence and Entry Regulations*.

PROCEDURES FOR BUYING OR STARTING A NEW BUSINESS

Buying an Existing Business.

Since the paperwork involved in setting up a business is both prolific and timeconsuming, it is no wonder that some prospective proprietors look for a going concern which they can take over. Small businesses are, needless to say, cheaper to buy in Portugal than in the UK or USA. It is still possible to sell your house in the UK, buy a home in Portugal and still have enough surplus to invest in setting up a small business. In order to get some idea of the price range of the type of enterprise in which one is interested, it is advisable to ring and check with a few UK-based property bureaux; many are listed in the overseas property columns of national newspapers. Alternatively a list of UK-based property agents who deal with Portugal can be obtained from the Portuguese UK Chamber of Commerce in London. Although the majority of the properties on offer are villas and apartments, many bureaux also deal with business premises for rent or sale. Anyone buying a business should note that about 10% will be added to the price by transfer tax ((*SISA*) and an additional 23% by the notary and registration fees. For details of purchase procedures, please see Chapter Three, *Setting up Home*.

Creating a New Business

In order to create a new business it is necessary to find a gap in the market that has a realistic prospect of success. For instance a bar situated in an isolated village would almost certainly be doomed to failure. We have already mentioned that the task of assessing what kind of business is likely to be profitable can only be done on the spot. Many businesses started by northern Europeans in Portugal are aimed either at the foreign residents or the tourists. Despite the fact that Portugal has one of the lowest per capita incomes in the EU and a quarter of its population lives below the poverty line, the betteroff local Portuguese residents are also a potential target for goods and services. The aspiring entrepreneur should therefore include the needs of local Portuguese residents when canvassing ideas (e.g. selfservice laundrette, film processing laboratory, fax bureau etc.).

The type of person intending to create a new business will probably fall into one of three main categories: firstly those who are already experienced in running a particular type of business, (e.g. a restaurant or boarding kennels) and would want to find out whether a similar enterprise would be viable in Portugal; secondly those whose entrepreneurial flair will help them to spot a lucrative gap in the market. This usually means supplying a product or service familiar at home but not available in Portugal. Food, outlets are often successful. Homemade sausages, pies and bread are some of the products that have so far resulted in nostalgic expatriates keeping their fellow nationals in business in Portugal.

The third category is professional services (e.g. legal, medical) for which there is always a demand.

Raising Finance

Those contemplating opening a business in Portugal should note that UK banks in Britain will not usually be able to provide startup loans in cases where the prospective proprietor intends to become resident outside the UK, although this is now theoretically possible within the EU and not just in Britain. Some UK banks have Portuguese branches (see the *Directory of British Employers* in the previous chapter). Unfortunately Portuguese banks are unlikely to lend money to start up a business, except in certain circumstances (e.g. if the business deals with manufacturing and guarantees jobs for the Portuguese). But readers should check on this. In addition, Portugal has base lending rates which may be higher than those in the UK. Many of those who have founded small commercial enterprises in Portugal have had to rely on money raised from the sale of a UK home. If this proves insufficient it might be worth considering taking out a mortgage on your Portuguese home through a Portuguese bank in Portugal. One of the biggest banks is the Banco Espirito Santo e Commercial de Lisboa, with branches throughout the country. Needless to say, the branches in places like Loulé, Faro and Portimão in the Algarve will be more used to dealing with such requests than branches in the back of beyond. When making enquiries one should ask to speak to the manager (*gerente*).

Government Investment Incentives

If raising finance proves a problem it is certainly worth investigating whether the proposed business qualifies for an incentive grant from one of the various Portuguese bodies empowered to allocate grants to certain types of enterprise. This should be considered as an addition to your investment, not of course something which can in itself justify starting a business, which should be viable in and of itself. This is how government grants are looked on in Portugal as in many other countries nowadays; and the prospects for the business from a commercial point of view will usually determine whether or not you can receive an additional grant. If you cannot persuade your bank, or other investors, of this, you are unlikely to persuade the relevant Portuguese government body.

The Portuguese definitely wish to encourage foreign investment. It is to this end that the government has devised a series of incentive packages for agricultural, industrial and touristic projects:

Agriculture. Cash grant incentives for agriculture are available for schemes that contribute to the efficiency of Portuguese agriculture generally, or promote agricultural development in the less developed regions of the country. The grants are distributed by the Financial Institute for the Development of Agriculture and Fisheries (IFADAP), after approval for the project has been granted by the Regional Agricultural Department (*Direcção Regional da Agricultura*). In the first instance the promoter should contact: Information Services, IFADAP, Av João Crisóstomo 11, P1000 Lisbon; ☎21-3558337; fax 21-3528030. Forestry projects including afforestation, reafforestation and forest improvement are also eligible for IFADAP grants.

Industry. In order to attract a range of projects (e.g. mining, manufacturing, catering, vehicle hire, travel agents and transport enterprises) to less industrialised regions, a new industrial incentives scheme, *Programa Estratégico de Dinamização e Modernização da Industria Portuguesa* (PEDIP II), has been set up. The aim is to create balanced regional development and the continued growth of Portuguese industry; and the scheme has been organsed within the framework of the EU, which provides 75% of the funds. Cash grants awarded under this scheme vary; and this new scheme relies more on interest subsidies and private sector involvement than previous ones. One of the conditions of eligibility is that the proposed business must be itself financially feasible and assistance is given for investment or expenditure, and employee training, 'only if it forms part of an overall strategic plan of the applicant company.' All applications for the various programmes which come under PEDIP II (known by their acronyms SINDEPEDIP, SINFRAPEDIP, SINAIPEDIP, SINETPEDIP, and SINFEPEDIP) must be submitted to the Institute for the Support of Small and Mediumsized Enterprises, IAPMEI, (*Instituto de Apoio às Pequenas e Médias Empresas e Investimento*, Rua Rodrigo da Fonseca 73, P1297 Lisbon Codex; ☎21-3864333; fax 21-3863161). The most important subprogramme of PEDIP is SINDEPEDIP, a form of subsidy towards projects in the manufacturing and mining industries, and medium and long-term development plans. There are four main categories of project that fall within the SINDEPEDIP ambit:

> ○ Projects designed to produce advanced technology and raise the quality of existing products.
> ○ Quality control projects aimed at bringing production methods into line with EU requirements.
> ○ Investment in machinery designed to improve productivity, hygiene and the protection of the environment.
> ○ Investments in equipment on the basis of individual assessment.

SINDEPEDIP grants vary according to the type of project; the maximum is about £125,000 for investment in purchasing and developing technology; and interestfree loans are available. Regardless of their size all companies applying for SINDEPEDIP should contact IAPMEI (see above) or a Portuguese bank with contacts with IAPMEI.

If all these acronyms seem bewildering, and you wish to pursue your enquiry further, recommended reading are the leaflets *Practical Aspects of Establishing a Business in Portugal* and *Investment Grants and Other Incentives* which form part of the *Portugal Guide for Investors* published by ICEP (Av 5 de Outubro 101, P1050 Lisbon; ☎21-7930103; fax 21-7952329) and also available from their office in London..

Tourism. SIFIT III *(Sistema de Incentivos Financeiros ao Investimento no Turismo)* is a programme of incentives which deals with investment in tourism including the construction, refurbishment or extension of all types of accommodation used for holidaymakers. The scheme lays special emphasis on developing under-exploited areas of the country. SIFIT III is also available for restaurants, spas, marinas, pleasure craft and hunting regions. Cash grants of up to one million euros or 65% of the cost, whichever is the lower, are allocated on the basis of geographical location and the number of jobs created. The promoter is committed to maintain the level of jobs for four years and provide 25%-30% of the required equity (new or existing schemes respectively). Applications should be send to the Institute of Tourism Funding and Support, Tourism Investor Support Office; Rua Ivone Silva, lote 6 ; 1050124 Lisboa; ; ☎21-781 0000; www.ifturismo.mineconomia.pt). It is important to note that a grant cannot be allocated if the project has already commenced. In order to qualify, investment expenditure must amount to at least £30,000 except for residential tourist accommodation, farmhouse accommodation and other forms of rural tourism which can be less.

In many cases a feasibility study will need to be carried out to enable prospective developers to prepare a Tourism Investment File.

The Portuguese UK Chamber of Commerce & The Portuguese Government Trade Office (ICEP)

The Portuguese UK Chamber of Commerce and the Portuguese Government Trade Office (ICEP) are two invaluable bodies for the aspiring investor and entrepreneur to know about. Although they share the same address and work closely together, they have different objectives:

The Portuguese UK Chamber of Commerce: 22-25A Sackville Street, London W1X 1DE; ☎020-7494 1844, fax 020-7494 1822; www.portuguese-chamber.org.uk. The PUCC is an independent body which exists to promote twoway trade between Britain and Portugal and to promote UK investment in Portugal. A list of companies who are members of the PUCC is kept by the Chamber; and many of its other invaluable services are outlined in the previous chapter.

ICEP (Investment Trade and Tourism of Portugal: 22-25A Sackville StreetLondon W1X 1DE; ☎020-7494 1517; fax 020-74941508; www.icep.pt). ICEP combines the functions of promoting trade, tourism and investment in the country. The Tourist Office provides fact sheets and leaflets on the different regions and the Trade Office can supply much trade and commercial information. The head office of ICEP/Turismo is: Avenida 5 de Outubro, 101,1050 Lisbon; ☎21-793 0103; fax 21-793 0103; website www.portugal.com.

Both the Chamber of Commerce and the Trade Office are invaluable sources of information for the prospective business entrepreneur. These two organisations have at their disposal uptodate information on all aspects of the economic and business scenes in Portugal. They can provide appropriate contact addresses in Portugal for all types of commerce. Booklets on investing in Portugal, including how to start up a business, are available free on request. Enquiries which comprise a range of questions are better submitted by post or fax.

Employing Staff

As mentioned in the *Employment* chapter, labour laws until recently were biased heavily in favour of the employee, making his or her security of tenure almost unassailable regardless of the prevailing economic state of the company. New legislation has made some improvements in the employer's favour.

Any company employing more than five staff is legally bound to recruit a workforce that is 90% Portuguese. The only exception is for specialised technical staff on whom there is no restriction. As Portugal is a full member of the EU, this restriction does not however apply to Britons and other EU nationals, only to those from outside the EU. The two main forms of contract, the fixed term and the uncertain duration, are for a minimum of six months but differ in certain other respects. The fixed term contract must specify the exact date of termination up to a maximum of three years. Even though the termination date is specified, the onus is on the employer to inform the employee eight days before expiry that he does not wish to renew the contract otherwise the employee may stay on for longer.

The contract of uncertain duration is applicable where the employee is replacing a temporarily absent employee, for seasonal work, for civil construction work, public works and industrial repairs, and lasts until the regular employee returns or the conclusion of the work in hand. The employer must give the employee seven, thirty or sixty days notice depending whether the work period lasts six months, six months plus, or up to two years. If the employer fails to comply with the notice period, the same regulations as for the fixed term contract (see above) apply.

There is one other main type of contract, the temporary employment contract which is applicable to temporary employment firms. In such cases the employer uses a third party (the temporary employment firm) to recruit temporary labour. If however the employer maintains the temporary employee longer than ten days after the contract should have terminated, the employee may stay on permanently. The permission of the Ministry of Employment and Social Security and a licence (*alvará*) is required before a temporary employment company can begin to operate.

No employee or employer rights are in operation during trial periods which can be from fifteen to thirty days depending on the length of the contract. Where employment is of a particularly complex and technical nature, the trial period can be six months.

Staff are entitled to thirteen public holidays and one local holiday. In addition the minimum annual holiday is twentytwo days. Minimum wages are fixed by the government annually. However wages are normally agreed by Collective Labour Agreements between the employees (or trade unions) and the Employers' Associations. Two extra monthly salaries are paid annually: one at Christmas (not compulsory) and one during the annual summer holiday (compulsory by law).

Largescale dismissals of personnel require prior notification to the Minister of Employment and Social Security and to the company's employee committee or the unions.

Staff may resign without just cause provided they put their resignation in writing either thirty or sixty days in advance depending on whether their contract is for less or more than two years.

Taxation

Businesses whether commercial, industrial or agricultural are subject to taxation on their profits in the form of corporate income tax (*Imposto Sobre o Rendimento das Pessoas Colectivas*) or IRC. The normal rate of IRC is 36% with an additional municipal tax in some areas (e.g. Lisbon) of up to 3.6% (i.e. an effective maximum tax rate of 39.6%).

Businesses are required to make three IRC tax payments annually in June, September and December. Each payment must amount to 25% of the previous year's liability. The difference between the amount paid and the amount actually due, is paid when the tax return is submitted (before 30 April).

Capital gains tax will also be levied where appropriate, normally when disposal of assets takes place two or more years after acquisition.

Profits of a Portuguese branch or subsidiary of a foreign company are also liable to the above taxes.

All businesses must register a record of their company accounts with the local tax office.

Portugal has its own version of VAT, IVA which applies to a wide range of goods and services. The standard rate is 17%; the intermediate rate of 12% applies to some food products, restaurants and diesel fuel; and the reduced rate of 5% applies to some food products, books, medicines, water, electricity etc.

Tax Free Zones: Madeira and the Azores have tax free zones. Madeira offers long-term tax and trade incentives to foreigndomiciled corporations who wish to develop their activities within the free zone. Incentives include exemptions from corporation tax until 2011 and local taxes. Further details may be obtained from the Madeira Development Company (*SDM – Sociedade de Desenvolvimento da Madeira, SA*), SDM Building, Rua da Mouraria 9, 1st floor, 9000, Funchal, Madeira; ☎291-201333; fax 291201399; www.sdm.pt.

Santa Maria, the Azores 'free zone', offers similar incentives. For the Azores, requests for information should be addressed to the Governo Regional dos Açores, Rua 16 de Fevereiro, P9500 Ponta Delgada; ☎9624694; fax 9623648.

Accountancy and Legal Advice

Accountancy Advice. Anyone intending to go into any form of business in Portugal will need expert advice to guide them through the fiscal jungle. There are several UK accountants with branches in Portugal and the Portuguese UK Chamber of Commerce in London, or the British Embassy in Lisbon, will supply a list on request. There is also a selection of British accountants with branches in Portugal in the *Directory of British Employers* at the end of the previous chapter on *Employment*.

Legal Advice. The prospective business person in Portugal would be ill advised not to seek out specialist advice on setting up a business and all the procedures that this entails. As well as several British legal firms with knowledge of the Portuguese legal system there are Portuguese firms which are able to advise business people in a variety of specialities. Some British firms in Portugal, and Portuguese firms with British connections, are listed in the *Directory of British Employers* at the end of the preceding chapter. A full list of British legal firms operating in Portugal may be obtained from the Portuguese UK Chamber of Commerce in London; and it is recommended in the first instance that you contact one of its members.

IDEAS FOR NEW BUSINESSES

As already mentioned, starting a business from scratch requires thorough background research, preferably on the spot, and if possible conducted for longer than a few weeks. If you have already lived in the area where you wish to start a business, so much the better, particularly if you have made a point of getting on good terms with anyone who can use their influence in your favour. In Portugal, knowing the right people can make the difference between falling over every obstacle in your path or negotiating each stage painlessly. One aspect of doing business in Portugal is worth noting: the Portuguese have a relaxed attitude to business dealings; deals are more likely to be struck over a drink in a bar than from either side of a desk. So part of your business plan should certainly be to cultivate new contacts.

Many of the existing possibilities for businesses have already been mentioned, from selling handicrafts to practising medicine. Small garages, plumbers, gardeners, legal advisory services, caretakers, delicatessens, bookshops, desktop publishers, dairy farms, trout farms and English language publications are just some of the businesses being operated at present. There are a number of other possibilities connected with Portugal's burgeoning tourism trade, which is moving upmarket and towards more independent holidays.

Accommodation

One area that looks promising for the future is the area of tourist accommodation and facilities. The Portuguese Tourist Board is keen to promote Portugal as a Year-round destination. The Algarve is also becoming more popular with those (like elderly and retired people) who stay there over the winter because of its mild climate. This means that businesses in this area, hitherto dependent on a seasonal tourist trade, may in future be able to benefit from a more regular income. The Tourist's Board's other aim is to increase the number of Pousada and manor house holidays available around Portugal. Pousadas are historic hotels run by the state, but manor houses are privately owned and usually less grand than pousadas. This is a growing sector of the market and a pricey one. A two-week holiday at a manor house can cost the customer upwards of £600. The customers are increasingly likely to be Japanese, American and Canadian, as the Portuguese National Tourist Office looks further afield; and it now has offices in these countries. An additional attraction for anyone thinking of starting a business around manorhouse holidays is that they could be eligible for a Portuguese government development grant (see *Tourism* above.

Car Hire

Another possibility for new businesses connected with the increase of tourism, and in particular independent and tailormade holidays, is car hire. This has experienced something of a boom recently, particularly in Lisbon, Oporto and the Algarve. Many UK tour operators book cars for their clients at very competitive terms, so the market is operating on low margins. Three-day rentals of small Seats start at £40 and minibuses from £160 for the same period. However it may be possible to compete with onthespot rentals for casual customers in the Algarve, or land a lucrative contract with a tour operator. Car maintenance is another need, as more British people live there or choose to travel around by car.

Adventure Holidays

As the Portuguese Tourist Organisation, seeks increasingly to promote the remoter regions of Portugal, possibilities for holidays-with-a-difference will arise (e.g. walking, riding etc.) Packhorse holidays, where a 'packer' accompanies a group of riders whose luggage is carried on packhorses or mules, are an adventurous variation on the riding holiday. This has already proved popular in Spain and could easily catch on in Portugal. If Portuguese roads, horsedrawn holidays which are common in Ireland, are another possibility. In addition to mainland Portugal, the Azores are being promoted for walking and biggame fishing holidays and there are opening here too for adventure holiday organisers.

Sports

The most popular sport with visitors to Portugal is golf. There are signs that the existing facilities are under pressure and that there is scope for additional golf courses; and many more permanent developments for visitors and expatriates are growing up around golf courses. Tennis and watersports facilities, and marinas are also current growth areas.

FORMS OF BUSINESS ENTERPRISE

There are at least six main forms of business enterprise that are recognised in Portugal. These include commercial activities carried out by individuals as well as companies. Certain financial activities including banking, insurance, venture capital and leasing, are subject to legal restrictions and supervision by the Bank of Portugal.

Business Structures for Individuals

There are two forms of business possible for individuals:

Unlimited Sole Trader. this type of sole trader is responsible without limit for debts which he may incur as a result of his trading activities.

Estabelecimento Individual de Responsabilidade Limitada (EIRL) (Sole Trader With Limited Liability. Under this the trader can safeguard his personal assets by limiting liability to the company's assets only. The registration procedure is the same as for companies (see below). An EIRL requires minimum investment capital of 1995 euros.

Business Structures for Companies

Sociedade por Quotas (Lda). An Lda is a private limited liability company and is the most widely used form of company. It is suitable for small businesses generally because the administrative and supervisory control by overseeing bodies is kept to a minimum. The main characteristic of an Lda is that all partners are liable not only for their own contributions but also for all contributions required to realise the full amount of the company's share capital. The minimum capital investment is 1995 euros (about £1,250). The minimum value of each quota is 99 euros (about £61). The Articles of Association by which a Lda is bound to operate must include by law, shareholders' names and contributions. Contributions must always be in cash. However as a transitional measure 50% of capital contributions may be postponed to fixed or determinable future dates. Contributions must be lodged with a credit institution (*Caixa Geral de D[ac]epositos*) in the period prior to notarial registration of the Articles of Association. This is by way of a deposit.

Deferred contributions ultimately fall due at the expiry of a fiveyear period from the signing of the Articles of Association. An Lda is required to maintain a legal reserve of a minimum of 1,000 euros. The governing bodies of an Lda are the shareholders and director(s). Shareholders' meetings may decide on supplementary provisions of capital, disposal and reorganisation of contributions (quotas), expulsion of members, dismissal and appointment of managerial staff, approval of accounts and distribution of profits and handling of losses. The Shareholders' meeting can also arrange the alteration of the Articles of Association, and approve mergers, demergers and any other transformations of the company.

One good piece of news for the smaller businesses is that only companies which exceed two of the following for two consecutive years: a balance sheet over 897,000 euros, a turnover of 1,845,000 euros, or fifty employees, need appoint a statutory auditor to examine the company's annual accounts.

Sociedade Anónima SA Corporation. An SA has a more complex system of supervision and administration than the allpurpose Lda. It is suitable for large and international concerns. The SA form is essential for companies who wish to have their shares quoted on the Lisbon Stock Exchange. Shareholders' financial obligations differ from an Lda in that they are only liable for the amount equivalent to their individual contributions to realize the shares subscribed by them. A minimum of five shareholders who may be either individuals or corporations, is required for the incorporation of an SA. The procedures of incorporation are broadly similar to those of an Lda. There are however additional regulations and larger financial considerations in the structure of an SA.

The minimum capital required is 24,940 euros (£15,625) and the shares must have a value of not less than about 5 euros (£3). Not less than 30% of the share capital must be deposited with a credit institution (see Lda's above) before the final registration of the Articles of Association.

The incorporation of an SA is usually made partly by private and partly by public subscription when one or more individual promoters subscribe for shares (*acções*). The shares represent the capital of the company and their issue price cannot be less than their nominal value. Except in exceptional circumstances it is forbidden for the company to own in excess of 10% of its own share capital.

Definitive conditions governing SA's are set out in the statute entitled *Código das Sociedades Comerciais*. The promoter(s) must prepare a draft of the Articles of Association in which should be included, a precise description of the activities in which the company will be involved and the number of shares not yet subscribed for. The draft Articles should then be submitted for provisonal registration. When this has been carried out the promoters place the shares for private subsription and offer the others for public subscription. Upon completion of these preliminaries each promoter and subscriber is entitled to one vote per share at a meeting for all promoters and shareholders. The minutes of the meeting are registered with a notary and incorporated into the deed. A copy of the minutes is also filed with the *Conservatória do Registo Comercial* (Commercial Register).

The final articles of Association should include details of the categories of shares, the procedure (if applicable) for the issue of bonds or debentures, and the organisation and supervisory structure of the company, and the conditions, if any, governing the transfer of shares. A share register must be kept at the head office of the company and be available for inspection by any member.

STEP BY STEP FORMALITIES FOR FORMING A COMPANY

O *Provisional Registration* at the *Registo de Pessoas Collectivas* (Companies Registration Office) and application for an approval certificate and a *Cartoa Provisorio de Pessoa Collectiva* (Provisional Business Identity Card). The national registry office in Lisbon is : *Registo Nacional de Pessoas Colectivas*, Praça Silvestre Pinheiro Ferreira 1C, P1500 Lisbon.

O *Declaracao Previa de Investimento Estrangeiro:* File a declaration of intent to invest foreign capital in Portugal at the *Instituto do Commercio Externo de Portugal* (ICEP).

O *Articles of Association:* Deposit a copy of the company's memorandum and articles of association a *notario* (public notary), for evaluation.

O *Caixa Geral de Depositos:* Deposit the initial capital of the company with a branch of the CGD.

O *Escritura do Contrato de Sociedade (company constitution):* Deposit a copy of the company's constitution with the notary.

O *Declaração de Inicio de Actividade)(declaration of intent of business):* File a declaration of intent of business at the local *Repartido de Financas* (revenue office).

O *Registering the Company at the RNPC and on the Commercial Register):* Apply to register the company's constitution at the RNPC and request the full business identity card. Also register the company on the *Conservatoria do Registo Commercial* CRC, (commercial register). The Commercial Register will carry out the gazetting of the memorandum and articles of assocation in the appropriate newspapers.

O The official books of the company, including the minute book, must be registered with the tax authorities, the Commercial Registry Office and the Bankruptcy Court.

O *Registration of Employees at the Social Security Centre:* Companies are obliged to register their employees into the social security system, at the *Centro Regional de Seguranca Social.*

The supreme governing body of an SA is the Shareholders' Meeting presided over by a *Mesa da Assembleia Geral* (Board). A chairman of the board is elected for a maximum period of four years. Ordinary Shareholders' Meetings must normally be called annually by means of a public announcement in the Official Gazette and a daily newspaper of Lisbon and Oporto. Extraordinary Shareholders' Meetings are instigated on the advice of the Company's Board, Management, or Audit Board. They can also be called by the President of the Shareholders' Meeting or by the Courts if the shareholders' request is ignored. The Board usually consists of an odd number of directors, but only one director is allowed in the case of capital not exceeding 99,759 euros. The Board is subject to dismissal by shareholders' meetings at any time.

The supervision of a corporation is handled by an Audit Board or a single statutory auditor if the capital does not exceed 99,759 euros (about £62,350). The Audit Board must meet at least quarterly and minutes of meetings must be recorded and signed by all present. Disapproval of resolutions must also be summarised in the minutes.

Although the traditional form of the administrative and supervisory structure of an SA consists of a Board of Directors and an Audit Board, a new structure is also available, comprising a General Board, an Auditor and the Management.

Sociedade em Comandita (SC) (Partnership Association). This form of business comprises two categories of partners: *Sócios Comanditários* (dormant partners), whose liability is limited to to the amount of their shares. *Socíos Comanditados* (Full Partners) who are liable without limit for company debts jointly with other partners. Public corporations and private limited liability companies are usually partners of the latter sort. There are two types of Sóciedades em Comandita depending on the form in which their capital is represented.

Sociedades em Comandita por Acções (Partnerships by Shares): when the captial is in the form of shares. Partnerships by shares require a minimum of six partners i.e. at least one full partner and five dormant ones. Only full partners can contribute services in exchange for their share in the partnership. A minimum capital of 25,000 euros (about £15,625) is required as capital.

Sociedades em Comandita Simples (Simple Partnerships): when the capital is not represented by any shares. Simple Partnerships require a minimum of two partners (i.e. at least one full and one dormant partner) and do not require any minimum capital.

In both types of SC it is normally only full partners who may be appointed managers. The partners' resolutions are adopted in general meetings and the partners' voting rights are in proportion to their stake in the company. However the full partners together, cannot be granted less than 50% of the votes to which the dormant partners are also jointly entitled.

Sociedade em Nome Collectivo (SNC), (General Partnership). A General Partnership is one based on personal relations and mutual trust. Partners are jointly liable without limit for the company's debts except where they have no financial stake i.e. partners may contribute services in exchange for their share in the company without liability for debts. Each partner is entitled to one vote. All partners are managers and each may represent and bind the company.

Branch Office of an Existing Foreign Firm. This form of enterprise is a possibility for foreigners wishing to create a branch office in Portugal of an existing UK-based firm. Opening a branch office requires presentation of a translation of the foreign company's Articles of Incorporation, a certificate of the company's legal existence, a translation of the minute that includes the board's decision to create a branch in Portugal and the appointment of a legal representative empowered by the head office to administer the affairs of the branch. The translation should be duly legalised and posted in the *Portuguese Official Gazette*. When all the necessary documents have been assembled the branch office must be registered at the local Commercial Registry. The branch requires no minimum capital to operate.

European Economic Interest Grouping (EEIG). This is a relatively new business form within the European Union inauguarated in July 1989. The EEIG can be conducted by individuals and companies and is designed to facilitate cross border cooperation between businesses in different parts of the European Union. The EEIG is governed by EU regulations rather than the narrow and diverse constraints of individual countries' company laws. The aim is that the EEIG will be subject to identical legal and tax regimes regardless of the country of operation; and it purpose 'is to facilitate or develop the economic activities of its members.' For other information on EEIGs see *Spain, Chapter 7, Starting a Business.*

Other Procedures

Licensing: Licensing is required for industrial activity but other commercial activities, e.g. running a shop (except food shops) do not in principle require a licence. A licence is obtained from the regional delegation of the Ministry of Industry and Energy (MIE). In the case of activities closely related to public health or security the *Direcção Geral do Comercio Interno* DGCI (Internal Commerce General Office) should also be consulted.

Approval of the Projected Work Schedule: The projected work schedule and engagement contracts of any foreign employees must be presented to the *Ministerio do Emprego e Seguranca Social* (Ministry of Employment and Social Security) for approval.

Useful website

www.portugaloffer.com – a resource for finding a supplier, customer, agent or business partner in Portugal.

APPENDIX I

PERSONAL CASE HISTORIES

SPAIN

DAVID TARN

David Tarn, 37, was offered a position as an accountant in an enterprise in Málaga, providing accounts for Gibraltar and the United Kingdom as well as Spain. Although he was already a qualified accountant, this meant that he had to learn the Spanish Accounting Plan. He says he found his stay there 'pleasant and frustrating by turns;' the business eventually folded, and he returned to the UK, but he would be 'pleased to work in Spain again.' We asked him:

How did you organise accommodation?
You need to look around first, or have friends who can help. I moved in with a friend who eventually loaned me his apartment, so I was lucky. A detached house with two bedrooms is less than £300 a month. I was paying about £175. Don't try holiday rentals if you can avoid them. Look around first and make up your mind then, when you have seen the area, so I think long-term is best when you have definitely made up your mind.

How did you find working there compared with home?
Much more relaxed. Although you are expected to wear a shirt and tie for meeting clients, you don't have to be formal in the office; and you get on first name terms with colleagues and clients quite easily. Socialising is also part of doing business in Spain. There is not quite the same work ethic; and the afternoon is siesta time. Everything shuts down. I enjoyed meeting and mixing with Spanish people.

What about red tape? Any problems?
To work in Spain you need to get a *residencia* and join the Spanish social security scheme which gives you free medicine from a state appointed doctor. When you have twelve years of contributions you are entitled to a pension which is 80%

of your average salary over the previous five years if you are staying that long. Prepare to be flexible when dealing with officialdom or doing business.

Have you travelled around? And do you have any tips?
Yes. Getting away from the tourist spots was the most pleasant aspect of living there, and travelling up to the 'white villages' inland from Marbella, a completely different country and lifestyle with unspoilt roads, ideal for walking, and my hobby which is painting. Away from the tourist spots are also the best restaurants where you will be treated like a friend, not just a customer. A good meal is less than £6. There are marinas all along the coast for those that like boats and yachting. I enjoyed travelling up to Sierra Nevada, a skiing resort about three hours' drive away, the highest road in Europe.

Did you find it expensive to live there?
No. Prices are similar to the UK, at least you tend to spend the same amount but the standard of living seems higher. Clubs like leisure and golf clubs are very expensive and worth avoiding I think unless you like that kind of socialising. Travel to and from the UK is cheapest at Easter and Christmas, outside the main holiday season.

What else do others living and working in Spain need to know?
The main thing is to be flexible. If you are starting a business, be prepared to change tack and try a different course.

KAREN GUY

Karen, aged 27, is a nursery nurse who worked in a family centre in London with 'parents and children with special needs' before deciding to move to Seville, where she found work through the newspaper *SUR in English* and 'word of mouth.' We asked her:

How easy is it to mix with people and what kind of social life is there?
To start with you need the language, because they are very closed people. I've been very lucky, but it is very difficult. Social life and going out in Sevilla is fantastic though.

What about red tape? Any problems?
Getting electricity, gas or a telephone installed is a complete disaster. Everything you do takes so much longer. Also getting the *residencia* is a huge problem. My advice is to have patience; and if you have money, employ a *gestoria* to do things relating to documentation for you as it saves time and effort. Don't give up when trying to organise utility services, buying cars etc.

Have you travelled around? And do you have any tips?
Yes, I have travelled through many provinces. You should always ask prices before buying in a bar, as they will always try to rip off foreigners in my experience. Get out and about and see the country!

JOANNA MUDIE

Joanna Mudie, now in her fifties, was a private language teacher in the Midlands, she says, before trying the same thing in Spain. She got a first job through the British press, one advertised by Nord Anglia; and then subsequent ones by either 'going to check' in June or September or checking in the Yellow Pages and then phoning and visiting. We asked her:

How have you found working there compared with home?
In one word, good; but there's much more uncertainty and insecurity about all aspects of work: hours, days, rates of pay, dates, insurance, contracts (invariably, if you're lucky enough to get one, a load of rubbish because employers put down less hours on paper to avoid paying so much insurance, and also to protect themselves if business dwindles and they can't offer you so much work). All of this is compensated for by mostly pleasant students interested in learning, small groups, and the pleasure of working in an attractive foreign country.

What about red tape? Any problems?
Horrendous, at least in the days of having to get a work permit, and my boss saying 'yes he was getting one' and it turned out to be lies. So, my advice is, forget your English sense of honesty and obeying the law. Relax, and 'when in Rome, do as the Romans do.' Simply don't worry too much about the 'legalities.' It usually seems to work out OK; and if not, well, it's a nice life in the sun.

Have you travelled around? And do you have any tips?
Around Andalucia, around Madrid, and on the Costa Blanca. Public transport is good value, punctual, clean and comfortable. Reasonable rooms in *hostales* are always available, except for festivals and *Semana Santa* (Easter). Costs are generally lower than in England. Before you go, begin learning Spanish and reading up about Spain. Thieving is prevalent, so open up a bank account immediately so you only carry the minimum with you, best in a money belt if you're travelling.

Do you find it expensive to live there?
No, except for manufactured items like electrical goods, and also clothes (which you can buy in the summer in England). Buy fruit and veg in the local market. For flats, there are many opportunities for sharing, so see local ads.

What are the advantages and disadvantage of living and working in Spain?
Advantages are the climate – but the sun really is strong from June to September from noon to 6pm and is best avoided – being with happy, relaxed people, music, dancing... Disadvantages, well, things are a bit 'wonky', taps, drains, showers, doors. In Spain, you're not going to make a fortune, or have the security of work that you might expect in England.

PETER SIDERMAN

Peter, an economic researcher, moved out to Madrid when he was offered a job researching EuropeanLatin American relations for a small, private research institute in Madrid. Peter was keen to work abroad, and to increase his knowledge of European languages and working environments. His Spanish girlfriend also provided a strong incentive to move! We asked him:

How awful is the notorious Spanish red tape in practice?

Spanish bureaucracy truly deserves its reputation as a lumbering, inefficient and frustrating machine. It is often longwinded and petty, yet many British people used to dealing with the Department of Work and Pensions will already be familiar with the delays and being shunted around endless departments. However, for many expatriates, the bureaucracy, partially at least, is irrelevant since most big firms take care of all formalities on behalf of their employees.

How do you find working in Spain compared with the UK?

In terms of pay and benefits, executives working for the Spanish subsidiaries of UK firms do exceedingly well. Coming from relatively lowpay Britain, the financial rewards of working in Spain were a major incentive for me to move. The Spanish work hard and long but manage to stay relaxed at the same time, rejecting the fraught British work ethic of arriving at work on time, wolfing down lunch, outworking colleagues and then taking work home at night...

How easy is it to mix with Spaniards and what kind of social life do they lead?

Spaniards are noisy and friendly, even in Madrid where city life makes anyone a little more arrogant and impatient. I have found the Spaniards hospitable and open to contact although perhaps a little insular – is this any surprise when they have a climate which ranges from that of Ireland in the North, through Alplike ski country, to flat endless plains and mile upon mile of beaches? The Spaniards quite simply do not have to go abroad to get away from it all, so many don't. Although it is possible to live and work in Spain without ever understanding a word of Spanish this tends to encourage an arrogance towards the Spanish and their culture which will only serve to alienate you. However, British 'colonies' are to be found all over Spain, although by joining one of these groups you will not learn very much about the language or the country. The Spanish take their social life seriously, have beautiful manners, want to have a good time and take their time in doing so. In terms of nightlife, Madrid can only be boring if you want it to be. There is absolutely no reason to miss anything you enjoyed doing in London and of course you can go on doing whatever it is much later into the night here. Alcohol remains very cheap for the huge quantities which are poured into your glass.

Any other tips for anyone considering taking the plunge themselves?

The best piece of advice is to come to Spain with an open mind, having learnt as much Spanish as possible and having sorted out all possible arrangements in the UK before getting on the plane. If you do this, no other tip is necessary.

Appendix II

PERSONAL CASE HISTORIES

PORTUGAL

MARY SWORDER

Mary Sworder had five years of working in public relations in London and one year working in France before coming to Portugal because her husband (then boyfriend) was offered a job there, with a Portuguese subsidiary of a British software company. Mary's husband had already worked in Portugal previously for Lloyds Bank. We asked her:

How easy was it to move to Portugal?
The move was relatively easy because it was a company move which meant most of the red tape was taken care of. There is plenty of rented accommodation available (start by looking in the *Anglo-Portuguese News*).

Was it difficult to find work?
There is always work as long as you have something to offer, for example teaching English, translating, secretarial work etc. I did a TEFL course at International House in Lisbon in order to be qualified to teach English. There is a great demand for English Language teachers so I had no problem finding a job.

How do you find living and working in Portugal compared with the UK?
Living and working in Portugal is a combination of pleasure and frustration. It is a beautiful country with a great climate and social life if you are prepared to mix in. Working is sometimes frustrating because you often come up against the bureaucracy; initially you are in unfamiliar territory so that even simple things are time-consuming and sometimes the telephones don't work! However, for me, it is interesting working in a country which is still developing and by being flexible it is enjoyable.

TEFL teachers earn less than some other places. Teaching privately you earn more. Rates of pay are not high compared with the UK, but they are enough to live on.

What kind of recreation is there and does it include mixing with Portuguese?
Getting to know the Portuguese is not easy, especially if you are not confident with the language. If you like the outdoor life, especially sports, and are prepared to adapt to your surroundings you should have a good time in Portugal.

Any tips for anyone considering taking the plunge themselves?
It is a good idea to spend some time learning the language. As a way of getting to know people I suggest joining a club like the Lisbon Casuals, a sports club which operates from the grounds of St Julian's school in Carcavelos on Wednesday evenings and all weekends. It has cricket, football, rugby hockey, badminton and basketball sections and has probably the cheapest sports facilities available in the Lisbon area. There is also a convivial bar.

SAM DUNLOP

S am Dunlop is in his thirties and was a journalist in Britain, worked as a technical artist in Switzerland, and taught English in Poland, Slovakia, Turkey and Greece, before moving to Porto to teach after finding the job through the *Education* pages of *The Guardian*; and reports that 'the money's better than in journalism'. He made no particular preparations before departure; and says he has found living in Portugal a 'positive' experience. We asked him:

How easy is it to mix with people?
Not easy, students don't invite you out, but you can meet people in bars who speak English. The social life in Porto is OK, but concentrated in specific areas of the city.

What about red tape and the cost of living?
Water, electricty and phone bills seem high. Drink prices in bars vary a lot. Don't go into tacky-looking 'nightclubs' who can charge over £5 for a beer; and don't lose tickets you get in posh bars which show how many drinks you've had – the fine is about £45.

Have you travelled around? And do you have any tips?
Trains are slow but cheap. Road traffic is dangerous; cycling in Porto is certainly not recommended; and cars are more expensive than in Britain.

Do you have any moneysaving tips?
Generally it is not expensive to live in Porto. You can buy a ten-journey bus ticket or a monthly pass. Drink in cafés is half the price, or at home even less (about £3 for five litres of wine). If you want to save money, bank transfer charges are expensive. It is better to risk it and take cash home.

What are the advantages of living and working in Portugal?
There are nice beaches, and the hot weather. The Portuguese are polite but reserved people. The TV has subtitles and many people get cable. All films at the cinema or on video are subtitled.

MICHELLE HONE

Michelle Hone also found Englishteaching work through *The Guardian*, in Lisbon. She is in her thirties, and taught previously in Sri Lanka, Greece and the UK. We asked her:

How have you found working there compared with home?
Fine. In my profession it's not a huge culture shock as you deal with people in English. Red tape can be annoying and expensive.

What about red tape? Any problems? Advice?
Be patient, but also pushy. You get things done by being pushy or knowing the right people. Try to get or pay people to do the queuing for you.

How do you find the social life?
In Lisbon there is a fantastic social life – for all ages and sexual persuasions. The Portuguese are kind and friendly. However making firm friends is difficult in the city.

How about travelling around? Do you have any tips?
Public transport is good, but slow. Car hire is OK, but can be expensive. A car is definitely the best way to see Portugal as there are so many fantastic places off the public transport routes. Hitching is not recommended.

What about living conditions and expenses?
Accommodation and services (electricity, water, phone) can be very expensive. However eating out and having a drink are still reasonable. Eat in the basic 'Tascas' cafés/bars; and give up being a vegetarian/vegan – it's almost impossible unless you want an omelette for every meal.

Did you prepare beforehand?
I had people to meet me and help me find accommodation. Check the papers and University noticeboards for work opportunities. You don't need anything else but your passport.

What are the advantages of living in Portugal?
The country is beautiful, great beaches and good surf. A great nightlife in Lisbon and cheap cultural events. Very friendly, hospitable people. And there is a variety of scenery. Living and working here has been a very positive experience. I would like to have a house here; and many of my colleagues don't want to leave.

What else do others thinking of living and working there need to know?
The national health system is very overburdened, so get private cover and use the local, private international clinics if you can afford to. They expect a 20% deposit and a permanent job. It is cheaper sometimes to have a mortgage than rent but it is difficult to get a mortgage, so do it through a British company, like Abbey National. And if you have young children, there are good and bad crèches like any other country, but plenty of them and relatively cheap. However, children don't start school properly until they are six years old and private schools are expensive.

MAGGIE MILNE

Maggie Milne is in her forties and works for the British Council in Lisbon, after teaching in Britain, Italy and Greece. 'Working is not a problem as I am working for a British organisation,' she says. The British Council takes care of most of the red tape, but dealing with banks, post offices and public organisations can be 'gruelling' and 'the concept of customer care is nonexistent.' We asked her:

How difficult is it to mix with the people?
It is extremely difficult to integrate into Portuguese society – the Portuguese are very closed and very family-orientated. Opportunities for social life tend to fall into two distinct camps – one is for the below 30s, no children age group, the other is entirely 'family'. There is not much for 'inbetweens' except for cinemas and restaurants – which for vegetarians can be extremely restrictive.

Have you travelled around in Portugal, and do you have any tips?
Portuguese railways are efficient (better than in Britain) and reasonably priced. Staff in hotels are helpful and polite. There is still some tendency to regard female lone travellers as something of an abnormality, but providing one doesn't frequent 'dubious' areas at night, Portugal is generally hassle free from this point of view.

What about prices?
It is fairly expensive, especially clothes. Eating out and cafés are not very expensive. Electricity, gas, telephone are more expensive than in Britain; and supermarket shopping is about the same.

What are your impressions of the country?
In comparison with other Latin cultures, Portugal is quiet and can be quite dull. There is some spectacular scenery, though, and a fairly active traditional crafts movement. On the whole, my experience of Portugal has been mixed, and I am pleased to be moving on (to S.E. Asia) this year as any more time here would have the tendency of making me negative about the culture and the people. Only come and live here if you want a quiet life and don't mind living as an outsider.

DAVID SKINNER

David Skinner moved to Portugal permanently seven years ago. He was brought up abroad and worked overseas in Libya and Saudi Arabia since qualifying in dentistry at Guy's Hospital. He returned to university in the UK in 1987 to take an MA in investment and finance. He later moved to Portugal in order to set up a dental practice in Cascais. David is married, and he and his wife found a classic Portuguese house built in the early years of the century to move into. We asked him:

How awful is the Portuguese red tape in practice?
It's a matter of luck – we were on the whole very lucky. When you move to someone else's country you either have to put up with the red tape or go elsewhere.

How easy is it to start a business?
There is huge potential in Portugal for anyone wanting to set up a business. Of course it's a challenge, but one derives enormous satisfaction from coping with that.

How do you find living and working in Portugal compared with the UK?
I feel that making comparisons with the UK is irrelevant. We are only here because we want to be.

How easy was it to find accommodation; how expensive is it?
We never had any problems arranging accommodation; it is expensive but not by UK standards. It is possible to find cheap or expensive accommodation, just as in the UK.

How easy is it to mix with the Portuguese?
I would say that it is no more difficult than one might find if one had moved from the Home Counties to Newcastle, except possibly the language barrier. But even that's debatable!

Vacation Work publish:

	Paperback	Hardback
Summer Jobs Abroad	£9.99	£15.95
Summer Jobs in Britain	£9.99	£15.95
Supplement to Summer Jobs in Britain and Abroad *published in May*	£6.00	–
Work Your Way Around the World	£12.95	–
Taking a Gap Year	£11.95	–
Taking a Career Break	£11.95	–
Working in Tourism – The UK, Europe & Beyond	£11.95	–
Kibbutz Volunteer	£10.99	–
Working on Cruise Ships	£10.99	–
Teaching English Abroad	£12.95	–
The Au Pair & Nanny's Guide to Working Abroad	£12.95	–
The Good Cook's Guide to Working Worldwide	£11.95	–
Working in Ski Resorts – Europe & North America	£10.99	–
Working with Animals – The UK, Europe & Worldwide	£11.95	–
Live & Work Abroad - a Guide for Modern Nomads	£11.95	–
Working with the Environment	£11.95	–
Health Professionals Abroad	£11.95	–
Accounting Jobs Worldwide	£11.95	–
The Directory of Jobs & Careers Abroad	£12.95	–
The International Directory of Voluntary Work	£12.95	–
Live & Work in Australia & New Zealand	£10.99	–
Live & Work in Belgium, The Netherlands & Luxembourg	£10.99	–
Live & Work in France	£10.99	–
Live & Work in Germany	£10.99	–
Live & Work in Italy	£10.99	–
Live & Work in Japan	£10.99	–
Live & Work in Russia & Eastern Europe	£10.99	–
Live & Work in Saudi & the Gulf	£10.99	–
Live & Work in Scandinavia	£10.99	–
Live & Work in Scotland	£10.99	–
Live & Work in Spain & Portugal	£10.99	–
Live & Work in the USA & Canada	£10.99	–
Drive USA	£10.99	–
Hand Made in Britain - The Visitors Guide	£10.99	–
Scottish Islands - The Western Isles	£12.95	–
Scottish Islands - Orkney & Shetland	£11.95	–
The Panamericana: On the Road through Mexico and Central America	£12.95	–
Travellers Survival Kit: Australia & New Zealand	£11.95	–
Travellers Survival Kit: Cuba	£10.99	–
Travellers Survival Kit: India	£10.99	–
Travellers Survival Kit: Lebanon	£10.99	–
Travellers Survival Kit: Madagascar, Mayotte & Comoros	£10.99	–
Travellers Survival Kit: Mauritius, Seychelles & Réunion	£10.99	–
Travellers Survival Kit: Mozambique	£10.99	–
Travellers Survival Kit: Oman & the Arabian Gulf	£11.95	–
Travellers Survival Kit: South Africa	£10.99	–
Travellers Survival Kit: South America	£15.95	–
Travellers Survival Kit: Sri Lanka	£10.99	–
Travellers Survival Kit: USA & Canada	£10.99	–

Distributors of:

Summer Jobs USA	£12.95	–
Internships (On-the-Job Training Opportunities in the USA)	£18.95	–
How to Become a US Citizen	£11.95	–
World Volunteers	£10.99	–
Green Volunteers	£10.99	–

Plus 27 titles from Peterson's, the leading American academic publisher, on college education and careers in the USA. Separate catalogue available on request.

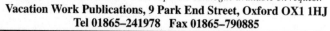

**Vacation Work Publications, 9 Park End Street, Oxford OX1 1HJ
Tel 01865–241978   Fax 01865–790885**

Visit us online for more information on our unrivalled range of titles for work, travel and gap years, readers' feedback and regular updates:

www.vacationwork.co.uk